COMMENTARY ON
DANIEL

COMMENTARY ON
DANIEL

HARRY BULTEMA

Foreword by
Daniel C. Bultema

KREGEL PUBLICATIONS
Grand Rapids, Michigan 49501

Library of Congress Cataloging-in-Publication Data

Bultema, Harry, 1884-1952

Commentary on Daniel by Harry Bultema

　　Bibliography.
　　Includes Indexes.

　　1. Bible. O.T. Daniel—Commentaries. I. Title.
BS1555.B85 1988　224'.507　88-777

ISBN 0-8254-2262-0　(Printed on groundwood-free paper)

1　2　3　4 5　Printing/Year　92　91　90　89　88

Printed in the United States of America

CONTENTS

12.   THE WISE SHALL UNDERSTAND

FOREWORD TO
THE ENGLISH EDITION

One of the amazing things in God's holy, infallible Word is the truth concerning God's love and His plan and purpose for His chosen people, the nation of Israel. Because of God's sovereign elective love, He bestowed great blessings and privileges on this chosen nation. Under divine inspiration, the apostle Paul wrote, "...who are Israelites, to whom pertaineth the adoption, and the glory, and the covenants, and the giving of the law, and the service of God, and the promises, whose are the fathers, and of whom as concerning the flesh Christ came, who is over all, God blessed forever. Amen" (Rom. 9:4, 5).

The apostle Paul's love for his own people was so great that he was led to write, "Brethren, my heart's desire and prayer to God for Israel is that they might be saved" (Rom. 10:1).

My father shared this all-consuming love for Israel and it became the hallmark of his ministry. This led him to an intensive study of God's Word and to prayerfully, carefully search out the prophetic truth of Scripture.

Regarding prophecy, my father writes in the *Introduction:*

When night falls in nature, the stars begin to twinkle. That was also the case with Israel's prophets. They were the shining stars in the night of Israel's sin and misery....The light of prophecy always shines in a dark place. For during the day, stars are not needed. We will not understand prophetism among Israel, if we regard it as a phenomenon that occurs among nations. It is not merely a psychological phenomenon in the history of the nations, but simply the shining among Israel of the light of a special grace of God. The prophet may justly be called a bright star in a black night.

This commentary on the Book of Daniel was written during the dark and tumultuous times of 1918. World War I, with its devastation of many lives and much property, was just coming to a close. In 1917, one year earlier, my father had published in the Dutch language *Maranatha!*, his famous book on unfulfilled prophecy. The storm surrounding that publication because of his premillennial stand concerning the second coming of Christ led him out of the Christian Reformed Church. He dearly loved these people and this was a very hard time for him.

But this was also a time when his soul was poured into a series of books with prophetic themes which came from his prolific pen. After *Maranatha!* there seemed to be among the Lord's people a special excitement and a spirit of expectancy for the Lord's imminent premillennial return. The first edition of *Maranatha!* was so blessed of the Lord that a second printing was released only a few months later. His two volume *Commentary on the Book of Daniel* soon followed. Then he produced his *Commentary on Revelation, Typology of Scripture, A Brief Commentary on Zechariah*, and a full *Commentary on Isaiah*. All these were written and published in Dutch.

Maranatha!, as well as the *Commentary on Isaiah* and *A Brief Commentary on Zechariah* have been translated and published in English. The remaining titles are now being translated and will be published as soon as possible.

My father wrote these books in the 1920's when few people in this country understood God's Word from a dispensational viewpoint. At that time, however, he was just beginning to see glimpses of light about dispensational truth. Nonetheless, my father's early grasp of the literal fulfillment of prophecy and the coming Millennial Kingdom, coupled with his recognition of the essential distinction between Christ as King of Israel and Christ as Head of the Church which is His Body, provided much help for many in a dispensational understanding of the Scriptures.

Some years later he was led more fully into the blessed truth concerning the special revelation and "fellowship of the mystery" (Eph. 3:9) given to the apostle Paul for this age of grace, "which was kept secret since the world began" (Rom. 16:25).

Seven decades have now passed since my father penned this *Commentary on Daniel*. We sense we are today even closer to the end of "the times of the Gentiles" and the fulfillment of Daniel's great prophecies—Revelation 22:20-21!

DANIEL C. BULTEMA

PREFACE

When writing this book on Daniel we had mainly three objectives in mind. The personal objective was to comfort our soul in these days of attacks from within and from without, regarding the glorious light of prophecy. By the grace of God we can testify that this goal has been fully obtained. Romans 15:4 has, as it were, imparted a new meaning to us. The higher goal that was sought was to put into the hands of our Dutch-speaking people a simple and concise explanation of the Book of Daniel. Until now they did not have one, nor was one available. A few of them had even begun, for the lack of something better, to pay attention to the writings of the Adventists. Whenever this was called for, we have, in the spirit of love, contested the errors of this group. We held to the opinion that there was also a real need for this kind of commentary. Finally, our highest goal was to glorify the triune God by cultivating greater knowledge of and a more ardent love for that part of the prophetic Word, which shines as a light in a dark place and, we may add, in a very dark time.

We have, as much as possible, guarded against anything that might discourage the uneducated reader. For that reason we have abstained from geographical and chronological explanations and illustrations. We very much welcome well-intended remarks and criticism for, in this undertaking, too, we have not been able to go beyond a "following after perfection." May the Lord sanctify these pages to all who love His appearing!

INTRODUCTION

The Time of Daniel

When night falls in nature, the stars begin to twinkle. That was also the case with Israel's prophets. They were the shining star in the night of Israel's sin and misery. Prophecy always presupposes apostasy and moral decline—we need only to recall the prophecy given at the gates of Eden's garden. The light of prophecy always shines in a dark place. For during the day stars are not needed. We will not understand prophetism in Israel if we regard it as a phenomenon that occurs among all nations. It is not merely a psychological phenomenon in the history of the nations, but simply the shining among Israel of the light of a special grace of God. The prophet Daniel may justly be called a bright star in a black night. For Daniel was made great by his God, and his time was made dark by the sin of his people.

For Israel it was the night of exile. Israel had experienced evil and dark days before but never to such an extent as in the days of the Babylonian Exile. The people of the Lord had been removed from the sanctified ground, from the city of the fathers, from the house of the Lord, because of its indescribable abominations, and was dispersed in the countries of the uncircumcised.

How oppressive this was to those among Israel who feared God and what emotions this evoked in them can be sensed from the stirring Lamentations of Jeremiah and from Psalm 137. Israel may have groaned under the hard yoke of servitude in Egypt, but it had at that time a free conscience. Israel had never known what it means to be an independent, free, and proud nation and, it had never possessed the luxury of a temple and a temple service. In Egypt Israel was a stranger, but in Babylon an exile, i.e., an expellee. Just try to imagine what that meant: the nation that knew itself to be the people of the Lord was now exiled from the face of God and from everything that once was precious.

But Judah received only a reward according to its deserts, for it had made things worse than Samaria and Sodom. It had made itself as unworthy of the theocracy as had the Northern Kingdom. From that time on, for Judah, also, the Davidic kingship was finished. We are greatly mistaken if we think that Judah, after its seventy year exile in Babylon was restored again as it had been in the days of old and that then the many promises of restoration and inheritance were fulfilled. Such promises as we find in Isaiah 52:9,10; 62:1; Jeremiah 32:41; Hosea 14:5-8; Amos 9:15; Obadiah 20, 21; Micah 7:19, 20; and Joel 3:17 are by no means fulfilled and are still awaiting their fulfillment. The absence of the theocracy among Israel, the presence of the kingdom of the world, and consequently Israel's dispersion among the nations are still continuing. The rise of the world power under Nebuchadnezzar has until this day made an end of the theocracy among Israel. Already in the days of Isaiah the formation of the world power began. Why? Because it was the time of the approaching end of the theocracy. The theocracy, i.e. the direct rule of the Lord upon earth, and the world empire, being absolute antipodes, exclude each other. Where the one appears, the other disappears. Babylon flourishes only at the expense of Jerusalem, and all world powers flourish only as long as Jerusalem, the city of the great King, is trodden down by the Gentiles (Luke 21:24; Rom. 11:25).

Nebuchadnezzar was the tool in God's hand to carry out the judgment upon Judah and Jerusalem and must establish the first world power, and whom all nations, Israel included, must obey for the sake of God and for conscience' sake. He also made an end of the Davidic kingship until this very day. After the return from Babylon this kingship was never restored again. Zerubbabel and Nehemiah were no more than Persian satraps. The kingship of the Maccabees was not the Davidic one and lasted no longer than a century. The Herods were Edomites and vassals of Rome.

Thus a new period in the great events of the world had dawned, the time of the vanished theocracy and the risen world empire, the time in which Israel, the chosen nation, is considered as *Lo-ammi*, not God's people (Hos. 1:9; 2:23). Now this was the time when Daniel commenced his office, and his prophecy covers the beginning, the nature, the long duration, and the end of the world empire. Daniel could be called the prophet of *Lo-ammi* or the prophet of the world empire.

The Personality of Daniel

Scripture contains three persons with the name of Daniel. We read of the first one in 1 Chronicles 3:1. He was a son of David, born at Hebron from the lovable Abigail, the Carmelite woman. The second person with this name is mentioned in Ezra 8:2 and Nehemiah 10:6 as a priest who accompanied Ezra from Babylon to Jerusalem. The third is the great writer of this prophecy. We think of him immediately when the name Daniel is mentioned. His name means "God is my Judge." However, from his day to our own people also have been his judges.

Present-day criticism usually brushes him aside with a single pronouncement as a pious fraud. But this does not remove the fact that Daniel now stands even taller before us than all his contemporary and present-day attackers piled on top of each other. In every chapter of his prophecy, except the third, we come across new beautiful facets of his sublime character. At relevant places we shall frequently have the opportunity to point this out. Here we only mention the main traits of his character when we say that he was a man of a tender conscience before God and men, a man of deep convictions with the courage of a martyr. He was as humble in dealing with those below him as he was before his God. He had the warm heart of a friend but was often lonesome, although always intimate with his God and, consequently, never altogether lonely. He was faithful in all things, in the small as well as in the great and over against the unfaithful as well as the faithful. In his conduct he joined the harmlessness of doves to the wisdom of serpents. He had all the characteristics of a great one in the Kingdom of God. He cared extremely little about money and fame, while God and His name, His people, His house and His Word were more precious to him than life itself. And he sought the blessed communion with his God through regular prayer and seclusion.

He not only possessed excellent moral and religious qualities, his mental gifts were also unequalled. When he was still very young, he was already at the head of all the sages of Babylon, and already during his lifetime his wisdom had become proverbial, so that it was considered utterly ridiculous to wish to be wiser than Daniel (Ezek. 28:3); and the heathen even compared his wisdom to that of the gods themselves (Dan. 5:11). They were certain that no difficulty was so great that he could not solve it, no problem was so knotty that he could not unravel it, no riddle was so dark that he could not explain it (v. 12). His influence upon the character of others bordered on the miraculous as well. His look caused others to bow, his word caused them to tremble. His friends considered him their superior, but his superiors manifested again and again, in spite of themselves, that Daniel was superior to them in mental power, so that he won them over to his will and viewpoint. Actually he was a man full of contrasts, which only grace can explain. Before Nebuchadnezzar he stood as a supplicant, before Belshazzar as a fearless and relentless judge, before his God he cast himself down as being deeply guilty together with all his guilty people, but before Darius he declared his innocence and dared with boldness to testify from out of the lions' den that even God had found no guilt in him. He was both a lamb and a lion and was a beautiful type of Him who was both in the fullest measure.

The Authenticity of the Book of Daniel

In this book on Daniel we proceed from the unshakeable presupposition that the prophecy which bears his name was written by Daniel the prophet during the time of the exile. The denial of this fact is not new, but was already voiced during the first centuries of our era. The opponent of Christendom, Porphyrius, already in his day defended the same sentiment that today has so many adherents, namely, that a certain Jew during the time of Antiochus Epiphanes, hence about four centuries later, invented this prophecy. The denial of the authenticity of this beautiful prophecy originated mainly from enmity against the miracle of literally fulfilled prophecy. We find here numerous predictions that have been fulfilled to a word. If the opponents would only acknowledge them to be true predictions, they would then also have to accept the miracle. And with the miracle they would have to acknowledge a wonder-working God. And it was exactly this they refused to do at all costs.

From the attacks launched against this book both in the days of old as well as today, we can readily conclude that the great enemy of souls hates this book with an extraordinary hatred. There are many reasons for this. This prophecy makes obvious Messianic predictions and foretells even Christ's first coming. It lets us see the weak foundation, the bestial nature, and the complete downfall of the entire world empire; it shows us that instead of development there is degeneration in the events of the world; to a large extent it reveals to us Satan's works of darkness, his hidden influence on the nations of the world and his secret counsels against Israel; and last but not least this prophecy describes the complete victory of the Lord Jesus Christ. This book repeatedly refers to the great end and emphatically tells God's children that they must do likewise. And now there is nothing Satan hates more than that believers look forward to the end with an eye of hope and longing. Even the Gentiles of old knew that this embodied the summit of all wisdom. For this reason and others the devil, who is the real father of higher criticism, always does everything that is in his power to do away with Daniel.

The hollowness and unreasonableness of unbelief is nowhere more evident than in the attack upon this prophecy. No matter how often it was refuted ever since the time of Eusebius and Hieronymus, the human heart, so rich in inventions, looked continually for new evasions and subtleties. But how unfavorably does the character of the enemies contrast with that of Daniel! This in itself is already a considerable refutation of all the criticism on Daniel. Porphyrius, the hater of Christendom; Spinoza, the father of pantheistic philosophy; the Jewish atheist, Uriel da Costa; the deist Anthony Collins; Johann Semler, one of the fathers of higher criticism; Corrodi, the hater of Chiliasm; Michaelis, the rationalistic corrupter of Scripture—behold, a list of men, from the days of old to the present day, who have launched a battle against the authenticity of Daniel. Only speaking of our degenerate time, there are a number of theologians who do bow before the Christ, but who, nevertheless, accept the unauthenticity of this Bible book as an established conclusion of modern criticism. We already stated that the many exact predictions in this book were the main reason why they came to this conclusion.

Now we shall list our basis for the authenticity of Daniel. First of all, we can provide exterior evidences that this book was written before the time of Antiochus Epiphanes. This ruler did not ascend the throne until the year 175 B.C. Well then, we find Daniel in the Septuagint, and this translation dates from the year 286 B.C. It also contains some stories about Daniel, which shows that, already, then there existed a tradition regarding the author, for traditions take time to develop. Daniel's history is quoted in the first book of the Maccabees as something that happened in a time long since past. This, too, points to an origin before the time of Antiochus Epiphanes. Josephus says that the high priest, Jadduah, showed Daniel's prophecy to Alexander in 311 B.C. There is no reason to doubt this account.

In the second place, other parts of Scripture prove the genuineness of this Bible book.

• The prophet Ezekiel, who was active in the time of the exile, mentions Daniel in three places as a very well-known and famous person (Ezek.14:14, 20; 28:3). The critics claim the Daniel mentioned here must have lived long before that, as he is twice mentioned before Job. But Dr. Abraham Kuyper recently proved conclusively in *De Heraut* that we must view the Book of Daniel our way and not otherwise.

• Christ calls Daniel a prophet and not a storyteller or fictioner (Matt. 24:15).

• Hebrews 11:33 does not mention Daniel's name, but it clearly refers to his act of faith in Daniel 6:23, when it says, "stopped the mouths of lions."

• In the Revelation of John many of Daniel's images are imitated. We mention only these few—Revelation 1:13 (cf. Dan. 7:13); Revelation 14, 15 (cf. Dan.10:6); Revelation 10:4 (cf. Dan. 8:26; 12:4, 9); Revelation 10:5 (cf. Dan. 12:7); Revelation 13:1, 2, (cf. Dan. 7).

In the third place, the form of the book itself proves sufficiently that we are not dealing here with the work of a novelist from the time of the Maccabees.

Almost half of the book is written in Chaldean. Things that deal with the world empire are written in the language of the empire. This phenomenon could hardly be explained if the writer had not lived until the second century B.C., but it is very natural for a composition dating from the time of the exile, as is also partly the case with Ezra.

• The description we find here of Oriental court life and of all kinds of customs is so exact that we can only expect this from an eyewitness and not from someone who lived in Palestine centuries later.

- Both language and style are pure, according to experts, and resemble that of Ezekiel who also wrote during the exile.

In the fourth place, the contents of this book sufficiently indicate its authenticity. The succession world empires, described in the second and seventh chapters can, on the basis of criticism, be explained only in a forced, deliberate manner. It has been the opinion for ages that these chapters are speaking of the Assyro-Babylonian, Medo-Persian, Greco-Macedonian, and Roman-Germanic empires. The last-mentioned world power is replaced by the eternal dominion of Messiah. Regardless of all devious attempts, the prophecy in this book cannot be ignored. The holy sublimity of this book is of such a nature that no genius, no matter how great, could ever produce such a piece of writing on his own. When Daniel is placed alongside the Apocryphal books from the time of the Maccabees, it becomes evident that there is a great difference, not merely in degree but in essence.

Finally, we can boldly declare that the testimony of the Holy Spirit tells us that the Lord Himself speaks to us in this book, and that the reverent reading of and searching in this writing is a blessed joy to the soul and has a sanctifying influence on a person's heart and life, whereby we see also Daniel standing among that cloud of witnesses counseling to lay aside every weight, and the sin which doth so easily beset us, and to run with patience the race that is set before us, looking unto Jesus the author and finisher of our faith.

The Purpose of Daniel

The purpose of Daniel's writing is, first of all, to be found in Israel. God had promised Israel in His covenant with the people at Horeb (Exod. 19:5, 6) that if it remained obedient, He would make it the nation of nations. But instead of ruling in obedience over the heathen, it came by its sin under the dominion of heathendom. Now the question presented itself quite naturally to the faithful remnant: What will now become of God's plans, God's people, and God's promises? To this question the prophecy of Daniel is the answer. Israel as a whole will from now on be *Lo-ammi*, i.e., not My people. As the prophet Hosea had foretold, Israel would abide for many days as a totally forsaken woman and the big world would rule over her.

God's intent for Israel as a nation was to be the recipient and bearer of and the witness to God's promise, but in this prophecy we do not see Israel as carrying out these tasks. Indeed, we find Israel mentioned only in a derogatory sense by the heathen and in a covenantal sense in the prayers of Daniel. And yet, no matter how contradictory it seems, we find Israel mentioned also here on every page. Whereas Ezekiel affords us a look at hardened Israel among the heathen, Daniel gives us a look at the faithful remnant which he and his friends represent. This faithful remnant represents the entire nation. The remnant continues the link with historic Israel, preaches the steadfastness of its election, its calling, and the covenant, and answers to the goal which God had set for the nation. Whereas Daniel in his entire ministry must, first of all, show that Israel as a nation had been temporarily put aside, he had, on the other hand, the most glorious comfort for the elect remnant.

The manner in which he comforts the people of the Lord is totally different from that of the other prophets. Not precepts, but the whole appearance of his example is a convincing way of preaching to Israel. He does not teach, but his whole life's history shows that God remains faithful to those who remain faithful amidst the heathen, that He honors everyone who honors Him and that He will make him a shining light among the heathen, mentally, morally, and religiously. Did not Daniel and his companions climb from the deep humility of slavery to the highest rung in the ladder of honor and power? Should this example not excite Israel to follow it? In the historical part of Daniel it is empirically shown that the faithful remnant conquers both the wisdom and the power of this world. At that time the wisdom of this world was embodied in the wise men of Babylon. The scientists of today still mention the heights of learnedness those men had already achieved. According to some German scientists, even all learning originated in Babylon. Well then, the remnant, as representing the entire nation, conquers worldly wisdom every time. And it is the same with regard to world power. Every chapter in the first part of this prophecy provides a striking example of this.

If the examples of the God-fearing remnant particularly point out God's faithful and often miraculous preservation of Israel, the apocalypses or revelations of Daniel turn Israel's eye to its

immediate and far future and ultimate delivery. It is clearly
pointed out that the world empires will last a long time and
consequently, also, Israel's dispersion and rejection, that these
empires will rage fearfully like wild beasts and not the least
against Israel, and that, as the ages roll on, it will become darker
all the time for *Lo-ammi*. Nevertheless, also, in this part words of
comfort are not lacking. It points to the indestructible kingdom,
which shall not be left to other people (2:44). The joyous prospect
is held out that the sanctified nation shall receive the kingdom
forever and ever (7:18); that the transgression shall be finished, an
end made of sins, reconciliation made for iniquity, and everlasting
righteousness brought in (9:24), and that all the people shall be
delivered (12:1).

Of particular comfort, moreover, is the disclosure of the world
of angels to Israel's view. It deserves very much our attention that
since Israel came into the power of heathendom the Lord afforded
His people a deeper look into the world and activity of angels. In
this writing of twelve chapters, more is written about angels than
in any other book of the Old Testament. That is by no means
accidental. It seems to us that there are mainly two reasons why
Israel's horizon was broadened with regard to the spiritual world
just at this point in time. The first reason for it must undoubtedly
be sought in the environment in which the people would find
themselves from then on. The religion of the Babylonians and
Medo-Persians gave the teaching of spirits a great place. Israel
would continually come in contact with that false teaching and
adopt many errors from it. To safeguard His people from this
pollution, and at the same time to make them recognize the
elements of truth among heathendom, the Lord, through Daniel,
gave these revelations concerning the higher world of the spirits.

Secondly, in this way Israel must understand the nature of its
struggle as well as of its protection. Israel would dwell for a long
time as an exile in a foreign country and see all the evil passions
of anti-semitism released against it. Now it could easily happen
that Israel, blinded with hatred, saw only the physical enemy,
thinking that all men were determined to seek its downfall. And
nothing was further from the truth than that. Not just the one world
of heathendom, but two worlds, also that of the evil angels,
conspired to seek its destruction. But—and observe here the
comfort of these revelations of angels to Israel—over against

these evil spirits stood the archangel, Michael, as"the great prince," standing for Daniel's people (12:1) with his hosts of mighty warriors. Furthermore:

• The Lord confirms His covenant to the faithful remnant, even in the midst of the heathendom.
• Israel's future may be dark, but the ultimate deliverance is glorious.
• In the meantime, the evil angels attempt its downfall, and there is a world of good angels, headed by Michael, that does battle for the children of Israel.

Thirdly, the object of this peculiar prophecy was also the world empire. Daniel, unlike the other prophets, was not active in the Holy Land, but in faraway Babylon, in the midst of sterile heathendom. And as far as the contents of his predictions are concerned, he is not admonishing Israel but the princes of the world, and we see here all the glory of this world appear and disappear. These undeniable facts give us a hint that, at least in part, the objective of this important book is also to reach the nations outside of Israel. And the usage of the Chaldean language makes this a certainty. What is this secondary objective, we may ask? It is this: that the heathen would know that Jehovah as the God of heaven stands above all other gods and all the great rulers of the world, and that this great God is Himself the cause of the various world empires. Furthermore, that this God of heaven in a special sense is the God of the Jews, who preserves His people under all oppression and persecution and will one day lead them to the eternal glory of the indestructible kingdom.

Again, it is not accidental that the first or historical part of this book, on every possible occasion, points out that Daniel and his friends are Jews, carried off as prisoners from Judah (see 2:25; 3:8,12; 5:13; 6:13). And the various royal proclamations at the occasions of God's miracles done on behalf of the remnant, and promulgated to all the nations of the world empire, are, from this point of view, very important. They always point out that the God of the Jews is the Most High, the everlasting and sovereign God. Just as at one time Dagon of the Philistines fell down before the ark of the Lord, which had been incarcerated as a prisoner in the house of that idol, so we see in Daniel the world empires and worldly wisdom fall down before Daniel's God and imprisoned people. All these things must be seen as typical images of that which one day will be glorious reality from pole to pole (cf. Ps. 68:31; 72:10, 11).

The Division of Daniel

On this matter we can be brief, as we have already indirectly indicated a few times that Daniel's book divides itself into two parts. These parts are of a dissimilar nature, but of the same size, each containing six chapters. The first part can generally be called historical and the second more prophetical. We intentionally add these qualifications, for the first part contains many types and a very important prophecy, and in the second part we find many historical notes. The first part (chapters 1-6) sketches the main features of the history of Daniel and his friends, but the second part (chapters 7-12) supplies at the same time a summary of the beginning, the decline, and the downfall of the world powers. It gives us a bird's-eye view of the history of the whole world.

This first part from verse 4 in chapter 2, continuing up to chapter 8, is not written in Hebrew but in Chaldean. The reason for this phenomenon must undoubtedly be sought in the fact that this part refers mostly to the Chaldeans, so that they could read this part of Daniel's writing in their own language. Another distinction between the first and second parts of Daniel is that in the former he speaks in the third person singular and in the latter in the first person singular. A conclusive reason has never been given for that fact, but we may definitely not argue that this is proof for a dual authorship. The second part (chapters 7-12) is apocalyptic, revealing the future. It describes in a sublime manner four visions of Daniel. The main thought of all of them is that Israel will suffer much under the various world dominions, but will be preserved under all oppression, and one day be delivered from all its suffering and, together with its Messiah, obtain world dominion.

Daniel's Place in the Canon

In the Hebrew text of Scripture we do not find Daniel grouped among the major prophets and hence, unlike our translations, not after Ezekiel but with the much later writings between the books of Esther and Ezra. The reason for this must probably be sought in the fact that Daniel actually did not belong to the common class of prophets. He never received, as did the others, a definite call or appointment to the office of prophet, and he never spoke to Israel, which actually was the nation of revelation. He did possess the gift of a seer in a high degree, but not the official office of a prophet. He was more a statesman than anything else and, therefore, fits better in the company of Mordecai, Ezra and Nehemiah than in that of the major prophets. In any case we should not conclude from the special place of Daniel in the canon that he was not held in high esteem. Both from sacred and secular writings it is abundantly clear that he was greatly esteemed.

In this respect his lot was considerably different from that of his contemporary, Ezekiel, who was always of little account among the Jews, and over against whom not only his contemporaries but equally as much their descendants were like scorpions, and it took quite a bit of doing to get his book accepted into the canon of holy writings. Daniel, on the other hand, was from the very beginning held in great esteem by his people, and his prophecy, which upheld the honor of Israel in such a magnificent manner over against heathendom, was incorporated in the collection of sacred Scripture without any opposition. Even though Daniel may not have been incorporated until late, and hence among the youngest collection of Israel's holy books, the fact that he does appear in the canon is for us proof that he belongs there, for the Holy Spirit, as the actual author of the Bible, has, as our Heidelberg/Westminster Confession states, "by a particular care" seen to it that the infallible revelation of God was preserved for the Lord's people.

The Explanation of Daniel

Principally there are three kinds of interpretations of Daniel. In about the same manner as with regard to the last book in the Bible, its expositors are divided into three groups:

- Those who view it in terms of church history.
- Those who interpret it in a modernistic vein.
- Those who concentrate on the explanation of the revelations regarding the future.

The first group is the most general. As the name indicates, its adherents view Daniel's prophecy as dealing with all or part of the history of the Church. All earlier Protestant expositors are adherents of this manner of explanation, although there is, naturally, no lack of variations. Calvin centered his view mainly around the first coming of Christ. Roman Catholic expositors belong to the same class. The main difference between Protestant and Roman Catholic expositors is that the Protestants, following Bishop Newton in the English-speaking world, and the followers of Cocceius and Vitringa in the Dutch-speaking world, apply much of this book to the papal hierarchy and persecutions, while the Catholics apply it to the Mohammedans. For the rest they agree that the book contains Messianic prophecies and that the Church can be substituted for Israel. The Adventists, too, adhere to this view, but they form still another group again. They agree with the earlier Protestant expositors that the Jews come to naught, that Daniel has much to say about the Church, the pope, and the end of the world. But they differ from them in this respect that they seek in Daniel a basis for their so-called year-day and sanctuary idea, and on the basis of the former idea they think that they can determine the end of the papacy and of the world.

The second kind of interpretation we call the modern(istic) one, since modernists of all hues have adopted it, and, consequently, it can be called an invention of the modern day. We may also call it *de Critical*, *Zeitgeschichtliche* or Rationalistic exposition. It proceeds from the idea that everything in this book is fiction, invention, written by a pious Jew who was contemporary with Antiochus Epiphanes, and whose purpose was to comfort the Jews in those evil times. According to them, this unknown author, with allegedly pious deceit, dressed all his writing in the form of miracle stories and predictions, so that the gullible, believing people would more readily accept them. Also among this kind of expositor we again find widely diverging views, but as a rule they are generally agreed that here we do not have a description of miraculous things that actually happened or of future events, nor does the book contain Messianic prophecies. In order to excise all prophecy, they considerably mess with the four world empires. From their point of view they can naturally not agree that Daniel predicts the Roman empire, nor that it speaks of a future Messiah. For that reason they consider the second world power not to be the Medo-Persian, but only the Persian; the third, the Persian; and the fourth, the Greco-Macedonian. Even the so-called "ethicalists" in the Reformed Church in the Netherlands accept this viewpoint by and large.

In the third place, of late a totally new explanation has appeared on the scene which we call the futurist exposition. Also this name is not correct, since the first-mentioned kind explains much in terms of the future as well. The English term for this kind is "Futurist Interpretation" and in German it is called *Endgeschicht-lich*. Among these expositors there is unanimity regarding the following matters.

1. They accept elements of truth in the first-mentioned sort, but reject as something coming from the evil one the last-mentioned kind of exposition.

2. They believe that not a word is mentioned about the Church or the dispensation of the Church in which we are said to believe in now. It is not the Church as the mystical body, but Israel and the world empire that are the objects of these predictions.

3. With regard to the seventy year-weeks of 9:24-27, they follow what is called the intercalation method, that is to say, they insert this whole dispensation between the sixty-ninth and seventieth year-week. Just as the sixty-nine year-weeks were literally fulfilled in the first coming of Christ, so will most certainly also the last year-week of Daniel be fulfilled in the future. They identify the last seven years with the time of the Antichrist. According to them the Jews will again have a temple in Jerusalem at the time of the end, in which they will bring sacrifices, but "in the midst of the week" (verse 27) the Antichrist will terminate this service of sacrifices and inaugurate the Great Tribulation upon Israel. After three years and a half Christ, together with those who are His, will return to destroy the Antichrist and his followers.

4. This kind of expositor has an aversion to mystical and symbolical interpretations and follows the simple and verbal meaning of the words. In the English-speaking world, Tregelles and Darby are called the fathers of this interpretation. In Germany it was followed by Auberlin, Gartner, Mayer, Hoffman, Fuller, Dachsel, Bettex, and others; in England and America by nearly all students of prophecy. If we were to join one group or another, it would, out of full conviction, be with those just mentioned, for we owe much to the expositions by Darby, Dennet, Kelly, Seiss, Gaebelein, Ironside, Burton, Jamieson, Fausset and Brown, Gray,

Scofield, Sir Robert Anderson, and others. The writings of these men have the merit of having made the difficult Book of Daniel approachable and enjoyable to the simple child of God, for whom it is intended in the first place, and of having unfolded the rich comfort as well as the wide scope of these predictions.

Finally, we wish to make a few remarks concerning the guiding principles to which we adhered while explaining this prophecy.

* We tried to keep in mind that the Lord has revealed His Word (and also this difficult part of it) not unto the wise but unto little children, and He has done so for a very practical and exclusively religious purpose (see Rom. 15:4; 2 Tim. 3:15, 16; 2 Pet. 1:19, 20). If this was the objective at the time of its inspiration, then the exposition should have the same objective.
* On the basis of 2 Peter 1:20 we have attempted to explain the book as much as possible on the basis of itself and of other parts of Holy Scripture. Hence, we have constantly sought for correspondence with the infallible explanation the Lord Himself gives us here and elsewhere. The heavenly explications we come across in Scripture may not always give what we would call a complete explanation, nevertheless, it cannot be denied that they are infallible as far as they go and that no expositor or Bible reader can ignore them with impunity.
* It is a firm rule of Scripture that it does not put the world powers on the scene, except insofar as they stand in some relationship to the people of the Lord. We too may never disregard this rule and in this case this also meant, in our judgment, that with a book like this, which tells us more than any other Bible book about the world empires, we may not lose ourselves in secular history, as all too often is done by the expositors of Daniel. How laudable it may be to read the books by Rawlinson or any other historian on Babylon, but Scripture itself mentions the glory of Babylon sufficiently.
* In closest connection with this last statement we have followed the rule that Scripture must be interpreted not on the basis of history, but vice versa—history must be explained in the light of Scripture. This is a far-reaching principle with regard to the explanation of prophecy. It has been for centuries the custom to explain the infallible predictions of Scripture

with the help of historical events. Whoever adopts this point of view says at the same time that to the simple reader prophecy is of no practical use but rather a deterrent, for he or she knows next to nothing of historical facts, nor do they care little or anything about them. This principle does not mean to deny at all that the pages of history have recorded many literally fulfilled prophecies, or that we can use them very profitably. As helpful resources they may not, especially in a case like chapter 11, be totally rejected out of hand. But with this rule we do deny that historical books are the means par excellence to understand and explain the fulfilled portions of prophecy. There simply is no human means whereby we can explain Scripture. Even knowledge of the original languages and the help of the most excellent commentaries, however indispensable and inestimable they may be, are no more than aids, as only the Holy Spirit Himself, through the channel of a sanctified personality, makes the secrets of God known. Here we must be on our guard against what Kuyper calls "the curse of the intellectual mind-set."

• For the rest we have followed a natural, literal exegesis. This is by no means something new. Luther said,"Every word must be taken in its natural meaning." Tyndale said this about it: "Thou shalt understand, therefore, that the Scripture hath but one sense, which is the literal sense." Kuyper writes, "That rarified, formless spiritualism in which so many today lose themselves, is not according to Scripture."

• Finally, it is not superfluous to point out emphatically that we consider the future of Israel to be an absolute reality and that what some like to call pipe dreams may in a mediative sense, more than anything else, be called the key to the exposition of Daniel. We cannot refrain here from quoting a paragraph from the booklet by Professor E. F. Stroter, *Israel, the Miracle People:*

All nations pass away; their splendor disappears swiftly; their beauty withers like a flower and their place does no longer know them. But the misery and scorn of Israel continues until this day. Of the powerful Pharaohs, only the mummies speak to us. Of Babylon, the beautiful, only the clay tablets. Of luxurious Greece, only broken pillars and cold marble statues.

Of proud Rome, only massive ruins and triumphal arches. But the sin and scorn of Judah is alive and has flesh and bones. Israel's wounds bleed anew every morning. Its timorous footstep skulks uncertainly and everywhere around us. Yet it is not a bogey. It is a living, dreadful, tangible reality. This looks to us as though nothing but dead people were walking among us. According to all the rules of logic and philosophy we all should have been dead, buried, and decayed long ago. But of what concern is our logic to Israel—and to Israel's God? There is no nation on earth, no language or tongue where Israel's lamentations and sighs are not heard.

But soon Israel's sighs will no longer be heard. Soon the Lord will create Jerusalem a rejoicing, and her people a joy (Isa. 65:18-25; Jer. 31:35, 36; 46:27, 28). Israel's unbelief does not cancel out God's faithfulness (Rom. 2:3, 4). If its fall is the riches of the world, and its decrease the riches of the Gentiles, how much more will its fullness be (Rom. 11:12)? If its rejection is the reconciliation of the world, what will its acceptance be but life from the dead (verse 15)? Israel's restoration is guaranteed by no one less than God. Despite the unbelief of men, God will most assuredly do it in His time.

And so we say after Da Costa, the great one among Israel, when in his poem *Chaos and Light* he expresses himself thus:

> Open up, Divine Word! Prophets from olden,
> But never antiquated, day, on whom the Apostles built!
> Enlighten us, but not by means of this false science
> (Greatly glorified as it is), whose delusion at each step,
> While she with new insipidities honors Unbelief,
> Imagines that the world owes her new praise and laurels;
> Not by means of this dead knowledge, which, indeed! and all too well!
> With ice-cold eye and hand and sharply whetted scalpel,
> Dissects like a corpse, knows how to grub in the Word of God,
> But, therefore, in that Word will not find the beat of a pulse,
> No more breath of life, no heavenly harmony,
> From whence proceeds no perfect whole built up from prophecy.
> Beam Thou Thyself down on us, Spirit of truth and of life!
> Thou who in the beginning deignedst to hover over the abyss,
> And to brood there, until presently, at the powerful word of God's mouth
> From out of the darkness the animating light came into existence,
> And give us eyes to see the calling of Today,
> The hope for the Future, and the riddles of the Past.

Chapter 1
THE YOUTHFUL EXILES IN BABYLON

Jerusalem Besieged

In the third year of the reign of Jehoiakim king of Judah came Nebuchadnezzar king of Babylon unto Jerusalem, and besieged it (v. 1).

In the first chapter of his book the prophet gives an introduction in which he tells of his position and that of the nation of the Jews. In these first verses he points out that the Lord had literally fulfilled what He, through Moses and the prophets, had foretold long ago. The first verse briefly mentions a specific time, the theocratic ruler, the world monarch, and his siege of Jerusalem.

The contesters of Daniel and his prophecy made much ado about the contradiction which seems to exist between the time reference in Daniel 1:1 and that given in Jeremiah 25:1; 36:1; and 46:2, which verses refer to the same event but speak not of the third but of the fourth year of the reign of Jehoiakim. This seeming contradiction can easily be solved when we assume that Daniel, being in Babylon, not only adheres to Babylonian time but also reckons from the time of Nebuchadnezzar's advance to Jerusalem, whereas Jeremiah in denoting the time is thinking rather of the result of that campaign against the holy city. Besides, there is still another way of dissolving this objection.

Without doing violence to the original language we can read this verse as saying "marched against" instead of came to Jerusalem. But the other, most commonly accepted solution is in our opinion also the most likely. At any rate, we may safely conclude from this seeming contradiction that it was not a pious deceiver who wrote this introductory verse. Such a one would have anxiously guarded against even the semblance of contradiction.

The condition of the kingdom of Judah during the last years of its existence was lamentably bad. In the year 722 B.C. the northern kingdom had been sacked, but Judah had not taken this to heart. It was blind to this alarming example and deaf to all admonitions (Jer. 3:6-12). During the reign of Manasseh and Amon, unspeakable abominations had been committed. The God-fearing King Josiah courageously undertook the work of reformation, but he was not able to stop the vile stream of unrighteousness (2 Kings. 22; 23:1-30; 2 Chron. 34 and 35). Years before, Isaiah had already cried out, "From the sole of the foot even unto the head there is no soundness in it; but wounds and bruises, and putrefying sores: they have not been closed, neither bound up, neither mollified with ointment" (Isa. 1:6). Such a sickness could no longer be cured, and the Lord had become weary with repenting (Jer. 15:6).

Josiah's death in the battle of Megiddo was an enormous disaster to the theocracy. Already after three months, Jehoahaz was deposed by Pharaoh-Necho of Egypt. His older brother, Eliakim, was appointed as his successor, whose name was changed to Jehoiakim as he is called in this verse. This name means "God shall establish" in the sense of cause to excel, make excellent among his people. But Scripture depicts him as a ruler who excelled in wickedness. He was treacherous, hot-headed, cruel, lascivious; he caused idolatry to thrive and hated the Word and the servants of the Lord. This theocratic king was not only a vassal of Egypt and Babylon but even more of Satan and his evil schemes. As the leader is, so is the nation. His example, which should have been a warning to Judah, was all too eagerly followed. Thus the measure of sin had at last been filled and judgment upon Judah and Jerusalem was inevitable. From then on the theocracy must make place for the world empire.

Jehoiakim, the king of Judah, is the manifestation of the vanishing theocracy; Nebuchadnezzar, the king of Babylon, is the incarnation of the emergence of the world empire. It is not these kings who are absolute opposites and antipodes, and who cannot exist alongside of each other, but rather their kingdoms. The world empire appeared the moment the theocracy on earth disappeared, and the moment the world empires will disappear, the theocracy will again be restored. The instrument God used to officially remove the theocracy from Judah, and thereby from the earth, was Nebuchadnezzar, the king of Babylon.

Nebuchadnezzar! The name of this world ruler is as equally well known in Scripture as in history. In Scripture his name also appears as "Nebuchadrezzar". This form is the more correct one and means, "Nebo protects the crown." Scripture calls him several times "the servant of the Lord," not to indicate that he wished to serve the Lord with his whole heart, but that, in spite of himself, he must serve the Lord in fulfilling the judgment upon Judah, just as seventy years later Cyrus the Great was called His servant, because he must restore Israel. When God puts someone to work and gives him an important task, He makes him prosperous until that given task is completed. That is what happened to Nebuchadnezzar.

One of his most famous battles is described in Jeremiah 46 in a divine manner. There, in the battle at Carchemish, the mighty Pharaoh-Necho of Egypt had found his Waterloo, and the lot of the world at that time was sealed. With that victory the young crown prince, Nebuchadnezzar, had obtained his greatest laurels. Already the Lord had used him as His executioner to carry out the sentence on Pharaoh-Necho and Egypt, on account of the injustice Egypt had done to His people. In the same way Cyrus would come one day, and in his turn and for the same reason execute judgment upon Babylon. At the establishment of the covenant of grace it had not been said in vain that whoever cursed Israel would be cursed (Gen. 12:1-3). Nevertheless, it must be said to his honor that Nebuchadnezzar always treated the Jews with respect.

After the conquest of the city of Carchemish on the Euphrates, Nebuchadnezzar advanced on Palestine to make the nations subjected by Necho tributaries to the crown of Babylon. From the Euphrates to the Nile he subjugated one nation after another, so that he struck terror all around, and from that time on Necho had neither the courage nor the strength to venture outside his own borders.

Whereas all nations round about were seized with fright, the frivolous inhabitants of Jerusalem continued to hang on to and trust in the invincibility of Jerusalem. Had not a man like Isaiah shared this opinion and in that confidence sung:

Look upon Zion, the city of our solemnities: thine eyes shall see Jerusalem a quiet habitation, a tabernacle that shall not be taken down; not one of the stakes thereof shall ever be removed, neither shall any of the cords thereof be broken (Isa. 33:20)?

Was Isaiah mistaken then? Believing Judah might have asked, and we may ask too. The answer to this question must be that Judah already applied to blood-guilty Jerusalem that which will not be perfectly applicable until the time of the truly theocratical Jerusalem of the future. Isaiah was not mistaken, as unbelief scorns. Just as Micah's prophecy concerning blood-guilty Jerusalem was fulfilled—that it would become ruins (Mic. 3:12)—so will also this glorious fact become reality one day, when Jerusalem will be established in the top of the mountains (Mic. 4:1). The bloody city screamed for God's vengeance. Had not Jerusalem become like unto Sodom and Gomorrah (Jer. 23:14)? And vengeance did come. For if God's words do not avail, He then comes with deeds. If the manifestation of His grace is rejected, then He comes with the manifestation of His vengeance. And then the latter will be more fierce to the extent that the former is greater.

Sacred history makes no mention of the actual siege of which verse 1 speaks (2 Kings. 24 and 2 Chron. 36). Apparently Jehoiakim, who until then had been a vassal of Necho, offered no resistance but voluntarily subjected himself to Nebuchadnezzar. It is not stated he was actually carried away to Babylon, only that Nebuchadnezzar took him prisoner to carry him off. In Ezekiel 19 Jehoiakim is compared to a devouring lion pursued by the aggravated nations around, caught in a net, taken in a pit, and put in ward in chains with rings through his nose. So Jehoiakim was taken to the king of Babylon, always supposing his voice would no longer be heard on the mountains of Israel. His ready subjection, combined with the promise that he would be Nebuchadnezzar's servant, apparently caused the latter to decide to return the throne to Jehoiakim as his vassal. For the rest the conqueror satisfied himself by carrying away a number of hostages to Babylon, as well as a considerable part of the precious vessels of the temple.

King Carried Captive

And the Lord gave Jehoiakim king of Judah into his hand, with part of the vessels of the house of God: which he carried into the land of Shinar to the house of his god; and he brought the vessels into the treasure house of his god (v. 2).

In this verse we find the striking contrast between what the Lord did and what Nebuchadnezzar did; between Adonai as the Mighty One of the whole earth and Bel, the god of Babylon. Numerous times the Lord through Moses and the prophets had foretold that if Israel were to break the people's covenant, the nation would be banished from its inheritance (Exod. 19:5, 6). The Lord had always emphatically pointed out that He Himself would deliver them into the hands of their enemies and carry them away (see Lev. 26:33-45; Deut. 4:27; 28:25-37; Jer. 18:16; 19:8; 42:18; 43:10; 44:22; 51:37; Mic. 3:12 and many other places). Those predictions had now been fulfilled, and see how the Lord once again emphatically points out that it was He Himself who had given Jehoiakim into the hand and into the power of Nebuchadnezzar, together with part of the holy temple utensils. The reason why the Lord re-emphasizes this here, it seems to us, is threefold.

First of all, this proud and stiff-necked people (as we learn to know them especially in Jeremiah and Ezekiel), could be divested of the illusion that they had been delivered in order to perpetrate abominations (Jer. 7:4-10; Ezek. 8) or to think the Lord did not see them doing these things. They could learn from this word that, far from being delivered, they were imprisoned because of these abominations. Their exile was the fruit of their thoughts (Jer. 6:19). Let Israel in exile realize that God is not an idle spectator of evil!

Secondly, the statement that the Lord had delivered Jehoiakim into the hands of Nebuchadnezzar contained no small comfort as well. Exile as such was a terrible thing to the God-fearing mind. For Israel did not merely go to Babylon to sojourn there as strangers as it had once done in Egypt, but definitely as exiles, banned from their own inheritance, from the face of God, and moreover as a conquered people under the dominion of their uncircumcised conquerors. How the God-fearing people looked upon their exile can be gathered from the words of Jeremiah in Lamentations 5. Also these God-fearing people could so easily make the mistake of looking only at secondary causes or viewing God as having become totally indifferent to His land, His people, His house, and His service (Lam. 2:1-9). To comfort these people the Lord points out His power and His truth. He who had the power to deliver them into the hand of the enemy also had the power to deliver them from the enemy. If He, as the true God, had at last carried out His threats, then He would in the end also not fail to fulfill His promise of deliverance after seventy years.

Thirdly, Nebuchadnezzar received here a divine hint. Nebuchadnezzar was a heathen, but there is no doubt that several times he was influenced by divine revelation. It is quite likely Jeremiah and Ezekiel frequently addressed him; that Daniel did so we know for a fact. As Jeremiah tells us more than once, and as is sufficiently evident from Daniel's prophecy, Nebuchadnezzar, with all his excellent character traits, was extremely proud. Well then, as a proud person, as a conqueror, and as a heathen, he could only think that he had subjected Israel by his power and by the power of his god. Daniel 4:30 shows us clearly what he thought of himself and his kingdom. Only as a pious heathen did he share the honor with his god, as this verse indicates. He took, or rather, he let his captives and the golden vessels be taken as the trophies of his victory to the land of Shinar, which is the old name for the land of Babylon, and put them in the house of his god, while he put the vessels in the treasure house of his god. The fact that this text speaks of his god twice points out not only that he was a heathen, but also that he considered Bel, the chief god of Babylon, his special property and as someone whom he allowed to share in his favor and glory. But even though this ruler ascribed his victory over Judah to the power of his weapons and of his god, the Lord made him realize here that it was He who had delivered Jehoiakim, Judah, and the holy vessels into his power. Daniel constantly and with emphasis points this out (2:37, 38; 4:20-22; 5:18, 19).

"The Lord delivered Jehoiakim, the king of Judah, into Nebuchadnezzar's hands." It is generally little realized that this brief statement provides the key to the understanding of the prophecy of Daniel. It clarifies many of Daniel's actions and words and also sheds a surprising light on the sad history of Israel to this very day. This statement does not merely tell us God is mighty and His thoughts are wholly different from those of His instrument Nebuchadnezzar, but that a new era, totally different from all previous eras, had now dawned. The time of the theocracy had passed and that of the world empire had come.

What does it mean that the time of the theocracy or the reign of God was past? It implies that from then on the Lord was no longer on earth with His glory and immediate authority. Ezekiel describes how he saw the glory of the Lord depart from the temple (Ezek. 9:3). Going hand in hand with this departure of the glory of God was that His immediate government on earth was placed in the hands of the mighty ones of earth. Today God still rules on earth. He never lets the reins of government slip from His hands. They are fools who think He does not cause the wars and destructions on earth (Ps. 46).

But once He had a special people who, as a nation, were to stand at the head of the other nations. According to His covenant with the people (Exod. 19:5, 6), Israel was His peculiar treasure, the nation of all nations. Isaiah frequently calls this people His servant who was to serve Him in order to bless all nations. But this people had become worldly-minded and, therefore, the Lord now abandoned them, as a nation, to the world, for He often punishes with the same thing with which sin is committed. Now these world powers, namely, their rulers, such as Nebuchadnezzar and Cyrus, are called His servants in the execution of His counsel. A beginning had been made with what the Savior later called "the times of the Gentiles" (Luke 21:24). Jerusalem will continue to be trodden down by the heathen as long as these times of the Gentiles last, and during all that time it will be *Lo-ammi*, "not My people," and *Lo-ruhama*, "unpitied" by the Lord. Hence as a nation among, or above, the other nations, Israel has now been rejected for many centuries, because it has broken God's covenant with the people (Exod. 19:5, 6; 24:7-18; 34:10-28), just as Adam once broke the covenant of works. But as the elect covenant people of the Lord, Israel can never be rejected, for the calling and election of God are irrevocable. Israel had now become *Lo-ammi*. Hosea's prophecy had been fulfilled.

In Daniel the Lord never once calls Israel His people, and He never uses His covenantal name, Jehovah. That is why He does not say here that Jehovah gave the king of Judah into the hand of Nebuchadnezzar, but Adonai, the Omnipotent One of the whole earth, whom everyone must obey as His servant. Also the temple is not called here, as usually, the house of Jehovah, but simply the house of God. There is progressive development in evil! Already in the day of Hezekiah, the Babylonians had cast covetous glances at the temple treasures; now part of these treasures had been taken by them. After a few more years all of them would be carried off to add glory to the gods of Babylon, until finally Belshazzar would even use these God-dedicated things to provoke the Lord!

Choice Children

And the king spake unto Ashpenaz, the master of his eunuchs, that he should bring certain of the children of Israel, and of the king's seed, and of the princes; children in whom was no blemish, but well favored, and skillful in all wisdom, and cunning in knowledge, and understanding science, and such as had ability in them to stand in the king's palace, and whom they might teach the learning and the tongue of the Chaldeans (vv. 3, 4).

Ashpenaz was the master of his eunuchs. The word "eunuchs" means castrated men. But this by no means indicates we are to think of such a mutilated person here, or that Daniel and his friends were castrated, although it is somewhat remarkable we do not read that any of these four young men led a married life. Since Ashpenaz apparently was in the army with Nebuchadnezzar, it is quite likely that the term refers to a general title and that this man belonged to the bodyguard of the king or was the head of all the courtiers. When it is said here he should bring certain of the children of Israel, it means he had to take these young men to Babylon. We must not picture Nebuchadnezzar as being in Babylon himself, for he had not yet completed his campaign. The word "bring" is the same as that used in verse 2 of the bringing of the holy vessels to the land of Shinar.

This account speaks of the first deportation to Babylon, and is commonly considered the beginning of the seventy-year exile. After this carrying away there were five more, not just two as is usually stated. The idea there were only three and not six different deportations originated apparently on the basis of Jeremiah 52:28-30, which makes mention of three different abductions. But this passage speaks exactly of the three which are not mentioned in the histories of the Kings and in Chronicles.

The second deportation took place, according to Jeremiah 52:28, in the seventh year of Nebuchadnezzar, when only 3,023 Jews were carried away to Babylon. The third exile to Babylon is described in 2 Chronicles 24:8-16. This took place in the eighth year of Nebuchadnezzar, hence one year after the second. Figured according to the number of captives, it was the largest. Among the captives were also Ezekiel (Ezek. 1, 2) and Mordecai's grandfather, Shimei (Esth. 2:5, 6).

The fourth exile is mentioned in Jeremiah 52:29. This took place in the thirteenth year of Nebuchadnezzar, during the siege of Jerusalem. At this occasion only 832 persons were taken from Jerusalem. The fifth exile took place a year later at the destruction of Jerusalem itself (Jer. 52:15). And for the sixth time a deportation took place in the twenty-third year of Nebuchadnezzar, hence some four years after the actual destruction of Jerusalem. At this time only 745 of the poor remaining people were taken. As some of these captures took place soon after each other, they are sometimes taken together as, for instance, the second and third, and the fourth and fifth.

When Moses and the prophets speak of the future exile, they always present it as one event. This shows that time distinctions do not play the greatest role in history. At the same time we can derive the hint from this that in the one "day of Christ" many and great acts of God may take place.

But we return to the charge given Ashpenaz. This charge insisted these first captives must consist of the choice of the people, young men whose glory is their strength. The word "children" used in the King James Version is a pliable concept; here we must think of the ages between fifteen and twenty years. They must be young men of royal and noble blood. Nebuchadnezzar was very ambitious. When soon these persons of royal blood would be serving him, this would greatly increase his royal splendor. Young men of courtly manners and civilized deportment would be all the more capable to stand in the king's palace.

These young men must not only be of high birth, but also in excellent physical condition with beautiful features. A beautiful form was, according to Eastern concepts, most closely connected with excellence of mind and spirit, and this was even considered as a sign of a favorable disposition on the part of the gods. Moreover, we must not forget that we are dealing here with "the civilized world." Being externalized by sin, it is always obsessed with external beauty. This holds true for the entire classical world as well as present-day "decent" heathendom. To the extent there is less interest in the internal beauty of things, to that extent people get all excited about external beauty.

Furthermore, these young men must excel in spirit. As a further requirement, Ashpenaz was told they must be skillful in all wisdom. This does not mean they must already possess all wisdom. Their youth alone made this impossible. What is meant is that they must be bright and intelligent, so that if so desired they could eventually master all wisdom. What has been said about beauty applies even more to the wisdom of this world. It has always been one of the things highly rated by men, and frequently also highly rated in the estimation of Christian men. Beauty, wisdom, power—these are the three great qualities the world restlessly pursues. Daniel's prophecy demonstrates strikingly how God puts all three to shame.

Cunning in knowledge was another quality Ashpenaz was to look for when selecting his elect men. Literally, it says knowing knowledge, which is to say they must be eager to learn and have a burning desire to study and apply themselves to the utmost to obtain knowledge. Man has never completely taken leave of the tree of knowledge. In a metaphorical sense it may be said that he, like Eve before him, casts a longing look at its desirable fruit.

And understanding science was a further demand of the king. What he meant is no doubt penetrating discrimination or discernment. It is evident that the king's demands were by no means moderate. The Lord Jesus is satisfied with far less in His servants. He does not, in the first place, look at the head but at the heart. And, rightly considered, faithfulness is the only thing He demands of His servants. But then faithfulness in all things, the small as well as the big, with respect to the unfaithful as well as the faithful part of the flock.

Finally, the dual purpose for this elect body and its requirements are mentioned in these words: "and such as had ability in them to stand in the king's palace, and whom they might teach the learning and the tongue of the Chaldeans." They must be educated to become courtiers and wise men. In worldly terms, a brilliant future opened up before these young men. Honor, riches, and power all lay within their reach if they only had the right ambition to make good in the world; an ambition that is also found in many young men from Christian homes today. The Bible knows nothing of this kind of getting ahead in the world, however. Scripture does not point forward but upward, and, therefore, makes the forward subservient to the upward. Paul pressed toward what lay ahead, because he desired to go upward, and reached forth with both hands unto eternal life. Later on we shall see that these young men also totally rejected this kind of ambition which has no scruples and thinks only of honor, riches, and power.

The learning of the Chaldeans that must be taught these young men does not refer to books as we know them, nor scrolls, but to clay tablets of which lately numerous samples have been found. Already many books were written and made, and they were read over and over again. These books contained the history and religion of the people as well as the science or wisdom of those days, of which we in our proud times must not have too low an opinion, for these ancient Chaldeans had made great advances in certain branches of science, such as higher geometry and star gazing. The clear skies at night in which the stars sparkled with exceptional brilliance greatly facilitated these sciences.

These young men must, of course, also learn the tongue of the Chaldeans. It is not sure whether this refers to the Chaldean language as we find in a large part of Daniel's prophecy and which is also called Aramaic, or to the original language of the Chaldeans, which was related to the Scythian languages further north. In opposition to the first idea, it has been argued that between the Aramaic in Daniel and Hebrew there is little difference. Well-educated young men of royal and noble blood must already have known this language or at least could have learned it without any trouble. The learned people of today all too often forget they know practically nothing of the original pronunciation of this language, and it may have differed greatly from Hebrew. These two ideas by no means exclude each other. It is quite possible these young men were taught the original language of the Chaldeans which was still preserved among the caste of these learned men, just as those who wish to study English thoroughly must devote considerable time in studying Anglo-Saxon.

We find here the literal fulfillment of the Word of the Lord which He, through Isaiah, addressed to Hezekiah, berating him for having shown all his treasures to Merodach-baladan: "And of thy sons that shall issue from thee which thou shalt beget, shall they take away; and they shall be eunuchs in the palace of the king of Babylon" (Isa. 39:7). The Lord is a fulfiller of His Word, never allowing a jot or a tittle to fail by not fulfilling it. He is not a man that He should lie. His promises are fulfilled as precisely as His threatenings. His Word is true.

Severe Trials

And the king appointed them a daily provision of the king's meat, and of the wine which he drank: so nourishing them three years, that at the end thereof they might stand before the king. Now among these were of the children of Judah, Daniel, Hananiah, Mishael, and Azariah: unto whom the prince of the eunuchs gave names: for he gave unto Daniel the name of Belteshazzar; and to Hananiah, of Shadrach; and to Mishael, of Meshach; and to Azariah, of Abed-nego (vv. 5-7).

These youths had to endure three severe trials. We must keep in mind that Chaldean wisdom was inseparably connected with the heathen religion of the Babylonians. If anywhere then it was here that truth was mixed with falsehood. We need only remember in this connection the defilement attending the eating of certain food, but the spiritual food they had to take in from day to day was no less unclean. There is also a defiling and poisoning of the spirit, although it must be admitted that in our materialistic days people, even in Christian circles, often hardly think about that. We can safely assume the study of these young men must have been a daily ordeal to them. Yet the study as such did not deter them. By God's common grace it contained good elements, and by constantly praying for the light of special grace from above, they must have proved all things, but only to hold fast that which was good. This is a precious example to young people from Christian homes who study at agnostic universities!

Not only their education but also their food immediately presented a serious problem. The royal order to Ashpenaz covered everything pertaining to the training of these youths. Thus he also decreed they should be given royal food. When the text speaks of provision of the king's meat, we must not think of the leftovers of the king's table. In verse 16 we come across the same word and that would make little sense there. Many people marvel at the magnanimity of the king in that he determined to let these captive slaves eat from his own table. But most likely we are dealing here with a smart demonstration of statecraft rather than with a character trait on the king's. For no doubt it was not pity for these young men, so far removed from their parental home and native country, that motivated his action, but rather the ambitious and at the same time wise intent to give these young men a royal status by providing them royal food (cf. v. 15). And most of all thereby to flatter them, so that by this means they would that much sooner forget their cares, their parents, and their God in order to devote themselves with an undivided heart to the interests of the Babylonian kingdom. Meanwhile, this royal nourishment presented a great dilemma to Daniel and his friends. Later on we shall see how they passed this test of faith most gloriously.

The third trial lay in the changing of their names. It is true it is not specifically stated that this constituted a trial, but by logical deduction this can be fairly and sufficiently assumed. Verses 3 and 4 speak of the election by the king; verse 6 mentions the elect of God by name. Naturally, countless young men had been taken from Judah to Babylon. They were all young men who had the sign of the covenant on them. But once they were in Babylon, we neither hear or see them again. Did they, after their arrival in Babylon, become Babylonians? We do not know, but it would not surprise us. The attraction of the world was strong in Babylon, especially to a young mind. In any case, God did not count them worthy to be named in His Word. Here God is present with His elect group: a foursome chosen from among the masses, and then from these desirable four the man greatly loved, Daniel, as the one specially favored by God.

They are fools who do not believe in election, for it affects all of life. Both Scripture and history are equally full of it. From among the many thousands of warriors in Israel, David possessed thirty special heroes, but there were three among these thirty who exceeded the rest and who stood out among them in brilliance; but even these three could not measure up to "the first three." This selection or election by God is also found with regard to the patriarchs, the psalmists, the prophets, the apostles, and even to the women whom Scripture mentions. A Dorcas stood higher than a Euodia and a Syntyche. Persis, the beloved sister, who labored much in the Lord, is carefully distinguished by Paul from two other sisters. The latter do not receive the high praise of being beloved and of having labored much in the Lord as Persis did.

Both from the names as well as from the conduct of these four young men we can almost certainly conclude they had had a God-fearing mother. The special tenderness of conscience these youth manifested later on is as a rule only instilled in early youth by the tender godliness of a mother. All four of their names refer to Israel's God. They were glorious names! And what horrible names they were given instead! Daniel, "God is my Judge," was called Belteshazzar, "Prince of Bel," according to Nebuchadnezzar's own explanation in 4:8; Hananiah, "Gift," or "favored one" of Jehovah, received the name of Shadrach, "Enlightened by Rag," the sun-god; Mishael, "Who is like unto God?" became Meshach, "Who is like unto Shach?" (the goddess of lust); Azariah, "Help of Jehovah," received the idolatrous name of Abed-nego, "Servant of Nego," another idol, probably the same as Nebo the moon god.

This is not an ordinary change of names as in other instances, such as Pharaoh-Necho changing the name of Eliakim into another Jewish name, Jehoiakim (2 Kings. 23:34), and as Nebuchadnezzar himself did with the name of Mattania, for which he substituted the Jewish name of Zedekiah. We are not dealing with merely a custom or with a facilitation of pronouncing foreign names, but with a Satanic drive to make these young men forget the Name and Being of the God of Israel and at the same time to familiarize them with the abominable gods and goddesses of Babylon.

We find here the diabolic opposite of what the Lord Himself did with the names Abram, Sarai, Jacob, and Simon. It needs no argument that these name changes were a severe trial to them. For the sound of their new names was a daily mockery of their upbringing, their religion, and their God. Besides, Jews attached much greater value to a name than we do. To us names are usually mere sounds, but Jews often conceived of names as agreeing with the essence of things. Added to this was the fact these youths were unable to resist this trial. With regard to the study of heathen wisdom they could, with their enlightened consciences, distinguish between what was good and what was bad. With regard to food, they could simply leave everything untouched and ask for cereals. But this changing of names they simply had to accept, whether they wanted to or not. Hence the trial came down to this, that they had to put up with a daily lie, an indignity, an attack against their own God, and a mockery.

It is evident that Daniel considered his own name most preferable, since he always calls himself by his Hebrew name. Others called him Belteshazzar, but he himself never (7:1; 8:1, 15, 27; 9:2). And when heaven addressed him, it too was always by his Hebrew name, Daniel (9:22; 10:11; 12:9).

These young men must be educated for three years according to the order of the king. They were to be housed in royal quarters, fed royal fare, and be given royal instruction. This length of time and special treatment was considered necessary to become fully acquainted with the Chaldean wisdom, language, and manners of the court. Interestingly, still today three years of intense study at a seminary is also considered long enough to prepare oneself for the service of the Lord.

Faith Honored

But Daniel purposed in his heart that he would not defile himself with the portion of the king's meat, nor with the wine which he drank: therefore he requested of the prince of the eunuchs that he might not defile himself. Now God had brought Daniel into favor and tender love with the prince of the eunuchs (vv. 8, 9).

A moment ago Daniel was mentioned in one breath together with his friends, but here we already see him outshine the others and take a leading position in behalf of the others. These verses speak of his choice of faith, his act of faith, and his reward of faith.

It is a remarkable fact that so many men of God in the Old Testament have names whose meaning agrees with their task in life. This holds true of Moses, Joshua, David, Solomon, Elijah, Isaiah, Micah, Malachi, and many others. This can now also be said of Daniel's name. It points to the justice and judgment of God. What has Daniel's entire life been but a divine judging of heathen wise men, kings, and gods? Already at the inauguration of the covenant of grace itself, God had said, regarding the Egyptians, that He would judge the nation that would make His nation serve it (Gen. 15:14). In essence the same sentence was foretold regarding the Chaldean oppressors. The exile had commenced and the Lord already started His moral judgment. Just as Noah by the building of the ark condemned the first world (Heb. 11:7), so Daniel by his faithfulness and tender conscience condemned Babylon.

"But Daniel purposed in his heart." In this phrase Scripture describes his choice of faith. Josephus, Calvin, and others make it sound as though Daniel acted that way for physical reasons, but we obviously must think of religious reasons. It is true Daniel's conscientious objection originated from a desire to be moderate, but even at a luxurious table Daniel could have practiced moderation, so it is preferable to think purely of religious objections. The ceremonial law was of such a nature that a strict Jew could actually not eat with a heathen. Hence Israel was a people that must dwell alone and should not be reckoned among the nations (Num. 23:9; Deut. 33:28). Also by means of the ceremonial law the Lord forced Israel in every respect to dwell alone. Hence by virtue of the divine law there were at least three objections that made it impossible for Daniel and his friends to partake of the royal fare.

In the first place, unclean animals would be constantly served. The Lord had made for Israel a separation between clean and unclean (Lev. 11; Deut. 14). Secondly, in many cases food for Israel had to be prepared a certain way and not otherwise. Clean animals had to be butchered in a manner that absolutely no blood remained in the meat. The Jews were forbidden on pain of death to eat fat and blood (Lev. 3:16; 17:10-13). But now they would be constantly confronted with such unclean things at the heathen table. The third and most important reason for this action must have been the wine, which was not forbidden as such, but was first dedicated to the gods as a libation before it was brought to the table. This was to the heathen what prayer at the table is to us. Hence there were sufficient reasons why Daniel absolutely refused to partake of it.

People have wondered and have been puzzled by the fact that a young man like Daniel, who had hardly outgrown the shoes of his childhood and who was a slave besides, and who had, moreover, been treated very nobly by Nebuchadnezzar, could manifest such an exaggerated scrupulousness, as it has been called. The people who speak that way have, obviously, never known what living by principles, living with a clear conscience, is all about. Daniel was a person in whom the fear of God dwelt. This fear had become the power of his life. He had given his heart to God and, consequently, lived by his heart. He would rather risk all that Babylon would array against him than to pollute his heart. He would rather be at odds with the whole world than with even a part of the truth. A sly policy of weighing the odds was alien to him. To give and take and compromise was a foreign art to him. Steering a middle course was impossible to him. Running back and forth between Bel and El was out of the question. While he was in Babylon he was not of Babylon. So away with all these delicacies! Away with them for the sake of God! It is only the Esaus who for a dish of pottage sell their birthright, but not so the Daniels. Therefore, we had better admire this young lad rather than wonder at him.

It is difficult to say what is most admirable in him—his self-denial by which he pushed the royal food aside, his childlike fear of doing something against God's law, his trust in God, or his calm courage of faith by which he even dared to resist the ordinance of Nebuchadnezzar. From whatever angle we look at him, the gold of his faith sparkles on every side.

After the choice of faith follows the act of faith. If our walk is to be good, then first of all things within us must be in good condition. From the heart issue forth all acts of life. Before Daniel resisted the ordinance of the mighty king of Babylon, he had Babylon, in a moral sense, already under his feet, and in his heart he had completely conquered Babylon.

A choice of faith precedes an act of faith. That is the right order, which, alas, is all too often lost sight of by people who are engaged in what they call Christian action, without first having made an inner and firm choice. But a choice of faith, no matter how pleasant in itself before God, is nevertheless insufficient for life in its rich variations; it is not real in the sense that it is not realized. Speaking in a broad sense, religion implies two kinds of relationship and calling; with respect to God and with respect to men. That is, the first and second tables of the law. For that reason the choice of the heart must always be succeeded in life by the active carrying out of its implications. This is what Daniel did.

"Therefore, he requested of the prince of the eunuchs that he might not defile himself." Faith makes courageous, as is evident here, for it was indeed a brave undertaking to come to the fore with such a request. A head of the eunuchs was a great lord and a heathen besides who could not possibly understand this request and therefore could not justify it either. How many critics and expositors are there who can barely control their anger with this young man who, by worldly standards, could in such a way spurn his fortune. Who could immediately upon entering the world destroy his brilliant career in it! Would it have been any wonder if this man Ashpenaz had seen it as stupid resistance against his lord and king, or consistent fault-finding in the young man that he dared consider such delicious food unclean? True faith of the heart, however, is not only courageous but also tender and tactful. Daniel did not storm toward Ashpenaz with loud steps and theatrical gesticulations to tell him in no uncertain terms what he thought of it, and that he wanted none of this heathen junk, etc., etc. No, he did not come with a protest, but with a request.

A good matter can be handled in a very bad manner, and that happens all too often in life. But Daniel had a good matter and he also presented it in the right way. He who was like a lion in his courage of faith was also like a lamb in his humility. So he does not come roaring like a lion to Ashpenaz but approaches him like a lamb. Daniel was, as we shall see again and again, a faint image of the Lamb that one day would take away the sin of the world.

Such a faith that expresses itself so courageously, freely, and humbly, always obtains from God the reward of faith. God gave Daniel grace and mercy. Daniel had believed the words of Deuteronomy 8:3, "Man doth not live by bread only." Daniel believed the God of his fathers, who at one time by His almighty power had fed Moses and Elijah for forty days, lived still, and would do the same for him, even for forty years if necessary. He had believed the entire ceremonial law. He had believed and therefore he had spoken. On his part he could do no more. Now it was up to God to intervene actively. And He who keepeth truth forever did not fail him. We read of the Savior that He increased in wisdom, i.e., in favor with both God and man (Luke 2:52). Hence with Him the twofold relationship had harmoniously become one. Now God did the same for Daniel.

God inclined the heart of Ashpenaz so that he, too, looked upon Daniel with favor. It is quite possible Ashpenaz was already favorably inclined toward this youthful captive. In any case take into account the omniscient guidance of God who inclined the heart of this heathen to His darling and gave him a listening ear for his petition. "Those who honor Me I shall honor," the Lord has said. To him who orders his ways aright, God will show His salvation. According to His rewarding justice this can never fail.

Daniel's Proposition

And the prince of the eunuchs said unto Daniel, I fear my lord the king, who hath appointed your meat and your drink: for why should he see your faces worse liking than the children which are of your sort? then shall ye make me endanger my head to the king.

Then said Daniel to Melzar whom the prince of the eunuchs had set over Daniel, Hananiah, Mishael and Azariah. Prove thy servants, I beseech thee, ten days; and let them give us pulse to eat, and water to drink. Then let our countenances be looked upon before thee, and the countenance of the children that eat of the portion of the king's meat: and as thou seest, deal with thy servants. So he consented to them in this matter, and proved them ten days (vv. 10-14).

Faith is often sorely tested. Daniel experienced this more than once. Ashpenaz was by no means unfavorably inclined toward Daniel. He even looked upon him with favor and tender love when the youth stood there before him with his serious and polite request. Nevertheless, mountains of objections arose before his eyes. For he was not master alone. His own master was the awesome Nebuchadnezzar who killed whomever he wished. And Nebuchadnezzar had given him the express command to feed these young men thus and no other way. Was he now simply to grant the request of this young man, squarely contrary to the king's instructions? If he allowed this, and the king were to learn of it, would he not knock his head off?

We sense the burden of this man. And he frankly admitted it by saying he feared the king, that the latter had given a clear command, and that Daniel and his friends by their lessened attractiveness would give themselves away to the king and him also. There seemed to be a conflict of obligations within this man. He dared not cast Nebuchadnezzar's command to the winds and he wanted not to refuse Daniel's request. At last he seems to have found a way out. As head of the eunuchs he had merely given general rules and instructions. He had appointed a certain person as cook and food master for these four young men. While he did not openly want to grant Daniel's request and thereby rescind Nebuchadnezzar's command, he could quietly condone that Daniel and Melzar decide this matter. It is, moreover, not unlikely that he even dropped Melzar a hint.

So Daniel went to Melzar with his request. We must not think of Melzar as a proper name but as the name of an office, for the text says that Daniel spoke to "the Melzar." The definite article points out that we are dealing here with some lower official such as a kitchen chef. Ashpenaz was more than willing to grant Daniel his request, as long as it would not put him in danger. For Melzar, a lower official, this danger hardly existed. So Daniel came with his request to him who was in charge of food preparation.

It was no longer what we might call a request that he made this time. He went a step further. He fully realized now what lay at the root of all this concern. Those heathen officials were afraid that if the young men did not get their specially selected menus every day, they would soon visibly lose weight and emaciate. Daniel, however, firmly believed this would by no means be the case. The Lord their God would not allow this calamity to happen to them in the way of obedience. For that reason he approached the Melzar with a proposition, namely, that he would allow them a trial period of ten days, during which they would be fed only pulse—food made of ground seeds, fruits, and vegetables, mixed with water. After ten days a comparison could be made with the young men who ate from the king's table. Depending on how this comparison came out, it could then be decided what course of action to take. Daniel was so certain of his case and his victory that he dared to say the courageous words, "And as thou seest, deal with thy servants."

Almost automatically the question presents itself, what would have happened if the Melzar had decided they did not look too well and had ordered them to return to the former food. Would Daniel and his friends have done so? The answer to this question can only be that such an outcome was totally unthinkable to Daniel. We are seeing here true miraculous faith in action. He simply believed a miracle would happen to him and his friends. His faith rested only in God, and he was not put to shame.

"So he consented to them in this matter, and proved them ten days." There is one special trait in Daniel which we observe again and again. It is that he knew how to captivate men's minds in a very special way. This is a unique gift which becomes ours only by God's sovereign creation ordinance. Daniel possessed this gift to a high degree, for whether he stood before his friends, before high officials, over against his conquerors or other mighty rulers, he always commanded respect and people bowed to him. He was a king in the realm of spirits! A king who was able to govern his own heart; a king able to conquer others' hearts. So he also won over this Melzar. Here again we must, in the first place, think of the grace of God, who also inclined the heart of this official as He had done before in the case of Nebuchadnezzar and Ashpenaz. We shall observe further how this trial of faith ended.

Fairer Countenance

And at the end of ten days their countenances appeared fairer and fatter in flesh than all the children which did eat the portion of the king's meat. Thus Melzar took away the portion of their meat, and the wine that they should drink; and gave them pulse (vv. 15, 16).

These verses tell us about the outcome of the trial period. We see here that the Lord performed a miracle by which the heathen were put to shame and the faith of the youths was gloriously rewarded. "Whoever puts in God his trust, builds surely not on sand or dust" It had been the good favor of God that for the second time He had inclined the heart of a heathen official. But His grace shone even more brightly in this feeding miracle. He most clearly showed here that His favor strengthens more than the choicest food. Unbelieving expositors may shut their eyes to this miraculous element and a lukewarm Christendom may prattle in this connection about the value of moderation in eating and drinking. Certainly, moderation has great value, but that is not the issue here. Is it not obvious that this is nothing less than a miracle of the Lord's hand? A miracle not only in the heart of Melzar, but also in the bodies of the young men.

It was clearly visible that their bodies were in better condition than those of the others. Melzar and the others who examined them could see this with their own eyes. These boys were definitely fatter, brawnier, smoother, and better looking than the other young men. Had they on this sparse diet been just as healthy looking, this would already have been a remarkable fact, but they were definitely healthier. Therefore, praise be to the God of Israel who alone performs miracles!

This miracle must have amazed the heathen officials. They had been worried that the king would soon discover Daniel and his friends were failing in health if they were given such simple meals. As heathen they had not taken into account the wonder-working God of Israel. Whether they actually saw the hand of the Lord in all of this is not mentioned, but one thing is certain, Daniel was a mighty witness in that heathen Babylon to the God who performed miracles. He was a witness both in his person and in his words.

Once again the faith of Daniel was gloriously crowned. Just as long ago Elijah had taken on a mighty match amidst his heathenized people, so Daniel had taken on this proposition of a trial period amidst heathendom. And his faith was not put to shame. Nor that of his friends. For although Daniel as the leader stands in the foreground, his three friends, too, shared in that firm trust that can never be put to shame. Thus these four young men were an example that was both humiliating and worth imitating to the other young men who had been carried away from Judah and who, without any qualms of conscience, continued to banquet at the king's table. They not only embodied an example but also a protest against their fellows who forsook God's law in heathen Babylon.

Divine Gifts

As for these four children, God gave them knowledge and skill in all learning and wisdom: and Daniel had understanding in all visions and dreams (v. 17).

It is clear that this whole chapter is an introduction to the entire book, the purpose of which is to point out the position of Daniel and his friends. We may consider them as the representatives of the God-fearing remnant which the Lord, according to the election of His grace, even during the darkest times of the history of His people, has always preserved and for whom He continues to fulfill His promises. So this verse tells us God gave these four faithful young men the special blessing of wisdom, and to Daniel, moreover, the special gift of explaining visions and dreams.

The previous verses showed us that the Lord took care of the physical well-being of His own; the rest of this chapter points out the well-being of their spirits. Earlier the chapter spoke of their health and beauty; here of their wisdom. The Lord had a great task for these young men, and for that reason He gave them an excellent preparation and great wisdom for this work.

We see again and again in Scripture that as a rule the Lord is very sharing with the gift of science and general wisdom, but He nevertheless grants this gift in a special measure to those who have a special position in His kingdom on earth and who must carry out a special task. Thus He gave this special gift at one time to Joseph, to Moses, to David, to Paul, and in the history of His church to

William the Silent [William I, founder of Dutch Republic and first governor of the Netherlands; d. 1584]. All these men occupied extraordinary positions and were called by Him to carry out very special tasks, and, therefore, He also granted them very special training and extraordinary wisdom. Such was the case with Daniel. His position was extraordinary; a God-fearing child at a heathen court. So God gave him not only the most beautiful opportunity to acquire necessary and useful skills, he also gave him wisdom in an unusual measure.

He must have concerned himself very little with the illicit arts and sciences of the heathen Chaldeans but with the licit and beneficial ones all the more. He must have gone constantly to the source from which all wisdom originates (James 1:5), and he must have abhorred the wisdom that is earthly, sensual, and devilish (James 3:15). Daniel's wisdom must have been extremely great, for already in the time of Ezekiel his wisdom had become proverbial among the Jews in Babylon (Ezek. 28:3). God does not despise wisdom. He does not entrust His people to the leadership of ignorant men.

And whereas Daniel must be the spiritual guide and leader of Babylon and Israel at the court of Babylon, the Lord also gave him, in distinction from his friends, understanding in all visions and dreams. This does not refer to mere dreams but to visions and dreams as revelatory means, as is sufficiently evident from what follows. Interpreting dreams was also a secret art belonging to the general arts of the Chaldeans, but here we are emphatically told Daniel had not acquired this ability at the feet of his teachers, but as a gift from above, from God Himself. His three-year course at the heathen seminary could not possibly have provided him with this, no more than many years later the wise Gamaliel could have taught Paul to be content with whatsoever state he was in (Phil. 4:11).

The fact that only Daniel, with the exclusion of the other three young men, received this special gift points out once more the sovereign good pleasure of God, the same motive whereby He has mercy unto eternal life on whomsoever He wills. The purpose of this gift of interpreting dreams can easily be seen in the light of this entire prophecy.

God, in the days of the Old Covenant, revealed Himself many times and in many ways. Even though Israel was now in exile and thereby exiled from before His face, God continued to reveal Himself during that time. He revealed Himself in a different manner, however, as this prophecy teaches us, to other people and for another purpose. He revealed Himself here in the persons of Nebuchadnezzar and Belshazzar at the beginning and the end of the first world power. The Lord had never worked like this before. Nor had He ever announced the end of their empires and all world empires as He did here at the court of the mighty men of the earth.

Since it was God's intent to reveal Himself to the world powers, we see here so strikingly that He takes into account the perceptivity of the instruments of His revelation, and knows how to choose the right means for the right purpose. The ancient heathen were very much enchanted by dreams and visions. The Chaldeans, especially, considered them revelations from their gods. For that reason their sages exerted themselves in the secret art of interpreting dreams.

When we keep in mind that the state and religion in Babylon were absolutely one and the same thing, then we observe the wisdom of God in the sending of His revelatory dreams to Nebuchadnezzar (see chapters 2 and 4). Even though the heathen could receive revelations, they did not possess the light to explain the divine meaning of them. For that purpose did God now give Daniel wisdom in all manner of visions and dreams. This favored man would be the actual means of revelation, whereby God puts to shame both the power and the wisdom of this world. Daniel is the bright, shining star in dark Babylon.

Ten Times Better

Now at the end of the days that the king had said he should bring them in, then the prince of the eunuchs brought them in before Nebuchadnezzar. And the king communed with them; and among them all was found none like Daniel, Hananiah, Mishael, and Azariah: therefore stood they before the king. And in all matters of wisdom and understanding, that the king inquired of them, he found them ten times better than all the magicians and astrologers that were in all his realm. And Daniel continued even unto the first year of king Cyrus (vv. 18-21).

The three-year preparation at the king's training college had sped by. Experience teaches sufficiently that the harder one studies the faster time flies. Ashpenaz, the master of the eunuchs, gives us the impression he was a faithful and kindhearted courtier. According to the order of the king, when the appointed time arrived he led all the Jewish young men whom he had selected in Jerusalem three years before into the presence of the king.

Before Nebuchadnezzar! Ashpenaz's heart, like that of those Jewish boys, must have beaten faster. The king might be in a bad mood, or in a capricious or whimsical mood. And what if he was? Well, then he killed whomever he would, and he put down whomever he would, did he not? (5:19).

After careful preparations the Jewish youths finally stood before him. Nebuchadnezzar in highest grandeur would personally conduct the examinations. The one and only monarch manifested that he alone ruled absolutely. At this examination he was the professor, curator, and examiner all in one person.

We often speak of examination in the singular, but actually this was a twofold examination. Apparently all the Jewish candidates were first brought before him and then afterward the heathen ones, so that a comparative examination could be held between the two groups. Concerning the first examination we are told that among them all, i.e., among the exiles of verse 3, none was found like Daniel, Hananiah, Mishael, and Azariah. It must not escape our attention that they are mentioned here by their Jewish names. They had conducted themselves as true Israelites, and it is also in their quality as true Israelites that they are presented here as the favored ones of God. Had they become Babylonians, like the others, they would not have stood here before the king's face as favored ones, and we would not here read their Jewish names. "How good to Israel Thou art, to those who are the pure of heart!" We do not know how many Jewish boys stood there, but regardless there was not one as fair and as wise as these four.

Daniel stood at the head, probably as an indication that he again outshone his three companions. He was the first also, because he trembled most before God's Word. Is this not remarkable! All these young men from Israel had much in common with each other. They were of the same class and of the same country. They were all covenant children and all exiles. In general their lot and their education had been the same, yet now there was a difference. It was a difference of which the deepest cause lay most certainly in God, but that was due also, as we have seen, to the sin of the others and the fleeing from youthful lusts by these four.

Furthermore, we see in these four select young men the fulfillment of the promise once given at the establishment of the covenant to all who walk in uprightness before His face: "I am thy shield and thy exceeding great reward" (Gen. 15:1) With this statement the Lord promised them His safekeeping and reward. He would keep them safe from Satan, sin, and the world and reward them with the grace He Himself had first given. He had kept these four young men safe from the temptation of sin and from the anger of Nebuchadnezzar. From this examination it is evident to us—it was not to the examiner—that the Lord had, according to His covenant, not withheld from them the recompense of the reward.

After the brilliant examination of these four, whereby they scored off all their former countrymen, they were examined in the presence of the native sages. We need not think all the wise men of Babylon were actually present here or that they too were examined. We rather think these four select young men were evaluated against the wisest men in Babylon. If Daniel and his friends were ten times wiser than they, then it could be truly said that they were "found to be ten times better than all the magicians and astrologers that were in all the realm."

Note here also what great knowledge Nebuchadnezzar himself must have possessed to conduct a comparative examination in all the subjects of the Babylonian arts and sciences before such an assembly, and to ask the examination questions. Both Scripture and history record his great ability not only on the battlefield but also at his court. Furthermore, we must not only praise his knowledge but also his wise circumspection to seek the wisest and most capable men to serve him and his kingdom. The last king of Babylon was guilty of gross neglect in this regard.

Ten times better than all the magicians and astrologers. What a brilliant future lay before them! We must refrain here from making generalizations by saying that the most God-fearing students are also always the brightest, for that is simply not the case. It is indeed a rule that the students who fear the Lord from the heart, like Daniel and his friends, will do their utmost to accumulate useful knowledge, but simply for that reason alone they do not always succeed as brilliantly as these four youths. We are dealing here with a special case, a revelatory marvel, for God had a special purpose with them for Israel—for Nebuchadnezzar, for these young men themselves, for the wise men of Babylon, and most of all for Himself. Daniel and his friends were an excellent example for their people. Israel could see here that true wisdom is most closely connected with the fear of God and obedience to His Word.

Because of this examination Nebuchadnezzar's heart must have been favorably inclined to these Jews. This king, who in many respects was an excellent ruler, had never despised the Jews, but here he must have learned to definitely esteem them. Then, too, these young men must have been greatly encouraged by the outcome to continue to walk in the path of the fear of God. The wise men of Babylon had been put to shame. Their huge pride had received a blow. They had been surpassed ten times over by these four contemptuous Jews. How the king arrived at this score of "ten times better" we do not know, but Scripture says so.

The learned van Hamelsveld translates the word "magicians" as learned in pictography. The word "astrologers" could also be translated as sages, for the Hebrew word *ashaphim* is possibly the same as the Greek *sophoi*, sages. They were the men who by gazing into the eerie realm of the stars thought to discover true or imagined wisdom.

So we see here, and we shall see it again and again, that the wisdom of the world is put to shame by the wisdom of God which dwelt in Daniel and his friends. The God of Israel proved again and again to be the God of wisdom and of sciences and the God who alone performs miracles. Hence when He displayed His wonders before the eyes of heathendom, it was meant to be to the glorification of His name above all other gods and at the same time a preparation for that glad day when all nations shall praise Him, yea, all nations together.

The last verse of this chapter contains a striking hint concerning the duration of Daniel's activities. Thus far we have learned about his status, his fairness, his innate ability, his deportation, the tenderness of his conscience, his lion courage, his lamb-like character, his self-denial, his trust in God, his power over men's hearts, as well as God's favor bestowed upon him and his friends, far above that bestowed upon his fellow exiles and all the sages.

In this final verse we are told of his many years of service. We purposely speak of service, for it is certain he did not die in the first year of Cyrus. For 10:1 tells us during the third year of Cyrus

Daniel still received visions, which are recorded in the last three chapters. The little word translated "unto" by no means excludes the events following it. What must be meant is that Daniel was at the court during the whole time of the first world empire, during the whole seventy-year exile. He saw famous rulers come and go and he saw his people enter exile and leave it. Hence we can conclude from this note that Daniel came to Babylon at a very young age and passed away at a very old age.

The first year of Cyrus the Great was the important year of Israel's release, the year of the famous edict of Cyrus, in which he proclaimed Israel's liberty to all nations, and which reads in the last chapter of 2 Chronicles and the first chapter of Ezra as follows:

> Now in the first year of Cyrus, king of Persia, that the word of the Lord by the mouth of Jeremiah might be fulfilled, the Lord stirred up the spirit of Cyrus, king of Persia, that he made a proclamation throughout all his kingdom, and put it also in writing, saying, Thus saith Cyrus, king of Persia, the Lord God of heaven hath given me all the kingdoms of the earth; and hath charged me to build him an house at Jerusalem, which is in Judah. Who is there among you of all his people? his God be with him, and let him go up to Jerusalem, which is in Judah, and build the house of the Lord God of Israel, (he is the God,) which is in Jerusalem. And whosoever remaineth in any place where he sojourneth, let the men of his place help him with silver, and with gold, and with goods, and with beasts, beside the freewill offering for the house of God that is in Jerusalem (Ezra 1:1-4).

Would not the conjecture be justified that Daniel, whose noble heart was always with his people as is evident from his prophecy and also because of his influential position, had a hand in this important proclamation? If we assume this, then light is shed on the apparent contradiction of this verse with 10:1, for then what is meant here is to simply refer to the most important year of his life—the year of the release of his people. This brief statement then depicts at the same time the most important fruit of his wisdom and power and of his whole long, well-spent, and godly life.

Chapter 2
THE PROPHETIC ALPHABET

A Significant Dream

And in the second year of the reign of Nebuchadnezzar, Nebuchadnezzar dreamed dreams, wherewith his spirit was troubled, and his sleep brake from him. Then the king commanded to call the magicians, and the astrologers, and the sorcerers, and the Chaldeans, for to shew the king his dreams. So they came and stood before the king (vv. 1, 2).

A. C. Gaebelein rightly calls this chapter "one of the great pivotal chapters of the Bible." We might very fittingly call this chapter the prophetic alphabet. The first verse contains a chronological difficulty, which has been seized by the unbelieving in an attempt to prove their theory, that a pious Jew from the period of the Maccabees wrote this book. In Jeremiah 25:1 the fourth year of King Jehoiakim is identified with the first year of Nebuchadnezzar. (See also Daniel 1:1 and our comment.) These young men had already been in training college for three years. How then could the event in this chapter take place in the second year of Nebuchadnezzar?

The solution to this problem as given by believing scholars is very simple. Nebuchadnezzar ruled for some time together with his father as the crown prince and when Jeremiah spoke of the fourth year he counted from the time of the co-regency, whereas Daniel counts from the time Nebuchadnezzar was ruling alone. The critics can score no points from this solution since a "pious deceiver" would have guarded against such a seeming contradiction. This is all the more so since we can gather from chapter 9 that Daniel knew Jeremiah and read his writings constantly.

The bedrooms of the great monarchs of the world, together

with the prisons and hospitals, are as a rule the places of the greatest unrest. The people in the cottage of a day-laborer usually go to bed in far greater peace of mind than is the case here. And so during the second year of his sole kingship, the mighty ruler of Babylon lay restlessly tossing and turning in his bed one night. From verse 29 we learn that one thought in particular occupied his mind. And it is of the utmost importance to realize this well, because the dream was the answer to this one thought and hence also the interpretation. We can say it contains the key to this prophetic chapter and at the same time a refutation of the foolish notion that this book deals first of all with the time of the Maccabees. The thought which troubled the king was the question of what would happen in the future.

This reveals the greatness of character of Nebuchadnezzar. It is the fickle little souls without a care who only drown themselves in the speedily passing present. Souls who are more idealistic try to cast a glance into the future. Nebuchadnezzar's character differed greatly from that of Belshazzar, who threw a big party, a drinking bout, when the enemy stood before the gate. This would be unthinkable to Nebuchadnezzar. He was too farseeing, too serious of mind, and his kingdom weighed too heavily on his heart for such a thing. And so on that particular night he lay thinking about the future of his world empire. Man cannot look an inch into the future, yet he has a strong desire within to lift a tip of the black veil that hides the future and to cast a glance into the unknown. This desire, found among all people of all times, manifests itself in many different ways; one day in anxious concern, another time in a running to the fortune-tellers and sorcerers, and not seldom in bed in the form of the strangest of dreams. This last example was the case with Nebuchadnezzar.

Nebuchadnezzar dreamed dreams. A dream is a mystery. In connection with the vast advances psychology has made in recent years, scientists have paid a good deal of attention to dreams, but they have never succeeded in satisfactorily solving this mystery of the human mind. The human soul in all its activities is a mystery. Dreams can be so sweet that they please the mind, and they can be so bad that they disquiet the soul. The latter was the case with Nebuchadnezzar's revelatory dream. This dream of the heathen king proved to be a means of revelation sent by God.

We might ask whether the Lord still causes such dreams to be dreamed, and then the answer must be absolutely in the negative. All the wondrous dreams which sometimes even pious people trot out, and on which they often build their hope for eternity, must absolutely be rejected. They are as a rule only proof that these people have either eaten too much or have not worked hard enough or maybe have slaved too much (Eccl. 5:3).

Quite frequently among the Mormons the greatest crimes are covered by their so-called revelation dreams. Often they use them as a means in the defense of polygamy. And yet regardless of how firmly we reject present-day revelatory dreams, because the Lord has brought His revelation to a close (Rev. 22:18, 19); every person knows by experience that dreams are mysterious both in origin and in nature.

For example, recently a lawyer in London had been writing letters until late in the evening. After midnight he went out to put them into a mailbox. Upon his return he undressed to go to bed but discovered that he missed a check for a considerable amount of money. Anxiously he started to search for it but all his efforts were in vain. Finally, he went to bed, fell asleep, and dreamed he saw the check lying on the sidewalk not far from his house. He woke up, dressed himself hurriedly, and ran immediately to the spot where, to his great amazement, he indeed found the check. Examples like this could be multiplied many times.

A revelatory dream, however, is one in which God gives a revelation of divine thoughts. It is this kind of dream we have here. People have wondered at the fact that a heathen king was given a revelatory dream, and one of such far-reaching implications at that. This case is by no means unique in Scripture. In Genesis 20:6 we read of a revelatory dream given to Abimelech, the king of Gerar; Genesis 31:24 speaks of such a dream given to Laban; Genesis 40 tells us about the dreams of the Egyptian baker and butler; Genesis 41 tells about Pharaoh's dream. From these examples we can conclude that a dream is one of the lowest, if not the lowest, forms of revelation, and that it is a means used mostly for the heathen or, on special occasions, for His people (see Gen. 31 and 37). Judging by the books of Moses and the prophets, such dreams apparently seldom, if ever, occurred.

It is even very remarkable that for the dreams of Pharaoh and Nebuchadnezzar, interpreters were needed from among His chosen people. The significance of Joseph and Daniel consists to a large extent in the fact that they were famous interpreters of the dreams of heathen kings. For that reason we can continue to call Israel the people of revelation in the fullest sense of the word, for neither Pharaoh nor Nebuchadnezzar would have viewed his dream as a divine revelation without the Jewish interpretation of it. Besides, we can easily understand why Nebuchadnezzar received this dream. For was not Israel at that time *Lo-ammi?* At least that is the way this prophecy views it. Daniel was prophet to Israel only in a secondary degree. Added to this was the fact that the Lord here wished to give a prophecy concerning the character, the unity, and the breakdown of the world monarchies. What would have been more fitting and effective than that Nebuchadnezzar, the golden head of the first world power, received this prophecy himself?

Nebuchadnezzar was deeply troubled by the strange dream he had dreamed. This, too, is nothing strange when we realize:

- People at that time attached special supernatural importance to dreams.
- The Chaldeans were especially very superstitious with regard to men's dream life.
- Nebuchadnezzar apparently realized that it concerned him.
- This image was not only huge and striking in splendor, but according to verse 31 its form was terrible.

Nebuchadnezzar wanted to know the dream and its significance. He was not the kind of man to let an important matter, as he considered the dream to be, evaporate. For that reason he called on the wise men of his realm. We need not assume he called all the wise men to his court and that all there appeared. We need to think only of the most important representatives of the different groups of sages. Four classes are mentioned. The first and second we already met in 1:20. "Sorcerers" must be seen as the spiritists of that time, people who consulted the dead, just as today thousands of apostates ardently pursue these devilish arts. The word sorcerer always appears in the Bible in a negative sense. The "Chaldeans" formed the proud caste of wise men, adorning themselves with this name as if they alone represented the entire nation.

From verse 4 it is evident that this name was also taken in a broad sense as indicative of all the different kinds of wise men. It is evident that men always remain what they are—like unto themselves. The wise men of the world were then, as they are now, swollen with philosophical pride. And also the mighty men of earth remain like unto themselves in the sense that, when they are in trouble and the power of weapons is insufficient, they do what Nebuchadnezzar did and betake themselves to the wise men of the world. Then they run to the soothsayers, the spiritists, or to the Edisons and Marconis to see if they can supply light. It is an unchangeable rule, as history has always shown, that when world power proves insufficient men seek help outside of God from the wisdom of the world. And the wisdom of the world, which knows not God, is ever ready to offer its services to the world powers, as did the wise men of Babylon.

Nebuchadnezzar commanded they be called, and he was immediately obeyed. The wise men came and stood before the king. They were afraid and had every reason to fear, for the king was overwrought and curt.

The King's Demand

And the king said unto them, I have dreamed a dream, and my spirit was troubled to know the dream. Then spake the Chaldeans to the king in Syriac, O king, live forever: tell thy servants the dream, and we will shew the interpretation. The king answered and said to the Chaldeans, The thing is gone from me: if ye will not make known unto me the dream, with the interpretation thereof, ye shall be cut in pieces, and your houses shall be made a dunghill. But if ye shew the dream, and the interpretation thereof, ye shall receive of me gifts and rewards and great honor: therefore, shew me the dream and the interpretation thereof (vv. 3-6).

As soon as the wise men stood before him in stately rows, the king began to speak and explained the purpose for which he had ordered them to the court. All this solemnity seems ridiculous to us now, but not to Nebuchadnezzar and the sages. The former, obviously, had a dark premonition that the gods had revealed the future vicissitudes of his kingdom, while the wise men, whether they did or did not believe in the gods (according to verse 11 they seem to have been rather pious heathen), must have secretly hoped for honor and rich rewards. Soon, however, they had a rude awakening, for the king told them only that he had dreamed, but not what he had dreamed. He first demanded to know the dream and its context and then its meaning. If he had asked only the latter, they would come up with something, but collectively they shrunk away from the twofold demand.

People have wondered if it was indeed true that the king had forgotten the dream or that he kept it back for the purpose of testing the wise men and so to defend himself from their flattering deceits. For if they first correctly recalled the dream, they would then surely also be able to come up with a trustworthy interpretation. A clinching argument for this understanding based on the expression "the thing is gone from me" cannot be produced, for what the king really and literally says here is: The word, i.e., the command, has gone out from me, namely, that if they failed in their interpretation they would be cut in pieces. That is the way the Septuagint, the Vulgate, and other translations have rendered it.

There are four arguments in favor of denying that the king had not really forgotten the dream, but that he wished to test the wise men to protect himself from their tricks.

1. As pointed out above, we cannot say the king specifically said he had forgotten the dream.

2. The king was not as unreasonable as is usually thought, but rather even very wise. For these sages themselves pretended to be able to know everything by means of their communication with the gods and their knowledge of the secret powers of nature. And so here again they pretended to be able to produce an infallible interpretation of the dream. But for that reason it was then quite natural to demand from men with such lofty claims that they first reveal the dream.

3. The argument can be made that on this view the perplexity of the sages makes more sense to us. If they had really believed that the king had forgotten everything, then, being as smart as they were, they would certainly not have desisted from fabricating something beautiful and flattering to the king, rather than allowing themselves to be threatened by death. But now they could not do so, for if they came up with something different from what the king had dreamed, they would be caught and his anger with their discovered deceit would know no limits.

4. We might call it a psychological impossibility for a dream which could terrify a king to that extent and which of itself was so simple to escape him completely.

We may by no means tamper with the glorious divine thought that both the power and the wisdom of the world were at a loss here and were put to shame by Israel's God and people. For even if we assume that the king knew the dream as such, neither he nor his sages were capable of fathoming the correct meaning of it.

After the wise men had greeted the king and had taken cognizance of his desire, they responded with the polite request for the king to tell them the dream, adding hastily the promise that they then in turn would give him the interpretation. All the wise men are presented here collectively as "the Chaldeans," unless we assume that only the last-mentioned class in verse 4 answered on behalf of all of them. They addressed the king in Syriac, as Aramaic or Chaldean is also called. The name Aram or Syria was sometimes taken in a broad sense for the entire territory of the first world empire. And so, in the middle of the verse, Daniel begins to write his prophecy in Chaldean. The reason for this is clear enough. He simply recorded the words as they had been spoken. It is, however, not so clear why he continued writing in this language to the end of chapter 7, and then begins again and continues with Hebrew. Scholars have written a great deal about this, but the best explanation is, undoubtedly, that what concerned mostly the Chaldeans was written in their language, and what concerned mostly the Hebrews in theirs. Hence the request of the wise men was that they might hear the dream from Nebuchadnezzar's lips. That was a smart idea. For if the king told them the dream they would at once have a basis on which they, with the imaginations of their hearts, could invent its interpretation.

We usually see three factors at work in these sages as well as in their spiritual offspring of today—the spiritists, the theosophists, and others—by which they could and can perform miraculous things, namely, knowledge of unknown powers of nature and secret psychological capacities, cunning deceit, and Satan's operation. Only the first factor was present in Daniel and his friends, together with special enabling grace of the Holy Spirit. So the sages made use of their cunning adroitness to see if they could extract sufficient information from their ruler to compose the evil inventions of their hearts.

If indeed they had hoped for this information, they had reckoned without their host, for the king was extremely curt and had already decided what to do with them. Although we are not told so, it seems to us that the assumption is not too bold that the king was still very dissatisfied with them, since he had recently discovered at a comparative examination that some of his captive slaves from Judah had ten times more ability and knowledge than all the sorcerers and astrologers in his entire kingdom. To learn a thing like that about his own subjects must have hurt him.

On the basis of this natural and obvious assumption, it is even more understandable that his decision had already been made and their doom sealed in order to be carried out immediately, if they did not at once furnish him the dream as well as its interpretation. Far from allowing himself to be caught in their cunningly woven net, he was determined to catch and kill them if they did not provide him the dream. Here we must not view Nebuchadnezzar merely as a capricious despot who with inner glee only mocks the wisdom of the wise. He did seem to be tired of the boasting and flaunting of these pseudo-sages. And since they seemed to leave him in the lurch exactly at the occasion when he yearned for light on his dream, he did not shrink from threatening them with the most horrible punishment. He threatened to cut them in pieces.

Scholars are not agreed on the exact manner in which this punishment was administered. Moses' law knows of no such punishment, yet it frequently occurs in Scripture. So, for instance, did Samuel cut King Agag in pieces (1 Sam. 15:33); David apparently executed this same punishment on the children of Ammon (1 Chron. 20:3), although we must admit that there is no agreement on this text (see Exodus 23:27).

The king did want to vent his wrath not only on their persons but also on their homes. Their houses would be made into dunghills. The Septuagint translated it "your houses will be plundered," the Vulgate uses "confiscated," Luther by "ignominiously disrupted," Van Hamelsveld "thy houses will be made inheritances dedicated to the gods." Then the intent would be that they could never become the property of the rightful heirs. Still others translate it by ruins, manure pile, or cesspool. In any case it is clear that this punishment expressed deep disdain, dishonor, and shame. Havernick writes:

> According to an Eastern custom hostile houses or dwellings which belonged to criminals, even temples and holy places, were, as an

expression of the highest contempt, not only flattened but also expressly made into dunghills, mud holes, dumps, manure piles and used for other dishonorable purposes.

Hence the wise men could know that their doom was irrevocably sealed if they did not succeed in making the dream and its meaning known to the king. In that case they could know that nothing but a miracle could save them from certain destruction. Thus it was, obviously, the intent of the Lord to lead them to the acknowledgment of the wonder of His hand that would soon take place by the mediacy of Daniel.

The king, however, did want to make an appeal not only to their sense of fear but also to their covetousness. He must have felt instinctively that most of all the sense of desire and dislike, of fear and covetousness, drives a man to action. And so he placed a bait alongside his threat. Just as surely as they and their possessions would be shamefully destroyed if they did not satisfy him, so surely would they receive presents, rewards, and great honor if they did. Verse 48, which speaks of the rewards of Daniel, sheds some light on these promises of the king. But no matter whether the king threatened or promised, it was not in his power to obtain from them what they did not have or ever could give.

The world possesses two kinds of great power: its carnal power of weapons and its knowledge, which represents its spiritual power. Both forms were represented here and both were equally powerless and empty-handed over against one revelation of God. They were capable of receiving a revelation, but by no means of understanding and assimilating it. We have here a striking example of the absolute powerlessness of the world over against the celestial and the divine. At the same time we see here clearly that a subjective revelation in man must be preceded by an objective revelation to man.

Wisemen Dumbfounded

They answered again and said, let the king tell his servants the dream, and we will shew the interpretation of it. The king answered and said, I know of certainty that ye would gain the time, because ye see the thing is gone from me. But if ye will not make known unto me the dream, there is but one decree for you: for ye have prepared lying and corrupt words to speak before me,

> til the time be changed: therefore tell me the dream, and I shall
> know that ye can shew me the interpretation. The Chaldeans
> answered before the king, and said, there is not a man upon the
> earth that can shew the king's matter; therefore there is no king,
> lord, nor ruler, that asked such things at any magician, or
> astrologer, or Chaldean. And it is a rare thing that the king
> requireth, and there is none other that can shew it before the king,
> except the gods, whose dwelling is not with flesh (vv. 7-11).

Although the king had already pronounced the sentence of
death upon them if they did not fulfill his wishes, the wise men
nevertheless remained outwardly calm. They did not at once voice
a loud protest but tried again to persuade the king to tell the dream.
So they repeated their request and their promise.

But the king was by no means ready to acquiesce. He replied
with two accusations. When we compare the king's behavior here
with that which he displayed to the three young men as recounted
in chapter 3, where he was even very lenient with deliberate
disobedience, then, so it seems to us, it is clear that the king was
prejudiced with regard to the wise men. We already expressed our
opinion earlier that the superior wisdom of Daniel and his friends
had something to do with that. Hence we see in verse 8 that he did
not allow the wise men a moment of procrastination, whereas,
according to verse 16, he readily granted this to Daniel. It must be
considered very likely, it seems to us, that not only the greater
wisdom of the Jews, as compared to that of the Chaldeans, but also
the pure uprightness of these young men, in contrast with the lying
and deceitful attitude of his wise men must have filled him with
repulsion towards his counsellors. If we assume this, then it is
psychologically much easier to explain why, in this mood of
prejudice, he exclaimed bitterly, "I know of certainty that ye
would gain the time." Only one who has been already looking for
a long time for an opportunity to catch someone in the act, and who
has finally succeeded, speaks this way.

Usually these things are explained by the worn-out remark that
we are dealing here with an unreasonable Eastern despot. An
Eastern despot the king most certainly was, but he was not an
unreasonable man. Most recent expositors have often acknowledged this. "I know of certainty," he said, a statement based on the
natural assumption that he did not consider them to be above
doing such a thing.

"Gain time" is an expression that is also found in Ephesians 5:16 and Colossians 4:5, where it refers to a Christian virtue recommended to a believer. This shows how much a thing can differ according to circumstances and persons.

Once more the king hurled a threat at the wise men, who by now must have stood trembling before him, by saying that their sentence had gone out from him, meaning that he was not going to change or recall the sentence he already had pronounced but would execute it to one and all, as he manifestly considered them all equally guilty. If the king had really believed that these sages, as they claimed, were in close contact with the gods, then he would not, so it seems to us, so rashly have ordered them to be killed, for in many respects he was a pious heathen.

The second accusation he hurled at them was that they with lying evasions and imaginations tried to stretch the time. Correctly considered, we find here only one accusation: "You seek in a sly and lying way to hoodwink me in order to escape your sentence." We get the impression from the words used here (and it is, moreover, very likely) that much more was said than is recorded. Once more the king repeated his demand, as he was not the kind of man to let go of his original intent just like that. He deliberately described his demand more elaborately than he had done before. He now made clear that he was first of all and mainly interested in hearing the dream itself from them in order thus to have a guarantee as to the veracity of its interpretation. Instead of calling this unreasonable and unfair, as is often done, we consider this instead a wise move and by no means a cruel whim. For if these people could truly produce an infallible interpretation, then they could also easily produce the dream. The former they pretended; and the latter he demanded as a guarantee for a correct interpretation.

When the Chaldeans saw that they made no headway with their polite requests, they switched to a rather vehement protest. They began burning with indignation. But before their speech grew into a protest, they made a confession of inability. How difficult it must have been for them to let such a confession come over their lips! Man does not easily admit his own powerlessness, and especially the wise men of the world do not easily come to an acknowledgment of their own inability. Here we can truly say in the words of C. van Proosdij, "The Lord God let the bank of heathen wisdom crash!" Still, these sages were not about to admit without a whimper to the absolute powerlessness of their own wisdom. No, they persisted in hovering in vague generalities, as sinners can do so skillfully. To confess that all men are sinners is quite different from confessing with David, "Against thee, thee only, have I sinned," or to beseech God with the publican, "O God, be merciful to me, a sinner!" (Ps. 51:4; Luke 18:13) And so these wise men came with the general and meaningless confession, "There is not a man upon the earth that can shew the king's matter." Their confession was too general and, therefore, untrue because Daniel also was a man and, in the power of the Lord, could indeed do it.

After having told Nebuchadnezzar that there was nobody who could give the dream to him, they continued to say there had never been a king who had asked a thing like that. His demand, they told him, was unheard of and did not find its equal in all of history. Thereby they conveyed, by no means obscurely, that he was a tyrant and a brute and that he should be ashamed of himself to come to them with such unreasonable demands. They quite cleverly placed an allegation of his lack of understanding and goodwill alongside their general acknowledgment of powerlessness.

The second part of their protest was closely related to their acknowledgment of powerlessness. "It is a rare thing that the king requireth." Alongside the unconscionable they place the impossible. And to prevent the king from thinking they cut such a lamentable figure before the king due only to a lack of wisdom, they again added immediately, that there was nobody else who could give the desired information either. They allowed only one exception—the gods. But this exception, coupled with the added concession that their dwelling is not with flesh, must have goaded the king to even more opposition. For there is no doubt that he had always heard from the sages that they lived in special communion with the gods. And now to hear from their own lips that the gods' dwelling is not with flesh must have angered him still more.

This concession reminds us of the exclamation of the Egyptian magicians in Exodus 8:19, "This is the finger of God!" The Lord, who had His hand in all this, would meanwhile gain a victory with this statement by the Chaldean wise men. When soon, thereafter, the God of Israel, the God of Daniel and his friends, would make known and interpret this dream, these proud sages would have to agree that they were not in communion with this God. When at that time Daniel would become president of them all as a reward for his action, they would have to acknowledge him as their superior; Daniel who lived in real communion with this one exalted God of Israel. The obvious purpose of it was that both the power and the wisdom of the world would be forced to acknowledge its own powerlessness and the exaltation of Daniel's God.

Call for Daniel

For this cause the king was angry and very furious, and commanded to destroy all the wise men of Babylon. And the decree went forth that the wise men should be slain; and they sought Daniel and his fellows to be slain. Then Daniel answered with counsel and wisdom to Arioch, the captain of the king's guard, which was gone forth to slay the wise men of Babylon: he answered and said to Arioch, the king's captain, Why is the decree so hasty from the king? Then Arioch made the thing known to Daniel. Then Daniel went in, and desired of the king that he would give him time, and that he would shew the king the interpretation (vv. 12-16).

To learn from the sages that the gods would be able to tell the dream must have made Nebuchadnezzar even more eager to know the dream, while at the same time their acknowledgment not to be in communion with the gods must have been no small disappointment to him. In any case, this last statement was also the last straw and aroused his full wrath. He was practically beside himself with fury and vindictiveness. This strong king, who ruled the entire world, could not even control his own passions. In his boiling anger he called for Arioch, the head of his bodyguard, and ordered him to put the wise men of Babylon to death. This was a command of far-reaching consequences, for there were many wise men in Babylon and they were highly respected. The regulation of the arts, science, and religion was in their hands so that they were the recourse of all who were oppressed in mind and spirit.

It is a rule confirmed throughout all the ages that the common people are always more attached to the representatives of religion and the caretakers of their souls than to their rulers. That must have been more or less the case in Babylon as well. Only a ruler like Nebuchadnezzar, who knew himself to be firmly established on his throne, could issue a command like that, and which could be so momentous in its results.

The question is, however, how far-reaching this command was and whether Babylon here means the city, the province, or the entire world realm. No sure answer can be given. It may be safely assumed that most of the wise men at least lived in the city. That the king meant not just the men who stood before him is sufficiently evident from the fact that also Daniel and his friends, who were not present there, were sought in order to be killed.

The king's dreadful command was sped along swiftly and immediately executed by his servants. A beginning was made with the slaughter of the sages. For this is the meaning of the words, that the wise men should be slain. The Dutch translation agrees with the Greek and the Latin: the wise men began to be killed, and this undoubtedly renders the participle *mithkatlin* correctly. The reason why some translators and expositors wish to read this differently seems to be based on verses 14 and 24, but incorrectly so. These verses only show that the execution was stopped before all the wise men were killed. In this contested verse it is not stated they were actually all killed but only that at the command of the king the killing had already commenced. The wise men standing before the king were killed first of all, of course.

Since Daniel and his friends also belonged to the rank of the wise men, soon some government officials hastened to their home. They were in a hurry with the king's command and everything was done posthaste. Daniel and his friends were totally unaware of the threatening danger hanging above their heads.

He must have looked surprised indeed when Arioch, the chief of the royal bodyguard, entered his house with his soldiers to take him prisoner, and that for the dreadful purpose of putting him to death. He was still so young. Must he now die already and so far away from home? The thing that hurt most must have been that he was not conscious of having committed any felony. Still, he made no outcry and did not become the victim of despair. Calmly and with self-possession he reasoned with Arioch. That is to say, he made a wise and sensible proposition to Arioch so that the officer was compelled to listen to him.

Here we see once more Daniel's noble traits in brilliant action. Admirable here is his calmness amidst deathly danger, his kindheartedness and willingness to forgive, so that he did not explode in anger at such a cruel command. If the other wise men might at times have deceived the king, he and his friends had never done so, had they? We further observe here his self-denial. He was obviously not thinking of himself in the first place or of the dangers threatening his friends, but of the thing that so concerned the king. What is striking above everything else is his exceptional influence upon others. We have already seen evidences of that in chapter 1 in regard to Ashpenaz and his servant. Here we see it again, and we shall over and over have the opportunity to observe it in Daniel.

Daniel was a Napoleon in the realm of the mind. Whether he was confronted with the powerful men of the earth or dealing with his friends, or whether we see him facing his waylayers, he ever stood there calm and serene with a clear conscience before God and men, compelling all of them to listen to him as well as extracting from them the respect and reverence due to him. Arioch must have been anything but a meek little lamb; besides he was goaded by the command of the king, which demanded unconditional obedience. He knew it would cost him his life if he did not promptly obey the wrathful king, and yet, despite all of this, we see him yield to Daniel's courageous spirit.

Daniel asked him, "Why is the decree so hasty from the king?" Many translations have, "Why has the king pronounced such a hard sentence?" The original text allows for both translations. It contains the ideas of both cruelty and exceeding haste, which are always closely connected. He told him what had taken place at the king's court—all the wise men of Babylon were to be executed.

As soon as Daniel learned this state of affairs, he made up his mind. He understood there was no time to delay. Therefore, he set out at once for the royal palace, to which Arioch, the commander-in-chief of the bodyguard, must have given him admittance. Lowth writes:

Four things are strange and amazing here:

1. That Arioch, instead of speedily carrying out the king's command, stops here.

2. That he dared to appear before the king, who was so angry, instead of doing what his command demanded of him.

3. That Daniel had the courage to go in to the king while the latter was so furious.

4. That he requested and obtained a delay of execution, which the king had refused the wise men.
To which we answer:

- The mighty hand of God was behind all these things.
- Daniel enjoyed the esteem of the king above all the wise men.
- He provided both Arioch and the king a good prospect that he could make known the king's dream and its interpretation.

Daniel was great, but he owed his greatness only to the greatness and the favor of his God, whose hand is so manifestly evident in this whole event. Daniel's request actually contained two elements. First of all, a promise that he would satisfy the king's demands. It is true that is not expressly stated, but this is quite self-evident. Secondly, for the fulfillment of his promise to the king, Daniel asked for a specific time within which he would make known the dream and its interpretation. He asked for the latter so that he might consult his God and his friends. When believers are in great perplexity, they should follow Daniel's example and tell it to God and to His people. That was also the constant rule of George Müller of Bristol.

We must observe that apparently Daniel firmly trusted in his soul that he could satisfy the king, hence that he could do more than all the wise men together. He must have realized his punishment would be terrible if he would raise high the expectations of the king only to disappoint them later. Daniel, however, dared to do many things with and for God. Do we, too, not often sing, "Blest is the man who trusts the Lord, will always strength and help afford!"?

Secret Revealed

Then Daniel went to his house, and made the thing known to Hananiah, Mishael, and Azariah, his companions: that they would desire mercies of the God of heaven concerning this secret; that Daniel and his fellows should not perish with the rest of the wise men of Babylon. Then was the secret revealed unto Daniel in a night vision (vv. 17-19a).

Here we have a striking prayer service of a young men's society in Babylon! Young men are able to serve their God in the midst of much temptation in Babylon. These verses show this in a striking manner. The question has been asked whether Daniel addressed his request personally to the king or through someone else. It has been thought on the basis of verse 24 and especially verse 25, that he did not personally appear at the court. But these verses by no means compel us to think that. On the contrary, the words "Then Daniel went to his house" indicate he had been away from his house. In this context, what is more natural than to assume he had been in audience with the king, unless we want to assume he was indeed at the court but conveyed his request through an intermediary.

Upon his return home he gave a detailed account of all his experiences to his friends. We meet here a delightful young men's circle, a group that reminds us of the little Scholte group at the University of Leyden in the first half of the nineteenth century. Here, too, we find a separated group of those pious people who are in Babylon but not of Babylon, who being in a foreign land, nevertheless, kept themselves free from foreign pollutions, who belonged to the institute of the wise but not to that of the worldly wise who were wise only in their own eyes. For that reason they had not come to the court with the other Chaldean wise men. Already in chapter 1 we saw that these young men were separated from Babylon; here we see in a striking manner that they were separated unto God. The former alone would have led them to a pharisaical exclusiveness, but the latter brought them to a hidden relationship with God, to the right practice of godliness.

Observe well that here these young men are again called by their Jewish names. This is a divine hint that we are dealing here with the elect remnant of Israel, which always represents the entire nation. It was Israel, the nation of revelation, that made this dream known; it was the seed of Abraham, in whom one day all the nations of the world will be blessed, by whom the sages of Babylon were saved from death.

Daniel was a warm-hearted friend. Although he exceeded the other three in wisdom, he nevertheless did not look down on them. He, their guide and leader, was always open-hearted and humble before them. So here, too, he carefully brought them up to date. True soul-friends have no secrets to hide from each other. However, it was not merely for friendship's sake that Daniel told his companions everything. The purpose is clearly mentioned. His purpose was that these young men would wrestle with God on their knees together with him until the Lord would give light on the mysterious dark dream and they themselves might be spared with the rest of the wise men of Babylon. The expression "rest of the wise men" further confirms our opinion that already a beginning had been made with the killing of the wise men.

Obviously, the young men were in a state of dreadful distress. And when God's children are in great distress here below, they always flee to the throne room of God, there to pour out the needs of their hearts. That is what David did, for he says, "In my distress I called upon the Lord, and cried unto my God: he heard my voice out of his temple, and my cry came before him, even into his ears" (Ps. 18:6). It was precious indeed that Daniel already knew the special power that is to be found in praying together and that he put this into practice. The only true High Priest Himself pointed this out in Matthew 18:19. The Apostles were acquainted with it (Acts 12:5), and Paul highly valued it and often begged for it (Rom. 15:33; (2 Cor. 1:11; Phil. 1:19).

Hence they turned to the Lord in their distress and asked Him for His tender mercies with regard to the secret of the dream. They considered themselves to be miserable and hence desired mercy. They considered the dream to be a revelation of God, and a secret that could be known only by them that feared Him. And they desired all of this of "the God of heaven".

This name of God is very meaningful throughout Daniel. In this prophecy, in which the Lord views Israel as a nation as *Lo-ammi,* He does not reveal Himself with His covenant names and in a covenant relationship, but as "the God of heaven." This is the name He uses in connection with the world powers just as He uses Adonai Jehovah and Jehovah Sabaoth with regard to Israel and the theocracy. With the exception of only a few times when Daniel himself addresses the Lord with the name Jehovah, this most beautiful of all names is not found in the book of Daniel, but instead usually the name "God of heaven" (see vv. 19, 28, 37, 44; 4:37; 5:23).

These four young men experienced the truth that God answers prayers and that the upright in heart do not call on Him in vain (Ps. 34:4, 5). We do not know how long of a delay Daniel had requested and obtained. One thing is certain, however, and that is that the Lord, who never comes too soon or too late, but always at the right time, came exactly on time for them also. Then was the secret revealed unto Daniel in a night vision. It is very possible Daniel dreamed the same dream as the king and that he received the interpretation with it by the extraordinary enlightenment of the Holy Spirit, although a night vision is usually something that man receives in a state of wakefulness. He at least was certain God had not only heard their prayers but graciously provided for them to know the solution to the great dilemma they faced.

Song of Praise

Then Daniel blessed the God of heaven. Daniel answered and said, Blessed be the name of God forever and ever: for wisdom and might are his: and he changeth the times and the seasons: he removeth kings, and setteth up kings: he giveth wisdom unto the wise, and knowledge to them that know understanding: He revealeth the deep and secret things: he knoweth what is in the darkness, and the light dwelleth with him. I thank thee, and praise thee, O thou God of my fathers, who hast given me wisdom and might, and hast made known unto me now what we desired of thee: for thou hast now made known unto us the king's matter (vv. 19b-23).

Here we have the sevenfold song of praise for the answer to their prayer. Daniel, as usual, appears in the foreground and is mentioned alone, although we may safely assume the others did not refrain from expressing their gratitude. Daniel was a man in whose life God always came first. Here, too, he did not run immediately to the king, shouting, "Eureka!" but was thinking first of all of the glorification of God's name.

The beginning and the end as well as the main idea of this song of praise is that the wisdom and the power, which, as we saw earlier, are the two great world concerns, do not belong to the world but to God, and that He had now given these to Daniel for the purpose of interpreting the dream. The Lord is the only wise God. That is what He is called in Scripture (Rom. 16:27; 1 Tim. 1:17; Jude 25). He revealed this wisdom in creation (Ps. 104:24), in providence (Ps. 113:5-9), and in salvation (2 Cor. 1:21; Eph. 1:8; 3:10). In Christ He has hid all the treasures of wisdom and knowledge (Col. 2:3). The gospel of Christ is the wisdom of God (2 Cor. 1:24; 2:7), and Christ Himself is Wisdom personified (Prov. 8:12-14). This wisdom is usually understood to mean that

God, by way of the best means, obtains His most glorious goal. For that reason this wisdom will one day be praised for evermore after God's purpose with all the elect will have been obtained.

"He changeth the times and the seasons." Here Daniel is undoubtedly, referring to the succession and vicissitudes of the various world powers. God has determined their seasons. "Their times are in His hands" refers not only to individuals but to world dominions as well. After the time of the first world dominion passed, the fingertips of His hand are seen when He writes, "counted, counted, weighed and divided" above that dominion.

"He removeth kings, and setteth up kings." This is most closely connected with the previous statement and is also an allusion to the dream and the experience Daniel would gain during his eventful life. Kings rule by Him. Only by His power and wisdom are they both installed and deposed. Both the prophets Jeremiah and Daniel emphasize that the Lord Himself, as the Creator and Ruler of heaven and earth, is the author of the world powers (see, for instance v. 37 in this chapter). With bonds and yokes upon his neck Jeremiah must bring the following message to Judah and to the messengers of the surrounding nations:

> I have made the earth, the man and the beast that are upon the ground, by my great power and by my outstretched arm, and have given it unto whom it seemed meet unto me. And now have I given all these lands into the hands of Nebuchadnezzar, the king of Babylon, my servant; and the beasts of the field have I given also to serve him. And all nations shall serve him, and his son, and his son's son, until the very time of his land come: and then many nations and great kings shall serve themselves of him (Jer. 27:5-7).

"He giveth wisdom unto the wise, and knowledge to them that know understanding." We must not turn these words around nor identify them with the words of Psalm 19:7 and Psalm 119:98. They are often misquoted as if they were saying, He gives wisdom to the unwise and knowledge to those who lack it. This is indeed true with regard to the enlightenment of the mind in God's work of regeneration. This passage refers specifically to those children of God who have already received such enlightenment. Here applies the word of the Lord that whoever has, to him will be given, and whoever does not have, from him will be taken even what he has. Here then it means specifically that the wise men receive their wisdom alone from the only wise God. We must not forget that here Daniel is praising the wisdom and the power of God.

"He revealeth the deep and secret things." Once again the wisdom of God is specifically mentioned. Only God has knowledge of the most secret things (Job 26:6; Ps. 44:21; Eccl. 12:14; Matt. 6:4, 6, 18; Rom. 16:6; 2 Cor. 4:5). Thus all the wise men of Babylon had been at their wits' end with regard to a secret of God, because He had not revealed it to them. But Daniel, on the contrary, had just experienced that God reveals deep and secret things, even hidden dreams.

"He knoweth what is in the darkness, and the light dwelleth with him." With this Daniel penetrates the wisdom of God even deeper. He points out that to Him there is no distinction between light and darkness and that light dwells with Him. God Himself is a Light and no darkness dwells in Him (1 John 1:5). We men already achieve quite a lot when we cause light to shine in darkness, but God in creation caused light to proceed from darkness, and He still does so repeatedly in the preaching of the Word and in the conversion of a sinner.

Finally, Daniel cries out in ecstasy, "I thank thee, and praise thee, O thou God of my fathers, who hast given me wisdom and might, and hast made known unto me now what we desired of thee: for thou hast now made known unto us the king's matter."

That is the climax of the very simple song of praise on the wisdom and the power of God. It is obvious that a godly Israelite is speaking, and also note that Israel as *Lo-ammi* is loved for the sake of the fathers. We hear the grateful words of a heart giving thanks for the benefits bestowed and of someone who is absolutely certain his prayer has been answered. When Daniel spoke these words, he had not yet compared his insight with that of the king, but still he was absolutely sure the Lord had heard and answered their supplication, and that soon when he appeared before his king he would by no means be put to shame.

Bring Me to the King

Therefore Daniel went in unto Arioch, whom the king had ordained to destroy the wise men of Babylon: he went and said thus unto him, destroy not the wise men of Babylon: bring me in before the king, and I will shew unto the king the interpretation.

Then Arioch brought in Daniel before the king in haste, and said thus unto him, I have found a man of the captives of Judah, that will make known unto the king the interpretation. The king answered and said to Daniel, whose name was Belteshazzar, art thou able to make known unto me the dream which I have seen, and the interpretation thereof? (vv. 24-26)

It sounds like a royal command when Daniel said to Arioch, "Destroy not the wise men of Babylon." This shows courage, for what he said was contrary to the king's command. Nevertheless, it was not foolhardy courage, for he was very sure that he knew the dream. We see once again in this intercession for the wise men a characteristic of self-denial and love of fellow men on the part of this man of God. He did not come out of the house that morning after the night vision with a loud hooray or a quieter, "Thank God, my life is saved," or with a prayer to Arioch or the king, "Now, don't take our lives, please!" Even though we may safely assume that although Daniel thoroughly abhorred the superstitions, deceits, and devil's witchcraft of these men, he nevertheless was concerned about their well-being.

Had he lived under the theocracy, we would most likely not have heard this plea for the wise men, for according to the law of Moses all sorcerers, fortune-tellers, soothsayers, astrologers, and all similar magicians had to be exterminated. But Christ Himself taught us that on the field of this world the weeds need not, indeed absolutely may not, be pulled up. Hence in the world unrighteous things, which may not be tolerated in the midst of His people, must be tolerated. Well then, this concerned weeds which were rampant in the world power, although we may not lose sight of the fact that amidst all these weeds some good ears of wheat were hidden. And in His relationship to the world, the Lord always thinks of His elect first of all. The tares of this world owe their temporary preservation and well-being to the wheat that grows among them. This is strikingly evident from this story. God-fearing Daniel was the intercessor for these wise men like all God's children have always been the intercessors for the entire world. Had Daniel not been one who constantly prayed to the living God, he could not have made intercession for these wise men now.

We further see that Daniel desired of Arioch to take him as the true interpreter of dreams to the king. Daniel put a difficult request to the commander of the royal guard. When we read these words, it looks to all appearances as if he were Arioch's commander. The man obeyed Daniel at once. Daniel had first made him stop the sentence of death, then revoke it, and now he ordered him to take him to the king. We already had the opportunity before to remark that Daniel exercised much power not only over his own spirit but also over that of others. We may safely assume that Arioch raised objections, but Daniel must have continued assuring him that he would satisfy the king's ardent desire, that he was the God-appointed interpreter of dreams, and that he, in case Arioch was in danger, would exercise his influence on the king. "I will shew unto the king the interpretation," was his self-assured statement to Arioch. There was not the faintest doubt in his soul that the Lord had made known to him the dream and its meaning. He considered erring to be out of the question, for he spoke with the certainty of infallibility. And that is something to keep in mind with regard to the significant interpretation of the dream itself.

If indeed Arioch had objections, like Obadiah once had in a similar situation, he soon acquiesced. No doubt the bloody command had been extremely repugnant to him, so that he gladly cast off his burden and hastily took Daniel inside before the king. It seems that he cherished the secret hope of honor and reward, for having come before the king, he acted as if he took a great interest in the dream of the king, and as if it had been his constant concern to find a sage who could satisfy the king's desire, and as if he had finally succeeded after much trouble in finding such a man.

The Holy Spirit, who is the first Author of Scripture, concealed in the insincere language of this courtier a precious hint with regard to Daniel and this whole story. For Arioch said here, as if in passing, that he had found a man of the captives of Judah. A captive Jew would turn on the desired light in the dark heathen world. It cannot be emphasized enough that, although Israel is considered *Lo-ammi* in this prophecy, the God-fearing remnant, beloved for the sake of the fathers, nevertheless represents the nation of revelation, and is a glorious prophecy for the future, when the entire world will be blessed through this nation. Here this God-fearing remnant was already a light unto the entire world kingdom, and one day Israel's acceptance and restoration will be as life from the dead (Rom. 11:15).

The king apparently responded to Arioch's boastful words with a certain reservation and very few words. He turned at once to Daniel, who is here also mentioned with his Chaldean name; Daniel and Belteshazzar. These two names point out the double position which this man of God occupied in Babylon. Daniel is the name that depicts him as the man of God who always stood for the justice of God and thereby judged Babylon in a moral sense and shed the right light on Israel, if it were faithful to its God. The heathen name, Belteshazzar, depicts him as the most important wise man and high dignitary of the whole world power.

It may not be deduced from his question, as some do, that the king did not know him and hence that Daniel, according to verse 16, had not been personally before the king. The king considered his youth and only doubted his power since all his older sages had failed. As a heathen he, of course, had no eye for the supernatural help Daniel had received. Besides, he made it abundantly clear to Daniel that he wanted to know not only the interpretation but also the dream itself.

Revealer of Secrets

Daniel answered in the presence of the king, and said, the secret which the king hath demanded cannot the wise men, the astrologers, the magicians, the soothsayers, shew unto the king; but there is a God in heaven that revealeth secrets, and maketh known to the king Nebuchadnezzar what shall be in the latter days. Thy dream, and the visions of thy head upon thy bed, are these; as for thee, O king, thy thoughts came into thy mind upon thy bed, what should come to pass hereafter: and he that revealeth secrets maketh known to thee what shall come to pass. But as for me, this secret is not revealed to me for any wisdom that I have more than any living, but for their sakes that shall make known the interpretation to the king, and that thou mightest know the thoughts of thy heart (vv. 27-30).

In answer to the king's question, Daniel first of all emphasizes that the wise men are incapable of furnishing him the dream and its interpretation. So if the king saw him as just another wise man, then he must answer the king's question in the negative. In passing he made another plea for the sages, but that was not his main purpose here. Many expositors wrongly present it as such. It is obviously God's purpose here to emphasize that the wisdom of the world, which at that time was personified by Babylon's wise men, was absolutely incapable of knowing anything about the future and the secrets of God. We must not forget what many expositors all too readily forget when explaining this chapter that, theologically speaking, it was obviously God's purpose to put to shame the wisdom of the world and the power of the world (the two great powers of the world) and to display them in their hollowness and futility before the eyes of the heathen themselves. The wisdom of the world proved to be worthless with respect to the interpretation, and the world power futile with respect to receiving the mysteries of God, especially in the destruction of the world image by the stone that came rolling down from above.

But there is a God in heaven who revealeth secrets. It was always Daniel's goal to give the honor to God. In contrast to the powerlessness of the worldly wise, Nebuchadnezzar must soon acknowledge that Daniel's God possessed both the power and the wisdom. Daniel himself had already done so at the unmistakable answer to his prayer. Nebuchadnezzar must soon do this in his way after the interpretation of the dream, so that Israel might be comforted by all these things and heathendom might think highly of Israel's God, who is the God of heaven.

It further seems to us that here the key to the correct interpretation of the dream is given in the words "in the latter days." We come across this expression very often, especially in the prophets, but we meet it already in the books of Moses (Gen. 49:1; Num. 24:14). The phrase literally means in the end of the days. Scholars such as Lowth, Dachsel, Zoeckler, and Kranichfeld agree that it is always used in connection with Messianic times. There is no doubt that this expression must be understood in that sense here as well, for the dream image of the king reaches to the end of times at the re-establishment of the Messianic Kingdom. Hence, it is not correct to translate later times or successive times. Such general translations do not render the correct meaning of these words and totally overlook that this standing expression in the prophets is always closely connected with the so-called Messianic time. We consider this expression to be the key to the correct understanding of the world image in the dream, for it justifies our declaration that all interpretations that go no further than historical events are wrong and that this dream points us to the Messiah and His kingdom. This expression points out that the stone which smashes the image is far more important in God's sight than the whole image itself. Regarding verse 19, see our comment on verse 1 of this chapter.

In a rather complicated way Daniel had already modestly retreated to the background by stating that not a single wise man as such could furnish the dream and that only God in heaven reveals secrets and that He had also made known to Nebuchadnezzar what would take place thereafter. In the first part of verse 30 Daniel once again takes special pains to explain that the honor of interpreting the dream must not be given to him. When Nebuchadnezzar still wanted to give the honor to him afterwards (see verses 46 and 48), then this was not Daniel's fault. Furthermore, he wanted to prevent the king from getting the idea the was standing tbefore him with the secret desire for receiving manifestations of honor and presents.

It, moreover, seems that Daniel wished to intercept another objection of the king. For the king might ask how it could be possible that only God reveals secrets, since Daniel as a mortal stated that he could do it. For that reason Daniel stressed the fact of revelation in a way that could be understood by Nebuchadnezzar as a heathen, for the heathen Babylonians did believe in revelations given by their gods. We must once more admire Daniel's humility. He was indeed much wiser than all the sages of Babylon and they were the wisest people in all the world, so that he actually towered above all the living in wisdom. His wisdom was already proverbial. But true humility is not conscious of its own greatness.

This section points out the twofold purpose of the dream. This purpose concerned Babylon and Israel. "That thou mightest know the thoughts of thy heart;" the purpose with respect to Babylon and its ruler. Nebuchadnezzar, being a serious king, had been lying in bed pondering the future, especially the future of his realm. He was not like Louis XIV and his courtiers who at one time exclaimed, *Apres nous le deluge!*—"Let the flood come after us!" The thoughts of this heathen king were much nobler than of this said "most Christian" king. God rewarded Nebuchadnezzar by making known to him the desire of his heart. But Scripture never dwells long on Babylon. Let us not do so either.

The other and higher purpose of this dream lay in the interpretation given by Daniel as the representative of Israel. The original contains an indefinite, impersonal, and plural verb; the author of the action is purposely omitted. So the question is, who is not mentioned? Some students think it is angels. Many think Daniel omitted himself out of modesty. But we prefer to think of Daniel and his friends (see also v. 36) as representatives of Israel, which, being *Lo-ammi*, is not mentioned. Hence we accept the English rendition, "for their sakes that they shall make known the interpretation to the king." God had ordered everything in such a way that the light would be shed in dark Babylon by the exiles. The real blessing was, according to His promise, provided by Israel. And *Lo-ammi* would be comforted by the dream.

The Terrible Image

Thou, O king, sawest, and behold a great image. This great image, whose brightness was excellent, stood before thee; and the form thereof was terrible. This image's head was of fine gold, his breast and his arms of silver, his belly and his thighs of brass, his legs of iron, his feet part of iron and part of clay. Thou sawest till that a stone was cut out without hands, which smote the image upon his feet that were of iron and clay, and brake them to pieces. Then was the iron, the clay, the brass, the silver, and the gold, broken to pieces together, and became like the chaff of the summer threshingfloors; and the wind carried them away, that no place was found for them: and the stone that smote the image became a great mountain, and filled the whole earth. This is the dream; (vv. 31-36a)

It was very fitting that Nebuchadnezzar saw a large image. He did not see a picture of an image but a concrete image, a statue of a human form. Such images were much liked by the Chaldeans. It was further fitting for another reason. Nebuchadnezzar received here a view of the entire day of the heathen, as "the times of the Gentiles" is called by Paul. Was it not very natural that the heathen king saw these times from a human and humanistic point of view, whereas later on Daniel discerned with a spiritual eye the bestial and demonic character of them?

We further observe that the kingdoms of the world, different as they may be from one another, are nevertheless essentially the same. All world powers, with all their pride and splendor, were only lamps of the one, ungodly, humanistic, and Christ-hating world, which as such is wholly damnable before God. They are inspired by the one evil spirit of the god of this age. They are one in their chasing after happiness outside of God and they have one and the same future!

We further find here an irrefutable rejection of the philosophic idea of world evolution and development which has governed our age. Auberlin in his excellent exposition emphatically pointed this out for the first time, saying that in this world image there is absolutely nothing to be found of evolution and development but exactly the opposite, namely, degeneration and bastardization. The line runs downward from shining gold to muddy clay. The wise men of this world draw their line upward from muddy slime to the *Uebermensch*. If only the Church of Christ had continued to adhere to this clear prophecy it would always have retained the true view of the world and never have become enamored by a so-called Christian evolutionism.

With regard to the explanation of the world image, there is now great unanimity among the positive theologians. Generally speaking, there are now only two different interpretations, that of the modern critics and that of the various orthodox scholars. The modernists are all agreed on this point, namely, that this cannot be a prophecy concerning times later than that of the Maccabees when, according to them, the writer of this historic novelette lived. Orthodox expositors are all agreed that here we are given a look at all four world powers; the Assyro-Babylonian, the Medo-Persian, the Greco-Macedonian, and the Romano-German. And at the end thereof comes the eternal, indestructible kingdom of our Lord Jesus Christ. That will be the most absolute world dominion of all. It must not escape our attention that the emphasis is especially on this kingdom (see vv. 34, 35 and 44, 45).

The entire history of the world is explained and dealt with in the scope of seven verses (see vv. 37-43). Scripture is almost as marvelous in the things it is silent on as in those it mentions. It silently passes by the things that are high in the estimation of the children of men. It records extensively and at length the history of a small slave nation, while silently passing by Egypt's glory. It speaks much about the small flock in the midst of grasping wolves, while it hardly considers Rome's power and Greece's wisdom worthy of any mention, or it mentions these things only in order to condemn them.

Meaning of World Image

And we will tell the interpretation thereof before the king. Thou, O king, art a king of kings: for the God of heaven hath given thee

a kingdom, power, and strength, and glory. And wheresoever the
children of men dwell, the beasts of the field and the fowls of the
heaven hath he given into thine hand, and hath made thee ruler
over them all. Thou art this head of gold. And after thee shall arise
another kingdom inferior to thee, and another third kingdom of
brass, which shall bear rule over all the earth. And the fourth
kingdom shall be strong as iron: forasmuch as iron breaketh in
pieces and subdueth all things: and as iron that breaketh all these,
shall it break in pieces and bruise. And whereas thou sawest the
feet and toes, part of potter's clay, and part of iron, the kingdom
shall be divided; but there shall be in it of the strength of the iron,
forasmuch as thou sawest the iron mixed with miry clay. And as
the toes of the feet were part of iron, and part of clay, so the
kingdom shall be partly strong, and partly broken. And whereas
thou sawest iron mixed with miry clay, they shall mingle themselves with the seed of men: but they shall not cleave one to
another, even as iron is not mixed with clay (vv. 36b-43).

This section provides us with the infallible interpretation of the
world image. It is emphatically said that the interpretation of the
dream is given. Hence, all expositions that do not agree with that
interpretation cannot possibly be the right ones and must be
rejected out of hand by every believer of Scripture.

"Thou, O king, art a king of kings." Whoever does not know
Daniel and does not believe his words may very well consider
them to be flattering court language. But those who know him also
know that flattery was an unknown art to him. He was modest and
courteous. He could be a Chaldean to the Chaldeans and to the
courtiers a courtier.

It was indeed true that Nebuchadnezzar was a king of kings, for
several kings served him as vassals (Jer. 27 and Ezek. 26:7). But
Nebuchadnezzar must know that the God of heaven had made him
the golden head of the first world dominion. Once again we come
across the name God, of heaven, which appears so often in Daniel.
It was the name by which he was known among the Jews, and is
still known today, after the theocracy had disappeared and the city
and temple of God were destroyed. It is the name that implies that
the immediate authority of the Lord moved from between the
cherubim in the temple in Jerusalem to the heavens, while in the
meantime the world power reigns (cf. Ezra 1:2; 5:11, 12; 6:9, 10;
7:12, 21, 23; Neh. 1:4, 5; 2:20).

Much has been written about the question why, for instance, the mighty Pharaoh-Necho or one of the mighty kings of Assyria was not rather named the golden head, and why it is so emphatically and repeatedly written that God had given everything into Nebuchadnezzar's hand (Jer. 27; 28; Dan. 4:17, 25, 32), since he did not actually rule the entire world. The answer is that the reason must not be sought in Nebuchadnezzar. It was not because this ruler was better or would act better than the other mighty rulers, or because he allegedly had a desire to serve the Lord. The solution to this problem is found in Israel alone. If all exegetes only had an eye for the unchangeable rule that the world power made its appearance as soon as the reign of God disappeared, just as one day the world dominion will disappear as soon as the reign of God returns, they would have seen at once that neither Necho nor Sargon, Esarhaddon or Sennacherib could be the head of gold in the world dominion, since at that time the theocracy still existed and with that the sovereignty of God was still present on earth. But as soon as all this disappeared at Jerusalem's destruction, the times of the Gentiles began and all became ready for the world dominion, which is never founded on justice but always on power.

And now Daniel says in verses 37 and 38, as well as in other places, that God according to His righteous judgment, in a juridical sense, had given all this power, strength, and honor. When Daniel emphasizes so strongly the absolute dominion of the various world powers, then the implication is not that they had in fact conquered the whole world, but rather had received the power to do so from God, and also that they stood at the head of all nations and reigned over the whole known world. Even the beasts of the field, the birds of the sky, and the fish of the sea had God given into his hand. These expressions are no reference to the original appointment of man as head of the animal kingdom (Gen. 1:26; Ps. 8), but simply an Eastern manner of expression as an indication of absolute dominion. We would say that Nebuchadnezzar had a monopoly over hunting, fowling, and fishing.

When Daniel said to the king, "Thou art this head of gold," he meant, of course, not only his person and kingship, but his whole dominion. If ever any earthly ruler could say, "My kingdom is I," it was Nebuchadnezzar, for he was absolutely an absolute monarch. It could well be said that he was the head of *gold*. When history writers come to the glory of Babylon, they wrestle with the language to describe the grand, massive, and awe-inspiring splendor of this city.

Babylon was a kingdom of gold. Today luxury is finer and most beautiful, but we of today can no longer imagine all that solid gold, all the amazing splendor as was seen in this kingdom (DaCosta).

Never was there on earth any city greater and more awe-inspiring. Even Rome in its greatest splendor was, comparatively speaking, no more than an unplanned pile of palaces and temples placed on seven hills (F. Bettex).

To know Babylon we need not resort to the secular writers of antiquity or of today. It is a great and fatal error to think that we must know a lot about secular history to study and love a book like Daniel. Fatal is this error, because it scares off many simple God-fearing people from starting to read and study this prophecy. There is a kind of scholarship as well as a kind of exposition that obscures the Word rather than clarifies it for the simple people. So we must maintain that this prophecy is revealed to babes and is given to Israel and the church, not to the learned only. This Scripture must and can be explained by Scripture. Isaiah calls Babylon the glory of kingdoms (Isa. 13:19); the golden city (14:4); and the queen of kingdoms (Isa. 47:5). Jeremiah calls it a golden cup (Jer. 51:7), abundant in treasures (v. 13), and the praise of the whole earth (v. 41). These words of God are clear enough and point out again the harmony of Scripture.

"And after thee shall arise another kingdom inferior to thee" (cf. v. 32). It might have been pleasing to Nebuchadnezzar's pride that he was the head, even the golden head of the world image, but he had to also hear from Daniel hard and very unpleasant things. First of all, that he had not built mighty Babylon and, secondly, that the golden head would come to an end and would be followed by another kingdom lower than his. Already a century and a half earlier the prophet Isaiah had repeatedly depicted the downfall of Babylon in the most touching manner (see Isa. 13, 14).

This second world power would be inferior, as could already be deduced from the *silver*, the less precious metal of which the chest and arms of the image consisted. The difficult question here, however, is what is the real point of comparison? The fact that with this kingdom is meant the Medo-Persian, of which Cyrus the Great was the soul, cannot be denied on the basis of any reason whatsoever, for Daniel 6:8 and 10:1 tell us infallibly that the Medo-Persians succeeded, as Isaiah had predicted this long ago

(Isa. 45:1-3; see also Jer. 51:11 and 2 Chron. 36:20). Nor have we ever met any recent orthodox expositors who dared to doubt that.

But why and in what respect was this second kingdom lower than the first world power? The answers to this question vary considerably. Was it because of the degenerated character of the Persian kings? But see Daniel 5. Or because of their many defeats, such as at Thermopolae and Salamis in their battle with the Greeks? Or are we to think of their lesser riches? (see Esther 1). If anything, this kingdom was even richer than Babylon, for God Himself has said that He would give Babylon's treasures to Cyrus. Also, secular history tells us of the immense treasures of Persia's kings. Must we with others think of the lesser moral values of the kingdom? But Babylon is also called the golden cup by which all nations were made drunken (Jer. 51:7). It smote the nations in wrath with a continual stroke (Isa. 14:6). Nor can we think of decreased power and dominion, for the Medo-Persian kingdom conquered the Assyro-Babylonian and possessed the far greater area of land of Babylon, Media, and Persia together. Neither was the second world power less in military power, for the Persian kings had the greatest armies in all of antiquity. In what respect was this kingdom inferior?

It was lower in the nature of its government. Scripture itself points out that we are not dealing here with an absolute monarchy, with a strict central government as was found in the first world power. Already the form of the image points this up—the two sides of the chest and the two arms. Daniel 7 depicts this second kingdom as a lumbering bear, which is higher on one side than on the other, with three ribs in its maw, while the complexity of this kingdom is depicted by the ram with the two horns in Daniel 8:3, 20. God's ideal of authority and government is total centralization of government, absolute monarchy by a perfectly righteous One. This divine ideal will one day be realized in Christ, the righteous King (Isa. 32:1, 2). Hence we can say that the absolute monarchy of Babylon's king was more according to God's will than the division and scattered condition of the second world power.

The third kingdom is of *brass*, which also shall bear rule over all the earth. The famous Dutch exegete Hermannus Venema, born in 1697 at Wildervank and for half-a-century professor at the University of Franeker, spent much time in studying the prophecy of Daniel. Besides a commentary on chapter 11, a treatise on the four kingdoms as they are dealt with in chapters 2, 7, and 8 appeared after his death. He was one of the first expositors who, with regard to the four powers, took the wrong road, which today is still followed by so many exegetes. According to him the head of gold is the kingdom of Nebuchadnezzar, and the silver chest and arms are the Medo-Persian dominion. So far he was correct. But with respect to the belly and thighs of brass he gets confused. According to him, with this third kingdom is meant the Persian monarchy under Cyrus the Great; then the iron feet are the kingdom of Alexander the Great, while the toes represent his army generals. The stone, cut out without hands, allegedly represented the generation of Maccabean heroes, which ended not too long afterwards in the birth of the Messiah. The Dutch scholars Van Vloten, Van Hamelsveld and, partly, Klinkenberg, Van der Palm, and J. W. van Lennep followed him in this viewpoint, as well as countless foreign scholars.

The writers of the marginal notes in the [Dutch] States' translation adhere to the most generally accepted view that the brass monarchy represents the Greek world power. Today this is still the viewpoint of all positive expositors, and that could hardly be otherwise, for Daniel 8 states, infallibly, that the king of Greece will conquer the kings of the Medes and Persians. Compare this with 7:17 and 11:2, 3 and then we see that Scripture itself sheds sufficient light on that matter. And what Scripture teaches so clearly can be found in every history book on old-world history. Just as Nebuchadnezzar was the main figure in the first and Cyrus in the second, so was Alexander the Great in the third or Greco-Macedonian world empire. These three heads of the first three world powers occupy such a prominent place in prophecy because they were, in spite of themselves, the servants of the Lord in the execution of His divine counsels. Cyrus the Great is even called, in the prophecy of Isaiah, a messiah, an anointed one, since he had to deliver Israel from Babylon. And thus he is a type of the Messiah, the Deliverer of the nations. We shall meet Alexander again in chapters 7, 8, and 11.

A few more words about the inferiority of the third kingdom are in order. Brass is of less value than silver, and so in God's sight the third dominion was again of less value than the preceding one. If we do not look at it from God's point of view, then it will amaze us, because the years of the Greco-Macedonian monarchy (300 -

146 B.C.) were a period during which human ingenuity obtained its greatest triumphs. It was the era that followed the golden age of Greece, and all secular historians deal at length with these years. But to God all the arts and sciences are comprehended under the symbol of brass.

The focal point of comparison lies once again in the unity of authority and government. The monarchy of Alexander was very complex and became even more fragmented after his death. It consisted of the fiery people of Greece's free cities and Macedonia's provinces, which are probably represented by the thighs or loins of the image, while the weakened nations of the East are depicted by the belly. The land area of this realm was much greater than that of both preceding ones. That is the reason why it is emphatically stated here that it ruled over the whole earth. Reread what we said earlier about this expression.

The fourth kingdom shall be strong as iron. We still have to discuss a few parts of this image of a man: the shanks are the part of a leg located under the loins and run downward to above the knees, and the feet are figured from the knees down to the toes. From earliest times the Jews had always felt that this referred to the Roman empire. This idea, Josephus tells us, was even the main reason why the Jews thought that they would conquer the Romans under the Messiah. This was also the reason why they were always easily moved to rise up against the Romans. We know many Jews, even at the destruction of Jerusalem in A.D. 70, continued to cherish the silent hope that the Messiah would come when things were at their blackest to save them and crush the Romans. Seven features of this fourth kingdom need to be mentioned:

1. It will be as strong as iron and be able to break and grind everything to pieces. In size it will be much greater than all the preceding ones, for the Roman empire swallowed up all the previous world empires and dominated almost all of Europe.

2. It will be very cruel. In Daniel 7 this empire is represented as a terrifying monster for which no name can be found which in an indescribably cruel way devoured and trod everything under foot.

3. It will last long. Not only is this indicated by the long legs of this colossal image, but it will continue until the establishment of the kingdom of Christ. Since 146 B.C. it continues and we are

still living in it. It has often been correctly noted that Roman law is the foundation of the judicature of all civilized nations, and that the Latin or Roman language is considered a sign of civilization and as being indispensable to any scholar. Furthermore, the Church of Rome still rules over millions of docile subjects. This kingdom may be temporarily wounded, but one day it will, to the amazement of all, revive (Rev. 13:3).

4. It will be a very composite and divided kingdom. The text points out the fourfold composition of the shanks, the feet, the toes, and the mixture of iron and clay which will not bond. Besides it is by no means unlikely, although it cannot be proved, that both legs are a representation of the Roman and Greek churches, or of the Western and Eastern Roman Empires.

5. Despite the lack of all coherence, there will, according to verse 43, always be a striving for unity. They, that is to say, the kings of this realm will indeed mingle themselves with the seed of men, but their striving for unity will not succeed; they will not adhere. Van Hamelsveld translates verse 43 thus:

> That you have seen the iron mixed with clay means that they will try by means of mutual marriages to unite, although they will never adhere to one another any more than iron melts together with clay.

We have here a striking prophecy, which in the past and until this very day is promptly fulfilled. Has there not always been an attempt at unity in the Roman empire? Have not a Charlemagne, a Charles V, a Louis XIV, a Napoleon the Great, and Napoleon III always been inspired by the idea of unity in order to obtain, thereby, power over the entire world? And when they saw that the power of the state, the power of weapons, was insufficient, did they not then call upon the wisdom of statesmanship for help to obtain this goal? How much guile and cunning has always been displayed by the royal houses of Europe to obtain unity and power by the means of mutual marriages! We need think only of Napoleon and Josephine and of present-day relationships among the kings, who fight each other to the death. Neither human power nor wisdom (and remember that these are the two great powers of the world) have proven themselves to be sufficient to establish the desperately and long hoped-for one-world dominion. Someday soon, Satan, by means of his instrument, the Antichrist, who will be the head of the revived Roman empire, will for a brief period succeed in it, but then in him the absolute bankruptcy of all world dominion will become clearly manifest.

6. From this kingdom, ten democratic kings will emerge. This is represented by the ten toes of the image. It is true this cannot be concluded from this text alone, but it can be sufficiently deduced from a comparison of Daniel 7 with Revelation 13 and 17. When commenting on chapter 7 we shall point this out further, so we need not go into it here.

The prophets, and Paul in Romans 9, use clay as the symbol for weak, dependent children of men. These toes are made of clay, and all orthodox expositors are agreed that clay is an indication of unstable and shaky human government, of which we see sufficient examples in Russia and other countries.

7. This world power will last the longest but will also be the last one and will not be succeeded by another world empire in the real sense of the word. In the days of these kings, which undoubtedly mean the ten kings (cf. Dan. 7:24; Rev. 17:16, 17), God will raise up a kingdom that will nevermore be disturbed or destroyed.

Thus we have looked briefly at this image and have seen that it rested on a shaky foundation. Imagine it, a massive metal image of gold, silver, brass, and iron that rested on feet of clay! All that is needed is for a stone to roll against it and it is smashed.

Stone From Heaven

And in the days of these kings shall the God of heaven set up a kingdom, which shall never be destroyed: and the kingdom shall not be left to other people, but it shall break in pieces and consume all these kingdoms, and it shall stand forever. Forasmuch as thou sawest that the stone was cut out of the mountain without hands, and that it brake in pieces the iron, the brass, the clay, the silver, and the gold; the great God hath made known to the king what shall come to pass hereafter: and the dream is certain, and the interpretation thereof sure (vv. 44, 45).

The great and terrible image Nebuchadnezzar had seen apparently stood in a valley at the foot of a mountain. The image itself was terrible in appearance, but this would not have terrified the king as much as the sudden rolling of a stone against the clay feet of the image, whereby it was totally pulverized and blew away like the chaff of the threshingfloors. Nebuchadnezzar saw first the pulverization of the image and then the growing of the stone into a mountain which filled the whole earth.

Daniel speaks first of the mountain of the kingdom and then of the falling of the stone. Three matters call for our attention. 1) What this stone meant. 2) What this stone did. 3) What became further of this stone.

Many different explanations of this stone have been given. That need not amaze us, for we are dealing here with the stone of offense. The matters themselves are not obscure, but many people have obscured this text by words without wisdom. More than half a century ago, Professor Berg at the Reformed Seminary, New Brunswick, declared this stone represented the United States of America. The USA would one day destroy all the kingdoms of the world. If he were still alive today, he would no doubt cry out, "See, I have told you so!" for it really almost begins to look like it.

Very common is the view that Christianity is meant by this stone. It is the interpretation of Postmillennialism. But there are insurmountable objections to this view:

- Christianity existed before the toes of the image came into existence.
- This stone becomes a kingdom, and true Christianity never was a state power, still is not one, and never will be.
- Christianity does not pulverize the kingdoms of the earth.
- Christianity will not be forever. Indeed, true Christianity will endure into all eternity, but Christianity as Postmillennialism pictures it, and as it exists today, approaches fast its pitiful end.
- Christianity does not fill the whole earth.
- Neither with regard to this stone nor to Christianity can we speak of a gradual development as Postmillennialism does.

Dr. Samuel Tregelles, who may be considered to speak for all Premillennialist expositors, gives his opinion as follows:

> The falling of the stone on the image must mean destroying judgment on the fourth Gentile power, not gradual evangelization of it by grace, and the destroying judgment cannot be dealt by Christians, for they are taught to submit to the powers that be.

Some say Christ, at His first coming, is meant by this stone. This, too, is subject to several serious objections.

1. Christ at His first coming could not roll against the feet of the complete world power, since the image was not complete and the feet and toes were not yet there. The Antichrist will come in the days of the ten kings, and then Christ will also found His kingdom.

2. Christ at His first coming has smashed neither the Roman empire nor any other kingdom. On the contrary, the world power arose against Him and crushed Him.

3. The expositors who think to see Christ here at His first coming lost sight of the fact that the Old Testament never makes the distinction between the first and second coming of Christ as conceived separately from His return, for the simple reason that they did not know this whole dispensation at all. Furthermore, all too often the predominant characteristic of prophecy is lost sight of, namely, that it always looks at the consummation and the end time. This is true even of the very first prophecy, the so-called Mother Promise (Gen. 3:15).

4. On this interpretation it could not be said that this kingdom would not be left to any other nation, for Christ's Church is gathered from among all nations (Mark 16:15, 16).

5. The world image is completely destroyed by this stone. It becomes like chaff before the wind. No place was found for them. This simply cannot apply to the first coming of Christ.

The stone is most certainly Christ. But Christ as a stone has various meanings. This was true with Moses already as the rock that was struck, so that water might flow out of it for the believers. With regard to the Church, He is the Foundation and the beautiful and supporting Corner Stone. To unbelieving Israel He was, at His first coming, the rock of offense, but at His second coming He will be, to the world powers, the stone cut out of the rocks without hands, which pulverizes and grinds everything to dust. Most likely Christ Himself was thinking of this prophecy of Daniel when he said, "Whosoever shall fall on this stone shall be broken" — His first coming? — "but on whomsoever it shall fall, it will grind him to powder"—His second coming?

The second question we asked was, What did this stone do? This stone was hewn out, torn loose from the mountain at the foot of which the image stood. Maybe we have an allusion here, as some expositors think, to the miraculous incarnation of Christ. This would in no wise be at odds with what was said above, for the prophets in many places connect His miraculous incarnation with His future coming (see Isa. 11; 53; Jer. 23 and Micah 5). When speaking of His future coming, His first coming is always assumed or implied, just as sure as the greater comprehends the lesser.

But what must be understood by the mountain from which the stone was hewn? Most expositors usually pass this mountain by as though it was merely a part of the image. It seems to us we must take this to mean the mountain of Zion, where Christ at His return will reveal Himself (Isa. 59:20), the mountain He has chosen to dwell in forever (Ps. 68:16). Symbolically, this name then stands for Israel, just as Bashan's high hill stands for the world monarchy, so that here we have an indication that salvation is of the Jews. The fact that Israel is not indicated more clearly need not amaze anyone, for, in Daniel, God is a God who hides Himself from His people, whom He considers as *Lo-ammi*.

The stone was hewn out without hands. This expression is of the highest importance over against all the Pelagian and semi-Pelagian fanaticism of the Postmillennialists. Nowhere in His Word has the Lord promised us that we can cause the kingdom to come or even prepare or enlarge it by the hand of man and human strength or even by Christian action. He has enjoined us to pray for it daily. "Thy kingdom come," for everything is dependent on Him. And those who are truly praying for His coming will not be lazy and indolent Christians.

It is further said that this stone smote the weak clay pedestal of the image. It does not say that it rolled or fell against it, but that it struck the image, i.e., collided with it with great force. The Postmillennialists, who with regard to this stone usually make beautiful and elaborate speeches about the glory of Christianity, completely lose sight of the deliberateness, the juridical and catastrophical nature of this smiting. This striking of the stone against the beautiful but terrible world image shatters the foundation of all unscriptural optimism. Note also the awesome result of this impact of the stone. It pulverized the image and turned it into chaff. Remarkable also is the place where the stone struck. It did not beat against the head. God shows in all of Scripture, and He shows it here again, that He desired a long history even though this meant a constant struggle between light and darkness.

The result of the falling of this stone was to grind up all the elements of the image. When this is stated so clearly, how can anyone say that after the impact of the stone there can still exist something like a world monarchy? By saying that all the metals of this image became like chaff, this text says that all the glory of these world powers have no real value before God. For to God nothing of real value gets lost. Even the images used for the ungodly, who perish in judgment, point this out. They are always compared to worthless things like chaff, dross, stubble, ashes, etc.

No place was found for them. After Christ will have returned, there will be peoples walking the earth, as Scripture teaches us clearly in many places. But here it is taught just as clearly that there will never follow another world empire again.

In the third place, we asked what happened afterward with this stone. "And the stone that smote the image became a great mountain." Here we are confronted with a stark contrast between the image that disappeared completely and the stone that grew out to a great mountain, which filled the whole earth.

Two miracles are told of the stone. First, it was hewn out without hands. Second, it grew into a mountain. Both facts are supernatural. "The stone which the builders refused is become the head stone of the corner. This is the Lord's doing; it is marvellous in our eyes" (Ps. 118:22, 23). What is meant by this mountain that filled the whole earth can be answered by Scripture. Isaiah 2:2; Micah 4:1, 2 also speak of the glorious kingdom under the symbol of a mountain (compare vv. 35 and 44 of this chapter).

Derisively people have taunted, "Where does Daniel speak of a kingdom of peace?" The answer is, here. And furthermore in chapters 7 and 12. If someone says that here no mention is made of a thousand-year kingdom, then the answer is that no one has ever claimed that here the thousand-year duration of that kingdom is mentioned. We must not forget the following facts:

- Christ's kingdom of peace has a temporal side and an eternal side.
- The temporal side is the least important and consequently never stands in the foreground.
- The temporal side has no reference to Israel, the Church, or creation as such, but to Satan, sin, and its result.
- That is the reason why the temporary side of this kingdom could not be mentioned until after the final revelation.

• This temporary side is mentioned six times at the end of the Book of Revelation.

We must call attention to the fact that the kingdom of Christ does not become manifest and reach its full development until after the pulverization of the kingdoms of the world, that it comes from above, that it comes by Christ Himself without the hand of man; and that it is created, not obtained by conquest. Hence, He does not have His kingdom on this earth yet. The church, according to Van Andel's beautiful simile, is only a small colony of the heavenly motherland. The Evil One, the god of this age, still has his kingdom here.

Many expositors are always quick to emphasize, in this connection, that we are dealing here with a spiritual kingdom. If we use this word as a contrast to the sinful and the carnal, then it is a correct statement, but if we mean by it that the kingdom will not be visibly and gloriously physically present on earth, we are completely mistaken. Judge for yourself.

• The stone, from which this kingdom originated, was also visible and material.
• This kingdom is placed alongside of or, rather, opposite the other kingdoms, and is it not true that they were also visible?
• A spiritual kingdom can purify earthly kingdoms, but it cannot destroy them.
• It takes the place of the smashed image, which blew away like chaff before the wind. There is never a vacuum anywhere in the world.
• This is perfectly analogous with the teaching of Scripture.
• It is in agreement with the confession of the bodily resurrection.

This kingdom will fill the whole earth and will nevermore be disturbed or destroyed. Also the "quick" resurrection of which the apostle John makes mention in Revelation 20:7-10 does not take anything away from this last word. It is a very foolish and unscriptural presentation when people, often derisively, present it as though the thousand-year kingdom will come to grief again. This kingdom will be the absolute monarchy of Christ.

That Christ's people will reign with Him follows from the

statement that it will not be left to any other people. They will reign with Him eternally, but this, too, does not take anything away from Christ's supremacy. After Daniel had produced the dream and its interpretation he once more pointed out that the great God had made known the dream of Nebuchadnezzar; that things of the future were revealed, as Nebuchadnezzar had desired; and he finished by saying that the dream was certain and the interpretation sure. The dream was true because it had been revealed by God and at God's time the interpretation would be literally fulfilled. Let us give heed to Daniel's implied warning, for everything in the past that is related to the first three kingdoms, as Scripture itself points out, has been promptly fulfilled.

Daniel Made Ruler

Then the king Nebuchadnezzar fell upon his face, and worshiped Daniel, and commanded that they should offer an oblation and sweet odors unto him. The king answered unto Daniel, and said, of a truth it is, that your God is a God of gods, and a Lord of kings, and a revealer of secrets, seeing thou couldest reveal this secret. Then the king made Daniel a great man, and gave him many great gifts, and made him ruler over the whole province of Babylon, and chief of the governors over all the wise men of Babylon. Then Daniel requested of the king, and he set Shadrach, Meshach, and Abed-nego, over the affairs of the province of Babylon: but Daniel sat in the gate of the king (vv. 46-49).

Nebuchadnezzar must have listened to the interpretation of the dream with silent amazement. Here we see the impact on him and the result of it for Daniel and his friends. As a true heathen Eastern ruler, Nebuchadnezzar fell on his face and worshiped Daniel. Some people do not like to think of actual veneration, since the word can also be translated as pay honor, pay homage, pay respect. They also consider it below the dignity of the king to worship a foreign exile. Further, they point out Daniel's fear of God would prevent him from accepting such veneration. It seems to us that we most assuredly are dealing with a case similar to that in Acts 14:9-13 and 28:6, for the sacrifices he ordered to be brought to Daniel also point this out. From the introduction to the dream it can almost be concluded that Daniel had already feared this. That he must have emphatically and with disgust refused this worship is certain. It may not be stated in as many words, but from the answer of the king in verse 47 it is clear that Daniel pointed away from himself. From the further part of this verse it can be safely concluded that he pointed to the God of gods. Then we need not assume that these sacrifices were really made to Daniel. It is only stated that the king wanted to have them made.

Daniel must have advised him to bring praise to the God of Israel. When Nebuchadnezzar said, "Of a truth it is, that your God is a God of gods," we can deduce from these words that he had already heard and thought about this God before. Jeremiah had earlier not neglected to point him to the God of gods. But we must not ascribe too much to this expression of praise. It was still a heathen who was talking here, and one who only made Daniel's God the greatest among many other gods. Shortly after having said that he destroyed the Lord's temple. Still, this praise was of great value to Nebuchadnezzar, Daniel, and Israel.

Nebuchadnezzar also further glorified the wisdom of God when he said that he reveals secrets. All this had glorious results for Daniel. This favored man always obtained what he desired. As a reward Nebuchadnezzar gave him both riches (many great gifts) and power (he made him ruler over the whole province of Babylon). The kingdom of Nebuchadnezzar was subdivided into sections or provinces. Daniel was appointed governor of the chief province of which Babylon was the capital.

Furthermore, he was elevated as president of all the wise men in Babylon. The sages of Babylon were subdivided into different ranks or classes, each of which had its own supervisor. Now Daniel was elevated to be the superintendent of all these supervisors. Hence he received a very high scientific position. He, a foreigner, a Jew, and so young, was placed above all the proud wise men. How hard that must have been for these gentlemen!

Also it had the most glorious results for Daniel's friends. When Daniel had been in distress they had supported him with collective prayer, but now he did not forget them. He requested the king to set them over the affairs of the province of Babylon. Here we see again the lovely characteristics of Daniel. He was indeed a knight without fear or reproach. It is not clear what he requested of the king for his friends. According to the original, he may have asked the king to just pass his position as ruler over the province of Babylon on to them, or more likely, he requested that his friends might be his lieutenants, his commissioners, in the province of

Babylon, so that he could spend more time in the gate, i.e., in the presence of the king as his highest judge and counselor. Nebuchadnezzar was now even more favorably inclined toward Daniel than ever before and granted him his request. And the Lord obtained with all these things His goal. The God-fearing remnant that walked in His way was great even in Babylon.

Chapter **3**
THE BURNING FIERY FURNACE

Image of Gold

Nebuchadnezzar the king made an image of gold, whose height was threescore cubits, and the breadth thereof six cubits: he set it up in the plain of Dura, in the province of Babylon. Then Nebuchadnezzar the king sent to gather together the princes, the governors, and the captains, the judges, the treasurers, the counsellors, the sheriffs, and all the rulers of the provinces, to come to the dedication of the image which Nebuchadnezzar the king had set up. Then the princes, governors, and captains, the judges, the treasurers, the counsellors, the sheriffs, and all the rulers of the provinces, were gathered together unto the dedication of the image Nebuchadnezzar the king had set up; and they stood before the image that Nebuchadnezzar had set up (vv. 1-3).

There may be only a few chapters in Scripture as vehemently contested as this one. Critics have found in the form of this image, in the names of the statesmen and musicians, and in the miracle of the preservation of the young men in the burning fiery furnace all kinds of inaccuracies, impossibilities, and absurdities. Dean Farrar of England expresses the general view on this chapter when he says, "...historic fiction...superb in its imaginative grandeur." He does admit it is one of the most precious stories in Scripture.

The chapter does not say at which time this statue was erected. The Greek translation of the Old Testament, which is freer in Daniel than anywhere else and sometimes incorporates totally foreign pieces in the text, adds here a time reference. According to this Greek text, this statue was erected in the eighteenth year of Nebuchadnezzar. This would mean fifteen years had already passed since his remarkable dream and it would not surprise us at all that he once again esteemed the idol Bel higher than the God of gods and the Lord of kings in Daniel 2:47.

If we cannot pinpoint the time with certainty, the same must be said about the purpose of setting up the image. Much has been written about this and guessed at. Some people have thought it was an expression of pure pride and suspected Nebuchadnezzar wanted to contradict the interpretation of the dream by demonstrating that he was not only the head of gold but best represented by a totally golden statue. Others were of the opinion he wanted to purify himself from the suspicion that he had forsaken the religion of his fathers by elevating the God of Israel so high. Still others think he wished to celebrate his great victories in this way. The old Rabbis suspected the same motive as that of the builders of the Tower of Babel. There are some who see it as an anti-Semitic demonstration.

There is something to be said in favor of the last-mentioned motive. Apart from the idea held by some that this image was set up after the destruction of the temple and Jerusalem, it seems to us there are, nevertheless, some things which hint that the king put up a snare to catch Daniel and his friends. The terrible threat of verse 6, for example, was totally unnecessary for the Chaldeans and seems clearly to have been made with an eye on Israel. It is evident that opposition and disobedience were expected since not too far from the image the burning furnace for the disobedient had already been put in readiness. We also know that Israel in exile was despised and hated by everybody (Dan. 9:16; Ps. 137), and in the prophecy of Daniel we find several manifestations of anti-Semitism. Ever since the days of the Pharaohs the world has hated Israel. It cannot be otherwise, for the world always hates what God loves, and God loves Israel as His chosen people. These Chaldean men accused the Jews, and they emphasized that the latter were Jews.

We do not believe, however, that Nebuchadnezzar had such low intents in mind. He thought too much of the Jews for that. We much prefer to think that Nebuchadnezzar wanted to celebrate some great victory and at the same time to strengthen his monarchy, for he always had its glory in mind. And how better to further the unity of his domain than by the unity of religion? He was of the opinion, of course, that others could worship other gods as easily as he could. But then it seems quite probable that as far as his dignitaries were concerned, base motives played a role. Evidently, they would not fall down on their faces—then they could not have seen the young men standing—but cast furtive glances around to see how the Jews would behave and if they could not cause their downfall.

The image was made of gold and had a height of sixty cubits and a width of six cubits; about one hundred feet high and ten feet wide. As a representation of a human body this was a disproportionate ratio, for the average ratio of a person's height and width is six to one. Hence this image was either too high or too narrow, depending on how one looks at it. But this objection can be met with four arguments.

First of all, it is by no means sure whether this was a statue of a human being. The word in the original does not indicate this. It may very well have been an obelisk or some other pointed pillar. Secondly, the disparity between height and width need not surprise us, for excavations have clearly shown that Chaldeans had a taste for the grotesque and the monstrous. Thirdly, it may be noted that here the Greek translation mentions a height of six cubits and is silent on the width. But it seems best to include the pedestal in the height. Gaebelein makes the observation that this image had the number of man (Rev. 13:18).

Another objection centers around the gold. But here we must remember that we can hardly imagine the fabulous riches of Babylon. Besides, there are four possibilities with respect to the "golden image." The best thing to do is make a selection from the first three.

1. It may have been made of solid gold.
2. It may have been made of gold, but with a hollow inside.
3. It may have been made of wood, stone, or some other metal but overlaid with gold.
4. It may have merely been gilded.

The place of the image was the plain of Dura in the province of Babylon. This notation is of importance with respect to those people who hold the opinion that Daniel did not live in Babylon but in Palestine and hence was not, or could not be, well informed about situations and customs in Babylon. It has recently come to light that there were two additional Duras. Daniel knew this very well and so makes a careful distinction. A Palestinian Jew in the time of Antiochus Epiphanes could not possibly have given the details mentioned in this chapter.

The second verse tells us Nebuchadnezzar invited all the office-bearers of his kingdom to be present at the dedication of the image. Much archaeological study has been done to find which various officials are meant here, but always without success. We do know, however, that it was a Babylonian custom to place as governor over a conquered nation or people, one chosen from among these people. And since Babylon ruled over many conquered countries, there were many of these governors. This idea sheds light on Nebuchadnezzar's wise purpose in calling all these various governors together. Religion was used as a tool to promote the power of the state. By unity in religion he sought to obtain power, whereas God, contrariwise, uses it to promote holiness.

Seven kinds of officials are mentioned here. The mysterious number seven plays a key role in Daniel. Three of these names of officers are still used today, namely, satrap, ruler, and sultan. Generally speaking, we can say that all civil, military, and judicial high dignitaries were present here. At the end of verse 2 they are all taken together under the one general name "rulers of the provinces." The third verse tells us all these people obeyed the order of Nebuchadnezzar and took their places before the statue on the day of its dedication. It was a very solemn affair.

Fall Down and Worship

Then an herald cried aloud, to you it is commanded, O people, nations, and languages, that at what time ye hear the sound of the cornet, flute, harp, sackbut, psaltery, dulcimer, and all kinds of music, ye fall down and worship the golden image that Nebuchadnezzar the king hath set up: and whoso falleth not down and worshipeth shall the same hour be cast into the midst of a burning fiery furnace. Therefore, at that time, when all the people heard the sound of the cornet, flute, harp, sackbut, psaltery, and all kinds of music, all the people, the nations, and the languages, fell down and worshiped the golden image that Nebuchadnezzar the king had set up (vv. 4-7).

In the East there were royal heralds who were assigned to render the service which today is provided by our state journals and bulletins. They were men who could run fast and talk loud. Scripture often alludes to the work of such a herald. The word that is often translated as preaching is derived from it.

A military fanfare would give the sign to begin the public homage to the image. Music has always been one of the most tempting powers of this world. In the hand of the wicked it is always aimed at bewitching and intoxicating the senses. The generation of the Canaanites invented it and it has remained in the power of the world until this day. People may sometimes speak in a superficial idealism of taking this away from Satan or the world, but the fact is that this will remain impossible for the simple reason that God, the Giver of genius, does not bestow musical genius on His children apart from a few exceptions. One day it will be taken away from Satan (Rev. 14:2; 15:3), but that is reserved for the great Representative of the Father at His coming. As long as He tarries, however, the most beautiful music will be heard in religious Babylon and in apostate churches, and the apostate masses will continue to let it intoxicate them.

Some of these musical instruments have names of Greek origin. On this fact a gigantic argument has been based against the genuineness of Daniel. The argument goes as follows. In the sixth century B.C. the Greek language was not known in Babylon, yet Greek names appear here. Hence this book must have been written in the time of the Maccabees. The argument of Professor Driver is well known. It runs as follows:

> The verdict of the language of Daniel is thus clear. The Persian words presupposed a period after the Persian empire had been well established; the Greek words demand, the Hebrew supports, and the Aramaic permits a date after the conquest of Palestine by Alexander the Great (332 B.C.).

Although Christ called Daniel a prophet, this and similar criticisms reduce Daniel to a novelist from the time of the Maccabees on the basis of a few musical instruments. We wish to answer this argument with a few pointers.

- Babylon had assimilated all the glory of the conquered nations, and since the names of such instruments usually go together with the objects themselves, it is very possible the people already, at that time, knew the names of these instruments.
- Babylonians loved music and song, and Psalm 137 shows us that they demanded music and songs from their captives. If

they demanded this from the Hebrews, they could also do so from the nations that already had such instruments.

- We know from Scripture itself as well as from secular history that at about that time there were already trade relations between Asia and Greece. Why, then, could the Babylonians not have imported Greek musical instruments?
- We can, furthermore, add that even a learned man such as Michaelis doubts whether even one of these names is really Greek. It is quite well possible that the Greeks borrowed these names from the Chaldeans.

What has been said above about the names of the officials can also be said of the musical instruments. It has been thought that the words psalter, symphonia, and cither were Greek names. The message which the herald had to exclaim in the name of the king was that when this orchestra began, the entire multitude must fall down before the image. It can be safely assumed that the dazzling brilliance of the great golden image, the huge and grand assembly, the music and singing were fully intended to intoxicate the senses and overwhelm the minds of Nebuchadnezzar's lords.

Added to this was the special threat to the disobedient. Whoever did not fall down and worship would be cast into the midst of the burning fiery furnace. This kind of punishment was apparently quite common among the Chaldeans. In Jeremiah 29:22 we read that the king of Babylon roasted Zedekiah and Ahab in the fire. The Persians did not administer this kind of punishment since they worshiped fire as a divine element. Hence we see that Darius did not burn Daniel, but cast him into a den of lions. How these ovens were constructed we cannot say with certainty. At any rate, they were not similar to our baking ovens, but rather more like kilns and smelting furnaces.

That the Near East and also Israel were acquainted with great fiery ovens is evident from Malachi 4:1, where the burning day of the Lord on which the fire will be unleashed is compared with such a fiery furnace. And the punishment would immediately be applied to the disobedient. By way of a deterrent, the furnace could probably be seen burning near the image. In verse 6 the word "hour" appears for the first time in the Bible. It is believed the Chaldeans, who had made great advances in astrology and mathematics, were the first to invent time division.

Thus we find here again a true example of the tyranny of Oriental despots. Apparently they seldom gave an order without adding the most terrible threats to it. People have been amazed that Nebuchadnezzar, who at an earlier occasion had spoken such lofty words about the God of Israel, could here give a command like this; the more so since he had a certain respect for the Jews. We must hereby keep in mind that Nebuchadnezzar did not wish to be a religious persecutor. As a heathen it was an easy thing for him to fall down on his face before a Daniel (2:46), and now he was motivated by the same respect for others. Assyriologists have discovered and related that Nebuchadnezzar was very religious and especially venerated the chief god of Babylon, Bel Merodach, on all special occasions.

Verse 7 tells us his subjects complied with his wishes. There were but a few spoilsports at this world festival. A similar feast will one day be repeated on a much greater scale (Rev. 13:8).

Accused the Jews

Wherefore, at that time certain Chaldeans came near, and accused the Jews. They spake and said to the king Nebuchadnezzar, O king, live forever. Thou, O king, hast made a decree, that every man that shall hear the sound of the cornet, flute, harp, sackbut, psaltery, and dulcimer, and all kinds of music, shall fall down and worship the golden image: and whoso falleth not down and worshippeth, that he should be cast into the midst of a burning fiery furnace. There are certain Jews whom thou hast set over the affairs of the province of Babylon, Shadrach, Meshach, and Abed-nego; these men, O king, have not regarded thee: they serve not thy gods, nor worship the golden image which thou hast set up (vv. 8-12).

This section deals with the public accusation leveled at the Jews. It seems to us it contains a hint that we are dealing here with anti-Semitism. It is not stated that they were openly accusing merely the three young men but the Jews. Anti-Semitism is one of the great sins of the so-called Christian nations and at the same time one of the greatest sins of the church of Christ, although there it manifests itself in a totally different way, even in a pious garb. Especially of late this hatred has obtained even philosophical aid. Its adherents are opposed to the Jews becoming a nation of their own or even forming a unity of race. The erudite criminologist C.

Lombroso, himself of Jewish blood, did not count the Jews among the Semites but, like the Romans and Germanic tribes, to the Arians. Such a viewpoint leads fundamentally to the same attempt as that of Babylon and Edom—to raze and destroy them (Ps. 137).

Of the same nature is the mocking with Israel's restoration in Palestine. Many people have the idea that the Jews in the various countries are doing too well in order to return to a small and poor little country. They succeed in enumerating all kinds of objections to prove that this would be impossible if not foolhardy. The fact that God has nevertheless said so and (all opposition notwithstanding) will gloriously bring it to pass does not enter their mind. His arm has not become shortened. One day He will gather together Israel's exiles from the four corners of the earth. Anti-Semitism, which dates back many centuries in many forms, is the absolute antithesis of Christ's prayer at the cross and the wish and prayer of Paul in Romans 9:1-4 and 10:1.

These Chaldean princes had a cunning plan to cause the downfall of the hated Jews. Whether these Chaldeans are to be identified with the class of wise men mentioned in Daniel 2:2 and 4 is not certain. If they were one and the same, then they were maliciously ungrateful, for the Jew, Daniel, had saved the lives of these men. Still, everything seems to indicate that they had been lying in wait. For one thing, they literally quoted the king's command, which shows that before the service they had with malicious pleasure peered at that command with the hated Jews in mind. Furthermore, they emphatically reminded Nebuchadnezzar of his threatened punishment, as though they wanted to drive home that it would not do for him to retreat from it even one step. They also called his attention to the fact that the disobedient offenders were strangers, Jewish men. And they presented these young men as ingrates by pointing out to the king that he had favored them by appointing them over the realm of Babylon.

"These men, O king, have not regarded thee," they accused further. They thereby depicted them as miscreants who had not the least respect for the high majesty of the king. "They serve not thy gods," they added to the incriminating list. This accusation, however, implied great honor to the young men. The worst abomination, according to the accusers was that these young men had not worshiped the image of Dura. That there may be such a thing as conscientious objections lay totally beyond their vision.

This is sufficient proof of their own lack of conscience. From everything they said and did it is obvious that they were not in the least concerned with the glory of the image, the upholding of the laws, the honor of the king, or the unity of his kingdom; but, rather, to see to it that the Jews were cast into the fire. Here we see a limited example of the battle of the seed of the serpent against the seed of the woman.

King in Rage

Then Nebuchadnezzar in his rage and fury commanded to bring Shadrach, Meshach, and Abed-nego. Then they brought these men before the king. Nebuchadnezzar spake and said unto them, Is it true, O Shadrach, Meshach, and Abed-nego, do not ye serve my gods, nor worship the golden image which I have set up? Now if ye be ready that at what time ye hear the sound of the cornet, flute, harp, sackbut, psaltery, and dulcimer, and all kinds of music, ye fall down and worship the image which I have made; well: but if ye worship not, ye shall be cast the same hour into the midst of a burning fiery furnace; and who is that God that shall deliver you out of my hands? (vv. 13-15)

The accusation itself, as well as the form in which it had been presented, had been successfully geared to make Nebuchadnezzar explode with anger. The fact that he wanted to deal with them in a lenient manner, however, became obvious at once from his command that the young men were to be brought before him. Hence they were not, as the original command had stated, cast without any further ado and in the same hour into the burning fiery furnace. He wished to exercise some patience and make attempts to move them to worship his image. Moreover, he figured the possibility of some misunderstanding was not entirely excluded.

Before long, the young men were standing before him to be judicially examined. There must have been a breathless silence all around when these three Jews stood there before him. There must have been a general amazement among the great men of the realm that these three young men dared to be so courageous as to publicly disobey the mighty Nebuchadnezzar before whom all nations trembled. Hear what Nebuchadnezzar said to them!

Let us listen to this examination. Is it deliberate, he asked them, that you do not honor my gods? The attempt on his part is undeniably that he wished to save these faithful servants of his. He obviously asked something to which he knew the answer, for he knew very well that these Jews were not so ignorant as to have misunderstood his clear and repeated command. Upon some reflection he could know that the Jews were particularly strict in their religion. We get the impression that he found himself in a tight place with respect to this ugly situation. Apparently, he wished to put the words into their mouths that they had not deliberately but by mistake or for some other reason acted the way they had.

He thus affords them postponement and once more offers them the opportunity to manifest their submissiveness and readiness. He thereby posed that a while ago they may have not been fully ready, as is evident from the words, "If ye be ready." It is evident from all he said that the king was by no means thirsting for their blood but, on the contrary, that he wanted to save them and at the same time uphold their honor before their enemies.

In the meantime it irritated him terribly that these stiffnecked Jews refused to bow before his image. He was not insisting on true worship, only the motion of worship, by casting themselves on their faces. To his mind it must have seemed nonsense to refuse to do something like that. That he exercised much patience with these young men is evident from the fact that for their sake, alone, he was willing to let all the singers and music makers play once more. But the threat he added to it shows that after that his patience would be exhausted. If they continued to refuse, they would be thrown post haste into the midst of the fiery burning oven.

"Who is that God that shall deliver you out of my hands?" Without thinking of his earlier confession of Israel's God, Nebuchadnezzar started to slander the God of the Jews. In this monarch we already see something of that pride which will have ripened to full fruition in the Man of Sin who, according to Paul's word, will oppose and exalt himself above all that is called God or is honored as God (2 Thess. 2:4). It must be admitted that he did not mention Israel's God here, but it is evident enough that he was referring to Him. Here he used the boastful and slanderous language of a Rabshakeh. The faith of the young men would soon give him the answer to his slanderous question. God Himself would soon cause him to change his mind.

God Is Able to Deliver

Shadrach, Meshach, and Abed-nego, answered and said to the king, O Nebuchadnezzar, we are not careful to answer thee in this matter. If it be so, our God whom we serve is able to deliver us from the burning fiery furnace, and he will deliver us out of thine hand, O king. But if not, be it known unto thee, O king, that we will not serve thy gods, nor worship the golden image which thou hast set up (vv. 16-18).

We find here the answer given by Shadrach, Meshach, and Abed-nego. Its characteristic aspects are its calmness and its brevity, its confidence in God's power and salvation, and its determination not to engage in idolatry. Regarding their calmness and brevity we cannot refrain from quoting a paragraph from F. Bettex:

Angry, threatening, the king arises. The furnace, at his command already stoked hotter, spews out flames. All around the courtiers are waiting, holding their breath, the one with malicious pleasure, the other in great suspense, to see whether the hated foreigners will humble themselves or will be destroyed. "We are not careful!" They are not anxiously and beseechingly asking, "May it please your majesty to grant us most graciously a brief historic-scientific explanation concerning our beliefs as to how we have believed ever since our father Abraham, etc." No! They are not spouting one word concerning such an evident matter. "We are not careful." Nor do they ask for exemption from the sentence; they are not conferring with each other...they had had all the time to do so; there had been much talk everywhere about the great feast of dedication. Shall we refuse the king, who has overloaded us with benefits and honor, and whom Jehovah himself has placed over us, and thank him by abruptly and proudly refusing all further obedience? Should we not thereby set a bad example to the entire nation with regard to the government? In little, secluded Jerusalem our peculiar religion was in its place and wholly justified, but here the relationships are different; here in this great world city, in which the heart of life of the whole world beats, we must take into account other circumstances and times and we must comply with them. How else can we keep touch with the people whom we are called to govern? And as far as the act itself is concerned, has not the great rabbi and exalted prophet Isaiah—peace be unto his soul—taught, "An idol is nothing!'"? Consequently, the worship of an idol is an insignificant act. How much more is a mere eternal bowing before him while one in his heart refuses him all worship? God considers the heart. Must we not manifest a heartfelt pity with and an understanding of these people, since there surely must be found among them wise men and high priests who honestly look for the truth and who in the form of this image approach a highest being and the invisible deity? And may we then bluntly hurt their deepest religious feelings? The outward form does not matter; only the religious feeling of the heart must be considered....

Am I here in the valley of Dura or in one of the world cities of Europe? Am I hearing capable Babylonian speakers or modern scribes? For cannot my ears hear such arguments daily? But these three men remained as solid and hard as a rock. These foreigners stood much taller than the mighty king who threatened them with death; they were bigger than this whole multitude and its princes, greater than the entire kingdom and all the power of Babylon.

Also manifest here is that characteristic of the nation which, although it often obstinately resisted God, later also often sacrificed their possessions and their blood for its faith and for the law of Sinai during ages of dispersion and slavery and which by the thousands even in death spoke: "Hear, O Israel: The Lord our God is one Lord" (Deut. 6:4). "Here we stand! We cannot do otherwise!" That is what God is doing in our days, now that so many people who call themselves Christians, and even their leaders, have proudly, broadmindedly, and very tolerantly chosen as their slogan, "Here we stand! But we can also do something different!"

When the young men said that they were not careful to answer the king, it did not imply disrespect of the king as though they did not consider him worthy of an answer. Far less did their reply suggest a proud challenge. The reason they considered it unnecessary is that they considered it futile, as the original implies. For that reason some translators want to substitute: "it will not avail us." But it seems to us that the [Dutch] State Translation can very well be maintained, provided we understand it to mean that the reason for it not being necessary lay in its being futile insofar as they had already decided not to worship the image, and the king on his part had once again expressed his determination to burn them. We must take it to mean that even though there might have been a severe struggle in their souls, at that moment there was absolutely no such struggle or temptation in their hearts.

There was absolutely no conflict of duties, as is sometimes supposed, between their devotion to Nebuchadnezzar and his kingdom and gods and their faithfulness to Jehovah. Jehovah their God, whom they had come to learn to know and love as the only God from their earliest youth, had long ago obtained the victory in their souls, so that here it was not necessary to wage a battle. It kept resounding in their souls, "Hear, O Israel, the Lord thy God is one Lord" and "Thou shalt have no other gods before me" and "Thou shalt not bow down thyself to them." Hence they had remained standing straight when all the others bowed down.

Faithfulness to God cannot exist without trust in His power and goodness. This trust was found in these three faithful young men. They gave a twofold glorious testimony. They confessed that they served the God of heaven, as the Greek translation has it, and that this God is mighty to save from the greatest exigency. The apostle Paul also once gave such a glorious self-testimony to his fellow shipwreck victims in Acts 27:23.

The testimony concerning their God who had power to save from the fiery furnace must have sounded strange in the ears of those heathen. If that had been merely a theoretical or rhetorical statement, well, their superstition would have been able to accept that. But this was speaking from full conviction, and that in full view of the furnace spewing forth sparks and flames. It is evident that they gave an answer to the taunting question of the king: "Who is that God that shall deliver you out of my hands?"

The heathen had gods who could not deliver, and they had no more than a faint idea of the omnipotence of God. Meanwhile, it is evident from the last part of verse 17 that the three young men did not merely dwell on the omnipotence of God but proceeded to fully trust His will to save them. Whether they were thinking here of the Lord's promise in Isaiah 43:2, "When thou walkest through the fire, thou shalt not be burned; neither shall the flame kindle upon thee," we cannot say, but it is not unlikely. Whatever, it is evident from their whole demeanor that they trusted fully in the Lord.

Most certainly they had as yet no knowledge or any idea as to how they would be saved, and afterward they would be just as astonished at the miraculous deliverance by God as were Nebuchadnezzar and his nobles, but they had the confidence and trust in their souls that the Lord would give deliverance in one way or another. We see a similar case in the life of Abraham (Gen. 22 and Heb. 11:19). Maybe they, too, already had the testimony of the Spirit in their souls concerning the coming miracle, but verse 18 does not support this idea.

From verse 18 it is evident they allowed for the possibility that the Lord, whose thoughts are always higher than our thoughts, might for some reason known, only to Him, consider it wiser for them to be burned. God is and remains always free and sovereign. At times He allows much to befall the objects of His love and favor. Moreover, the promise quoted from Isaiah pertained not to individuals but to Israel as a nation. The burning bush as a whole, as had been shown to Moses long ago, could never be consumed, but nevertheless it was possible for a few twigs to be burned. If, however, they left some possibility of burning as far as God's determination was concerned, there was no room for becoming unfaithful to their God by kneeling down before Babylon's gods. They wanted to obey God rather than men.

This was living by principle. They knew nothing of bending. They stood immovably fast when all of Babylon bowed down. They preferred to have all of Babylon rise up against them than to have God against them. They looked on the command and for the rest were blind to the future. They defied the torturing pain of the fire as well as all of Babylon. They would rather die a thousand deaths than for a moment become unfaithful to the God of their fathers. Their faith was of the purest gold. Purer than the gold of Nebuchadnezzar's image.

From Hebrews 11:34 we learn that through faith they quenched the violence of fire. Where is there a power like the power of faith? The story will teach us their faith was not put to shame. Ah, that all our young men were so polite, determined, God-fearing, and steadfast of principle so as not to bow to the gods of this age.

Cast Into Fiery Furnace

Then was Nebuchadnezzar full of fury, and the form of his visage was changed against Shadrach, Meshach, and Abed-nego: therefore he spake, and commanded that they should heat the furnace one seven times more than it was wont to be heated. And he commanded the most mighty men that were in his army to bind Shadrach, Meshach, and Abed-nego, and to cast them into the burning fiery furnace. Then these men were bound in their coats, their hose, and their hats, and their other garments, and were cast

into the midst of the burning fiery furnace. Therefore, because
the king's commandment was urgent, and the furnace exceeding
hot, the flame of the fire slew those men that took up Shadrach,
Meshach, and Abed-nego (vv. 19-22).

Pure faith gives no more an impure sound than pure gold does.
The three young men had made it abundantly clear to the king
what they wanted. They had made him realize they were not
motivated by a dependence on chance but only by obedience to
Jehovah. Whether they were saved or not, would perish or not,
they would not engage in idolatry. The fact they had not said at
once, "We will not worship your abominations," had been wise,
for now they had had an opportunity to give a brief explanation
and a twofold testimony in the presence of the princes of Babylon.
It is, mainly with regard to the end of the chapter, quite evident that
behind all these things lay the holy purpose of the Lord; that His
people must keep themselves pure from the abominations of
heathenism, in whose midst they had to dwell for seventy years.

When Nebuchadnezzar saw himself contradicted with such
boldness, and that in the presence of all his mighty men, he
swelled up with fury, as the text says. Never before had he heard
such contradicting before him. He had never encountered before
such despising of his might and threat. This must have seemed to
him the height of brazenness. Thus far he had maintained a
seemingly kind attitude, but now his facial expression changed.
He trembled and turned red and cried out with a raw, quivering
voice to stoke the furnace seven times hotter than usual. Deep
within his heart there was also a fire, which blazed in a terrible
hatred and vengeance. This fire leaped from him in wildly raging
flames to the furnace and was the cause of it becoming unbearably
hot. Soon God would show, however, that He could extinguish
this consuming fire of vengeance too.

When the king ordered the furnace to be stoked seven times
hotter than usual, he manifested that he was blind with rage, for
to the extent that the fire was hotter, to that extent the suffering of
the objects of his anger would be less and their death would be
hastened. A small fire would have slowly roasted them. Once
again the mighty king showed that he could not rule his own spirit.
Meanwhile, this again served God's purpose, for when soon they
would be delivered from the fire, this would make the miracle that
much greater.

After the king had commanded to heat the oven "seven times more than it was wont to be heated," as the text literally says, he turned to his bodyguard and commanded the greatest and strongest soldiers to come forward. Anger usually expresses itself in superlatives. That was also the case here: the furnace had to be made supremely hot. Among all the gods there was not one who could save from his power, and now the brawniest soldiers must bind the young men in their own clothes in such a manner that they could never free themselves. Maybe the king expected some resistance, but if so he was sadly mistaken and showed only too clearly that he did not know these young men, for they resembled the Lamb of which Isaiah 53:7 makes mention.

The king's bodyguard obeyed him immediately and threw themselves upon the three brave young men. When reading verse 21 superficially, we may easily get the idea that they were bound with their own clothing, but that is apparently not what is meant. What it implies is that everything went so fast and the strong warriors flung themselves so rapidly at the young men that they had no time to take off the beautiful ceremonial clothes with which they were adorned for this occasion. On other occasions it was the custom to clothe the criminals that were to be burned in clothing suiting their crimes, or to throw them into the fire naked. This did not take place here. Everything went very fast because the anger of the king was in a hurry.

Meanwhile, we observe again that God had a purpose with all this and was about to perform a miracle, for these clothes also had to contribute in order to magnify the wonder of His hand. These three men were bound—maybe even to each other!—and yet a moment later they were walking about in the furnace. These clothes were flammable and could easily be turned to ashes, yet they did not burn or even smolder, and afterward the smell of fire in them could not even be detected.

It is emphasized in this verse and the following that the victims were cast into the midst of the burning fiery furnace, so that no one might get the idea that they were there for just a few seconds and then fell out of it again. God wants to be clearly understood in this miracle, so that everyone will see and agree that in every respect it was a miracle of His almighty hand.

Verse 22 points out that the enormous heat of the furnace even killed the strong warriors. The king in his anger demanded all possible speed and urged the soldiers on so that they practically forgot themselves and could not take any precautions against the immense heat of the fire. The result was that they were killed and choked to death by the blazing and exploding sparks of the fire. That, too, was an arresting scene which manifested the miraculous act of God all the more gloriously. Whereas these strong warriors did not escape from the mouth of the furnace, the three heroes were soon to walk freely around in the midst of the furnace. Besides that, it manifested that the fire did not lack the power to consume. The fact that the three objects of the king's wrath got safely out of the fire after a while was by no means due to the nature of the fire. Furthermore, it is true what Henry remarks at this place:

> Thus God immediately championed the cause of His unjustly mal-treated servants. He took vengeance on their persecutors instead. He not only punished them at once but also by the means they used to carry out the sentence. Moreover, these people were only the tools of this cruelty. He who had given the order to inflict it had greater sin. Nevertheless they suffered justly for carrying out an unjust command. And it is most likely that they carried it out gladly and were more than happy that they were used to carry it out.

Four in Furnace

And these three men, Shadrach, Meshach, and Abed-nego, fell down bound into the midst of the burning fiery furnace. Then Nebuchadnezzar the king was astonished, and rose up in haste, and spake, and said unto his counsellors, did not we cast three men bound into the midst of the fire? They answered and said unto the king, true, O king. He answered and said, Lo, I see four men loose, walking in the midst of the fire, and they have no hurt; and the form of the fourth is like the Son of God (vv. 23-25).

In contrast to the soldiers who were killed by the flames that leaped from the entrance of the furnace, verse 23 points out that the young men landed in the midst of the fire, and since they were bound hand and foot, fell down in it. What a contrast! What will become of the wicked who one day will be cast into the fire of hell, when even the sparks of an earthly fire can already kill them? What a glorious contrast also between the young men now and Zion afterwards! Now they were bound and falling down; soon they would be walking about; now in the midst of the fire, soon, to the amazement of all around, they will be walking out of it!

Verse 24 does not say Nebuchadnezzar heard anything, but it does say he saw something and that it astonished him. Apparently, the door of the great furnace had been left open so the people could see the men burning. There were three things that astonished and shook the king: he saw those young men living in the midst of the heat of the fire; he saw them walking, even though they had fallen in bound; and he saw a fourth man walking among them.

Turning around agitatedly, he asked his courtiers if there had not been three men bound and thrown into the fire, to which they answered in the affirmative. Hence the mouths of many witnesses had to testify that three men had been thrown into the fiery, overheated oven, while they could see with their eyes that there were now four walking in the midst of the fire. The king was full of amazement. No doubt his conscience must not have been at ease either. Totally flabbergasted, he cried out, "Lo, I see four men loose, walking in the midst of the fire, and they have no hurt." It amazed him above measure that there were four men walking around freely and boldly without any hurt. And the appearance of the fourth drew his attention most of all. He compared this appearance to that of a son of the gods. This person was obviously the protector of the three. And, like the others, he, too, was unassailable and totally fireproof.

Among Bible commentators and readers the question has always been urgent as to who that fourth person might have been. This question may not be considered totally immaterial, as some exegetes do. We must only realize that in cases like this we cannot go beyond a certain degree of informed and sanctified guessing at a probability. For further light, there are two important questions to be asked about this affair: 1) What did Nebuchadnezzar mean with the expression son of the gods, and 2) who may this fourth person really have been?

As far as the first question is concerned, it must be considered certain that Nebuchadnezzar was not thinking of the second Person of the Holy Trinity. Shortly afterwards, in verse 28, he calls him an angel. There is absolutely no basis for supposing the king already possessed such a clear theological knowledge. As a rule three ideas have been advanced in connection with the second question. It has been thought that it was an ordinary angel, one of the servants who are sent out in the service of those who will inherit salvation. Many church fathers and other exegetes saw in him the Angel of the Lord, also called the Angel of the covenant of whom we read so often in connection with Israel's history. Others think of the archangel Michael, of whom Scripture says that he is especially charged with the guidance and protection of Israel as a nation (see Dan. 10:21; 12:1). A definitive answer cannot be given, but we prefer to view him as the One who is the focal point of Daniel as well as of the entire Scripture.

Come Forth From Fire

Then Nebuchadnezzar came near to the mouth of the burning fiery furnace, and spake, and said, Shadrach, Meshach, and Abed-nego, ye servants of the most high God, come forth, and come hither. Then Shadrach, Meshach, and Abed-nego, came forth of the midst of the fire. And the princes, governors, and captains, and the king's counsellors, being gathered together, saw these men, upon whose bodies the fire had no power, nor was an hair of their head singed, neither were their coats changed, nor the smell of fire had passed on them (vv. 26, 27).

The king arose from his seat and walked up to the door of the furnace. With this the sign, his humiliation has already started. A while ago he called the men to come to him, now he has already walked up to them. Meanwhile, observe that the fire did have the property of light, so that the four men could be seen in the fire. When the king had come to the mouth of the furnace he called them by name, and called them moreover servants of the most high God. What a glorious title he gave them in saying so. He thereby gave them, as well as their God, the highest praise. He considered the God who could thus miraculously save them the most high God. His Bel or Nebo could not save anyone that way. Hence, with this statement he returned to his earlier confession (2:47) and at the same time gave himself the answer to his bold question in verse 15: "Who is that God that shall deliver you out of my hands?"

"Come forth, and come hither!" the king had exclaimed. Although the young men had walked freely in the furnace, they nevertheless had not jumped out of it to escape. They continued to serve out their punishment. It is a glorious art to show obedience in the midst of the fire! The same faith by which they had extinguished the power of the fire also enabled them to remain in the intense flame until they were called to come out of it. But after they were called out, they immediately obeyed. After having obeyed their God first, they now obeyed the king. That is the right and glorious order.

Meanwhile the entire illustrious assembly in the valley of Dura had been witnesses of this miraculous spectacle. They had listened amidst breathless silence to the examination of these young men by the king himself; they had seen their ruler explode with vehement anger; they had heard his commands and had seen how the young men had been forcefully slung into the great fiery furnace. They had witnessed the entire bloody drama and Nebuchadnezzar's fierce exclamations. And as soon as the young men appeared from the furnace obviously unharmed, the chief advisors approached them full of curiosity. How is that these three men not only survived the ordeal but showed no sign of being in the fire?

The purpose of verse 27 is obviously to call attention to the miraculous and well-attested element of the miracle. Already three particulars in connection with this miracle were mentioned before, and here four more are mentioned when it is said that the fire had not had power upon their bodies; that even the hair of their heads, which can be so easily singed by fire, had not burned; that their beautiful coats had not changed; and that even the smell of fire could not be detected on them. Hence it is obvious that they had been examined thoroughly by the curious and astonished multitude. This one miracle was a sevenfold miracle. Just as the one white light can make seven colors beam forth in the rainbow, so this one miracle actually contained seven miracles.

God never performs a miracle without having a high and lofty purpose in mind. The essence of this miracle may be no more explicable than that of any other, but its purpose is clear enough. It was of great significance not only to the young men and the heathen Chaldeans, but its main purpose was obviously to be found in Israel, which could so easily give its heart and hand to Babylon's idols. But the next verses themselves shed a clear light on the purpose of this sevenfold miracle, so that we need not say anything more about it.

Praise of Nebuchadnezzar

Then Nebuchadnezzar spake, and said, Blessed be the God of Shadrach, Meshach, and Abed-nego, who hath sent his angel, and delivered his servants that trusted in him, and have changed the king's word, and yielded their bodies, that they might not serve nor worship any god, except their own God. Therefore, I make a decree, that every people, nation, and language, which speak any thing amiss against the God of Shadrach, Meshach, and Abed-nego, shall be cut in pieces, and their houses shall be made a dung hill: because there is no other God that can deliver after this sort. Then the king promoted Shadrach, Meshach, and Abed-nego, in the province of Babylon (vv. 28-30).

The Lord manifested here in a striking manner that He can turn the wrath of men into His own praise (Ps. 76:10). The entire multitude of dignitaries that crowded around the king and the young men had been witnesses of the king's mad temper tantrum and blasphemy; now they had to hear from his mouth this glorious praise. Hence by this glorious miracle God turned the blaspheming of His name into the praise of His name. He had performed a sevenfold miracle both in the furnace and in the king's heart. He extinguished a double fire—the fire of the furnace and the fire of wrath in the king's heart. Truly, He is a God who inclines the hearts of kings like waterbrooks unto all that He wills.

The praise concerned three parties: the king, the Lord, and the three young men. First of all, this praise contains a confession by the king. It may be true that the form of a confession of guilt is lacking, but it is nevertheless clear that in contrast with what is said in verse 15, where he blasphemed Israel's God, he now praised Him. He had blasphemed in the hearing of the entire multitude, now he extolled His praise before the same multitude. When, in the second place, the God of Shadrach, Meshach, and Abed-nego is praised here, then we find as it were Babylon's echo to the phrase "the God of Abraham, Isaac, and Jacob." Next he pointed out that this God is a Deliverer, who had sent His angel to deliver from the fire. The same person whom a while ago he had called a son of the gods (v. 25) he now calls an angel. It seems to us that it is not justified to deduce from this that the king already had a knowledge of angels. It is far more likely that he had heard Shadrach, Meshach, and Abed-nego call him that.

In the third place, this praise contains a eulogy of the three faithful young men. He called them servants again as he had done before, in the sense of bond-servants, slaves. He called them, further, servants who were delivered. He was of course thinking here only of the earthly fire of the furnace, but they had been delivered in a far greater sense from the fire of hell. They were delivered servants that trusted in him (Jehovah). In a causal sense deliverance is the result only of trust. Before this trio had been cast into the furnace, they had cast themselves upon God, and therefore, they had not been put to shame. God had been with them in the midst of the greatest danger and, by means of His angel, had separated the heat and the consuming power of the fire. He had shown that He does not always keep His children from dangers, but that He is always with them in dangers.

Next, he said of these young men that they had changed the king's word, i.e., had bypassed, trespassed, not obeyed his command. In saying this, the king dealt a blow to his imagined absolute world dominion. He expressed here that there could be cases in which he was not unconditionally obeyed and that the disobedient could get away with it without being struck down by his power. The young men, he continued his eulogy, had yielded their bodies to be burned. But if they had not had love, this would not have profited them anything (2 Cor. 13:3), but we know that it was exactly the love of God's commandments that had motivated them. It is specifically mentioned that the cause of their action was found in God, that they wanted to serve only Him and none other.

After his eulogy Nebuchadnezzar issued a manifesto to all nations, in which he threatened with complete destruction (see Dan. 2:5; 2 Kings 10:27; Ezra 6:11) all who spoke anything amiss against the God of Shadrach, Meshach, and Abed-nego. We would be concluding too much from this manifesto if we were to arrive at the conclusion that thereby the king wished to have their God served and glorified as the only true God. He apparently meant that this miracle-working and saving God—for there is, according to him, no other God that can deliver after this sort— must be elevated in his entire realm to the rank of an especially great and awe-inspiring God who demanded everyone's reverence. Furthermore, since he called Him the God of Shadrach, Meshach, and Abed-nego, and these three men were His servants par excellence, therefore, they were also to be considered and treated with special respect. There was no other God who could deliver in that manner. This word from a heathen, and that from a heathen world monarch, was fully capable to inspire Israel's confidence in Jehovah. For if no one less than the head of the world kingdom, in the hearing of all his great men of the world, hence in the hearing of the whole world, praised their God in such a manner, then it must be all the easier for them to keep themselves far removed from Babylon's puny idols and to put their trust in a God who could thus deliver by means of such inexplicable miracles.

> This was a tremendous message to the king and the entire nation of Babylon, for God had with power stretched out His hand over those who confessed Him and commanded His angel to protect them. And ever since that day hundreds of thousands have read their history for the strengthening of their faith, and thousands of His children have confessed Him in the midst of flames, also then when it did not please God to save them on earth but to grant them the palm branch of the martyrs' flames. How He will deal with us we will leave to Him, our task is to honor Him with our fearless confession. For without shall be the fearful! (F. Bettex)

Then we read in the concluding verse of this beautiful chapter that the king promoted Shadrach, Meshach, and Abed-nego in the province of Babylon. There are people who never forget or forgive an insult, but Nebuchadnezzar was not that way. Bearing a grudge was totally foreign to him. Although he had felt deeply insulted by these young men, and that in the presence of all his lords, he was nevertheless not bent on revenge. On the contrary, he magnanimously made up for the shame he had caused them, and who dares deny that thereby he put many present-day Christians to shame? How much vindictiveness, meanness, and secret and malevolent retribution we often find in Christian circles!

In which manner the king made this trio to prosper is not stated. Van Hamelsveld, who usually translates freely but as a rule carefully, renders this verse thus: "The king went on to restore Shadrach, Meshach, and Abed-nego to greater authority in their posts over the province of Babylon." He may have shown his royal favor in many different ways and elevated their position. The translation of the Seventy [Septuagint] adds here: "And he promoted them to be the heads of all the Jews who were in his realm."

From a historical and ideological perspective, much can be said in favor of this addition.

"Those who honor me, I shall honor." It is remarkable that this is the last thing we hear about these young men. Nowhere do we come across them again. Could it be that later on they were tempted by all their prosperity and, like Demas, had come to love this present world? We cannot consider this impossible with a view to the craftiness of the human heart and the alluring power of Babylon, but it is highly unlikely for young men who once went through a fire for God.

And while it may be called remarkable that we never hear again of these three, it is equally remarkable that in this entire chapter we do not meet Daniel. Where was he? We cannot answer this question with certainty, but what we can do is mention different possibilities to explain why we do not meet him here. He may have been present at this world festival—and, yes, as a sinner he may have bowed and knelt for a moment, only to humble himself afterward as a penitent sinner in dust and ashes. Knowing the human heart, we cannot agree with those commentators who hold this to be impossible. Look at the beloved disciple of Christ who denied Him and even cursed himself. And if a Peter wept bitterly, why can a Daniel not have done the same afterward? We think that if Daniel had been faithful in every respect, the Lord would not have weighted this greatly favored man down with even the semblance of unfaithfulness by not mentioning his name here. Understand us well. We are by no means saying Daniel actually knelt before the golden image, but we only defend its possibility.

Also, Daniel may have been present but since he was too highly placed, the enemies may not have dared to accuse him. He may have been on a journey, but against this it can be argued that the king had invited and ordered all the dignitaries to attend the dedication of the image. It is also very well possible that Daniel privately bared all his conscientious objections to the king and that the king had allowed him to sway him by the power of his spirit. But the most probable explanation is that we simply suppose with Klinkenberg and many other exegetes that he was legally prevented from being present at this feast by sickness or extraordinary weakness, as he seems to have been a weak person.

Chapter 4
FROM GLORY TO INSANITY

A Public Confession

**Nebuchadnezzar the king, unto all people, nations, and lan-
guages, that dwell in all the earth; peace be multiplied unto you.
I thought it good to shew the signs and wonders that the high God
hath wrought toward me. How great are his signs! and how
mighty are his wonders! His kingdom is an everlasting kingdom,
and his dominion is from generation to generation (vv. 1-3).**

The story contained in this chapter was not written originally
by Daniel, but by Nebuchadnezzar, and borrowed and most likely
revised by Daniel. The most recent exegetes have also levelled
their numerous objections against this chapter. According to
them, the language does not come from a heathen. In answer to
this objection it can be argued that the Lord so ordered it and
enlightened the heathen rulers in such a way by the empowering
grace of the Holy Spirit that they must continually declare the
greatness of His name and the everlastingness of His kingdom
(see Dan. 4:2, 3, 34; 2:44; 3:28, 29; 6:27; 7:14).

By means of all these things God wished to make preparation
among the nations for the coming of the Deliverer and at the same
time protect His people from the pollutions of heathenism. This
affords a prophecy of the future kingdom of peace when Christ
shall reign over the nations (Ps. 22:28-30) and all great men shall
worship Him.

Next, it has been thought improbable that Nebuchadnezzar ate
grass like an ox and that after seven years he became king again.
Of course, if we refuse to acknowledge the hand of God in these
things, then all this must be considered improbable; but it is a
totally different matter if we, with Nebuchadnezzar, consider all
these things as the signs and wonders of the Lord. Objection
against Nebuchadnezzar's madness has also been levelled, namely,

that the Babylonian chronicles have confirmed nothing regarding such a remarkable event. But this has often been refuted by the fact that the church father, Eusebius, refers to a legendary story about Abydemus, an old historian, which runs as follows:

> The Chaldeans have a tradition that he, Nebuchadnezzar, having ascended on his royal palace and there, inspired by a god, made the following prediction: "I, Nebuchadnezzar, predict to you, O Babylonians, an approaching disaster, which neither my forefather Belus, nor the queen Beltis of the goddesses will be able to avert. There will come a Persian mule and with the help of your own gods he will put you under the yoke. He will thereby make use of a Median of which Assyria greatly prides itself. Ah, that he might be carried away by a whirlwind or devoured by the sea before thus betraying my people! Or that he, being waylaid, might wander about between rocks and abysses in a desolate desert, devoid of cities and the footsteps of men and where nothing but predatory birds and wild animals roam about! Ah, that a better end were my portion before he undertakes this evil!"

When we remember that in those days insane people were often considered as being driven by a certain deity, then it is not all that difficult to see in this tradition a corruption of the true story contained in this chapter. The ancient historian, Berosus, who lived about 250 B.C., also tells us that Nebuchadnezzar had become the victim of an illness. It is in this connection noteworthy that, according to scholars, the inscriptions show an interim during which none of the great achievements of this renowned ruler are recorded, whereas it must by no means surprise us that for obvious reasons the animal-like conduct of the brilliant king was not given too much publicity.

The first three verses of this chapter contain the introduction to this royal testimony. In the first verse we hear again the voice of an absolute monarch. It is evident that he considers himself the lord of the whole earth. Above his circular letter he places a precious salutation. "Peace" was the common greeting of people in the East. As is sufficiently clear from the very many examples in Daniel, only kings were greeted with an "O King, live forever!," i.e., Long live the king! To people in the East, "shalom," peace, was the embodiment of all blessing. And that the Holy Spirit considers this to be the case, too, is evident from the song of the angels. This greeting was, therefore, a meaningful one, but the people must have fathomed the rich meaning just as little as we do today with regard to our old Dutch New Year's wish.

From the second verse it is evident that the king viewed Israel's God as the supreme Lord. A certain progress and development in his ideas of God is noticeable.

- In Daniel 2:47 he considered Him an important deity among the many gods of his country.
- In Daniel 3:26 he saw Him as the most high God, and furthermore, as a God who can deliver and send out His angels to save people (vv. 28, 29).
- He considers Him as the most high God who had performed signs and miracles for him, who now possessed an indestructible kingdom.
- In Daniel 4:34, 35 He gives expression to the absolute sovereignty of the Lord and depicts Him as a punisher of those who walk in pride.

It is hard to understand what the king's purpose was with this public testimony. To guess at it is to miss the point, but the most likely guess is that Daniel had a hand in it. In any case it is clear that God had a glorious purpose with it.

Flourishing in His Palace

I, Nebuchadnezzar, was at rest in mine house, and flourishing in my palace: I saw a dream which made me afraid, and the thoughts upon my bed and the visions of my head troubled me. Therefore made I a decree to bring in all the wise men of Babylon before me, that they might make known unto me the interpretation of the dream. Then came in the magicians, the astrologers, the Chaldeans, and the soothsayers: and I told the dream before them; but they did not make known unto me the interpretation thereof. But at the last Daniel came in before me, whose name was Belteshazzar, according to the name of my god, and in whom is the spirit of the holy gods: and before him I told the dream, saying, O Belteshazzar, master of the magicians, because I know that the spirit of the holy gods is in thee, and no secret troubleth thee, tell me the visions of my dream that I have seen, and the interpretation thereof (vv. 4-9).

Here Nebuchadnezzar tells us what befell him in connection with his dream and its interpretation. Already twice the Lord had revealed Himself in a glorious manner to the king, first by the marvelous interpretation of his strange dream and afterward in the miraculous delivery of the officers he had sentenced, and now for the third time by these signs and wonders, as he himself calls them in verse 2. The king was a very open-hearted man, as many great men after him have been. The first thing he tells in this official document is that he was at rest and flourishing in his palace like a tree full of leaves. He had caused many nations to bow under his scepter and now at last he had come home from his campaigns to enjoy the glory of Babylon and its wonders of the world. In Scripture the reference to a flourishing green tree is often the striking picture of prosperity and happiness (Ps. 37:35; 52:8; 92:14). Whoever has looked into the life of Nebuchadnezzar as a warrior will understand what this expression means in his mouth. "This rest had been bought at the price of forty years of unrest," says C. van Proosdij.

This rest of Nebuchadnezzar is a striking image of the natural rest of sinners. A sinner may be—as with Nebuchadnezzar—bent with old age and turn grey and see death and the grave come closer, and nevertheless be unaware of any danger. Still, the heart of man is never truly at rest until, according to Augustine's famous expression, it finds rest in God. And when God wants to give this rest of faith, He first makes the sinner restless.

Without wishing to say that God gave this kind of rest to Babylon's king, it is nevertheless true that He disturbed his rest. As He had done years before, He sent him a dream that disturbed and disquieted him. Like before, he was frightened and bewildered.

> The Judge of heaven sends His bailiff with the divine exhortation at the gate of the king's palace. Before confiscating the furniture of him who refuses to pay the taxes, he gives his third warning (C. van Proosdij).

As he had done before, he again sought his refuge with the wisdom of the world. That is something man does not easily give up, since this wisdom is part of the powers of the world that are highly esteemed by men. Again the wise men proved to be his obedient but powerless servants. The world monarch is forced once more to voice a public evaluation of the wisdom of the world. And it sounds like a lament when he says, "But they did not make known unto me the interpretation thereof."

At last Daniel appeared before him. To say the least, it is very strange that the king again first expected the interpretation from the heathen Chaldeans and that he did not at once call Daniel to appear before him, since the latter had already in such a remarkable manner made known a dream and its interpretation after the powerlessness of all his wise men had become manifest. Here again we must admit that the king acted that way for reasons unknown to us. If we knew fully the situation in Babylon and its customs at that time, then a difficulty like this could easily be clarified. Several possibilities may be mentioned as to why it was impossible or at least unwise for Nebuchadnezzar to summon Daniel immediately.

- Maybe it was the custom first to call the lower class of wise men.
- Daniel may have been far away or ill.
- Maybe in his hurry the king did not think of Daniel.
- Or Daniel's position may have been too exalted to call on him at once.
- It is also very possible that his conscience told him the dream portended not much good, and that in this case the severe solemnity of a true prophet did not look as attractive as the flattering words of false prophets.

Meanwhile, what is very clear is the purpose the Lord had with it. Once again the world power must first see and publicly acknowledge the absolute powerlessness of worldly wisdom. The world itself had first to struggle to deliver itself, before at the last the higher, the divine light through the mediation of Daniel was welcomed. That is exactly the way it has always been in the world and with the world.

Daniel, having appeared before the king, was joyfully welcomed and immediately flattered with praise. The king called him by the heathen name Belteshazzar, indicating at the same time that he was named after Bel, the god mostly revered by Nebuchadnezzar and all of Babylon. He next called him by his scientific title, master of the magicians. The word translated "magician" actually means interpreter of the cuneiform. The king told him that he had the greatest confidence in him and had called him to interpret the dream, since he knew that the spirit of the holy gods was in him. This strange expression contains a mixture of heathen and Jewish imagery; "gods" points to heathenism and "holy" to Israel. Actually, the gods were unholy, despicable abominations. What the king meant, of course, was that Daniel was a person to whom the gods revealed themselves in a special manner and with whom he had a very special relationship, so that, consequently, as he intimated further, no secret was too difficult for him, by which he meant that not a single secret could remain hidden from him.

It is remarkable that the king at this time, unlike before, did not want to know the dream but only its interpretation. That is why it is all the more curious that the wise men could not even give the interpretation. That exposed their worthlessness all the more in the sight of all the nations. All of Babylon must know that the wisdom of this world is foolishness. It is further noteworthy not only that Daniel was greeted here so extravagantly, but also that this was even incorporated in the proclamation. No doubt, this, too, was part of God's purpose to glorify the Lord's ambassador before all of Babylon, for the glory of the servant is the glory of the Master.

The King's Second Dream

Thus were the visions of mine head in my bed; I saw, and behold, a tree in the midst of the earth, and the height thereof was great. The tree grew, and was strong, and the height thereof reached unto heaven, and the sight thereof to the end of all the earth: the leaves thereof were fair, and the fruit thereof much, and in it was meat for all: the beasts of the field had shadow under it, and the fowls of the heaven dwelt in the boughs thereof, and all flesh was fed of it. I saw in the visions of my head upon my bed, and, behold, a watcher and an holy one came down from heaven; He cried aloud, and said thus, Hew down the tree, and cut off his branches, shake off his leaves, and scatter his fruit: let the beasts get away from under it, and the fowls from his branches: nevertheless leave the stump of his roots in the earth, even with a band of iron and brass, in the tender grass of the field; and let it be wet with the dew of heaven, and let his portion be with the beasts in the grass of the earth: let his heart be changed from man's, and let a beast's heart be given unto him; and let seven times pass over him. This matter is by the decree of the watchers, and the demand by the word of the holy ones: to the intent that the living may know that the most High ruleth in the kingdom of men, and giveth it to whomsoever he will, and setteth up over it the basest of men (vv. 10-17).

Already in verses 10-12 Nebuchadnezzar had compared himself to a great, green, leafy tree and had thereby most likely already alluded to the dream about the great tree. The description of the tree is grandiose, poetic, and totally illustrative of the greatness of Babylon's king and empire. Frequently a prosperous man, and specifically a prosperous believer is compared to some tree. We cannot refrain from once more quoting a paragraph by the able student of nature and Scripture, F. Bettex:

> Strikingly beautiful is this symbolism of the God-sent tree. The tree is, already by itself, a picture of man. Its roots are the feet; on it rises the trunk, and from there it stretches its mighty arms to heaven; it breathes through green lungs, and sap, like blood, courses its veins. Both the tree and man grow only by suitable nourishment; both wither and die when their time is up. Together with this outward similarity there is an inner likeness. The soul, implanted by God (Matt. 15:13; Rom. 6:5; 1 Cor. 3:6), seeks from the soil of the relationship and the occupation in which it was placed its appropriate nourishment, and has the ability, as does the nightshade and other plants, to convert this food into poisonous or healthy fruit; it also remains an indestructible entity, so that a linden can never become an oak. The grafting in of the noble cutting is God's prerogative (Rom. 11:17-23). Scripture points out time and again that the rearing of a plant and of man are similar (Matt. 21:19; Luke 13:6-9), and that God's Israel is a vineyard and the children of God are cedars of Lebanon, oaks of Bashan, and oaks of righteousness. A century-old giant of the woods is a beautiful image of a mighty warrior. Rooted deeply, it stands firm and has proudly braved all the raging storms for many years. As in silent prayer it lifts its mighty arms to heaven, shakes its blossoms, leaves, and fruit as a present, spreads protectingly its cool roof of leaves over man and beast, and with silent submission receives sunshine and fruitful rain, frost and heat from heaven.

The following traits point out the greatness and prosperity of Nebuchadnezzar, who is depicted by this tree:

1. The tree stood in the midst of the earth. That indicates the central place the king occupied in the entire world.

2, Its height was great, referring to the greatness of the king's glory. Just as God caused the tree to grow and become tall, so He had elevated Nebuchadnezzar to become a world monarch, so that he now was the tallest among all the trees of the forest.

3. This tree became tall and strong. It grew in height and in girth until its top finally reached the clouds of heaven and it became visible, as Nebuchadnezzar says, to the end of all the earth.

4. Its leaves were beautiful. Historians vie with each other in describing the great impressive beauty of Nebuchadnezzar's kingdom. Its fruits were many and the tree provided food for all. It is said that in the city of Babylon alone there was enough food stored for more than twenty years, so that the city could not be starved out by a siege. Moreover, there were wheat fields, meadows and hanging gardens in the city.

5. Forest animals found shadow underneath this tree and the birds of heaven nested among its branches. Behind Babylon's walls the people—think of Belshazzar who was feasting when Cyrus and his army stood before the walls—considered themselves as safe as the ox that peacefully ruminates its food in the cool shade of the trees and as the little birds that feel themselves safe in the tops of the trees.

In the visions of his dream, the king next saw a watchman, a holy one, descending from heaven, who cried out with a loud voice that the tree had to be hewn down. This "watcher" means an angel. It is believed the Chaldeans and Syrians called angels by that name. Also the nations outside of Israel had some idea of angels and even a distinction between good and evil spirits was not totally unknown. Although the name watcher for angel is nowhere else to be found in Scripture, the idea of a watchman and watching is always present when it speaks of angels (2 Chron. 16:9; Prov. 15:3; Jer. 32:19; Zech. 4:10).

It is very remarkable that in the book of Daniel we find a fuller revelation concerning the world of angels than in any other book of the Old Testament. Not until Israel had been abandoned to the world empire did it receive a deeper revelation concerning the spirit world of good and evil angels. Israel was comforted with protection by good angels while the exiles were also given a glimpse into the world of evil spirits bent on Israel's destruction. Hence the time had come that God's people must know that it had to fight against the evil spirits in the air (Eph. 6), and that good angels were always on their side.

A particular holy angel descended from heaven and cried with a loud voice. Already this loud voice as such was full of foreboding. Love whispers softly; anger and punishment cry loudly. Scripture frequently speaks of angels who cry with loud voices and that often spells bad things for the wicked (see Ezek. 9:1; Rev. 10:3; 14:7, 9, 15, 18; 16:1). The contents of the angel's command was that the proud giant of the woods had to be hewn down so that its leaves and fruit and the animals and the birds should leave it.

The word translated "hew down" means actually not so much to cut down as to remove the tops, shear, prune, to trim in such a way that the leaves are gone. From verse 14 it is clear that not only the stump but also the trunk must be left intact. The king was not to be destroyed, but his glory must depart from him, just as the beauty of a tree is gone when it is completely shorn. The band of iron and brass probably points to the chains with which the insane king would soon be bound, for this whole picture is full of the clearest hints regarding the king, his realm, and the fate that awaited him.

In the second part of verse 15 the imagery is abandoned and it speaks of a person who, although not mentioned by name, is easily recognized. For of a tree it could hardly be fittingly said that its portion would be with the beasts in the grass. Verse 16 speaks specifically of the change of the king's heart. Here it does not mean what we usually mean by a changed heart, but the angel in the dream already predicted that Nebuchadnezzar's spirit, his character, his mind would be changed, impaired. Also the expression "a beast's heart" in the same verse means the nature of a beast, bestiality. This description already indicates to some extent the nature of his insanity.

Seven times would pass over him. How long a period does this indicate? The word translated here into "times" appears nowhere else in Scripture outside of Daniel. In this prophecy it is always used for the same original word and with the same meaning (see 2:8, 9; 3:5, 15; 4:16, 23, 25, 32; 7:12, 25). The word can mean any length of time such as days, weeks, months, or years. Here it does not imply days or weeks, however, as that would obviously be too short a time. Thus it points out the miraculous aspect that after his illness the kingdom would be returned to him. This would not have been a miracle at all after only a few days or weeks, but it definitely would after a time of seven years. Generally speaking it could mean months, but they are usually called moons in Scripture. And since in 7:25, 11:13, and 12:7 this same word is obviously used for years, it is certainly advisable to take it in this sense here as well.

This has always been the most general interpretation. This points out the foolishness of the so-called year-day theory of the Adventists and other exegetes. According to their view all "days" in the prophecy of Daniel and Revelation stand for years, all "months" for thirty years, and all "years" for 360 years. If that were correct, then this theory must be "conclusive" here as well. And even if they were to take the word "times" to mean months, then, according to this view, Babylon's king would have been insane for 210 years, whereas, according to Scripture, the first world empire lasted for only seventy years! It gets even worse if we, with most exegetes, take the word to mean years. In that case, according to the above-mentioned theory, the king would still be stark crazy until this very day and for another half century to come! If Noah would have adhered to this foolish notion, then he would still not have to make the ark ready today. This foolish theory, which must lead to all kinds of absurdities, has already done great harm to the study of prophecy. In prophecy, as anywhere else, "days" means days and "years" means years.

Verse 17 points out both the certainty and purpose of all these things. This matter is the decree of the watchmen, it says. This does not imply that angels make decisions and so had decided to strike the king of Babylon with insanity. This would be at variance with the teaching of Scripture, for it clearly teaches that God in His counsel has decreed all things from eternity. Known unto God are all His works from the beginning of the world (Acts 15:18), and He works all things according to the counsel of His own will (Eph. 1:11). His hand has decreed beforehand all that will take place, but in His general government of all, God uses His mighty warriors.

Scripture teaches clearly that angels are not sent out only for the benefit of those who will inherit salvation. Thus this remarkable expression certainly means that the Lord placed the decree of the execution in the hands of His holy watchmen who are obedient unto the voice of His word. In the histories of 1Kings 22:19 and Isaiah 6:8 we see something similar. Here, however, this expression may also mean that this decree, in the sense of its punitive sentence, was pronounced at the request of these holy watchmen. The explicatory phrase following this expression justifies this idea somewhat. This matter is by the decree of the watchers, and the demand by the word of the holy ones means that this matter or case is the command or sentence of the holy angels.

> How important is this look into the celestial government. Hence on high there are thrones from which watchmen and holy ones with immortal, searching eyes observe all our actions, being constantly concerned with the honor of God, equipped with wisdom to deliberate, gifted with divine power to intervene when the poor child of the dust elevates himself too much to his own detriment and to that of others. Also now they watch and work invisibly, as sensed by men in great times, over countries and nations. At one time they empower and embolden the small army of Waldensians, of Puritans, of Huguenots, of Camissards so that it becomes invincible and defeats its enemies that are a hundred times stronger; at another time they strike fear in the heart, paralyze the arm, and the uplifted sword falls down; the battle is lost before it commences and the realm totters. Or suddenly they strike a monarch with insanity and the reins slip from his hands. Or they blind him so that he rushes toward his destruction, indeed, brings it about himself....If God wishes to punish the nations because of the guilt they have accumulated over centuries, then the watchmen take the small, lame Tartar or the commander of the Huns, supply him with a pitiless heart and a million wild warriors, protect him as with a shield so that nothing or nobody can harm him until he has mowed down the nations, burned the cities, and changed the lands into deserts. And then the command is given that the rod of God's anger must be broken and cast into the fire. That is the work of the watchmen and the holy ones, who behold God's face and read on it the vicissitudes of the universe (F. Bettex).

The second part of verse 17 points out the purpose of this unalterable decision. It states that Nebuchadnezzar, first of all, and all of his proud statesmen also, must acknowledge and confess that not they but the Most High has the rulership over the kingdoms of men. The last part of this chapter shows that this goal has been completely obtained with regard to the person of Nebuchadnezzar. This public letter is intended to convince his entire realm of this fact. The Lord gives the kingdoms to whomsoever he will, even to the devil (Luke 4:6). God alone is the absolutely Sovereign One, and when the devil says that he gives the kingdoms to whom he will, he then only imitates the absolute sovereignty of God. The last part of verse 17 adds that sometimes

God gives the kingship and the kingdoms to the lowest among men. Both Scripture and our times teach us this. We need only to recall David in the days of old and Trotsky and Lenin in recent time. One day the meek of heart will inherit the whole earth.

Astonished for One Hour

This dream I, king Nebuchadnezzar, have seen. Now thou, O Belteshazzar, declare the interpretation thereof, forasmuch as all the wise men of my kingdom are not able to make known unto me the interpretation: but thou art able; for the spirit of the holy gods is in thee. Then Daniel, whose name was Belteshazzar, was astonished for one hour, and his thoughts troubled him. The king spake, and said, Belteshazzar, let not the dream, or the interpretation thereof, trouble thee. Belteshazzar answered and said, My lord, the dream be to them that hate thee, and the interpretation thereof to thine enemies (vv. 18, 19).

We do not appreciate Daniel fully when we do not keep in mind that the Chaldean wise men were the chief wise men of those days and represented the wisdom of the entire world. And, further, that the world power was personified in Nebuchadnezzar. If we further keep in mind that the Chaldean wise men were at the same time the spokesmen for religion and the interpreters of the heathen gods themselves, then we realize that in the prophecy of Daniel God makes known again and again the emptiness and vanity of the power, wisdom, and religion of the world; and, as is the case here, makes this known to the world by means of its most authoritative spokesman. On verse 18, see the comment of verse 8.

Daniel was very astonished after hearing the dream from the king's lips. With increasing amazement he listened to every word that came out of the mouth of the king of Babylon, and he understood only too well the terrible judgment of God these words contained. This astonishment and the ensuing wish cast a striking light on the mutual relationship between these two great men.

As can also be gathered from the next chapter, Daniel was very fond of Nebuchadnezzar. Humanly speaking he owed his exalted position to his king. The latter had also been the royal benefactor of Daniel's three friends. Indeed he had severely afflicted God's suffering people and already Jeremiah had compared him to someone who had broken the bones of a bewildered lamb (Jer. 50:17), but Daniel knew that he had been the divinely appointed servant of the Lord and that his people, due to their rebellion against Him, had fully deserved the heavy punishments fully. According to his words to Belshazzar, he had great admiration for the glorious majesty and power of the king who elevated and humiliated whomever he wished. And when he realized that this mighty and dreaded king would be like unto the oxen for the long period of seven years, this thought was vexing and astonishing to him. How strikingly he saw the mighty and avenging hand of the Lord in all this! How pity must have filled his tender heart for this man who presently stood there before him in all his splendor, unaware of the terrible fate that awaited him, and who had to hear these things from his mouth!

It seems for almost an hour Daniel, due to his tremendous emotion, was unable to speak to the king. The latter had noticed Daniel's perturbation and understood the cause of it, so that he encouraged him by saying, "Belteshazzar, let not the dream, or the interpretation thereof, trouble thee." Apparently, the king had already suspected when he had the dream that the hewing down of the tree portended something bad for him. This suspicion must have been confirmed by the painful look on Daniel's face and his silence, which betrayed his inner shock. Now the king probably thought Daniel was also shaken and that he was prevented from telling him the whole truth out of fear for himself and of possible punishment. For that reason the king spoke this reassuring and encouraging word.

Now the prophet no longer hesitated. "My lord," he began, "the dream be to them that hate thee, and the interpretation thereof to thine enemies!" This is not an expression of vindictiveness toward Nebuchadnezzar's enemies but an Eastern courteous expression of his love for the king, so that he would gladly, if it were in his power, turn away all this calamity from him. For that reason we must not put too much emphasis on the word "be," which does not even appear in the original text (cf. 1 Sam. 25:22).

From Man to Beast

The tree that thou sawest, which grew, and was strong, whose height reached unto the heaven, and the sight thereof to all the earth; whose leaves were fair, and the fruit thereof much, and in it was meat for all; under which the beasts of the field dwelt, and upon whose branches the fowls of the heaven had their habita-

tion: It is thou, O king, that art grown and become strong: for thy greatness is grown, and reacheth unto heaven, and thy dominion to the end of the earth. And whereas the king saw a watcher and an holy one coming down from heaven, and saying, Hew the tree down, and destroy it; yet leave the stump of the roots thereof in the earth, even with a band of iron and brass, in the tender grass of the field; and let it be wet with the dew of heaven, and let his portion be with the beasts of the field, till seven times pass over him; this is the interpretation, O king, and this is the decree of the most High, which is come upon my lord the king: that they shall drive thee from men, and thy dwelling shall be with the beasts of the field, and they shall make thee to eat grass as oxen, and they shall wet thee with the dew of heaven, and seven times shall pass over thee, till thou know that the most High ruleth in the kingdom of men, and giveth it to whomsoever he will. And whereas they commanded to leave the stump of the tree roots; thy kingdom shall be sure unto thee, after that thou shalt have known that the heavens do rule (vv. 20-26).

The repetition Daniel gives of even the smallest details of the dream is not superfluous. This was evidence to Nebuchadnezzar that Daniel saw the dream clearly in his mind and understood it correctly. Moreover, this repetition was a slow and psychological preparation for the king for the dreadful fate that would soon be revealed to him. For the details of this tree and the watcher, see the comments made on verses 10-15.

From verse 24 on the meaning of the dream is given. First, it is stated with a few words that all of this reflects the irrevocable decision of the Most High. From what follows it is clear that it was not Daniel's intent to call the king's attention to an unavoidable fate, as the heathen viewed such things. His purpose was not to guide the king to a passive acceptance of fate but to a humbling of himself before the high God who certainly will execute judgment upon all arrogant pride (see v. 27).

1. The king would be driven away from men by men. What a punishment this was for a man who ruled over the inhabitants of the earth! But we see the reason for this divine punishment. By his pride he had wanted to soar high above that which was ordinary and common and human, and now he was banished from society and sank below the level of all that was human. He, who had wanted to deify himself, was turned into an animal by God. The

text does not say who would do this to him; an indefinite verb is used, as is often the case in Daniel. Exegetes have thought it was executed either by God, by angels, or by men. The last option seems the most likely of the three and does not, of course, exclude the first. In the heathen East there were no institutions of mercy for the insane. Without any pity such unfortunate people were driven out of the community and into uninhabited areas, far away from the people, as we also find in the Gospels (see Mark 5).

2. His habitation would be with the beasts of the field. It took courage on Daniel's part to tell this to the king. It must even amaze us that the king remained calm while listening to these words, and that he did not explode into a rage of revenge. But he had called the prophet himself and encouraged him to speak. Besides, his conscience also must have told him that these words were completely true. There have been those who have deduced from these words that the king truly underwent a physical change into an ox or a wild ass. Others gladly accepted this view in order to ridicule it as the presentation given by Scripture. But Scripture does not present such an image. On the contrary, the king would be with the beasts of the field, but not be one of them. He would be like an animal, but not be an actual animal; his dwelling and food would be with the animals.

3. "And they shall make thee to eat grass as oxen." The question has been asked how the man could possibly have lived a life like that for seven years, without perishing. In answer to this we mention the following:

- The king had been used to the privations of the life of a soldier for forty years.
- According to experts, the body of an insane person can sometimes endure a lot of abuse.
- We need not assume he had nothing to eat but grass and had no covering whatsoever against the elements. The word translated "grass" means, according to Van der Palm, all kinds of raw food, such as roots and wild fruits which grow in fields and woods.
- We must see this first of all as a miracle of God. And a miracle by the hand of God neither can nor needs to be explained.

The question may be asked what kind of sickness Nebuchadnezzar had. Some experts speak of a kind of insanity known as zoanthropy, which causes the patient to think that he or she is an animal. Such patients moo like a cow or bleat like a sheep. Lycanthropy is a form of insanity which makes the patient think he/she is a wolf and act like a wolf. A similar disorder, kunanthropy, makes a patient think he is a dog and act like one. Nebuchadnezzar must have had boanthropy, so that he imagined himself an ox. One of the characteristics of this form of insanity is that the patients retain a sense of who they really are. This seems to have been the case with Nebuchadnezzar. Then his punishment was all the more painful and touched him truly in his damnable pride.

The intent, the divine purpose of this severe punishment was that the king would acknowledge that the most High ruleth in the kingdom of men. The introduction to this public letter (see vv. 2, 3) clearly indicates that this goal was reached. He indeed acknowledged in a beautiful manner that the heavens, i.e., the God of the heavens rules. The question might be asked how anyone who suffered from insanity and whose senses had become totally dull and like those of an animal could come to acknowledge the sovereignty of the Lord. The answer is that this kind of insanity brings outward degeneration, but there remains an inner self-consciousness or, as it would be called today, a sound subconsciousness. From the rest of the story can be deduced that the symptoms of the illness slowly disappeared again and that probably long before his complete restoration Nebuchadnezzar could think clearly again.

> How now? Must the king in that animal-like condition, while still thinking he is a grazing ox, acknowledge the supremacy of heaven? Yes. We know from other examples that the soul of what are incorrectly called the mentally ill (the spirit does not get ill) and whose soul as it were is in chains and incarcerated in a dark dungeon and no longer knows the way outside and with whom no one can have intercourse, nevertheless in its deepest essence continues a life unknown to us, thinks, decides, grows, and matures (F. Bettex).

Closely connected with the divine purpose was the divine limitation of his punishment. The fact that the entire tree was not hewn down and that the trunk remained already clearly indicated a limitation and pointed out that there would be no total destruction. He was told that there would be two delimitations to his punishment. First, he would not stay insane but would bear this terrible punishment for only seven years; second, in spite of his prolonged animal-like existence he would remain king. His kingdom would be permanent, namely, for him; but not afterwards. Most likely his first minister Daniel took charge in the interim. In any case, during that time there must have been a strong hand at the helm if matters were not to come apart while Nebuchadnezzar was with the animals. Who else could have been better qualified to take charge than Daniel, whom we have learned to know as courageous and wise and with a special measure of spiritual acumen. For was he himself not a king?

Break Off Thy Sins

Wherefore, O king, let my counsel be acceptable unto thee, and break off thy sins by righteousness, and thine iniquities by shewing mercy to the poor; if it may be a lengthening of thy tranquility. All this came upon the king Nebuchadnezzar (vv. 27, 28).

The Lord did not allow the king of Babylon to run along blindly in the way of sin. Daniel knew what was the cause and the reason of the punishment of the king. As a faithful spiritual adviser he pointed this out to him. Only by recognizing and removing the cause of something can its inevitable results be prevented. "O King," he pleaded, "let my counsel be acceptable to thee." And then he admonished him to break with his sins. The verb translated "break off" means to redeem, in the sense of to compensate, to atone, to reconcile. The king was admonished to redeem his sins of pride by acts of righteousness and his unrighteous deeds by showing mercy to the poor. The first part of this admonition refers to his relationship to God and the second to that to men.

Verse 27 has always been a favorite one to Rome as one of the main proofs for its doctrine of the meritoriousness of good works. In his Apology in the Augsburg Confession, Melanchthon in Article 3 tried to wrest this prooftext away from Rome. He writes this under the heading of the love and the fulfillment of the law on the first part of this verse:

This is the brief content of a whole sermon; it means as much as: "Repent!" It is a fact that when we turn away from our sin we are delivered from it. Hence he says, "Make loose (break off)." From this it does not follow, however, that we can be delivered from our sins by our works, or that our works can be the payment for sin. Nor does Daniel emphasize only good works, but he says, by righteousness. Now everyone knows that in Scripture righteousness does not refer only to outward works but implies faith, as Paul says, "The righteous shall live by his faith." For that reason Daniel demands in the first place faith when he speaks of righteousness and says, "Break off thy sins by righteousness," i.e., by faith in God, that you may be justified. Add to this good works, namely, fulfill your calling, don't be a tyrant, but take care that your reign be beneficial for the country and the people. Preserve the peace and protect the poor from unjust violence. This constitutes royal alms.

It seems to us that we do not have to drag in the righteousness by faith in this context, for it does not refer at all to faith and eternal salvation but only in a general way to turning away from vice to virtue, which, as we see with Ahab and the Ninevites, is pleasing to God and beneficial to the persons themselves. In so doing the Ninevites saved their city for two centuries, and one day the men of Nineveh will arise in judgment together with the Jews and condemn them, for they repented at the preaching of Jonah (Matt. 12:41). We are dealing here with the law of retribution or, if you will, with the reward of grace, as we find this mentioned already on one of the first pages of Scripture: "If thou doest well, shalt thou not be accepted? and if thou doest not well, sin lieth at the door" (Gen. 4:7). Hence, the very first time that God acts as spiritual adviser He already points out this great law of retribution. If Rome had always had an open eye for this fact, it would never have arrived at the wicked and foolish doctrine of the meritoriousness of good works. And if Protestantism had developed the correct doctrine of the reward of grace, it would never have been so afraid of Rome's teaching and it would have combated it in a totally different way than it often did (see also Prov. 16:6; Zeph. 2:1-3; Acts 8:22).

The poor to whom Nebuchadnezzar had to show mercy are undoubtedly the Jews. Indirectly we have here a plea for the setting free of this opposed people, who always were uppermost in the noble mind of Daniel. The question has been asked how to square Daniel's words, "if it may be a lengthening of thy tranquility," with the determined decree of the Most High which would come upon the king and of which he spoke in verse 24. The answer is that many prophetic threatenings contain a provisional element. Jeremiah describes this principle most extensively when he says:

> At what instant I shall speak concerning a nation, and concerning a kingdom, to pluck up, and to pull down, and to destroy it; if that nation against whom I have pronounced, turn from their evil, I will repent of the evil that I thought to do unto them. And at what instant I shall speak concerning a nation, and concerning a kingdom, to build and to plan it; if it do evil in my sight, that it obey not my voice, then I will repent of the good, wherewith I said I would benefit them (Jer. 18:7-10).

Prophecy is not an inescapable fate and never works in a magical but always in a moral manner. Frequently, the Lord makes threatenings in Scripture exactly for the purpose of preventing the materialization of the threats. He always remembers mercy in the midst of His anger. This was the case with Jonah's preaching at Nineveh and Christ's lament over Jerusalem (Matt. 23:37, 38; see also Isaiah 38 on the story of Hezekiah's sickness).

> This way of preventing the threatened sentence from materializing was also open to Nebuchadnezzar, the more so since the time when the dream would be fulfilled was not determined and hence he was given time to repent (Keil).

The law of retribution was applicable to Nebuchadnezzar as well as to Cain: "If thou doest well, shalt thou not be accepted? and if thou doest not well, sin lieth at the door" (Gen. 4:7). "To him that ordereth his conversation aright will I shew the salvation of God" (Ps. 50:23).

Alas, the king of Babylon did not heed the deadly serious advice of the man of God. It is already remarkable that not a word is said about how he reacted to this advice. Apparently he dismissed Daniel in a cool manner, unpunished and unrewarded. All the calamity that Daniel had told him about came down on the king as a horrible reality. As is evident from the continuation of the story he did not humble himself before the Lord. Hence, he remained unbelieving with regard to these divine threatenings, otherwise he would have humbled himself instead of exalting himself. Now he would have to feel the striking hand of the Lord since he refused to listen to His voice. The following verses tell how Nebuchadnezzar called down the punishment of the Lord upon himself.

Kingdom Departed

At the end of twelve months he walked in the palace of the kingdom of Babylon. The king spake, and said, Is not this great Babylon, that I have built for the house of the kingdom by the might of my power, and for the honor of my majesty? While the word was in the king's mouth, there fell a voice from heaven, saying, O king Nebuchadnezzar, to thee it is spoken; the kingdom is departed from thee. And they shall drive thee from men, and thy dwelling shall be with the beasts of the field: they shall make thee to eat grass as oxen, and seven times shall pass over thee, until thou know that the most High ruleth in the kingdom of men, and giveth it to whomsoever he will. The same hour was the thing fulfilled upon Nebuchadnezzar: and he was driven from men, and did eat grass as oxen, and his body was wet with the dew of heaven, till his hairs were grown like eagles' feathers, and his nails like birds' claws (vv. 29-33).

The king had at least a year's time to repent. It is, however, a sad truth that the postponement the Lord in His mercy grants man in order to induce him to repentance is often used by the sinner as an occasion to put off his repentance. 2 Peter 3:4 teaches us that the scoffers who want to walk according to their own lusts turn the gracious postponement of the day of the Lord into an occasion of mockery and say, "Where is the promise of his coming?" (see also Rom. 2:4). Whether Nebuchadnezzar's attitude was similar we do not know, but we do know that he did not humble himself before the Most High. We prefer to picture him as having been deeply under the impression of the dream and Daniel's words for a few months and that his awakened conscience often accused him, but that the temptations of riches, the cares of life, the flattery of the people at his court, the lusts of the eyes and of the flesh, and the greatness of life—in short, everything in all of great Babylon slowly stifled the voice of his conscience, so that he became even more swollen with pride than ever before. And pride, blind and blinding pride, usually precedes an imminent fall.

A year after his dream he walked on a certain day on the flat roof of the royal palace, from where he could see the entire proud city. His victorious campaigns had come to an end. Now he could rest and he was flourishing like a strong, tall tree. A false peace and foolish pride go hand in hand. That had once been the case with David and it was the case with Nebuchadnezzar. In the barracks of the battlefield and near the campfires he would not have displayed such a foolish pride as he now did on the flat roof.

When he saw from the rooftop of his palace the magnificent city lie at his feet, he cried out in self-satisfaction, "Is not this great Babylon, that I have built for the house of the kingdom," i.e., as the royal residence, the capital. Hence he considered himself the builder, the founder of Babylon. Strictly speaking this was not true, for the actual founding of the city is ascribed to Nimrod or Bel (Gen. 10:10). But Nebuchadnezzar was referring here to the renovation and beautification of this city to make it the seat of his kingdom, and in that sense he indeed spoke the truth. He had enlarged the city west of the Euphrates so that the river now ran through the center of the town. He had built an extra new palace— maybe the same one he was walking on now. He had built enormous walls around the city. He had built aquaducts, the hanging gardens, (considered one of the seven wonders of the world), and he had considerably enlarged the famous temple of Bel. The evil lay not in the mere recounting of what he had accomplished in the area of military achievements and in architecture, but in his abominable and satanic pride, so that now he exclaimed that he had done all these things by the power of his strength and to the honor of his glory.

Two things always characterize the unrepentant sinner: his Pelagian trust in his own power and his constant working for his own glory. We are dealing here not just with the "manner of tyrants" but with the manner of all those whose hearts have not been broken and whose spirit has not been subdued. Not only Babylon and its king, but also the entire false church reveals itself in similar language, saying, "I sit a queen, and am no widow, and shall see no sorrow" (Rev. 18:7). By nature there is no one who seeks after God (Rom. 3:11). As a rule all people seek themselves and their own (Phil. 2:21). Pride, however, is an even more satanic sin than selfishness. The essence of sin is not selfishness but pride. Whereas the former is bent on seizing everything unto itself and consequently, is greed and avarice, pride vaunts itself and puffs itself up and wants to be like unto God.

A sinner can be viewed in three different relations: to God, to himself, and to the world around him. In relation to God and His Word he is motivated and driven by unbelief; in relation to the world by avarice; in relation to himself by pride. The last mentioned drive is greatly in evidence with Nebuchadnezzar. His self-glorification was in essence a dethronement of God. For that reason God dehumanized him and made him like an animal.

The king had hardly uttered these words—indeed his bragging words still floated in the air, as it were—when a voice resounded from heaven which told him that he would no longer be king for a season and would lead an existence that could no longer be considered human. What kind of voice this was we do not know. Both Van Hamelsveld and Van der Palm think it resembled the sound of thunder. It is true that in Scripture a thunderbolt is often called a voice, but for this idea there is no foundation here. Apparently it was a voice only Nebuchadnezzar heard. It seems most logical to assume that it was the same voice which cried in verse 14 that the tree must be hewn down, hence the voice of the holy watcher, who acted according to God's decree and now executed His sentence upon the king. We see that things followed each other in rapid succession after the king had sinned away and squandered the twelve months God had granted him. God's patience is great and lasts at times for centuries, but once the measure of iniquity is full, His judgments usually follow in accelerated succession. One of His purposes is to make the sinner fully realize the connection between his sin and its punishment. The last book in the Bible gives frightening examples of how quickly and rapidly the Lord will pour out His judgments upon a world that has filled the measure of its iniquity to the full.

On verse 32, see the comments on verse 25. The nature and purpose of the punishment are emphatically repeated here. All Nebuchadnezzar's subjects must know that not their king but the God of Israel was the Most High; He has the rulership over the kingdoms of men and gives them unto whomever He chooses (see also vv. 17 and 25). The conclusion of the chapter tells us God fully obtained His goal. His decrees are never frustrated.

Verse 33 states that the voice from heaven and the beginning of the king's insanity coincide. This man with the splendid mind suddenly became a brute beast. This verse gives a touching picture of his mental degeneration. People must first have tried to subdue him and calm him down, but he was untamable. He imagined himself an ox and wanted to eat nothing but raw food. The clothes he wore he tore to shreds so that he was reduced to walking back and forth across the open terrain, stark naked, and drenched by the dew of heaven. Since he constituted a danger to his fellow men they must have put up high fences around a certain area, probably the royal pastures, so that he was not exposed to the curious gazes of the rabble nor to their ridicule and maltreatment.

His shaggy hair was never cut or shaved so that it began to resemble the features of an eagle. The Greek translation has "until his hair became as shaggy as that of lions." His nails were never trimmed and reached an enormous length so that they turned back upon themselves and his toes began to look like the claws of a bird of prey. Hence the appearance of this erstwhile brilliant genius became totally repulsive and frightening. It revealed that the finger of God had touched him. "Pride goeth before destruction, and an haughty spirit before a fall" (Prov. 16:18).

In this connection we are reminded of Friedrich Nietzsche, the brilliant scholar who in Turin, Italy, January, 1889, was struck with the terrible calamity of complete and incurable insanity. Nietzsche, who in his aristocratic pride had wanted to trample down all that was weak, and for many years was cared for in the little town of Naumburg, Germany by his mother, a weak old lady whom he often stared at with either unmoving, unseeing eyes, or wildly rolling eyes, groaned, "Mother, I am dumb!" Nietzsche had striven to create or become the superman, but instead fell to a subhuman level. "Be not deceived; God is not mocked: for whatsoever a man soweth, that shall he also reap" (Gal. 6:7).

In our days of nervous running to and fro and back and forth and of endless racket, the string of life is drawn too tight and taut and is in danger of snapping. The specter of sleeplessness and insomnia rears its head everywhere. The suffering due to nervous breakdowns spreads its dark wings over all of mankind. Suicide runs like a black stream through all of life today. And with all these symptoms man simply harvests what he has sown (see Deut. 28:58, 59). Children do not become insane. If our contemporary fellow human beings lived more in a childlike manner, not so many of them would end up down and out in wild insanity.

King Restored

And at the end of the days I, Nebuchadnezzar, lifted up mine eyes unto heaven, and mine understanding returned unto me, and I blessed the most High, and I praised and honored him that liveth forever, whose dominion is an everlasting dominion, and his kingdom is from generation to generation: and all the inhabitants of the earth are reputed as nothing: and he doeth according to his will in the army of heaven, and among the inhabitants of the earth: and none can stay his hand, or say unto him, What doest thou? At the same time my reason returned unto me; and for the glory of my kingdom, mine honor and brightness returned unto me; and my counsellors and my lords sought unto me; and I was established in my kingdom, and excellent majesty was added unto me. Now I, Nebuchadnezzar, praise and extol and honor the King of heaven, all whose works are truth, and his ways judgment: and those that walk in pride he is able to abase (vv. 34-37).

The king describes his restoration in a beautiful manner. The judgment of God had lasted just as long as had been predicted (v. 16), and no longer. At the end of those days he says, "I lifted up mine eyes unto heaven." This is the opposite of what he had been doing during his animal state. Mentally sick people like that often heal slowly. Maybe the king, too, became gradually more tractable and more human. At last the storm of animal passions had spent itself. His wild madness had at last made place for quiet reasoning. And because his reason had returned to him, he lifted his eyes to heaven. An animal does not look up but always downward, and people who have become like animals do the same. But the mind, when it is not befuddled, lifts its look on high. Hence the king himself apparently knew that he had been like an irrational animal. An outstanding medic, Dr. Browne from Scotland, concluded on the basis of more than thirty years of medical experience that among the insane the mental image of themselves is seldom impaired to that extent and never leaves them completely. He expresses it thus:

All the angels, devils, dukes, emperors and kings and the many gods I have had in my care remained what they had been before they turned into what they imagined they had become. I have known a man who said he was the Savior, and called himself James Thompson and always attended the worship services as if he had never deluded himself....I consider it plausible that Nebuchadnezzar during the entire time of his humiliation retained the consciousness that he was Nebuchadnezzar. We cannot know for certain that this was the case the entire time, but he did know toward the end of his illness.

His look to heaven became a prayer to God who inhabits heaven as His permanent dwelling place. His was a double cure. The first thing he did after his cure was to praise and magnify the Lord. He manifested at once that the purpose of his malady had been obtained. He was cured from his megalomania as well as from his insanity. David once spoke the profound words, "Thy gentleness hath made me great." To some extent Nebuchadnezzar could stammer this after him. He praised and glorified God with the sacrifices of thanksgiving pouring from his lips, before whom he had to abase himself. In his arrogant pride he had, as it were, wanted to remove God from His throne. Now he acknowledged Him as the Most High. This God was higher than all his gods and all his great men.

He glorified the Everlasting One. Once again he used this name as a contrast to and as the opposite of the gods of his realm. The Everlasting One has an everlasting dominion. Generations of men and dynasties may pass away, but the Lord never changes.

In verse 35 he praised the absolute sovereignty of the Lord. In comparison with Him all the inhabitants of the earth were as nothing. The prophet Isaiah in writing 40:15, 17 expresses the same idea. God always carries out His will both in the heavens and on the earth, in the world of angels as well as in that of men. He works all things according to the counsel of His will (Eph. 1:11). Man may grumble and murmur against God's decree, but he can never bring it to nought. God always obtains His goal, as Nebuchadnezzar had experienced. Man is not even master of his own mind. Without the will of God he cannot move a finger. Part of the hosts of heaven may break out in rebellion against Him and become devils, but never fear, He will cast them out of heaven and sling them into hell. "None can stay his hand, or say unto him, What doest thou?" The text actually says, No one can strike Him on the hand. In the vernacular we would say, No one can slap him on the fingers and demand an account of his actions from Him. No one can forbid this sovereign God anything or prevent Him from doing anything.

The restoration of Nebuchadnezzar's kingship is described in verse 36. He received back his royal majesty, his former fame and glory, at the same time his mind returned to him. His advisors and officers apparently had not totally withdrawn themselves from him in his lamentable condition, for as soon as his mind returned they sought him again. It is not stated who they were. We have already expressed our opinion that Daniel, who knew the duration and purpose of this illness, was the most suitable person to make sure that Nebuchadnezzar received his kingdom back again. The fact that these counselors and mighty men, these learned men and soldiers, came and visited him indicates they were very devoted to him and that all those years they had silently hoped he would be restored again. Their hope, which had possibly been encouraged by Daniel, was not put to shame. Their king became king again and truly king-like. All the signs of his former animal-like existence disappeared and his majesty could, as in former days, once again command admiration and awe. It was God Himself who had cast him out, who had preserved his kingdom intact, once again established him in it, and gave him even greater glory.

The last verse apparently is not part of the remarkable proclamation. In these words he expressed his constant mode of behavior after his humiliation; he once again emphasizes that he extols and honors the King of heaven, because all His works are truth, and His ways judgment. The concluding words of this chapter are stirring. They contain a confession that he had walked in pride and that the mighty God of heaven, whom he now glorifies, had abased him.

Bible expositors are prone to bring up the question how Nebuchadnezzar must be viewed—as a truly humbled and saved sinner, or not. Many claim, among whom also Calvin, that we are dealing here with an outward humiliation but not with a true inner brokenness of soul, that his conversion went no deeper than the surface, that he was compelled to give God the honor, but that he did not despise and forsake his idols. Many others seem to be just as sure of his true conversion and hence of his eternal salvation. And there are several good reasons for this viewpoint:

1. This whole proclamation does give the impression that it was not the result of a spontaneous reaction to the impulse of the moment but of a well thought-out and thorough self-examination.

2. He was filled with zeal for Israel's high God and openly urged all the nations of the whole earth to fear Him.

3. He acknowledged the absolute sovereignty of God, i.e., God's right and power over man. In all of Scripture no text is found that teaches the absolute sovereign rule of God more succinctly than does verse 35.

4. A complete confession of sin contains three parts:
   • An admission of sins—and we find this in the entire proclamation.
   • Repentance of sin, which here is evident enough it seems to us, from the last clause of verse 37.
   • A promise to conduct himself better. This we find also in the last verse.

5. We must keep in mind that a heathen ruler is not as familiar with the language of Canaan as a pious Jew in Canaan was.

The wisest thing to do will be what other expositors have done and postpone our judgment consigning him neither to heaven nor to hell, but leaving him in the hand of the Lord, as He in any case surely must have done no injustice to him. But sweet is the thought that one day we might see and behold this king in righteousness.

Chapter 5
BABYLON FOUND WANTING

From Revelry to Destruction

Belshazzar the king made a great feast to a thousand of his lords, and drank wine before the thousand. Belshazzar, whiles he tasted the wine, commanded to bring the golden and silver vessels which his father, Nebuchadnezzar, had taken out of the temple which was in Jerusalem; that the king, and the princes, his wives, and his concubines, might drink therein. Then they brought the golden vessels that were taken out of the temple of the house of God at Jerusalem; and the king, and his princes, his wives, and his concubines, drank in them. They drank wine, and praised the gods of gold, and of silver, of brass, of iron, of wood, and of stone (vv. 1-4).

The first question confronting us is who this Belshazzar was. There are five different opinions on this question, but we shall not weary the reader with all of them. There was a time when unbelieving scholars simply denied there had ever been such a person. It was assumed he had been invented by a pious Jew, a Chasid, who allegedly wrote this book during the time of the Maccabees. Nebuchadnezzar, the golden head, had died in 501 B.C. and had been succeeded by Evilmerodach who, at his ascension to the throne, had shown mercy unto the captive king of Judah, Jehoiachin, and released him from prison and elevated him to the second place in his kingdom (2 Kings 25:27-30; Jer. 52:31-34). Hence thus far we are on solid biblical ground. In Josephus we find an account by Berosus that runs as follows:

Nebuchadnezzar was succeeded by Evilmerodach; he governed badly and was killed by the husband of his sister, Neriglassar, after he had reigned two years. This Neriglassar reigned for four years after him. His son, Laborosoarchod, succeeded him when he was still a boy and reigned for nine months, but since he showed many evidences of a bad character he was murdered by friends. Now his opponents, according to a mutual plot, charged one of the Babylonians, Nabonidus, who had been one of the conspirators, with the reign. [1]

Hence Berosus lists the following sequence: Nebuchadnezzar, Evilmerodach, Neriglassar, Laborosoarchod, and Nabonidus. No Belshazzar appears in this list. However, throughout the centuries all of them have had the honor of having been considered Belshazzar by various expositors. In any case there is no justification whatsoever for hastily saying that he never existed, for at that time kings often carried more than one name.

In the year 1854, however, light was shed on this king by excavations in the East. In that year the learned Sir Henry Rawlinson found inscriptions in the ruins of Um-Gheir (allegedly the old Ur of the Chaldees) which contain an account of the acts of Nabonidus, from which it appears that his oldest son was called Belshazzar and to whom he had given a share in the government. This confronted the scientists with the difficulty how this Belshazzar could have been called the son of Nebuchadnezzar (see Dan. 5:2, 11, 13, 18). One answer is that in Scripture the concepts of father and son are often very broad and elastic and that the word "father" often stands for ancestor, progenitor, grandfather, predecessor, or instructor. Moreover, Rawlinson assumes that Nabonidus had married the daughter of Nebuchadnezzar, and in that case Belshazzar would have been Nebuchadnezzar's grandson. Bettex and others consider it likely that he was one of several natural sons whom Nebuchadnezzar had sired with his concubines, since it is not very likely an intruder would have succeeded in occupying the throne of the mighty king Nebuchadnezzar and reigned for many years without opposition from anybody.

It seems to us, however, that the names son and father of Belshazzar and Nebuchadnezzar do not present such a difficulty as the remarkable prophecy of Jeremiah 27:7, which runs as follows:

---

1. Josephus, Flavius, *Complete Works of Flavius Josephus* in "Flavius Josephus Against Apion." (Grand Rapids: Kregel Publications, page 614. "And all nations shall serve him, and his son, and his son's son, until the very time of his land come: and then many nations and great kings shall serve themselves of him."

According to his prophecy only three kings would reign over Babylon—Nebuchadnezzar, his son, and his grandson—whereas it is obvious that there have been at least four or five. In total agreement with Jeremiah, Scripture mentions only three—Nebuchadnezzar, Evilmerodach, and Belshazzar. Scripture simply does not include the murderer who illegally ascended the throne, Neriglassar, nor his son, Laborosoarchod, who reigned less than a year, as is frequently the case in biblical chronology.

This Belshazzar made a great feast. The occasion for it is not mentioned. Here again, many guesses have been presented, but there simply is no certainty. Not the occasion but the end of the feast demands all our attention and is extensively described. This man Belshazzar was apparently a frivolous and lewd person. Dutch seamen of old used to say, "When a ship is about to sink it must not be caulked any more." But Belshazzar did far worse than that. According to Scripture and history the ship of state, his entire kingdom, was in great danger and the mighty emperor Cyrus, who had already vanquished many nations, was at the gates of Babylon with his armies of conquerors. At such a time when they should have fasted, Belshazzar, who knew this, or at least could and should have known this, decided to have a feast with his lords and generals. He trusted in his mighty men and the thick walls around the city so that it was thereby considered invincible. And were there not so many provisions laid up in the city that it could survive, if need be, a siege of twenty years?

Scripture describes Belshazzar's festive company. It consisted of himself, his one thousand officers, his wives, and his concubines. In the East it was not the custom for women to be present at carousals. But at this occasion there was a shameless trespassing of all morals and propriety. With this the chapter points out the contributing cause of the downfall of the first world empire. All world empires have come to ruin for the same reason. In this connection we are reminded of ancient Rome. The people threw themselves blindly into the maelstrom of unbridled sensual lusts. Also in the "eternal" city frivolity and wantonness had reached staggering proportions. Carousals and orgies were the order of the day. Often emetics were taken to be able to continue the revelry, and quite frequently the guests lay together in snoring heaps so that afterwards their slaves had to carry them home on stretchers. Crazed by sensual pleasure, besmirched with the most bestial and repulsive iniquities, mad with passions, totally leprous with the vilest of sins, many took their own lives, for they knew that those who committed such sins are guilty of death. Something similar took place at the end of the first world empire.

After the meal the wine was served. According to the custom of the day, the king took the first swallow. Our text only says that he drank. But Luther translates, "swilled himself full," and the beginning of the next verse finds him drunk. This is as good a description of the situation as any. "Wine is a mocker" and supplies the courage of a drunkard, which usually leads to the lowest form of mockery. This is evident here. If Belshazzar had been sober he would not have done what he did now. Under the intoxicating influence of the wine he commanded to bring the golden and silver vessels which his grandfather had taken out of the land of the Jews long ago. (For a similar use of the word "father" in Scripture, see 2 Sam. 9:7; Isa. 39:7; Ezra 6:14; Matt. 1:1.)

The sacred vessels were fetched at once. Nebuchadnezzar had considered these vessels so precious that he had carried them off from Jerusalem and had put them in safe keeping in the treasure house of his god, i.e., in that part of the temple of Bel which was to serve as the storehouse of spoils from conquered nations vanquished by the power of Bel. Already the capture of Jerusalem was considered a victory of Bel over Jehovah by Nebuchadnezzar, but this king was of too high a moral character than to mock at the vessels in such a base manner as Belshazzar did. After the vessels had been obtained and filled with the intoxicating liquid, the king and his officers and wives and concubines drank from them. As is the king so are the people. It has been said that such use of the cups must have seemed sacrilegious in the eyes of even the heathen Chaldeans; but since the king set the example, his guests did not hesitate to follow. In those days there were two kinds of mistresses, called wives and concubines here. The former were the most important. The most excellent and best-loved of this king was the queen whose children were the future crown princes and princesses. We already meet the two kinds with David (2 Sam. 5:13) and Solomon (1Kings 11:3).

Under the influence of the wine, and continuing to drink and toast, they lauded and sang the praises of the idols of Babylon. It was the custom of the chief festivities to place the images of the deities before the guests on the tables. Apparently this was also the case here. When these imagined gods stood before them, they began to toast them by singing their praises and blowing the trumpet. Note well that the sins committed here were staggering and cried unto heaven. There was frivolity and wantonness; there was sacrilege and mockery; but now they began openly to elevate Babylon's dumb gods above the God of Israel.

Moreover, it must not escape our attention that the various kinds of idols are specifically mentioned in exactly the same order as that of the metals of the great world image Nebuchadnezzar once saw. That is not an accident. This clearly contains an indication that the great ones of the first world empire had already advanced to the full measure of sin, that they had already come to a public sacrilege on a grand scale. All the metals of the world image, all the forms of blatant sin, were already manifest here.

Writing on the Wall

In the same hour came forth fingers of a man's hand, and wrote over against the candlestick upon the plaster of the wall of the king's palace: and the king saw the part of the hand that wrote. Then the king's countenance was changed, and his thoughts troubled him, so that the joints of his loins were loosed, and his knees smote one against another. The king cried aloud to bring in the astrologers, the Chaldeans, and the soothsayers. And the king spake, and said to the wise men of Babylon, Whosoever shall read this writing, and shew me the interpretation thereof, shall be clothed with scarlet, and have a chain of gold about his neck, and shall be the third ruler in the kingdom (vv. 5-7).

These verses speak of the sealed verdict in the hall of festivities and in the king's conscience, and verse 7 shows that in his fear he takes refuge with the wisdom of the world. When the measure of sin had become full, which we saw in the preceding chapter, then God's divine wrath suddenly exploded. In the same hour, i.e., at the same moment the carousal reached its zenith and the gods of Babylon were praised the loudest, their shouting and their wild joy died on their lips, for they saw the fingers of a man's hand on the white plaster of the wall. This appeared over against the candlestick. Some expositors think this means the seven-branched candlestick from Jerusalem's temple, but that cannot be proven. When it is said this was written against the corona of lamps, the chandelier, it means that all could see it clearly. Those fingers rapidly wrote some words on the plastered wall. People have been surprised to read that in a royal palace a wall was simply white-washed, but possibly this great feast was held in some large hall, as was the case with the feast of Ahasuerus (see Esther 1). From the ruins of Babylon it is evident that the architects did not build with marble but with bricks and plaster.

The king saw the extremity of the writing hand. There is a book of remembrance before the Lord and He is always writing in it (Mal. 3:16). He is always observing man; He is always watching men's ways and He registers everything—literally everything both the good and the bad. But men do not always see His writing hand, as they did here.

Not only did the Lord write on the whitewashed wall in the sight of that frivolous multitude, but at the same time he also wrote on the conscience of the king. His face turned ashen and he became as white as the white plaster of the wall before him. His thoughts terrified him. A moment ago he was still in a stupor and saw a fog before his eyes, and all his thoughts were drowned in drink. But now his thoughts returned. All of a sudden he became fully sober. And he had good reason to be troubled, for this writing came from the great Bookkeeper of heaven Himself and sealed the doom of himself and that of his kingdom. This writing was very mysterious and was fully meant and manifested to terrify him. For there was nothing else left in the world that could terrify him, not even the mighty and vengeful army of Cyrus the Great.

Strange thoughts must have crossed his befuddled mind. His entire sinful life must have appeared before his mind's eye. He must have thought of the writer and wondered about the possible meaning of this mysterious writing before him, and why this had to come and spoil all his fun. No doubt his conscience told him this writing contained something very important and forebode nothing good. Blessed are they who with another king can say, "My meditation of him shall be sweet."

For a moment the king was completely overwhelmed by the writing. His strength failed him. The joints of his loins were loosed, and his knees smote one against another; he trembled with fear and could hardly walk or stand any more. Oh, what must it be for a sinner one day when he must meet the righteous Judge in person! Here the king saw only His hand; but what would it be when His full anger would burn against him?

Verse 7 points out that the world empire always remains true to itself and seeks refuge with the wisdom of the world. He cried aloud—he screamed at the top of his lungs from fear—and ordered to convene the astrologers, the Chaldeans, etc. To entice them to come even more, he added alluring promises to his pleas. He promised three different things:

- A purple robe. What is meant is of course a royal garment. At that time it was a great honor to be given such a robe (Esth. 8:15).
- A golden chain about the neck. Such a chain was worn by the highest officials (cf. Gen. 41:42).
- To become the third ruler, because he himself was the second ruler. Actually his father, Nabonidus, was the true king. Belshazzar did not know that soon he would be divested from all this glory. See further the comments on 1:20; 2:2; and 4:6.

King Greatly Troubled

Then came in all the king's wise men: but they could not read the writing, nor make known to the king the interpretation thereof. Then was king Belshazzar greatly troubled, and his countenance was changed in him, and his lords were astonied. Now the queen, by reason of the words of the king and his lords, came into the banquet house: and the queen spake and said, O king, live forever: let not thy thoughts trouble thee, nor let thy countenance be changed: there is a man in thy kingdom, in whom is the spirit of the holy gods; and in the days of thy father light and understanding and wisdom, like the wisdom of the gods, was found in him; whom the king Nebuchadnezzar thy father, the king, I say, thy father, made master of the magicians, astrologers, Chaldeans, and soothsayers; forasmuch as an excellent spirit, and knowledge, and understanding, interpreting of dreams, and shewing of hard sentences, and dissolving of doubts, were found in the same Daniel, whom the king named Belteshazzar: now let Daniel be called, and he will shew the interpretation (vv. 8-12).

All their sharpness of mind, goaded on by the king's promise of royal favors, was not able to decipher the signs on the plastered wall and to interpret their meaning. No wonder. For to understand divine writing requires more than mere human wisdom. The men of science stood there before that wall with the divine writing like little children. They could read the stars; they could solve difficult problems; but here their insight failed and they had to confess together that their wisdom did not go that deep. This confession of inability frightened the king (J. J. Knap).

Scholars are by no means agreed on why these few words could not be read and explained. Some thought it was written in reversed writing (as when reflected in and by a mirror), in some mysterious cipher writing, in some foreign language, in the language of angels, in acrostic, or in unnaturally flashing signs. Van der Palm suggests a kind of calligraphy with intertwining letters, called *diwani*, which demand expertise in order to understand and comprehend it. Others hold the opinion that the wise men and the king and his mighty men were too shaken and confused to understand. The simplest and most acceptable interpretation is that the letters were familiar, but that the words seemed meaningless and incoherent. The words were short, unconnected, and as is evident from Daniel's interpretation, of the utmost significance.

The words—MENE, MENE, TEKEL, UPHARSIN—simply meant: counted, counted, weighed, divided. Even if the wise men had been able to sense the full weight of these words, they still would not have dared to tell the king the terrible news, being fawning courtiers. God guided things once again in such a manner that His servant was needed to read and interpret His writing.

When the king saw that his wise men also left him in the lurch and could not solve the writing for him, he became even more terrified than before. That flaming writing in front of him burned in his soul as well. He was no longer thinking of his gods and his happy feast. God's finger alone was sufficient to cause him to break out in a cold sweat. Nor were his thousand mighty men any comfort to him for they, too, were full of fear and astonishment. Neither the power nor the wisdom of the world was of any avail to him. He felt to be beyond the pale of reason, hope, and succor.

When a mighty monarch, surrounded by his great men, already cringes and becomes undone like this, how then will people react when the King of Kings appears on the clouds of heaven with majesty and glory! Heaven and earth and all their inhabitants will then shake and tremble (Hag. 2:7; Ezek. 38:20), and the kings of the earth, and the great men, and the rich men, and the chief captains, and the mighty men, and every bondman, and every free man, will hide themselves in the dens and in the rocks of the mountains, and say to the mountains and rocks, "Fall on us, and hide us from the face of him that sitteth on the throne, and from the wrath of the Lamb" (Rev. 6:15, 16). Until that time, no man on earth knows what it is to turn pale with terror.

Soon the general dread and consternation had reached the people outside. The royal bodyguard had been sent out to summon the wise men, and soon they came in great masses to the court. In the meantime the queen had also learned what was going on. We get a very favorable impression of this woman. She was manifestly a noble person. She had not attended the frivolous drinking bout, but she did appear on the scene as soon as there occurred an emergency. We are not told who this woman was. Some exegetes express the opinion that she was the wife of Belshazzar, but for various reasons that is very unlikely. In that case Belshazzar would have known Daniel just as well as she did, and from what she told him it sounds as though she addressed him as his mother or grandmother. Most recent expositors usually think of her as the queen widow of Nebuchadnezzar, and we agree with them, for in verses 11 and 12 she speaks of Daniel in the same manner as Nebuchadnezzar had done in 2:47 and 4:8, 9. That still does not mean she was the actual grandmother of Belshazzar. Since polygamy was very common at Eastern courts she may easily have been one of Nebuchadnezzar's many wives.

After the customary royal greeting she spoke a reassuring word to the king. She was calm and dignified in her whole demeanor. In verses 11 and 12 she gives her account and evaluation of Daniel. It has been correctly noted that only the fact that Daniel was such an unknown person at the court of Belshazzar speaks volumes—volumes of testimony against this frivolous monarch. How darkly he contrasts in this regard with Nebuchadnezzar, who could appreciate the great man. Van Hamelsveld holds the opinion that Daniel, in keeping with an Eastern custom according to which the physicians and wise men of the monarch had to be removed from the court after his death, had indeed been removed; but the first verses of chapters 7 and 8 by no means give that impression, nor does this story. Everything gives the impression that Daniel was close by, so that he could be summoned and rapidly appear at the court. What is evident is that Belshazzar coolly ignored the man of God. Van Oosterzee once used the expression that many a biography can be summarized in three words: "idolized, reviled, forgotten." Nebuchadnezzar once literally idolized Daniel; nor did the latter remain unknown to the other two Babylonian kings. We can be sure that their forsaking God grieved him more than their losing sight of himself. David once said, "Am not I grieved with those that rise up against thee?" (Ps. 139:21).

We do see, however, that God once again ordered matters so wisely that Daniel became the central figure in the next world empire. In Belshazzar's kingdom he was merely a forgotten man. The queen said that the spirit of the holy gods was in him. So in spite of all her high esteem for Daniel, she still remained a heathen lady. O sinner, learn from this that with all your possible respect for the ambassadors of Christ you still are not a Christian!

Three times over Nebuchadnezzar is here called the father of Belshazzar. Neither Hebrew nor Chaldean has a word for grandfather and grandchild. The same is true of the word grandmother. Maachah, a daughter of Absalom, is called the mother of Abijam, but also of her grandson Asa (1Kings 15:10; see also Gen. 28:13). The fact that the queen emphasizes the words "your father" has its reason. They contain a silent rebuke that the man who was held in such great esteem by his famous ancestor had been forgotten by him. And at the same time they contain an exhortation that he, if only for Nebuchadnezzar's sake, should listen to Daniel. She further pointed out that there was found in Daniel light, understanding, and wisdom and that he had an excellent spirit, knowledge, and understanding and was able to interpret dreams, riddles, and knotty problems. She recommended him as a person who could solve the most complex and difficult problems. That was a glorious testimony regarding Daniel before such a great multitude.

Daniel Brought In

Then was Daniel brought in before the king. And the king spake and said unto Daniel, Art thou that Daniel, which art of the children of the captivity of Judah, whom the king, my father, brought out of Jewry? I have even heard of thee, that the spirit of the gods is in thee, and that light and understanding and excellent wisdom is found in thee. And now the wise men, the astrologers,

have been brought in before me, that they should read this writing, and make known unto me the interpretation thereof: but they could not shew the interpretation of the thing: and I have heard of thee, that thou canst make interpretations, and dissolve doubts: now if thou canst read the writing, and make known to me the interpretation thereof, thou shalt be clothed with scarlet, and have a chain of gold about thy neck, and shalt be the third ruler in the kingdom (vv. 13-16).

The queen-mother, i.e., the grandmother, had urged Belshazzar to summon Daniel and had added, with the greatest confidence in his ability, the assurance that he would certainly make known the desired interpretation of the writing. Her wise advice was immediately followed. In the East, queen-mothers had great influence on kings. Without any further deliberation or hesitation Daniel was called and he, in turn, was willing to accompany the messengers at once to the palace. People might have forgotten him, but he had not forgotten his king. Even though his body had grown weak, he had always faithfully tended to the king's business (see 8:27). This time he went to the court, not to save what could be saved, but as Daniel, the judge of God, to judge.

It seems verse 13 contains a hint in that direction, since his Jewish name is mentioned no less than three times. The king first asked him, apparently in a choked voice—for the sentences are halting and incomplete—whether he was Daniel, a captive from Judah. Some expositors see this as an indication that he at least had heard about him. That must be considered very unlikely, but, while his servants had gone out to summon Daniel, he had no doubt gathered as much information on him as he could obtain, since he was going to ask a question. It is noteworthy that Daniel is twice said to have been taken captive out of Judah. Belshazzar may have meant very little with that, but the Holy Spirit all the more.

It cannot escape the attention of a serious reader of Scripture that every time Israel, or someone from Israel, is a blessing unto the heathen, it is always emphasized that such a person was from Israel, for the purpose of reminding the reader of the promise of the covenant that all nations will be blessed in Abraham. From this perspective read 2 Kings 2, Jeremiah 4, and Acts 18:24. So here again it is said of the person to whom such an excellent spirit and great wisdom was ascribed that he hailed from Judah. Salvation is of the Jews; light, knowledge, and wisdom are of the Jews. And Israel's God is the Source of all this blessing. In verse 14 the king declares he has heard about Daniel. It would have been more profitable to Belshazzar if he had listened better to the man of God. In his fear he was flattering Daniel. There was something beseeching in his voice, as if to beg for no personal disaster.

Verse 15 shows us once again in a striking manner that the highest power on earth must pronounce the bankruptcy of worldly wisdom. Belshazzar himself had put his trust in it, but he must acknowledge here before Daniel and all his great men that his trust in this wisdom was put to shame. But they could not shew the interpretation of the thing. Poor wisdom that fails in the approaching hour of danger and death! Poor people who put their trust in it! They will most surely be put to shame just as much as Belshazzar was. The need of a sinner is so great that he must not only have a wisdom to wrestle through this fleeting life, but also to get out of it. We must have a wisdom that knows how to lead and guide us past death and the grave and into the blessed courts of eternity. The true, personified Wisdom still lifts up her voice. Whoever finds her finds life and whoever hates her loves death (Prov. 8:35, 36). Meanwhile it need not surprise us at all that the present-day worldly wise hate Daniel's book so much, for no other book pronounces so often the total fiasco of worldly wisdom.

Daniel Refuses Gifts

Then Daniel answered and said before the king, Let thy gifts be to thyself, and give thy rewards to another; yet I will read the writing unto the king, and make known to him the interpretation (v. 17).

A breathless silence must have filled the festive hall in anticipation of what Daniel would say. The anointed man of God stood there, calm and dignified, over against the king with his mighty men and concubines. What a contrast between them and him! With him was found a quiet majesty; with them fear and a pounding heart. He was the great man there and they the lowly, base mockers. In times of prosperity men of God are often considered to be a dangerous lot, the spoil-sports of society; but in the day of calamity virtually all of society look up to them with great anxiety and expressions of hope.

Daniel, who normally was forgotten and neglected because the people could manage without him, was here the most wanted man. At this time he was already an old man, for it had been nearly seventy years since he had been taken from Judah. So he must have been a man of about eighty-five or ninety years of age. Much had gone over his hoary head. His life had indeed been very eventful. But during all this time he had remained faithful— faithful to his friends, faithful to his countrymen, faithful to his ruler. And above all, faithful with an unshakable faithfulness to his God.

When we compare Daniel before Nebuchadnezzar with Daniel before Belshazzar, we see a great difference. Daniel did not act here as a sympathetic friend and advisor but as a stern judge. He stood there indeed as Daniel. His Hebrew name, which refers to God's act in judging, is used here on purpose, for God through Daniel was pronouncing judgment on Babylon and its king.

It is remarkable that he did not even use the customary greeting for kings. A greeting is always more or less a sign of communion. At least that is the way Scripture views it. And even the least communion with this base mocker of Israel's holy things was repugnant to him. For the same reason he did not speak a word of sympathy to him as he had once done to Nebuchadnezzar (4:19). And again for the same reason Daniel refused his gifts and offers. The king could keep his gifts to himself and bestow his tokens of honor on others more like himself or more eager to receive such recognition. Like all great and wise men, Daniel cared nothing for gold or silver. Of all truly great men in the kingdom of God, three things can always be said:

- As a rule they had a God-fearing mother.
- They care nothing for money.
- And they read often in Scripture.

We know Daniel possessed the last two traits and the first trait in Daniel can easily be deduced from his steadfast fear of God. Daniel did not want to accept this threefold reward from the hand of Belshazzar. Yet we see that soon thereafter he did accept these powerful gifts. He must have accepted them as from the hand of the Lord who here again obtained His purpose; for it was His will that Daniel would also be a great leader in the second world dominion. But right now the king would believe Daniel's sad and discouraging message sooner if the great and deeply respected Daniel did not accept reward.

Glory of Belshazzar's Father

O thou king, the most high God gave Nebuchadnezzar thy father a kingdom, and majesty, and glory, and honor. And for the majesty that he gave him, all people, nations, and languages, trembled and feared before him: whom he would he slew; and whom he would he kept alive; and whom he would he set up; and whom he would he put down. But when his heart was lifted up, and his mind hardened in pride, he was deposed from his kingly throne, and they took his glory from him: and he was driven from the sons of men; and his heart was made like the beasts, and his dwelling was with the wild asses: they fed him with grass like oxen, and his body was wet with the dew of heaven; till he knew that the most high God ruled in the kingdom of men, and that he appointeth over it whomsoever he will (vv. 18-21).

Daniel as a judge had stiffly rejected Belshazzar's gifts. In these verses we read how he reminded him of what had befallen his grandfather Nebuchadnezzar in order to point out his ingratitude and his forsaking God. He called to Belshazzar's attention that Nebuchadnezzar had been very great. As king of Babylon he had had greatness, fame, and glory, so that all nations and tongues quaked and trembled before him. The nations stood in awe before him and did not break out into revolt but subjected themselves to him. He was an absolute monarch and decided even on the life and death of his subjects.

All this, Daniel emphasized in the second place, had been given him from above. He had not obtained this by his own effort, but it had been granted him by the Most High God; the God who was far above all the gods of Babylon had given him all this glory freely. God is the Author of the world power, Daniel emphasized. Hence this God must receive all the glory.

But Nebuchadnezzar had not given Him that honor. Paul's word also applied to Nebuchadnezzar that he, knowing God, had not glorified Him as God nor was thankful to Him but became vain in his imaginations (Rom. 1:21). Ingratitude is the first sin and actually the cause of heathendom. Unthankfulness soon turns into forsaking God, and forsaking God ends in the blasphemy of the

Antichrist. Nebuchadnezzar had found out that pride goes before a fall. God had cast him from his throne and not only taken away all his majesty and glory but also all his human dignity, and lowered him to the level of an animal.

It is further said here that his dwelling had been with the wild asses. A wild ass is one of the most timid animals that exist. He lives solitarily in the thickest woods and the deepest deserts. (On this animal see the beautiful description in Job 39:5-8; and see further Isaiah 32:14 and Jeremiah 2:24.) Israel is frequently compared to a wild ass (Jer. 2:24; Hos. 8:9). Hence it is not likely that the insane king actually lived with these animals. What may be meant is that he, like a wild ass, dwelt in the open field; but it is better to take the expression "dwelled with the wild asses" in the sense of "lived like an animal." There is also a reading that says "among the flocks."

The Lord had had a glorious purpose with this deep debasement of Nebuchadnezzar, namely, His own glorification. Babylon's monarch must glorify Him, the Most High, and not himself. Chapter 4 showed us how God obtained His purpose with him.

Pride and Blasphemy

And thou his son, O Belshazzar, hast not humbled thine heart, though thou knewest all this; but hast lifted up thyself against the Lord of heaven; and they have brought the vessels of his house before thee, and thou, and thy lords, thy wives, and thy concubines, have drunk wine in them; and thou hast praised the gods of silver, and gold, of brass, iron, wood, and stone, which see not, nor hear, nor know: and the God in whose hand thy breath is, and whose are all thy ways, hast thou not glorified. Then was the part of the hand sent from him; and this writing was written (vv. 22-24).

"And thou his son, O Belshazzar"—with these words Daniel began the description of Belshazzar's list of sins, which at the same time contained the reason for this writing there on the wall. Belshazzar's sin was actually twofold: a sin of omission and a sin of commission. His first sin of omission was that he did not wisely observe God's great acts in the life of Nebuchadnezzar his grandfather. That showed his lack of wisdom and his blindness. A wise man learns from all men and all things, the foolish man learns from nothing or nobody. Also, although he knew from the example of Nebuchadnezzar that God punishes all pride, he had nevertheless not humbled himself and not conducted himself in a humble manner. The third sin of omission was that he had not glorified the sovereign God who held his breath in His hand and on Whom depended his entire existence. This is the great sin of heathendom and too often also the sin of present-day Christendom.

Then there were further abominable sins of commission in Belshazzar's life. The proofs for this were to be found everywhere. He had lifted up himself against the Lord of heaven. Had he not insolently ordered to get the sacred vessels and cups which had been stolen from Jerusalem's temple? Had he not mockingly guzzled wine from them together with his mighty men and frivolous wives and concubines? Was this not defiant and insulting to heaven? Had this not been a declaration of war with Israel's God? And had he not, to the scorn of Israel's God, praised the dumb idols? And had he not raised a toast to those idols, which do not see nor hear nor have any knowledge? Then let his awakened and now accusing conscience testify whether his sins have not piled up to mountains and whether there was not sufficient reason for the damning sentence there before him?

Then, so says verse 24, after the measure of his sins was full, this writing was drawn. The stern judge facing the trembling king undoubtedly pointed his finger at the miraculous writing on the wall when saying these words. He had pointed the finger at the causal connection between Belshazzar's wickednesses and these marvelous letter-signs.

Weighed and Found Wanting

And this is the writing that was written, MENE, MENE, TEKEL, UPHARSIN. This is the interpretation of the thing: MENE; God hath numbered thy kingdom, and finished it. TEKEL; Thou art weighed in the balances, and art found wanting. PERES; Thy kingdom is divided, and given to the Medes and Persians (vv. 25-28).

After Daniel had read the text, he said, "This is the interpretation of the thing: God hath numbered thy kingdom, and finished it." This refers to the duration of the Babylonian world dominion. God in His counsel had determined the duration of it already a century before as recorded by Jeremiah (Jer. 25:12; 27:7; 29:10;

Dan. 9:2). The fullness of time had come for Babylon's kingdom and king. Time was past, and the measure of sin was full. God's longsuffering had ended. During Nebuchadnezzar's sin there was still the prospect of a future—"until thou shalt have known"—but here the future was no longer. The time of grace had passed, and therefore: MENE, and once again with emphasis: MENE. God is the great Numberer or Counter. Just as He numbered Babylon's years He constantly numbers our days and our sins. One day all the days of our lives will have been numbered, and for us too the total sum will have been reached. Oh, that we too might pray the prayer of Moses: "Teach us to number our days, that we may apply our hearts unto wisdom" (Ps. 90:12).

God is also the great Weigher, who weighs with the undeceiving balances of eternal justice. TEKEL: "Thou art weighed in the balances, and art found wanting." The Egyptians, Chaldeans, and Greeks represented judging as a kind of weighing. Thus, mention is made here of the balances of justice and judgment. All who despise God will be found wanting by Him. And that is what happened with the despiser of God's works, of His name, and holy vessels, with Belshazzar. He was found to be like the stubble that will be consumed and the chaff that will be scattered. God is also the Weigher who still weighs the nations, peoples and individuals who despise His holy things. All our righteousnesses are found wanting by Him. Only the precious blood of Christ counts with Him (see further Job 6:2 and 31:6 on the idea of God's weighing). PERES: "Thy kingdom is divided, and given to the Medes and Persians."

In verse 25 we have the word UPHARSIN, which is the same word, with the copulative U, i.e., "and," and a plural form, "They divide it." In this word we evidently have already an allusion to the Persians, the most important national half of the Medo-Persian empire. Cyrus the Great was a Persian and Darius a Mede. That is why it is emphatically added that the one indivisible empire of Babylon will be divided among the Medes and Persians.

They were the "mighty nations and great kings" concerning whom Jeremiah had prophesied (Jer. 27:7). That the Medes are here mentioned first, although they were the lesser nation, testifies again to the mathematical correctness of this book for, as we saw in 6:1, Darius the Mede was the first to attain the rulership. Once more the words of the Bible are proved true and accurate.

Belshazzar Slain

Then commanded Belshazzar, and they clothed Daniel with scarlet, and put a chain of gold about his neck, and made a proclamation concerning him, that he should be the third ruler in the kingdom. In that night was Belshazzar the king of the Chaldeans slain (vv. 29, 30).

We are not told in what kind of spirit the king received his sentence. However, he kept his word and gave command to put the scarlet robe on Daniel and hang a golden chain of honor around his neck. And, as he had promised, he further ordered his heralds to proclaim loudly that Daniel had been appointed the third ruler in the kingdom. The prophet made no objections. Apparently in the meantime, he had sensed that this was the will of the Lord. Thus he had an advantage in the next world empire, an advantage which had been given him by Babylon's last king in his last night. Bible students have been amazed that the king kept his word even though the old prophet had treated him so coldly and sternly. But note:

- His conscience had apparently been touched.
- He did not want to go back on his royal word in the presence of the queen and the mighty men and concubines.
- Most likely he silently hoped that in this way he might satisfy the angry god and obtain Daniel's favor and affection.

Meanwhile this was the only good deed he did that night. "In that night," solemnly concludes this story, "was Belshazzar the king of the Chaldeans slain."

The secular writers Herodotus and Xenophon both recount that while the city was engaged in wild celebrations, the enemy, who had besieged the city for over a year, had diverted the Euphrates into an artificial small lake. As soon as they had reached the dry bed at a shallow place, they jumped in and found the heavy brass gates open; according to some, due to treason, and to others, neglect. They seized the palace guard and entered the royal hall. Soon they found the king, sword in hand, and surrounded by his mighty men. A great massacre ensued. Both Scripture and history are in striking agreement on this matter.

Usually little attention is paid to the extensive and accurate description of Babylon's downfall given about two centuries before by the prophet Isaiah (21:1-10 NIV):

An oracle concerning the Desert by the Sea:

Like whirlwinds sweeping through the southland,
an invader comes from the desert,
from a land of terror.

A dire vision has been shown to me:
The traitor betrays, the looter takes loot.
Elam, attack! Media, lay siege!
I will bring to an end all the groaning she caused.

At this my body is racked with pain,
pangs seize me, like those of a woman in labor;
I am staggered by what I hear,
I am bewildered by what I see.
My heart falters,
fear makes me tremble;
the twilight I longed for has become horror to me.

They set the tables,
they spread the rugs,
they eat, they drink!
Get up, you officers,
oil the shields!

This is what the Lord says to me:

"Go, post a lookout and have him report what he sees.
When he sees chariots with teams of horses,
riders on donkeys or riders on camels,
let him be alert, fully alert."

And the lookout shouted,

"Day after day, my lord, I stand on the watchtower;
every night I stay at my post.
Look, here comes a man in a chariot
with a team of horses.
And he gives back the answer:
'Babylon has fallen, has fallen!
All the images of its gods' lie shattered on the ground!'"

O my people, crushed on the threshing floor,
I tell you what I have heard from the Lord Almighty,
from the God of Israel.

Besides this description we find more in Isaiah 45:1-3; 46; 47 and in Jeremiah 50 and 51. The Lord has given us an extensive description of the fall of the first world empire in Scripture.

Chapter 6
THE MOUTHS OF LIONS STOPPED

Darius Comes to Power

And Darius the Median took the kingdom, being about three-score and two years old. It pleased Darius to set over the kingdom an hundred and twenty princes, which should be over the whole kingdom; and over these three presidents; of whom Daniel was first: that the princes might give accounts unto them, and the king should have no damage. Then this Daniel was preferred above the presidents and princes, because an excellent spirit was in him; and the king thought to set him over the whole realm (vv. 1-3).

The golden head, Nebuchadnezzar, and his empire were now things of the past. The second world empire, the Medo-Persian, had now commenced. The gold had made place for the silver (2:39), the lion for the bear (7:5). We would prefer to read immediately about Cyrus the Great, as he was the man of the second world empire and since both Scripture and history tell us that Cyrus the Great, also called Cores the Persian, had conquered Babylon (see Isa. 21:1-10; 44:28; 45:1-4; 2 Chron. 36:20-22; Ezra 1:1). We must also marvel at the fact that Daniel does not mention one word of the important year of Israel's release from captivity, which had been looked forward to with such ardent longing by Daniel and which took place during the first year of Cyrus's reign. In answer to this and similar questions Bettex says:

Here again we find the liberty of the great mind that does not concern itself with shields and customs to which weaklings and conceited persons are so attached....No, he marches on like Durer's Knight, straight towards his goal without allowing himself to be bothered by all kinds of small arrogant spirits, indeed not by death or the devil. But the all-knowing wise men of our day lay the finger of their wisdom on the nose of their intellect and declare that this story is unhistorical and cannot stand the test of critical examination. Later critics will discover in the same manner that Goethe and Schiller are unhistorical, because they mention not a word about their contemporary, the world conqueror Napoleon!

We do not know positively who Darius, the Median, was. There are four different views on this. Recent criticism simply denies his existence and secular history is silent on him. According to them, the Maccabean author needed such a weak king in his religious-historical novel, his Haggada, for the purpose he had in mind. The existence of both the Assyrian king, Sargon (Isa. 20:1), and the Babylonian king, Belshazzar, has been denied on the same weak foundation, and yet God has caused the unearthed stones to speak to assure their historical existence. But to the believer in the Bible it is certain even without such finds that in Daniel's time there was such a person as Darius, the Median.

Daniel describes the tremendous transition from the one world empire to the next in one sentence: "In that night was Belshazzar the king of the Chaldeans slain. And Darius, the Median, took the kingdom, being about threescore and two years old." The ascent of a new world dominion is described by him in the same way we place a death announcement in a paper. In verse 28 he mentions that under his reign Daniel prospered and in 9:1 that he was a son of Ahasuerus and had been made king over the realm of the Chaldeans. From 11:1 we can gather that during the first year of the reign of this Darius a tremendous battle was fought over Israel in the realm of the spirits.

On the basis of Josephus and Xenophon it was generally thought in times past that this referred to Cyaxares of the Cyropaedia. But against this can be argued that Xenophon's Cyropaedia is actually no more than a historical novella and hence that his Cyaxares was most likely a fictitious person, that this Darius was already sixty-two years old and that his father's name was not Astyages but Ahasuerus (see 9:1). Others thought it was the father of Cyaxares, namely, Astyages, at whose court Cyrus, the Persian conqueror, had been brought up. In favor of this view can be said that the weak character of this king totally agrees with that of Darius as depicted by Daniel.

Mainly on the basis of a couple of expressions in the cylinder inscription of Cyrus the Great, most of the recent expositors identify Darius with an important governor-general of Cyrus by the name of Gobryas. According to that unearthed inscription this Gobryas entered Babylon without a battle at the head of Cyrus' soldiers. A few weeks later Cyrus himself entered the city, proclaimed peace to all the inhabitants and appointed Gobryas as governor of all the provinces of Babylon. And according to this cuneiform inscription of Cyrus, Gobryas appointed governors in Babylon (cf. v. 3). The last-mentioned idea seems the most acceptable, but we cannot obtain certainty from these guesses and the truth of what is taught here by no means stands or falls with it.

From the text it is clear that Cyrus, the conqueror of Babylon, did not at once ascend the throne himself but gave it first to a Mede, so that the latter might govern in his name, while in the meantime he could continue his conquests. Thus we understand why it is emphatically stated that he received the kingdom and in 9:1 that he was made or appointed king.

After the conquest of Babylon all kinds of changes and new arrangements had to be made with regard to the administration of the provinces, the more so since Cyrus followed a totally different policy with regard to the conquered nations than did the Assyrian and Babylonian kings. That is why Darius was pleased to appoint 120 satraps to govern the entire realm (compare Esther 1:1). The second world empire was by no means as absolutely monarchial as the first had been. In the silver empire insolent governors and unalterable laws had a great influence on the monarch.

Over these 120 satraps three presidents or ministers were placed, of whom Daniel was appointed as the first minister or chancellor. The satraps were accountable to him and had to give him a report from time to time. The object of this was that the king would not suffer any loss. In political life there has always been a lot of plotting and scheming. At his advanced age Darius had learned by experience that the greed and covetousness of the satraps caused them to steal and embezzle the king's tax money in an unscrupulous manner. From the fact that Darius appointed the satraps it has frequently been concluded that Darius himself was actually the sole and absolute monarch and that Cyrus was his general. But this verse tells us only that Cyrus gave Darius a free hand, and no more. Already two centuries before, the prophet Isaiah had said clearly and repeatedly that Cyrus was the actual conqueror of Babylon and the actual world monarch. This prophetic testimony is to us as certain and clinching as the testimony of history.

Verse 4 shows Daniel always representing the God-fearing and obedient remnant according to the election of grace—excelling the others, exactly as the Lord had promised ages ago if Israel would be obedient. In spite of all his shortcomings, Darius had the wisdom to be able to recognize and appreciate the wisdom and faithfulness in someone else and to make use of it to the benefit of his kingdom, for he was thinking of and planning to appoint him over his entire realm. He wanted to give him the highest power under him as once Ahasuerus did to Mordecai (see Esth. 10).

Trap Set for Daniel

Then the presidents and princes sought to find occasion against Daniel concerning the kingdom; but they could find none occasion nor fault; forasmuch as he was faithful, neither was there any error or fault found in him. Then said these men, We shall not find any occasion against this Daniel, except we find it against him concerning the law of his God. Then these presidents and princes assembled together to the king, and said thus unto him, King Darius, live forever. All the presidents of the kingdom, the governors, and the princes, the counsellors, and the captains, have consulted together to establish a royal statue, and to make a firm decree, that whosoever shall ask a petition of any God or man for thirty days, save of thee, O king, he shall be cast into the den of lions. Now, O king, establish the decree, and sign the writing, that it be not changed, according to the law of the Medes and Persians, which altereth not. Wherefore king Darius signed the writing and the decree (vv. 4-9).

These verses describe the envy of the governors and satraps; the innocence of Daniel; the trap set by the rulers, and the self-deification of the king. It cannot escape the notice of the serious reader of Scripture that it pays more attention to the one Jew, Daniel, than to the first three world powers together. This cannot be explained from the fact that Daniel writes this himself or possibly craves the center stage, but only because he represents the God-fearing people, the Israel of God. His life illustrates how Israel, by remaining faithful to its God, will always prosper on earth, and at the same time how the counsels of the nations are always forged against God's people. This is beautifully told here. Daniel's faithfulness and honesty escaped the attention of the satraps and the other two governors no more than it did that of Darius. The stories of Abel, Job, and many others teach us that the evil one and the wicked cannot bear the goodness of those who fear God. Daniel's conduct in life condemned them, just as the light cannot but condemn the darkness. Noah's building of the ark condemned his unbelieving contemporaries. Their crookedness and corruptness contrasted drastically with his pure uprightness.

Added to this was that the king thought more of this hated foreigner than of all of them together. This aggravated their envy and jealousy even more. Envy in the heart of man is something terrible. It is, like hatred, a rottenness in his bones. It causes his countenance to fall. It is the yellow horse which the devil likes to ride. So as soon as they learned of the king's intention to elevate Daniel even higher, they too made their plans. They had to get rid of him, that Jew, who always had his eye on them so that they could not make their move. They hated Daniel without a cause.

Still it seems to us that they were not motivated merely by jealousy but that the deepest motivation for their activity must be attributed to anti-Semitism, which is the raging of the seed of the serpent against the seed of the woman. There are two kinds of anti-Semitism: that of the nations and that of the church of the nations. The latter does not proceed from the principle just mentioned but from an entirely different one. Scripture affords us examples of both kinds, and so does history until this very day. That we must really ascribe their hatred to anti-Semitism is evident from verses 5 and 13. In the latter verse they deliberately make no mention of Daniel's office but refer to him as the captive Jew, although it had been seventy years since he had been carried away from Judah. Maybe only his features still showed that he was a Jew. His faithfulness condemned their unfaithfulness and his prosperity aroused their envy, and so he was a despicable Jew (9:16).

These reprehensible ideas motivated them to subject the hoary statesman daily to a microscopic examination. In nothing else were they so diligent, in nothing so conscientious, as in their attempts to cause his downfall. With eagle's eyes they watched his every move to see if they might succeed in placing him in a state of suspicion, in an accusation concerning the kingdom, that is to say, in his official relationship to the kingdom. They were more concerned with some crime against the state than with some personal misbehavior. Besides, the king would only be interested in the former. But as carefully as they watched him so carefully did Daniel walk before his God and his king. And no matter how attentively and how unitedly and ceaselessly they checked his movements, they could not possibly find a single spot in his life as an officer of the state, regardless of all their cunning and snares, forasmuch as the Scripture says he was faithful.

All this considered, faithfulness is the only thing the Lord demands of His own. Faithfulness in everything, in small things as well as in great things, over against the unfaithful as well as the faithful. At His coming Christ will never say, "Well done, thou brilliant servant," but, "Well done, thou good and faithful servant" (Matt. 25:21). Well, then, Daniel was faithful. Not a single offense, not a single misdeed was found in him, and that after such a careful scrutiny. When Satan and his henchmen are bent on finding spots on the clothes of God's children they usually succeed only too well. He even finds that the robes of the high priests are polluted (Zech. 3). But Daniel had kept his clothing spotless. He was untainted, unspotted, unimpeachable. He reminds us strongly of Him who is more than Daniel and in whom no fault was found either, the spotless Lamb of God.

"Then said these men." What could they have said? This man Daniel is better, nobler than anyone of us; we will esteem him very highly from now on. But, no, they continued with their evil intent; they were convinced that they had to change their tack. Willy-nilly they had to admit openly to each other that he was faithful in all things and that also in the future they would not succeed in finding anything against him. All their further plotting would be fruitless. But the evil heart of man has always been full of inventions. The evil imaginations of the heart under the influence of Satan can think of many things and be very resourceful. And whatever one evil man does not know another does.

Thus it occurred to them that as a Jew he had a totally different religion than they. Their Persian religion consisted of the veneration of Ormazd and Ahriman, and the four elements, fire, wind, earth, and water. His religion consisted of the worship of only one Deity. And he was very strict in it. If they could effect a conflict of duties toward his king and his God so that in order to remain faithful to his God he would have to disobey his king, they would have obtained their goal; he then would no longer remain above their reproach.

This trick was truly inspired by the devil. Scripture constantly emphasizes that here there was a concerted effort when it says that these men assembled together in troops, en masse, before the king. A wicked gang is always capable of doing more when they band together than when they act individually. No doubt they were grinning on account of the good-naturedness of the king. When together they would present a bill to him, he would not have the courage to refuse to sign it into law. Verse 7 points out that they came with a proposition that, as they emphasized to him, had been approved and accepted by all. All the presidents, the governors, the satraps, the counsellors, and the pachas had, as they claimed, put together this statute. This was a false statement, however, for Daniel, the highest officer, had not been consulted. It is obvious that only a powerful personality would have had the courage to oppose them. And they knew only too well that Darius did not possess this courage, for he was a weak and irresolute ruler.

In the second place, they had taken great care that this proposition contained nothing that could offend the king but, on the contrary, much that flattered his pride. For the bill said that nobody in the entire kingdom was allowed to ask a petition of any God or man for the next thirty days except of the king. The latter part could only be flattering to the vanity of the king.

In the third place, these men proved to be well acquainted with the penal code of the realm, for they added in their proposition that any offender of this prohibition must be cast into the den of lions. To them this stipulation was the main part, of course. For what did they really care whether their king was honored in this manner! What they really wanted was not that the king be elevated but that Daniel be cast down—in the deep den of the lions.

This penal provision affords a testimony that is above suspicion as to the genuineness of the book of Daniel, for it proves that its author was fully acquainted with the customs of these nations. Since the Persians venerated the element of fire together with the other three elements, the Babylonian death penalty by fire was an abomination. Hence this manner of capital punishment. Critics have considered the royal decree absurd. They say it betrays itself as being nothing more than fiction. However, we must take into serious consideration the following realities which make a strong contribution toward refuting the critics:

- According to the viewpoint of these heathen, the king of the realm was worthy of divine honor.
- A law like this, enacted by an Eastern despot contained nothing or very little that was strange to Eastern heathen.
- This law could be easily obeyed by heathendom.
- Especially at that time when the nation had just obtained new rulers, such a law was nothing to be amazed about.

No doubt the people's reaction must have been a casual remark such as "other lords, others laws" or "something new again." Besides, the law was in force for only one month. But to Israel this law was terrible. Darius was not thinking of that, but the satraps were all the more. The king did not see through their sly hypocrisy. He thought they were seeking his exaltation and the splendor and unity of his monarchy. Their purpose was to give the king that impression, for they knew not only what a preference he had for Daniel; but in this way they also had a chance of being rewarded. Their object was twofold: Daniel out and they at the top. But the bill must be ratified by the king and signed into law, for not a proposition but only a royal law was unalterable to the Medes and Persians. For that reason they urged the king to sign it and make it into a law and promulgate it as such. Moreover, they reminded him at once that the law then could or might not be changed afterwards.

Lowth has pointed out the fine distinction between verse 8 and Esther 1:19. With regard to Darius the Mede the expression is, the law of the Medes and Persians; in Esther, the laws of the Persians and the Medes, since Ahasuerus was a Persian. The critics have also denied that there has ever been such a law, since Greek writers make no mention of it. However, this can easily be explained from the fact that this law no longer existed when the Greek writers learned to know Persia better. The intent of this "unchangeableness" was obviously not that these laws could never undergo any change, but rather that the king, as long as he lived, could not revoke his commands.

Because he was really in a predicament from which he could not escape, Darius attached his royal seal. Without fully realizing what he did, he thereby proclaimed himself to be God. The second world empire had just commenced and already we see it, too, was not only idolatrous but harbored a self-deifying character. The principle of this we already see in Genesis 3:5, and the full fruition of it we find recorded in Revelation 13. Perhaps his servants are blameworthy, but Darius should have known better. Only God must be the object of all veneration and worship. Darius stands before us as the symbol of another king who will exalt and magnify himself above every god and God Himself (Dan. 11:36, 37; 2 Thess. 2:4).

Daniel Remains Faithful

Now when Daniel knew that the writing was signed, he went into his house; and his windows being open in his chamber toward Jerusalem, he kneeled upon his knees three times a day, and prayed, and gave thanks before his God, as he did aforetime. Then these men assembled, and found Daniel praying and making supplication before his God. Then they came near, and spake before the king concerning the king's decree; Hast thou not signed a decree, that every man that shall ask a petition of any God or man within thirty days, save of thee, O king, shall be cast into the den of lions? The king answered and said, The thing is true, according to the law of the Medes and Persians, which altereth not. Then answered they and said before the king, That Daniel, which is of the children of the captivity of Judah, regardeth not thee, O king, nor the decree that thou hast signed, but maketh his petition three times a day (vv. 10-13).

Daniel's quiet resignation reminds us of the Lamb (Isa. 53). He never mentioned a single word about the evil tricks of his enemies to the king. That was very wise. If he had started action against them they would have accused him of wanting to seek their downfall. If he had lodged a complaint against this royal edict, he would have put himself in the wrong light with Darius.

> Men may misjudge thy aim,
> Think they have cause for blame,
> Say thou art wrong!
> Hold on thy quiet say;
> Christ is the judge—not they:
> Fear not! Be strong!

The apostle Paul did the same thing Daniel did. He did not defend himself for merely personal reasons but simply said, "But with me it is a very small thing that I should be judged of you, or of man's judgment...he that judgeth me is the Lord" (1Cor. 4:3-5). It is, alas, all too often the case that the old Adam comes more to the fore in Christian polemics than the "precious principle" or the "proven teaching of the fathers." After having completed his official duties at the court, Daniel went home in order to there pour out his heart and needs before God. His custom in days of calamities was to lift up his lamentations to God. In his house he had an upper room. Such a room was often built on a corner of the flat roof. People would occupy it when they wished to be alone. However, it was also used for all kinds of other purposes such as a lodging room, bedroom, sickroom or death chamber. Such a little upper room had an exit to the inside as well as one to the outside, which connected it with the street (see Judg. 3:20; 1Kings 17:19; 2 Kings 4:10; Acts 1:13; 20:8).

Daniel's rooftop house had windows facing Jerusalem. This shows how his heart, after having served Babylon for seventy years, was still with Jerusalem. Jerusalem lay in ruins, but he could not forget it. It was more precious to him than all the treasures of Babylon. "Jerusalem never dies" in the heart of a God-fearing Jew. To him Jerusalem embodied all that was glorious. It is, therefore, the city of the great King, and the day is approaching fast on which the kings of the earth will carry their glory into it, thus putting to shame the unbelief of Christians (see Zech. 14 and the entire second part of Isaiah).

There in his little upper room with the open windows toward Jerusalem Daniel used to wrestle three times daily with his God. No wonder he was so wise and remained so resilient in his old age, that at the age of about ninety years he could still handle the governmental duties. He was a man of prayer par excellence. And prayer is the channel through which God pours out His blessings on us. God loves to grant us His gifts upon our prayer. And when Daniel prayed, he did so in a kneeling position. In Israel kneeling was especially the posture of supplication. In this position Solomon and Ezra supplicated (2 Chron. 6:13; Ezra 9:5). Often the apostles prayed in this manner (Acts 9:40; 20:36; 21:5; Eph. 3:14). F. Kramer writes of Calvin that the Reformer considered kneeling such a natural position for praying that he could imagine, by way of exception, a different position only for sick people.

It is further stated that when Daniel prayed he also always made confession before his God. What a marvelous characteristic this was. How every child of God must love him! What an excellent example he is to all Christians! For although he was so faithful in everything and so pure of walk that even his most bitter enemies had to admit, in spite of themselves, that he was above their reproach, he nevertheless felt himself to be such a great and condemnable sinner that every day "he made confession before his God" (Dutch version; KJV has: "gave thanks before his God").

Verse 10 adds emphatically that he did so as "aforetime" (Dutch version has: "he...made confession before his God, wholly as he had done before"). This statement is of the greatest significance and is usually overlooked. There have been those who wished to idealize Daniel and presented it as though he had opened his windows and as though now he wished to pray three times over. But that was not the case. That window was not opened [see Dan. 6:10], but simply faced Jerusalem, and it was his custom to pray this way.

> Daniel is not the youthful knight who, bent on adventures, goes out to perform chivalrous acts and to obtain fame. He never conducts himself at the court of Darius in such a way as to show these heathen with youthful indiscretion and flippant self-confidence what the faith of a Jew is capable of. In this way, alas, even many believers have come to grief. No, he did what God asked him to do, and he did so with all his might (C. van Proosdij).

Daniel quietly continued doing what he had always done in his usual course. He did not show off in order to provoke the heathen to a reaction by demonstrating that he was not at all afraid. For then he would have tempted God. But, on the other hand, he did not pray less in order to make himself less visible, for this would have betrayed a lack of courageous faith (see also Ps. 55:17).

The cowards still raged en masse against this lone old man. What a mutinous band it was that had chosen this God-fearing man for its prey! Here we have the same word which in verse 6 is translated "troops." It refers to a wild and noisy crowd. The word appears only in this chapter; once more in verse 15. Hence it also indicates that they started out for the express purpose of being able to make an accusation against him. And they succeeded; they were successful in their "courageous" attempt. Daniel's custom of praying before the window facing Jerusalem made it very easy for them. They did not have to break down doors, but could see him, with hands spread out and lips moving, from the outside. As soon as they saw, their decision was made.

It was evident enough that he had broken the law and that they could unanimously indict him before the king! They wasted no time. In great haste they marched off to the palace to request an audience with the king. They reminded him emphatically of the contents of the edict, the signing of it by the king, and the threatened punishment. The sly pack manipulated it so that the king himself pronounced, as this was a law of the Medes and Persians, that it was irrevocable. That was a security measure on their part, for they knew their king's affection for Daniel. So now after the king himself had first referred to the unchangeableness of his command they could, if this proved necessary, refer back not only to the edict but also to his present statement. For after the king had pronounced this in front of all his officers, he now could not easily revoke his royal word by withdrawing his edict or insist on some exception to it for the sake of Daniel.

The king had hardly stated emphatically that it was a law of the Medes and Persians when they made their accusation. They took great care not to mention even one word of his high office, for then they would remind the king of Daniel's merits to the state. In anti-Semitic hatred they pictured him as belonging to the despised people of the Jews. Moreover, he was not a born citizen but an exile who had been taken captive from Judah. And this foreigner dared openly to despise the king by flinging his command to the winds. Their intention was to exalt themselves and knock Daniel down.

The Den of Lions

Then the king, when he heard these words, was sore displeased with himself, and set his heart on Daniel to deliver him: and he labored till the going down of the sun to deliver him. Then these men assembled unto the king, and said unto the king, Know, O King, that the law of the Medes and Persians is, that no decree nor statue which the king establisheth may be changed. Then the king commanded, and they brought Daniel, and cast him into the den of lions. Now the king spake and said unto Daniel, Thy God whom thou servest continually, he will deliver thee. And a stone was brought, and laid upon the mouth of the den; and the king sealed it with his own signet, and with the signet of his lords; that the purpose might not be changed concerning Daniel (vv. 14-17).

King Darius is depicted as a man who sought the well-being of his kingdom, and to that end knew how to engage the service of the most capable men in his realm. For the rest he was not a very intelligent ruler and was burdened with great ambition. But he was extremely fond of Daniel, as is sufficiently clear from these verses and the rest of this chapter. After the king discerned the evil intent of his great men, he was very angry and ill pleased with himself. Truly he had every reason to be angry. Had he not allowed himself to be taken in by his vanity and put himself in the place of God? Monotheism was not unknown to the Medes, and, therefore, did not have to be unknown to him.

In the second place, he must also have been angry with the great men of the state who had tricked him in this manner and who had varnished their malice and their murderous intent with seeming noble purposes for his kingdom and his exalted state. Too late he saw through the web in which they had so cunningly spun him. And what was he to do now? Stand courageously up to them and save Daniel? He would have loved to do so, but the necessary courage failed him. The bill had been unanimously presented and had been ratified and made into a law of the Medes and Persians by himself! Especially under the present circumstances he could not rescind this constitutional law, for then the people would lose all their respect for the recently established government. Moreover, he had to think of Cyrus too!

We do not read one word about his being dissatisfied with Daniel. On the contrary, he set his heart on Daniel to deliver him. Only by sheer necessity could he ever deliver his most faithful and most capable statesman into the claws of the lions. Daniel was a man from whose mature experience he had apparently already profited a great deal and of which he hoped to profit even more in the future. Was he not intricately acquainted with all the manners and customs of the Babylonians, and had he not served the mighty king Nebuchadnezzar for some forty years? Moreover, Daniel had never, not even now, done anything wrong to him. And so he tormented himself and "set his heart on Daniel to save him" for himself and the kingdom.

He did everything he could think of to avert this irreparable calamity. To begin with, he postponed his predicament until the evening so that he might gain time and could grope for a way out until the setting of the sun. Meanwhile he must not have ceased speaking with Daniel to see if this man could give him advice or to convince him to postpone praying for a month. But if he made such overtones—and that is more than likely—he must soon have learned that this was to no avail. He might just as well have asked him to be dead for a month, or to be willing to stop the source of his faithfulness, wisdom, and power during that period or if he who served his earthly king so faithfully would be willing to quit serving his heavenly King. Poor Darius, he saw no way out whatsoever! He has often, correctly, been compared to Pilate. Both were convinced of the innocence of the accused; both made all kinds of attempts to save their victim; both feared the people; both condemned, contrary to their better knowledge and judgment, an innocent person. But Pilate had greater guilt than Darius.

Meanwhile, the princes saw that the king was determined to save Daniel from their and the lions' claws. Hence they trooped once more to the king (see vv. 6 and 12). With their arguments concerning the unchangeableness of the law they put on the thumbscrews. They apparently pointed out that it was unheard of for a Median constitutional law to be rescinded, and that all royal commands were unchangeable as well.

Ah, if these criminal men had only considered the law of the Lord or the natural law in their hearts as unchangeable! The nature of God's law is indeed such that it is absolute and unchangeable and never permits any exception. The moral law never changes, but remains the same for all nations, for all persons, for all times and under all circumstances. In this respect the law of God differs from all human laws, which always have the character of regulations and ordinances that allow for exceptions. Only when human laws are based on the divine law do they permit no exceptions and are even more unchangeable than the laws of the Medes and Persians.

From verse 15 it is also evident that the officials were playing on the king's patriotism. It was as if they said to him, "Stay with the tested and tried customs of your fathers; don't tamper with innovations." And they appealed to his vanity when they called to his attention that he himself had signed and ratified the bill.

At long last Darius yielded under their pressure. His vacillating and wavering character was no match for all these great men. He gave the command for Daniel's condemnation and the royal guard was ordered to take him prisoner. Meanwhile, the old man of God must have wondered why his God, whom he had always served so faithfully, sent him this heavy affliction. We can imagine, however, that he willingly surrendered to his captors, without murmuring against God's high decree, also without resentment or rancor against his vile ambushers.

No descriptions from antiquity have come down to us about the structure of lions' dens. It is known, however, how those of more recent times in the East appeared. Host describes the lions' dens at Fez and Morocco as follows:

> A lions' den consists of a square hole in the ground, divided by a wall into two parts. In this wall is a door which can be opened and closed from above. The keepers (usually Jews) throw food into the one part, by which they lure the lions to go there. Then they close the door and clean out the other part. The den is open at the top, surrounded by a wall, so that people can look into it.

From this description it is evident that these dens looked very much like our present-day bear pits in our zoos. It almost seems as though the king accompanied his condemned servant to the den of lions. At any rate he bade him a touching farewell: "Thy God," he cried, "whom thou servest continually, deliver thee!" This wish is striking indeed! He had exhausted himself in attempts to save him and now he makes an appeal to Daniel's God. Observe that this contains an acknowledgment, in the hearing of all his great men, that he himself was not the only god and that in any case he was not a god who could save. According to the King James translation, Darius expressed his full confidence in the help of Daniel's God. But this translation is a little too positive. Luther translates it as a wish. In any case it seems that he had a silent hope that Daniel would be delivered by his God whom he constantly honored.

No doubt he had heard from Daniel's lips about the miracle of the fiery furnace; nor must the man of God have neglected to talk every now and then about the God of Israel as the only true God. For in the hearing of all of Medo-Persia, as represented by the high officials of the kingdom there, he gave first a confession of his own importance and after that he said that in case Daniel were saved, this would be wholly due to the God of Israel.

The same can be said of the sealing of the den. Whether this was specifically commanded by Darius or whether this was done at the express request of the conspirators, as they might not otherwise trust the king, God had His own wise purpose with it, for when soon he would be saved, everyone would know that only Israel's God who alone performs wonders had saved him from the den and called him as it were back from death and the grave. Daniel descended not only into death but also into the depth of the grave. He is a shadowy symbol of Christ whose grave was also sealed by the mighty men of the fourth world dominion (cf. Matt. 27:60, 66).

Fasting and Fuming

Then the king went to his palace, and passed the night fasting: neither were instruments of music brought before him: and his sleep went from him. Then the king arose very early in the morning, and went in haste unto the den of lions. And when he came to the den, he cried with a lamentable voice unto Daniel: and the king spake and said to Daniel, O Daniel, servant of the living God, is thy God, whom thou servest continually, able to deliver thee from the lions? (vv. 18-20)

And there is, late in the evening and far into the night, joy in the houses of the princes and governors, for their design has succeeded; the weak king Darius has, albeit against his wishes, given in; the righteous controller is gone; now there are riches for their wives and children. They look at life from the practical point of view, and that old Jew with his strict principles, with his keen eyes, with his serious reprimands, with his incorruptible heart, with his unimpeachable faithfulness; that obstacle, that encumbrance, that lock on the king's treasury, that omnipresent eye is out of the way. Hurrah! long live the wisdom of life! (F. Bettex)

Whether all of them were indeed that happy is, psychologically viewed, subject to serious doubt. Every man has a silent witness inside of him, which refuses to be silenced. Not all men are like unto Haman (Esth. 5), or have sunk to the depth of Jesus' conspirators who continued to slander the bleeding, mute Lamb of God on the cross. The faithful look of Daniel, directed at them before he descended, must have struck them like an arrow.

We know for sure that he spent a very anxious night. Darius did not sleep all night long. There was sadness in his heart because of the loss of his best friend and servant of the state, but also a burning self-reproach because of his foolish vanity to proclaim himself a god, and shame because of his weakness over against his princes. He did not eat nor sleep that night.

Verse 18 is interpreted in various ways, especially the word translated "joyful music" (Dutch version). The Dutch and English translations mean about the same thing. Luther translates, "And remained uneaten and let no food bring before him." The Greek and Latin translations say about the same thing. Others have, "He allowed no incense to be placed before him." Still others have, "He allowed no dancing ladies to be brought in." And finally there are many who render it, "He allowed no wife or concubine to be brought to him." The verse indicates clearly enough that the king fasted that evening and night, stayed awake, and spent the time very sad and lonely.

At daybreak the king got up and hastened on his way to the den of lions. How fear and hope must have vied for the first place in his soul! Fear that soon he would see the crushed bones of Daniel; hope that his God had saved him from the wild animals! Although he was in a hurry, he nevertheless must have dragged his feet on his sad walk to the lions' den.

Having come to the den, he called out in a plaintive voice, "O Daniel, servant of the living God, is thy God, whom thou servest continually, able to deliver thee from the lions?" We must feel pity for this benignant king who had been caused so much trouble by his treacherous princes. We can tell from his early walk to the den of lions that he had indeed a great love for Daniel. Once again, as he had done in verse 6, he gave Daniel great honor for serving God continually. It would be glorious if the world round about us could testify something like that concerning us!

In this statement—"O Daniel, servant of the living God"—we find the most wonderful testimony concerning Daniel's godliness. Apparently, the king had often secretly admired him for his faithfulness to his God, as well as for his punctual performance of his duties to him. But the testimony he gave concerning Daniel's God is more glorious still. He called Him the living God. In saying this he once again testified against himself, the worm of the dust, who had wanted to put himself in God's place. Darius did not have a solid faith in the saving hand of God, and he could not have, but he still had a continual secret hope that Daniel's God would perform a miracle in his favor. That is sufficiently clear from his question whether God had been able to deliver him from the lions.

Ignoring for a moment the contents of the question, his secret hope is already evident from the fact that he did ask a question. For if he had definitely believed that Daniel had been torn to pieces he would not have had to call to the lions in their stinking den. We can even go back a step further and say that his going to the den was a proof of his hope.

Delivered From the Lions

Then said Daniel unto the king, O king, live forever. My God hath sent his angel, and hath shut the lions' mouths, that they have not hurt me: forasmuch as before him innocency was found in me; and also before thee, O king, have I done no hurt. Then was the king exceeding glad for him, and commanded that they should take Daniel up out of the den. So Daniel was taken up out of the den, and no manner of hurt was found upon him, for he believed in his God (vv. 21-23).

We can be sure that Daniel spent a far more pleasant night than Darius. In that cage, so full of terror, it must have been a night of much prayer and a close walk with his God. For it is a rule that when the Lord, for reasons known to Himself, casts His children into a calamitous situation, He then will give them grace to suffer, strength according to the cross, and the sweetest, most blessed communion so they can boast that His grace is sufficient unto them and that they take pleasure in infirmities.

While Darius on his splendid bed spent a miserable night, full of gnawing self-reproach and burning regret, Daniel enjoyed the comforts of the Lord. He had a pure conscience and the consciousness that the Lord watched over him. And so he also experienced an imperturbable quietude. Whoever believes is not afraid or nervously agitated.

He, Daniel, did not anxiously cry back, "Oh, please hasten and get me out of this horrible den!" No, very calmly his voice sounded back from the depths, "O king, live forever!" He did not even forget etiquette in this loathsome den of lions! Although the king had caused him suffering, he neither cursed nor reproached the king, but wished him a long life. Daniel's calm answer shows us that the inner condition of our souls does not depend on our outward circumstances. This brief answer, this single greeting of Daniel from the den of lions, provides conclusive evidence against the entire materialistic-socialistic theory. Believers carry God in their hearts and are, therefore, impervious to circumstances.

"My God hath sent his angel," Daniel said to the king. The Lord rules over everything. And he governs His obedient children with a special care. He has often delivered His dearest children as sheep to the slaughter, but frequently He has also saved them in a gloriously miraculous way. There have been those who have rationalistically tried to cut down this divine miracle by pointing out there are examples of lions showing an inexplicable preference and attachment to certain people. This may be wholly true and may be explained from different causes, but that is not the truth that is taught us here. This was a miracle, an inexplicable act of God.

It is emphatically stated that God sent His angel. Just as more than half a century before the angel had stopped the consuming power of the fire for Daniel's friends, so He now had shut the greedy mouths of these animals. That does not mean they could not open their mouths at all, but that they could not do so to devour him. Who this angel was cannot be ascertained any more than in chapter 3 of the angel in the fiery furnace. As was the case there, here, too, there are three views:

- It was an ordinary angel.
- It was the Son of God as the Angel of His presence.
- It was the archangel Michael.

The last of the three views seems to us the most likely one as the keeping of Israel seems to have been entrusted to Michael. But the other two views are just as worthy of God. In such cases we must not speak with exclusive certainty. We can say with certainty that Van Hamelsveld is totally wrong when he wants to rule out the angel and merely ascribes Daniel's preservation to the protecting omnipotence and providence of God.

If we do not know with certainty who this angel was, we do know for sure why he was sent. It was because before the face of God—and God sees sharply—innocence was found in him. God sends His angels for the benefit of the upright and innocent. The prophet experienced the glorious truth beaming forth from all Scripture that when our hearts are upright before the Lord He paves the way before us from step to step. Even though he had not obeyed the king, as he said emphatically from out of the den, neither had he committed a misdeed against his king. He had been disobedient and was nevertheless innocent, since he was more obedient to God than to men.

Exuberant with joy that his servant was still alive, the king commanded that Daniel be pulled out of the den. Soon this command was executed. Daniel was examined and, behold, not a scratch was found on him. This was a repetition of the miracle-experience by the three young men.

The key to this miracle is given in the last clause of verse 23: "Because he believed in his God." Thus also this miracle of the shutting of the lions' mouths is said to be by faith. Both the Old and the New Testament are in agreement on the power of faith. Faith had led to prayer; this had set God's omnipotence in motion, and He had sent His angel; this mighty warrior had shut the mouths of the lions. That is how Scripture presents this miracle. He is a God who alone performs wonders. He can still shut the mouth of the roaring lion from hell, the Devil, so that he cannot harm you!

Darius Praises God

And the king commanded, and they brought those men which had accused Daniel, and they cast them into the den of lions, them, their children, and their wives; and the lions had the mastery of them, and brake all their bones in pieces or ever they came at the bottom of the den. Then king Darius wrote unto all people, nations, and languages, that dwell in all the earth; Peace be multiplied unto you. I make a decree, That in every dominion of my kingdom men tremble and fear before the God of Daniel: for he is the living God, and steadfast forever, and his kingdom that which shall not be destroyed, and his dominion shall be even unto the end. He delivereth and rescueth, and he worketh signs and wonders in heaven and in earth, who hath delivered Daniel from the power of the lions. So this Daniel prospered in the reign of Darius, and in the reign of Cyrus the Persian (vv. 24-28).

Daniel's enemies could not have suspected that while they were digging a pit for someone else they would fall into it themselves, or that by all their evil activity they were effecting their own destruction. This is often seen on earth even before the final great judgment. The king, now that he had Daniel again and saw clearly through all the ruses of his servants, allowed himself no longer to be detained by fear. He seems to have been beside himself with rage, as he commanded that also the wives and children of these men, who no doubt must have been innocent of their crime, must also be cast into the den. We need not suppose that all 120 governors with their households were thrown into the pit. Apparently only the most vehement of Daniel's accusers were cast into it. Now there was no angel to protect them. Now the mouths of the wild animals were not shut. The starved animals caught them in their mouths and crushed their bones. The question has been asked why Daniel did not prevent this inhuman punishment or at least mitigate it. But who is to tell whether Darius in his fury asked him for his advice, or would have listened to him! Besides, here God acted according to the divine right of retribution. And Israel, whose representative Daniel was, is itself the instrument with which God avenges the nations, no matter how little thought this is given. We are here reminded of the Canaanites.

The king issued a glorious proclamation in which he glorifies the God of Daniel. He calls Him:

- The God of Daniel. That was a beautiful testimony to Daniel, which also had significance for Cyrus, the deliverer of Israel.
- The living God, who is exalted above the dead gods.
- The One who is steadfast forever, that is to say, the God who remains the same forever, the Eternal and Unchangeable One.
- The God who has an eternal kingdom. A God who delivers and rescues, and delivered Daniel from the mouths of the lions.

Darius wanted all his subjects to fear and tremble before such a God, by which he meant that the deepest homage and reverence must be paid to Daniel's God. We need not think this implied an enforced religion, because the heathen cared little whether they had to serve one god more or less. Neither did he abolish the service of idols, nor did he command that Israel's God alone must be served. He meant to emphasize that among all the gods

Daniel's God was the highest and must be held in reverence. To him Jehovah was the first but not yet the only God. Still this manifesto went as far as a previous one had gone (cf. 2:38; 3:29; 4:34).

Finally, it is said that Daniel prospered under Darius and Cyrus. The prophet experienced that after the bitter comes the sweet. In this miraculous event God had shown no matter how dark God's way may be, He nevertheless still looks down on them who fear Him, and that the enemies of His people are also His enemies; that they do persecute His people but cannot destroy them. Now if Daniel might become impatient at times with regard to his people, he then could always think of himself. The Lord in His time would also deliver His people from all the oppression of the exile.

How long Daniel lived afterwards, we do not know. It cannot have been all that long when we consider his then great age. Darius apparently reigned for only two years. Nevertheless Daniel is still mentioned during the third year of Cyrus.

With this we have come to the end of the first part of Daniel. This prophecy consists of two main sections, each containing six chapters. The first six chapters dealt with the historical part of this prophecy, while the last six are prophetical. Understand, however, that the historical part, as we have seen, contains the most glorious predictions and types, while later on we shall have the opportunity to convince ourselves that in the prophetic part much history is found. Scripture does not make the sharp distinction between history and prophecy as we commonly do.

Chapter 7
THE BESTIAL NATURE OF THE WORLD DOMINIONS

Daniel Had a Dream

In the first year of Belshazzar king of Babylon, Daniel had a dream and visions of his head upon his bed: then he wrote the dream, and told the sum of the matters. Daniel spake and said, I saw in my vision by night, and, behold, the four winds of the heaven strove upon the great sea. And four great beasts came up from the sea, diverse one from another (vv. 1-3).

As we observed before, the Book of Daniel divides into two main parts. This division is not made on the basis of language, for then the second part should begin with chapter 8, where the prophet writes again in the language of his fathers, whereas this chapter is still written in Chaldean. Nor is this division made on the basis of time, for the chronology of verse 1 shows that we are taken back a few years into history. We already saw the prophet under the first king of the second monarchy and these verses refer to Babylon's last king.

The basis of the division lies in the general nature of these two main parts. The first six chapters we have discussed so far are historical in nature and are a chain of six miraculous stories, whose purpose is, obviously, to depict the hollowness of worldly power and worldly wisdom. The second six chapters, which actually start here, contain four dreams and visions Daniel himself received. In the historical part, Daniel usually performed the function of interpreter of dreams, but here that of the recipient of dreams, while angels supply the meaning of the dreams. There he usually speaks in the third person singular; here in the first person. Nevertheless, this division into a historical and prophetic part is not sharply delineated, for the first part contains many predictions and types, whereas in the second or prophetic part many historical memories and personal particulars appear. By way of introduction to every vision the prophet indicates the time when he received it (see 7:1; 8:1, 2; 9:1, 2; 10:1-4).

So here, too, we have a significant chronological reference. The first year of Belshazzar must have been a sad one for Daniel. With grief he must have come to the conclusion that Belshazzar was a frivolous crown prince. It was a time during which Daniel was ignored. We saw earlier that Belshazzar did not even know him, and not to know a great man like Daniel is failure to appreciate him.

Viewing this time reference in connection with the nature of this prophecy tells us that Daniel knew infallibly that another world empire would succeed that of the Chaldeans even before he deciphered the miraculous writing. More than half a century had passed since Daniel had explained Nebuchadnezzar's remarkable dream in which the king had seen the end of the world dominions. The fact that the prophet was given a similar vision at this time, when Babylon's glory slumped towards extinction, was significant. For Israel could easily come to the conclusion that Babylon's downfall would usher in its complete deliverance, but in this vision the holy nation of the Lord is told that it would not assume world dominion until the downfall of all four world powers. Thus the time of this vision was the end of the first world dominion, and its object was Israel, although as *Lo-ammi* it is not mentioned by name.

As far as the form of this prophecy is concerned, it may cause astonishment, but here we are dealing with the lowest form of God's revelation. That is not due to the person who received it, for Daniel was the "greatly beloved man." Nor can we say that this revelation itself is of little importance, for it encompasses the whole history of this world and even the establishment of Christ's indestructible kingdom. The reason must be sought in Daniel's time and position. He is not considered as a prophet of and for Israel, but as the ambassador of Israel's God at the court of Babylon. Israel is viewed here as *Lo-ammi*, and the Lord systematically avoids His glorious covenant name and the name of His covenant nation. Just as the heathen, who do not know God, as a rule received God's revelations in an unconscious condition, in their sleep—think of Pharaoh, Abimelech, Nebuchadnezzar and

Pilate's wife!—so Daniel, too, who was so closely connected with heathendom, and whose people was *Lo-ammi*, received the truth with reference to the future in this form of revelation. However, there was this great difference between the revelations to the heathen and those given him—heavenly interpreters were sent to explain them to this greatly beloved man.

It was night in restless Babylon, and the very old, white-headed man Daniel lay on his bed, the place where all men ought to be during the night. Only those who have the calling and inclination of Paul may sometimes work through the night. From the second chapter we know that Nebuchadnezzar received his dream in answer to his desire to know the future of his kingdom. Might we not safely assume that here something similar took place, namely, that Daniel, like Nebuchadnezzar, was pondering the future destiny of his people? We cannot prove this, but it corresponds with the nature of the matter, with the character of Daniel, and with the nature of this dream and its interpretation as well as with the terrifying effect upon this old man of God. He knew at once that his dream was of extraordinary significance, for he wrote the sum and substance of it down. Calvin correctly observes that we must not think that Daniel suddenly jumped from his bed so as not to forget the dream. When it is said that he wrote down the sum of the matters in the dream, then an indication is given concerning the high and universal value of this revelation, for which reason it must be written down and passed on to later generations. The prophet did not dream this dream only for himself, but also for Babylon, for Israel, and for us, and it will never become obsolete, because God's unerring view of the world and His people remains unchanged to the end of the ages.

All expositors are in agreement that this dream deals essentially with the same subject as that contained in Nebuchadnezzar's dream in the second chapter. "For the prophecy of the four metals and the prophecy of the four beasts are one in meaning and in substance" (Kuyper). We might ask why then there was a need or necessity for a repetition in chapter 7? The answer is that this vision clarifies and completes the dream of Nebuchadnezzar. Although in essence both depict the same thing and both give a brief sketch of the downward course of development of world history, there are, nevertheless, also considerable points of difference.

The heathen king saw everything from the human and terrestrial point of view, and for that reason the world was a striking image of mankind. Daniel considered the world in its essence and judged its moral quality and so saw it as wild and savage beasts. The heathen king saw in Christ nothing more than a dislodged rock rolling down the mountainside; Daniel saw Him as the Son of Man, coming in majesty and glory. In Nebuchadnezzar's heart the world stood in the forefront; in Daniel's heart, the kingdom of God. In the second chapter we did not hear a word about Israel; here most attention is paid to the people of the saints, for the symbols of the various savage monsters tell Israel that the four world monarchies will want to devour it; while the following establishment of an eternal government can comfort the people sanctified to God (v. 18) for many long centuries and during all its wanderings.

Verses 2 and 3 make mention of three symbols: the great sea, the four winds of heaven, and the four great beasts. The question has often been asked why Scripture gives such strange images specifically to Daniel. Those monsters are considered very strange and almost terrifying. But when these same people ride home in a tram or train they consider it not strange at all that in their papers the daily world events are presented in fantastic and monstrous caricatures. Thus today we see Great Britain depicted as a lion, the United States as an eagle, Russia as a bear, and China as a dragon. Ages before God already made use of caricatures. The characteristic of a cartoon or caricature lies in the fact that a single picture contains much striking instruction. Daniel saw nothing especially strange in these wild animals, for in Babylon he found a natural point of contact with them. Babylonian statuary, that has been unearthed in recent years, presents exactly such monstrous combinations as we find here in this chapter.

> There is nothing strange in the appearance of these beasts. Take whichever family or national coat of arms you like from ancient history, and almost without exception they show figures of animals on it. That is the case with our own national coat of arms and with that of the House of Orange, and almost all noble families have on their escutcheon the head of an animal, often held by two animals in their forepaws. This was an established custom in all of the East and passed on from there to the West and all of Europe (A. Kuyper).

There was not only a natural but also a spiritual point of contact for this kind of symbolism of wild and savage animals, for Scripture often compares the heathen nations to wild animals (see Ezek. 29:3; 32:2; Hos. 13:7, 8). That was a thing that could not be unknown to Daniel. Hence we see he was not amazed and asked information concerning the animals in general, but particularly concerning the fourth monster (v. 19).

These beasts climbed one after another out of the Great Sea, as the Mediterranean Sea was usually called in contrast to the smaller seas such as the Red Sea or the Sea of Galilee. Yet it is not wrong to take this expression to mean the great waters in general as opposed to the land. This symbol, too, was not difficult to understand for Daniel. For the limitless sea in its vauntiness, in its boiling and seething, in its treacherousness and with its voracious monsters is a standard image of the impetuous and untamable nations. It is mentioned in many places in Scripture (Ps. 46:3; 65:7; Isa. 5:30; 57:20; Jer. 6:23; Ezek. 26:3). The stilling of its angry waves is a glorious manifestation of God's omnipotence (Ps. 107:24; Job 26:12). This hollow sea will no longer exist in the kingdom of glory, but be smooth and calm like glass and crystal (Rev. 4:6; 15:2; 22:1). In Revelation 17:15 a heavenly interpreter says emphatically to John, "The waters which thou sawest, where the whore sitteth, are peoples, and multitudes, and nations, and tongues." So there need not be any doubt concerning this symbol.

On this great sea of nations the four winds of the heaven strove. "The four winds" was the common expression in Israel for the four points of the compass, so that here they refer to the east, west, south, and north winds. Storm, like fire, appears in Scripture as one of the means of God's judgment. When the Lord appears in majesty, He is said to walk (or fly) on the wings of the wind, preceded by a storm (1Kings 19:11; Ps. 18:10; 50:3; 104:3; Isa. 29:6; 41:16; Jer. 51:1; Ezek. 13:11; Amos 1:14; Nah. 1:3). So we can describe these symbols thus: the wrath and judgments of God are poured out upon the apostate mass of people as a result of which the four world dominions appear on the scene. When we check history, we learn that all four world monarchies originate from tremendous convulsions of the nations. And it is the constant teaching of Holy Scripture that especially the eternal monarchy will be born from the birth pangs of this old world.

Glimpse of World Empires

The first was like a lion, and had eagle's wings: I beheld till the wings thereof were plucked, and it was lifted up from the earth, and made stand upon the feet as a man, and a man's heart was given to it. And behold another beast, a second, like to a bear, and it raised up itself on one side, and it had three ribs in the mouth of it between the teeth of it: and they said thus unto it, Arise, devour much flesh. After this I beheld, and lo another, like a leopard, which had upon the back of it four wings of a fowl; the beast had also four heads; and dominion was given to it (vv. 4-6).

The first beast Daniel saw in his dream was a lion. From the various names and descriptions of the lion given in Scripture we can deduce that to an Israelite of old a lion was a dangerous and much-feared enemy. In Scripture the lion frequently stands for wicked and mighty enemies (see Ps. 22:13; Prov. 19:12; 20:2; 28:15; Ezek. 22:25; Isa. 5:29; Jer. 2:15; Zeph. 3:3). Especially in Jeremiah, Nebuchadnezzar is depicted as the lion that pounces on and destroys Israel (see Jer. 2:15; 4:7; 5:6; 49:19; 50:17).

Here Daniel saw a lion with the wings of an eagle. Both in sacred and in secular history the eagle is a cherished symbol of swiftness as is the lion of destructive power. Scripture time and again uses the swiftness of eagles in comparisons (Deut. 28:49; 2 Sam. 1:23; Prov. 23:5; Job 9:26; Jer. 4:13; Lam. 4:19). Especially Nebuchadnezzar, who swiftly pounced on Judah and the nations, is frequently compared to an eagle. Jeremiah says of him that his horses are swifter than eagles (Jer. 4:13). "Behold, he shall fly as an eagle, and shall spread his wings over Moab" (Jer. 48:40; 49:22). Even after the destruction of Jerusalem, the sad, lamenting prophet sighs, "Our persecutors are swifter than the eagles of the heaven: they pursued us upon the mountains, they laid wait for us in the wilderness" (Lam. 4:19). In Jeremiah 49:19 and 22 he even calls Nebuchadnezzar in one breath a lion and an eagle. The same image is found in Ezekiel 17:3, 7. And with Habakkuk 1:8, where both images of the lion and the eagle are combined, we can, therefore, say that Nebuchadnezzar is presented here as the representative of the first world monarchy in his majestic power and swiftness. The lion is the king of the animals and the eagle is the king of the feathered creatures, so Nebuchadnezzar as the golden head of the first world dominion was a king of kings before whom all nations trembled. Regardless of how far the ideas in this symbolism range, all expositors agree that this lion with eagle's wings represents Nebuchadnezzar and his world power.

In his dream Daniel saw something very special happen with the lion. His wings were plucked out, he was lifted from the earth and placed on his feet like a man, and the wild beast received a man's heart. The plucking out of his wings is a reference to the disappearance of his swiftness, for an eagle with his wings torn out can do no more than flutter. It is not quite clear what is meant by the lifting up from the earth. Also regarding some of the other expressions there is quite a difference of opinion among expositors. Bishop Newton and others interpret the lifting up as the cessation of the destruction by the Babylonian world dominion. But that is certainly not the meaning, for in 4:34 the same word is used for Nebuchadnezzar's lifting up his eyes to heaven. It seems to us that it means no more than that the downward-looking animal figure of the lion was changed into an upright-walking human figure. The following words point in that direction. The lion was made to stand up straight as a man and received the heart of a man.

It is difficult to see how some expositors could take this last-mentioned expression as referring to the civilization of the Chaldeans. Then the explanation of the decline of the first world empire is much more acceptable. Nevertheless it seems to us that the most obvious explanation is that it means the same as the story told in 4:28-37. This last-mentioned clause is the natural continuation of the words in 4:16, where we read, "Let his heart be changed from man's, and let a beast's heart be given unto him; and let seven times pass over him." We are to think first of all of the personal experience of Nebuchadnezzar, but not with the exclusion but the inclusion of his kingdom, for he had every right to say, "The state am I!" Although we may not be justified in using this expression as clinching proof for his conversion, we nevertheless may safely conclude from it that he abandoned his savage nature, and due to his bitter experiences with the chastising hand of God had become near human.

"Put them in fear, O Lord: that the nations may know themselves to be but men," David once prayed. God-fearing people must often have prayed in this manner in the days of the exile. And if so, then their prayer with reference to Nebuchadnezzar was heard, for in the sight of his entire monarchy he confessed the sovereignty of the Lord. The lion was placed on his feet like a man and received the heart of a man. The savage lion became human and must have shown mercy to God's poor people (4:27). And that which happened to him was reflected by his whole kingdom, albeit in a lesser form.

After this clipped-winged and upright-standing lion Daniel saw a beast that looked like a bear. This is not the only place where a lion and a bear are mentioned together. "As a roaring lion, and a ranging bear; so is a wicked ruler over the poor people" (Prov. 28:15). The herdman of Tekoa in Amos 5:19 expresses it thus: "As if a man did flee from a lion, and a bear met him." Hosea in 13:7, 8 says it this way; "Therefore, I will be unto them as a lion: as a leopard by the way will I observe them: I will meet them as a bear that is bereaved of her whelps, and will rend the caul of their heart." The unquenchable rage of a she-bear upon the loss of her cubs is proverbial to express the greatest fury in Scripture (see 2 Sam. 17:8; Prov. 17:12; Hos. 13:8). Together with the lion the bear was the most feared predatory animal in Palestine. With the exception of the critics, who identify this bear only with the Median kingdom, wishing to exclude the Roman empire at all costs, almost all expositors hold the opinion that this is a reference to the Medo-Persian world monarchy. To him who believes the Bible, there cannot be a trace of a doubt about it, for it tells us repeatedly through Isaiah and Jeremiah that Cyrus, embodying the Medo-Persian kingdom, would conquer Babylon, and the infallible explanation of Daniel says this also. Isaiah 13 gives a beautiful description of Babylon's destruction by the Medes. In verse 17 they are even mentioned by name.

Which main idea in this symbol of the bear applied to the Medo-Persian monarchy is a totally different question, however. Is the bear possibly mentioned only because he lived in the mountains of Media? Or because he is so ponderous, lazy, slow, and far less high-spirited and majestic than a lion? We prefer to answer these questions with the picture Dr. A. Kuyper gives of it:

When afterward the Medo-Persian power emerges from the depth, we immediately see a decline and deterioration. Now it is no longer a lion in his beauty, but a bear in its lumbering shape and brute power. It is especially its ruthless power that characterizes a bear. That is why you see its image before you, having three ribs in its mouth between its teeth, and the only exclamation that is heard at the appearance of this second ponderous animal is: "Arise, devour much flesh!". This command to "arise" has reference exclusively to the unwieldiness and lethargy of the bear, which sometimes can hardly get up, but which nevertheless, once it starts eating, knows of no quitting. This seems strange only insofar as the figure of Cyrus or Cores is not done justice. Especially in Isaiah 45, Cyrus is presented as Israel's savior from its exile. This applied only to the beginning of the Persian reign, however. The subjugation of Babylon brought with it, automatically, that the conqueror attempted to restore to their original condition those nations that had been so sorely oppressed. But even so, in no way did Cyrus declare the land of Israel free and independent again. Under Cyrus and under all of the Persian monarchy the holy land remained part of the great Persian empire, and until the arrival of Alexander the Great, the Medo-Persian power continued its policy of impoverishment and extortion of the nations it subjugated. For that reason the Persian kingdom could not obtain much stability. It could not be compared with Babylon. It did not come into being until the sixth century B.C., and already in the middle of the third century B.C. it succumbed to Alexander. Hence the description given here of the Persian world empire is not very extensive. You see it emerge and sink away again into the depth of the world ocean.

The bear went off to one side. Some interpreters take this to mean that it leaned over to one side; and others that it leaned against one side of the first animal, since the Median kingdom already co-existed in part with Babylon. Again others see it as an indication that the bear got ready to take a deadly leap at the weakened lion. Several expositors view it as an indication that the Medo-Persian kingdom allegedly would keep itself to one side, i.e., separated, from Judah and Israel. This would further imply that instead of Babylon, Cyrus, eventually, would make Susa the capital of Persia and Ecbatan the capital of Media.

The best explanation is to see this as an indication of the two separate kingdoms of which this second world monarchy consisted. There is even a reading, accepted by man, which renders this clause thus: "he positioned himself on one dominion." But even if we reject this reading, it is nevertheless very likely that it refers to the Persian realm which elevated itself above the Median. At first the Median kingdom was stronger than the Persian. Even 5:28 and 6:1 still point in this direction, as well as the repeated expression law of the Medes and Persians. The Median realm was far more fertile than the Persian. The Medes were descendants from the third son of Japheth, by the name of Madai (see Gen. 10:2). They were renowned as being martial and courageous. Their language and religion agreed in the main with those of the Persians.

In 558 B.C. the youthful Cyrus gained a decisive victory over the Medes. Cyrus is the man who plays such a great role in the second part of Isaiah. He is presented as the servant, the shepherd of the Lord, the deliverer of Israel from Babylon. Cyrus is even called the Anointed, a messiah, who is a royal type from among the nations of the Lord Jesus Christ, who one day will deliver Israel from all its oppression (see Cyrus and his mighty acts: Isa. 13:14; 41:2ff.; 43:14; 44:24ff; 45:1-14; 46; 47; 2 Chron. 36:22ff; Ezra 1). These and other texts show instructively that the Bible is sufficient for its own exegesis. Secular history can confirm Scripture and serve as an aid here and there for greater clarity, but this is something quite different from being absolutely necessary for the interpretation of Scripture.

The bear had three ribs in its mouth. Luther, and others with him, translate ribs by great fangs, but the original word does not have this meaning anywhere. Literally the word means rib-sides, rib-pieces, and indicates that the beast had caught and devoured prey and was still gluttonously busy with it. For that reason we cannot interpret these three ribs as referring to the three main parts of the second world empire, Media, Persia, and Babylon. This would violate the symbol, because the bear itself represents the Medo-Persian empire. The view that sees in these three ribs only a completion of the symbol and merely a vague allusion to the conquests of the second monarchy is all too facile and does no justice to the words.

When interpreting symbols, we must always be on our guard against two extremes. On the one hand, symbols must not be taken rigidly literally but, on the other hand, neither must they be over-symbolized. The most general and at the same time the most acceptable interpretation in our opinion is the one that views the ribs as the three most important nations Cyrus conquered, namely, Libya, Babylon, and Egypt. For Libya we could also substitute Palestine with the inclusion of Syria.

The Medo-Persian bear was told, "Arise, devour much flesh." Who it was who said this is deliberately not mentioned, and exactly for this reason we conclude that it is Jehovah. Who, especially in the Book of Daniel, is a God who conceals Himself. He is the divine Author and Governor of the world empires. It is He who makes desolations in the earth (Ps. 46:8). He did not want the Medo-Persian bear to be satisfied with the three ribs and lie down, but rather that he should be insatiable in conquering nations. We see the same idea expressed differently in Isaiah 45:1, "Thus saith the Lord to his anointed, To Cyrus, whose right hand I have holden, to subdue nations before him; and I will loose the loins of kings, to open before him the two-leaved gates; and the gates shall not be shut." Other parts of Isaiah, Esther, Ezra, as well as history teach us that the Medo-Persian bear obeyed this command.

When viewed correctly, the one dream of Daniel consisted of different visions. The third vision shown to the prophet's soul's eye was a leopard with four wings on his back and with four heads. The original Rationalists and the Dutch supernaturalists (Venema, Van Hamelsveld, Van Vloten, Klinkenberg, Van der Palm and Van Rhijn), as well as modern critics, usually apply this animal symbol to the Persian kingdom under Cyrus the Great, as they do the brass belly and loins in 2:32. This explanation must at the same time serve to get rid of the Roman empire. But almost without exception all orthodox exegetes from Calvin to Kuyper interpret this symbol as referring to Alexander the Great and his conquests. As we shall see later on, in chapters 8 and 11 it is taught quite clearly that the king of Greece conquers the kings of the Medes and Persians. And that which Scripture teaches us quite clearly is also taught in every textbook of ancient history. Hence on the basis of Scripture and history there can be no reasonable doubt that this leopard is a symbolic figure of the Greco-Macedonian world power of which Alexander the Great was the embodiment, as was Nebuchadnezzar of the first and Cyrus the Great of the second world monarchy.

With the leopard is meant the long, spotted tiger cat. In earlier times he apparently was quite often seen in Palestine. In Jeremiah

5:6, Hosea 13:7 and Habakkuk 1:8 he is, like here, mentioned in connection with a lion and a bear and other wild animals. Like other wild animals, he often appears in Scripture in some form of comparison. He is as bloodthirsty as a lion and a wolf of the evening (Jer. 5:6), but in the kingdom of peace he has abandoned his bloodthirstiness and will peacefully lie down with the kid (Isa. 11:6). Habakkuk compares the swift horses of the Chaldeans with the swiftness of his movements (1:8). Swiftness is the main idea presented here. This idea is fortified by the four wings the animal had on his back. It says that they were the wings of a fowl, and this is a silent hint that they were not the wings of an eagle, as in the case of the first beast. Historians without exception make mention of the unbelievable speed with which Alexander, the Macedonian world conqueror, moved across the earth. He began his wars of conquest as a young man of twenty years of age and after a little more than twelve years he had, with a small army of thirty thousand men, brought the world of that time at his feet.

Nebuchadnezzar was able to make fast conquests too, but in the language of symbolism he had only two wings, whereas Alexander had four. A secular writer says of him that he was impetuous and swift in his campaigns, like a panther in pursuit of its prey, and attacked his enemies with a speed as if he had a double pair of wings. This corresponding language of history only confirms what Scripture teaches us here and in chapter 8. There it is said of the he-goat who symbolizes the king of Greece, Alexander, that he did not touch the ground because of his speed (see 8:5 and 21).

Further, this winged leopard had four heads. What this implies is not very clear. There are expositors who think it refers to the division of Alexander's army into four parts under his four commanders—Ptolemaeus, Seleucus, Philippus, Antigonus. Others think it refers to the four principal parts of his world empire—Greece, Egypt, Syria, Persia. Most expositors refer to Daniel 8:8 and 22 and interpret it as the four heads of the four parts of the Greco-Macedonian world empire after Alexander's death. Although it must be admitted that this partition was a historical fact, this is nevertheless apparently not what is meant here. The four horns in chapter 8 did not appear until after Alexander's death, after the great horn had been broken off.

If we take the four heads to mean the four kingdoms that came into being after Alexander's death, then this symbol loses its value to a great extent, for then Alexander is presented here as a beast without any head, whereas it is a rule that Scripture specifically calls our attention to the great personalities of Nebuchadnezzar, Cyrus, Alexander the Great, and the Antichrist, in whom the four world dominions are embodied. So for the sake of the symbol we need to do one of two things: either eliminate Alexander completely, or also apply these four heads as well as the wings to him and his conquests. And since the former cannot be done, the latter will have to be accepted.

Pusey feels this too when he, after having explained the meaning of the heads as being the partition of the kingdom, writes as follows: "Probably the multiplication of the heads means more than the partition. The human head in the image of Nebuchadnezzar was a symbol of the human mind." In our opinion these four heads represent the fourfold mind and the unique talent of Alexander as a general. There have been many great generals but Alexander comes across as peerless and inimitable. (Compare with these heads Rev. 13:1; 17:3.)

Finally, it is said that the beast was given dominion:

> This is said because the prosperity of Alexander the Great was incomprehensible. Who could have thought that when he crossed the sea he would be the victor over all of Asia and the East? He took thirty thousand men with him and did not even wage war on his own authority but had, by means of various tricks, succeeded in getting himself appointed king of Greece by the free states. Thus he was like a servant of the Greeks and could not muster more than thirty thousand troops. And he ran into 150,000 enemies, after that into 400,000, and finally even into almost one million. For Darius in the last battle had 800,000 men besides the auxiliary troops. Alexander did have some auxiliary troops from among the foreign nations he had conquered, but he could not rely on them. Hence his entire force consisted of no more than thirty thousand men; and on the day he conquered Darius, Alexander was so intoxicated that he could hardly be awakened. The historians who exalt his military prowess excuse this fact by the statement that he had been awake all night; for the rest all are agreed that afterward he was like a dead person and could hardly be awakened when all commanders had assembled; all deliberately made a great noise near his tent, as no one dared enter it. And yet he had hardly rubbed his eyes when Darius fled. That is why the

prophet says, not without reason, that dominion was given to the beast, because it is at variance with all natural order and contrary to the expectation of all men that he could defeat such a great army, which by its appearance alone could frighten all of Greece (Calvin).

Thus we see that God was also the Author of the Greco-Macedonian or third empire just as He was of the first two world powers. He who works all things according to the counsel of His will had His own purpose to work out and fulfill with each world empire. The first world power had to destroy Jerusalem and carry Israel to Babylon. The second world power had the divine order to build Jerusalem, to actually rebuild the temple from the ground, and to restore Israel (Isa. 44:28); the third world power had to take the Greek language and civilization to the East for the purpose of preparing for the entrance of Christianity into the world; and the fourth world power has the glorious calling of taking Christianity to the utmost ends of the earth. When this has been done, the end of this dispensation will have come. From the human point of view, all the world empires are nothing but gigantic, unsuccessful attempts at creating an ideal state, a utopia; but from the divine point of view they are the awe-inspiring means to the preparation of His eternal and indestructible kingdom which he has foretold throughout the prophecies of the Old Testament.

Vision of Roman Empire

After this I saw in the night visions, and behold a fourth beast, dreadful and terrible, and strong exceedingly; and it had great iron teeth: it devoured and brake in pieces, and stamped the residue with the feet of it: and it was diverse from all the beasts that were before it; and it had ten horns. I considered the horns, and, behold, there came up among them another little horn, before whom there were three of the first horns plucked up by the roots: and, behold, in this horn were eyes like the eyes of man, and a mouth speaking great things (vv. 7, 8).

Here we have the vision and the description of the fourth beast. It is evident that Daniel did not see all the beasts at once. He saw one after the other emerge from the turbulent waters. That we are confronted here with something very special is evident:

- Because of its horrifying looks, there is no name which could be given to it.

- Far more attention to and a much more extensive description of it is given than in the case of the preceding three.
- The sight of it affected Daniel in a special way, so that he desired and received more light on it.
- This beast was not succeeded by others but by the Son of man Himself.

Various interpretations have also been given in regard to this beast. Some want to make it part of the symbolism of the Persian bear. The critics usually think it refers to Antiochus Epiphanes. But all present-day conservative exegetes interpret it, and very correctly so, as referring to the Roman empire, sometimes also called the Romano-Germanic empire. All of the New Testament serves as proof that this empire succeeded the third world power and that it existed in the days of Christ and the apostles.

The first thing said of this monster is that it was dreadful and terrible and exceedingly strong. Those who think the author lived during the time of Antiochus Epiphanes and that this beast represents him teach that the writer of these expressions is describing such an insignificant ruler as Antiochus. No, he is wrestling here with the language in order to somehow depict an incomparable monster. The beast cannot find its peer in all of nature; no name can be found for it; it is unlike any other; it is virtually indescribable.

Its dreadfulness does not describe as much its dreadful form as its dreadful and horrifying nature. Terrible refers to its cruelty. There has been no world empire that spread so much fear among the nations as the Roman empire. And there was not one that behaved so cruelly and murderously. We need think only of the persecution of Christians and Jews, of the cruel treatment of slaves and the hatred of Christ, and of the earlier and later bloody wars it engaged in. Today's bloodbaths also fall under the terms of this world empire. For Rome's language, Roman justice, and Rome's church provide the threefold proof that until this very day we live under this bestial world empire. And it will not reach the pinnacle of its abominations until it has brought forth the man of sin.

The second characteristic of this monster was its great iron teeth with which it devoured and pulverized everything. There has been no other world empire that could devour and incorporate and assimilate the nations as Rome did. There were but three things Rome could not make identical with itself—Christianity, Jewry, and the fickle will of the people. Whatever Rome could not crush with its iron teeth and assimilate, it pitilessly trampled down and crushed under its feet, as the following clause tells us.

In the third place, the text says that the beast stamped the residue with its feet. All it could not grind with its iron fangs it trampled to mulch underneath its enormous brass feet. This again is another obvious characteristic of Rome. For political reasons Rome was always intent on incorporating the nations and making them Roman, so that they swear by the eternal city, but woe to those who refused to be Rome's allies! Christians, Jews, slaves, and many nationalities have experienced what it means to oppose and resist Rome. They were crushed to pieces underneath the beast's paws. Under Roman rule there was no other choice but to be devoured or trodden down. This beast was ever busily engaged in pulverizing with its teeth or crushing with its claws.

In the fourth place, the prophet emphatically states that this beast was wholly different from all the preceding beasts. To clarify in what way this beast was different from all the other monsters, the prophet points out that it had ten horns. That that is an important point of difference is evident from the comparatively extensive description given here. This is wholly in agreement with the nature of prophecy, which is never much concerned with secondary causes and side issues but concentrates on the final coming of the kingdom of God and its last great enemies. Thus, also, here in Daniel, divine prophecy remains true to itself when it calls special attention to the fourth monster, particularly its ten horns, and specifically to the eleventh horn.

There are four texts which shed light on these ten horns. First of all, Daniel 2:42 and 44. The ten toes on the feet of the world image are the same as the ten horns here. Already verse 44 tells us that these toes are kings, that is to say, kingdoms, as Daniel and Revelation use these terms quite often interchangeably. That this verse is not referring to the four world powers is quite certain, for at the time of those kings the God of heaven will set up His eternal kingdom and we know that the stone rolls down from above against the ten toes.

The second text which sheds light on the ten horns is verse 24 of chapter 7. It contains a brief but infallible interpretation of the ten horns in these words, "And the ten horns out of this kingdom are ten kings [with kingdoms] that shall arise."

A third clarification Scripture itself offers is found in Revelation 13:1, 2. There the same monster is described in features derived from the other three monsters (leopard, bear, and lion), whereby the significant hint is given that the fourth world power has not grown away from the others but has retained all their brute, bestial, and monstrous traits. Well, then, that beast appears there too with ten horns, and that they are the same as these and represent ten kingdoms is evident from the addition that there were upon his horns ten crowns.

Finally, Revelation 17:3, 7, 12, 16 speak again of these ten horns. Verse 12 reads, "And the ten horns which thou sawest are ten kings, which have received no kingdom as yet; but receive power as kings one hour with the beast." John had marveled at the drunken whore seated on the scarlet beast with its ten horns. Thereupon, the angel gave him an infallible interpretation from verse 7 to verse 18. In verse 12 he touched upon the horns and in complete agreement with Daniel says the ten horns symbolized ten kings. He further says:

- These ten kings would each receive a kingdom.
- They had not yet received them at that time, i.e., almost a century after Christ. So we see that anyone who believes the explanation of the angel cannot possibly interpret these horns as something going on in the days of the Maccabees.
- The celestial interpreter indicates in general the time of the appearance of the ten kings and kingdoms. They will receive their power one hour with the beast. When we learn from Revelation 13:3 and 17:8 that the beast will be mortally wounded and suddenly appear again, we can deduce from this that the Roman empire will revive once more before the end of days and that from that revived empire there will emerge ten kings who will receive kingdoms at the same time as the beast, which is the reincarnation of the revived world empire.
- In verse 13 the angel says these ten kings have one mind, i.e., together they have the same principle, insight, and purpose, namely, to be at the service of the beast with all their might. For that reason they give their might and power to the

monstrous beast which is the head and embodiment of the last world power.

- These ten kings of the revived Roman empire will, according to the same angel, wage war against the Lamb, but Christ will come in judgment against them, accompanied by His people, and He will conquer them. It is evident from this last statement that the beast and the ten kings will not publicly appear until the church has been taken up in the air to meet the Lord, for otherwise Christ could not very well come from heaven together with His people and use them as co-judges in His judgment on the beast and the ten kings.

- Before the ten kings will be judged, God, whose intent and plan they are carrying out, will first make use of them as the means of judgment for the false church. They will utterly destroy the whore, the apostate church (see vv. 15-18).

In the light of the full revelation in the last book of the Bible it is therefore, clear that the so-called historical interpretation does not hold water. Various Bible expositors have mentioned at least forty different groups of ten kings, and this great variety as such is already suspect. With regard to the futuristic interpretation there is in the main only one idea, namely, that in the restored Roman empire ten kings will emerge who will put all their authority and might in the service of this restored empire.

When the very sober question is asked when in history there was ever such a group of ten kings, the answer is that there never was. There were always either more or less. And even today, in the area of the erstwhile Roman empire as it is bordered by the Scandinavian countries in the north, the Atlantic Ocean in the west, southeast Russia in the east, and the Mediterranean Sea in the south, there are no ten kings or kingdoms to be found. What is to be found are kings, emperors, princes, counts, dukes, and grand dukes who together rule over some forty nations. Now when these ten kings as rulers over as many kingdoms did not exist in the past nor at present, then it is inevitable that we must expect them in the future, unless we assume with Dr. A. Kuyper that ten here is not a fixed number, but refers only to a certain number in general. This greatly learned man expresses himself thus on the ten horns:

Now what is broadly the prophecy regarding this fourth kingdom that is at stake here? This fourth monstrous animal had ten horns. In a context such as this, horns refer of course to mighty rulers, either as persons alone or with their realm and dynasty included. Hence from the one world empire with which it began there would soon emerge a tenfold dynastic power. The Roman empire would, when it went down, dissolve itself into a complete set of states. Ten in a designation like this is not the cipher ten. It simply means that from Caesar's empire there would emerge in Europe a certain number of kingdoms or states and that these together would remain the constant bearers of the great Roman world empire. All this is quite easily understood. Caesar's empire did indeed not remain one. Many powers arose under Rome's protection, even in Asia and Africa, as they are still found there today, and hence it would be, according to this prophecy, the spirit of the Roman empire that in principle would always govern these states. History shows that this is indeed the case.

Thus Dr. Kuyper still holds to the historical view. He comes to this view by symbolizing the number ten into something indefinite. When he gets to the number three and a half he makes that also into something indefinite. And the spiritualizers generally do this with all numbers in still-unfulfilled prophecy. We emphasize here, because with regard to fulfilled prophecy and to history these same people usually take numbers in their ordinary meaning. Moreover, this prophecy does not say it would be the spirit of the Roman empire that in principle would reign, as Kuyper says. It is neither the spirit nor the principle but the actual raging Roman empire which is presented here together with its ten horns as reigning at the coming of the Lord. Regarding this view both Daniel and Revelation are in agreement and so we have to accept it. At the Lord's time all these things will literally take place, just as the prophecies concerning the preceding three words have literally been fulfilled. Ah, why do exegetes not take this principle of interpretation for unfulfilled prophecy, as prophecy in the past was already so promptly fulfilled?

To us it is an absolute fact that we must expect these ten kingdoms in the future on the following grounds:

1. In Daniel 2 they are pulverized by the stone (Christ).
2. In Daniel 7 they are closely connected with the Antichrist and the Lord's return.

3. Revelation 13 fully agrees with Daniel.
4. Revelation 17 says—
   - The ten kings get power as kings one hour with the beast.
   - They war against the Lamb.
   - They are destroyed by the second coming of the Lord.

When Daniel looked at the ten horns more intently, he then discovered another small horn which arose among the ten. The attentiveness of the prophet and his interest in it contain a significant hint that we, too, must pay careful attention to this part of prophecy. It must grieve the Holy Spirit greatly that many Christians are so indifferent with regard to such predictions. When merely casting a glance, the prophet had seen no more than ten horns, but when he paid closer attention and looked longer at them he saw an eleventh horn taking shape. Apparently this horn was not there at first. The impression is given that it will not appear until late in history and further, that it will one day become visible and grow; in fact, it will grow so fast that by its growth it will uproot and pull out three other horns. It appears between the other horns. Hence, speaking without symbolism, we have something which is simultaneous with and similar to the ten kings.

"And, behold," the prophet says, again as a sign of his great amazement, "in this horn there were eyes like the eyes of man." This indicates intelligence and wisdom. In the symbolism of Scripture men's eyes are quite often used for discretion and wisdom (see Ezek. 1:18; 10:12; Zech. 3:9; 4:10; Rev. 4:6; 5:6).

Furthermore, the horn had a mouth with which it spoke great things, i.e., audacious language. As the following verses say more about this, we need not go into it further at the present. We only wish to ask the question, what is meant by this little horn? Here again the ideas of expositors vary greatly. For the sake of brevity we only mention in passing the most important ones, without refuting them, for Scripture itself refutes them.

Calvin says, "Hence I do not doubt that with the little horn is meant Julius Caesar, and the others, Augustus who succeeded him, next Tiberius, Caligula, Claudius, Nero, and others." Calvin simply had to come up with something of this nature because when interpreting this vision he accepted as a maxim that it did not go further than the first coming of Christ. The church of the Middle Ages usually saw in this little horn Mohammed and the

Turks. The men of Higher Criticism interpret it as referring to Antiochus Epiphanes. Bishop Thomas Newton is the father of the papal theory. Many an exegete saw in it Napoleon the Great, and others Napoleon 3. And all these interpretations always "fit" exactly! If they had only read the sequel in this chapter (vv. 20-26) soberly and without presuppositions, they would have seen that these ten kings and the eleventh horn will come into being immediately before the Lord's coming unto judgment and will be destroyed in this judgment. This fact alone is sufficient refutation of all the various interpretations of the historical school.

On the basis of the futuristic interpretation only one interpretation is possible, namely, that this is a reference to the Antichrist, the man of sin. This interpretation recommends itself by its simplicity, its unity among greatly diverging interpreters, and above all its perfect Scripturality. As far as the last-mentioned item is concerned, it can be said that the prophecy of Daniel agrees most beautifully with the Revelation of John. Only what was not yet revealed to Daniel was later told by the angel to the seer on Patmos—the Roman empire will run through three phases:

- A heathen phase in the past.
- A seemingly Christian phase in the present.
- An antichristian phase in the future (see Rev. 17:8, where we read of "the beast that was, and is not, and yet is").

This phrase is often considered an inexplicable riddle, but it is obviously not meant to be. In brief form this threefold course of development is given here:

- The beast was present under the emperors.
- It is not, since the Nordic barbarians in the fifth century broke up the Roman empire.
- It will be again in the time of the Antichrist. The last-mentioned development is the most terrible but also the briefest, as we learn from the following verses:

Empire Destroyed

I beheld till the thrones were cast down, and the Ancient of Days did sit, whose garment was white as snow, and the hair of his head like the pure wool: his throne was like the fiery flame, and his

> wheels as burning fire. A fiery stream issued and came forth from before him: thousand thousands ministered unto him, and ten thousand times ten thousand stood before him: the judgment was set, and the books were opened. I beheld then because of the voice of the great words which the horn spake: I beheld even till the beast was slain, and his body destroyed, and given to the burning flame. As concerning the rest of the beasts, they had their dominion taken away: yet their lives were prolonged for a season and time (vv. 9-12).

Until now the seer had seen nothing but a boisterous sea from which the four beasts emerged in succession. Here he turns his gaze upward. The sea monsters had filled him with terror, but the exalted sight he now beholds, and especially the killing of the last beast, must have been somewhat reassuring to him. Not from below but from above, via the pathways of judgment, would deliverance come.

Daniel saw that thrones were set (Dutch version). The King James translation, with a few others, says here that the thrones were cast down, and exegetes usually apply this to the thrones of the ten or eleven kings; but the Dutch translation [as well as the NIV] is better and agrees with the Greek, the Latin, and the German translation by Luther. The same word is used of the casting of the young men into the fire and of Daniel into the den of lions. This means judgment will be pronounced and that for that purpose the seats of the judges are set up. When the judges have ascended their seats, the Ancient of Days appears to assume the presidency at this juridical session.

The first question concerning this Ancient of Days is who is He? There are mainly four different ideas on this.

1. Most Jews hold the opinion that it is they who are represented here because on the basis of their Scriptures they are aware that they will be the future judges of the world.

2. Most expositors see here a presentation of God the Father, mainly because a little later mention is made of the Son of man. It is very much a question, however, whether the first Person of the holy Trinity ever manifests or describes Himself in bodily form.

3. Gaebelein and others think that the Lord Jesus is presented here. But who is the One who occupies the central place in this vision of judgment? There can be but one answer. It is our Lord

and Savior Jesus Christ. John 5:22 gives the conclusive answer. "For the Father judgeth no man, but hath committed all judgment unto the Son."

4. Many later expositors see in this person the triune God. In our opinion this is the best explanation, agreeing with the constant teaching of holy Scripture, for it is full of similar descriptions of God's appearance as Judge (see Exod. 19:18; Ps. 50:1-3; 68:1-3; 93:1, 2; 94:1; 96:12; 97:1-5; Hab. 3:2-5).

The idea that God the Father is presented here as a white-haired old man can safely be abandoned, for the original text itself is better translated "the constant, everlasting One in days." The text intends to indicate God as the eternal and everlasting One, with whom one day is as a thousand years and a thousand years as one day. To emerge, glitter, and disappear is the destiny of all nations.

> Whiter crowns
> Show forth brilliance,
> Nations, states bloom with prosperity;
> Longer is the hour
> Their sin lasts,
> But their evening nevertheless approaches rapidly.

Concerning the outward appearance of the Everlasting One, it is said His garment was white as snow. In ancient times kings were clothed in white, heavenly blue, and purple (Gen. 41:42; Esther 8:15). White indicates the purity and spotless holiness of this Judge. The color of the hair on His head, resembling pure, washed, white wool, points in the same direction. Black usually indicates sin and uncleanness.

His throne was sparks of fire (Dutch version), i.e., it glittered with sparks of fire. The King James version has "His throne like fiery flame." Fire is a means of God's judgment. The Lord ascended His judgment seat and fire will consume His opponents. In the East thrones quite often had wheels, so that these heavy golden chairs could be easily moved. That is why it is stated here that the wheels of the throne were a burning fire, which most likely is an allusion to the shooting red lightnings of God's consuming justice. Read in this connection the description of Ezekiel's throne-chariot in Ezekiel 1 (also Revelation 1) which derives several features from this vision and that of Daniel 10.

Verse 10 says an awesome stream of fire flowed out from Him and streamed before Him. This too indicates His holiness and majesty by which He with irresistible power consumes everything in His way. In nature there is practically nothing that has such an enormous power as a stream of water, but a stream of fire is even more consuming (for similar descriptions, see Ezek. 19:14; Ps. 18:8; and Rev. 4:5). Since this royal Judge is glorious, magnificent, and splendid beyond all description, so also is His retinue which surrounds and serves Him. Thousand thousands of holy angels ministered unto him and millions stood before Him.

There are ranks in the world of angels, and according to some interpreters two different ranks are mentioned here, but it seems to us that in this highly poetical description we must not see an indication of rank or number, for in Scripture "serving" and "standing before" someone are terms of similar meaning. The text contains nothing which demands such an interpretation. Compare this with Revelation 17:14, which undeniably refers to glorified believers. For that reason we prefer to think the text here speaks of both angels and glorified believers.

The Judge and His co-judges and servants were present and so the judicial examination commenced. The books were opened, i.e., the scrolls were rolled open. These words are not referring to the "books of God's omniscience," nor men's consciences (Article 37 of the Belgic Confession), nor the book of life, but the books of God's retribution in which are recorded all the sins of commission and of omission. Matthew 25 contains a touching page of this divine book of retribution (see also Ps. 56:8; Mal. 3:16, and especially Rev. 5:1-9).

According to verse 11, Daniel continued to watch attentively, because he wondered what would happen to the horn whose blasphemies he had heard. So without interruption he held his eyes riveted on the grand spectacle before him. He knew that the foolhardy horn could not remain unpunished, but that it would be swallowed up by the fiery stream of the Judge. And that was what happened. The beast was killed and assigned to be burned. Verse 26 speaks of this in more detail (see also Rev. 19:20; 20:10).

Verse 12 contains some difficulty. The Dutch version refers back to the beasts described earlier, but we know that their judgment had already taken place earlier, as is recorded above. For that reason some translators preferred to use the singular here, so that it would read that the rest of the beast, namely, its horns, existed for some time after their dominion had been taken away. However, the text does not justify such a change. According to Van Hamelsveld the text reads as follows: "Concerning the rest of the beasts, their dominion had already been taken away from them, their lives having been prolonged until a certain predetermined time." That would mean that the previous three world dominions had been destroyed long before. It seems to us that what is meant here is that the factual dominion of the earlier world powers had indeed been taken away but that their actual essence, or being (which according to Revelation 13:2 is embodied in the last beast) was only now, by the judgment executed upon the last beast, completely annihilated. The last beast was so terrible that it contained or comprehended all the others, and now not only its dominion but its very existence was taken away to be replaced by the Messianic kingdom.

We must not make the mistake of identifying the judgment these verses have been speaking of with the so-called last judgment mentioned in Revelation 20:11-15. According to the context there, the latter will take place at the end of the Millennium. It is not the Antichrist but the revolt of Gog and Magog that are its contributing cause. Here Daniel describes only the judgment upon the Roman empire and the Antichrist of which Revelation 19:11-21 speaks. Finally, we quote here the very correct notations of T. M. Looman. In his Bible commentary he notes on verse 12 the following:

> With the annihilation of the Antichrist, the horn that proceeded from the fourth empire, the power of the fourth beast is generally broken and at the same time all possibility for one of the four world powers which had existed ever being able to rear its head again was cut off (cf. v. 12). However, Ezekiel 38, 39 and Revelation 20:7-9 teach that thereby the emergence of another last enemy of the kingdom of God after the Millennium is not cut off. But this final enemy will emerge from a world dominion different from that from which the Antichrist emerges, who comes forth from the Roman empire. The northern parts of Asia and of Europe and their nations bring forth the last enemy according to Ezekiel 38:1-6, albeit that southerly nations must also serve him, whereas the Roman empire and the dominion of the Antichrist emerging from it belong to the southern part of Europe and

extend to the parts of Africa bordering on it. What at the same time also will take place, alas, is that the group of nations to which also the German nation belongs will also assume a hostile attitude against the kingdom of God. For, although the ruler who is in command of this revolt belongs to the northern part of Asia and Russia, nevertheless all of Gomer, according to Ezekiel 38:6, is in his service, i.e., also the Germanic nation. Preeminent, however, is the group of Romanic nations, the southern parts of Europe, from which emerges the first antichristian power.

The Son of Man

I saw in the night visions, and, behold, one like the Son of man came with the clouds of heaven, and came to the Ancient of days, and they brought him near before him. And there was given him dominion, and glory, and a kingdom, that all people, nations, and languages, should serve him: his dominion is an everlasting dominion, which shall not pass away, and his kingdom that which shall not be destroyed (vv. 13-14).

Daniel's attentive gaze remained rapt and now he saw the Son of man coming on the clouds of heaven. These two verses tell the same thing as the story of the stone rolling down against the feet of the world image and the consequent growth of the stone becoming a glorious kingdom (2:34, 35, 44, 45). The entire seventh chapter runs parallel to the second, but every feature is viewed from a different angle. What was but a broken-off piece of rock to the heathen king was to Daniel the glorious Son of man. And in John's book He is even more exalted, for there it is brought out even more clearly that He Himself is God (Rev. 1:13-20).

According to theologians, Daniel 7:13 in particular is the text from which the Savior derived His often-used name. The name Son of man does not merely designate Him as the ideal man, but as the revealed Head of the new mankind and as the Mediator between God and man. He Himself had a preference for this name, for by it He presented Himself as God manifest in the flesh, and as the great Representative and Vicar of the Father, who took the place of the first Adam and by His suffering death brings many children to glory. It is not enough to see in this glorious name only His humiliation or His true humanity, for Christ used it as much in connection with His forgiving sins and His exaltation as He does in this. This comprehensive name signifies what we often mean by the less suitable name of God-man (see Matt. 24:30; Mark 13:26; 13:34; 14:62; Luke 21:27).

That the Ancient of Days is not Himself the Lord Jesus Christ is sufficiently evident from the second part of verse 13. This tells us that the great Representative of God was led to the Everlasting One, the great Judge of all the earth. Scofield in his Reference Bible correctly says:

> This scene is identical with that of Revelation 5:6-10...Verse 13 describes the scene in heaven which, in fulfillment, precedes the events which Daniel sees in vision in verses 9-12. The historic order will be:
>
> 1. The investiture of the Son of Man with the kingdom (Dan. 7:13, 14; Rev. 5:6-10).
>
> 2. The "vexing" of Ps. 2:5, fully described in Matt. 24:21, 22; Rev. 6:18.
>
> 3. The return of the Son of Man in glory to deliver the "smiting" blow of Dan. 2:45 (Dan. 7:9-11; Rev. 19:11-21).
>
> 4. The judgment of the nations and the setting up of the kingdom (Dan. 7:10, 26, 27; Matt 25:31-46; Rev. 20:1-6).

It is almost incomprehensible how some exegetes can view this as a description of the Roman empire and others limit it to Christ's first coming. It is also incomprehensible that the men of criticism view the Son of man as do the Jews themselves. But all exegetes who do not want to recognize the full truth of prophecy must of necessity seek refuge in all sorts of artificial exegesis.

Verse 14 points out first of all that royal majesty and glory were given to Christ. Hence it does not speak of His rule as God, but of His mediatorial work, the Kingdom which He as the Representative of the Father receives as a reward upon the travail of his soul. The time when He receives the kingdom is His return on the clouds of heaven. It is amazing how many children of God are of the opinion that Christ already now reigns in fact as King. As if the Confession of Faith, which is read and heard every sabbath, does not already deny this clearly enough! For the sitting at the right hand of the Father indicates clearly enough that He is not yet actually reigning as King, but for the time being occupies the place of the Crown Prince, while in fact the god of this age still reigns. Certainly, in a juridical sense all things are already subject to Him and He can say, "All power is given unto me in heaven and in earth," but in an actual sense the words of the apostle prevail: "But now we see not yet all things put under him" (Heb. 2:8). Now He is still sitting with His Father in the throne of God, but at His return He will be sitting on His own throne (see Matt. 19:28 and Rev. 3:21). Both Testaments teach this abundantly and also agree on this matter in the most beautiful manner.

It is further said here that His mediatorial kingdom will be absolute, general, and comprise all nations, peoples, and tongues. In an absolute sense there have never been world powers, in the sense that all nations actually paid homage to the heads of these world dominions. But Christ's kingdom will be universal in the most absolute sense of the word, for at that time the earth will be full of the knowledge of the Lord as the waters cover the bottom of the sea, and then all nations will ask after the root of Jesse, and they shall find His rest to be glorious (Isa. 11:9, 10).

From the context as well as from the words themselves it is sufficiently clear, that this kingdom of Christ will be truly on earth. For in heaven there will be no peoples, nations, and different tongues. And the other powers that are replaced by this kingdom were also on earth. Hence we can safely assume that although Christ's kingdom is not of the world, not from below, but has its origin from above, it will nevertheless be definitely on this earth.

Finally, our attention is called to the permanency of this kingdom. The other kingdoms carried from the very beginning the germs of death within; whereas the kingdom of King Jesus will never be disturbed or destroyed. It was absolutely not the intent of the Holy Spirit to point here at the temporary millennial aspect. In Daniel several matters are generally combined which in Revelation are more particularized and separated by time and place. Here it is the express purpose to point out the eternal and imperishable nature of the kingdom of God in contrast with the fast-passing glory of the preceding kingdoms. For that reason it is simply foolishness to insist on finding here a reference to the one thousand years. That would be the same as demanding from Daniel to make a reference to or give an exposition of the covenant of works or of original sin.

As far as we know there has never been an advocate of the

Millennium who wanted to insist that this was indicated here in its millennial duration. For that reason it may be called a vain attempt to attack the doctrine of the Millennium on the basis of Daniel. If no one claims that it does exist, then there is no need for anyone to get all excited to claim that it does not exist. For wise reasons Daniel wished to emphasize not the duration but the eternal nature of this kingdom. The Millennium is found clearly enough in Revelation 20, where the number one thousand is found as often as six times. And between the presentation of Daniel and that of John there is no contradiction but the most beautiful harmony. The Millennium is part of the eternal kingdom as it is depicted here.

Daniel Is Overwhelmed

I, Daniel, was grieved in my spirit in the midst of my body, and the visions of my head troubled me. I came near unto one of them that stood by, and asked him the truth of all this. So he told me, and made me know the interpretation of the things. These great beasts, which are four, are four kings, which shall arise out of the earth. But the saints of the most High shall take the kingdom, and possess the kingdom forever, even forever and ever (vv. 15-18).

These night visions overwhelmed Daniel; he kept seeing more, his thoughts multiplied, and finally his spirit was overwhelmed by all these impressions. The question cannot be suppressed as to why the prophet was so grieved, literally, so struck, wounded in his spirit. In order to understand this, we must realize that the prophets were not soul-less tools, but receptive and often finely-strung minds on whom the divine revelations quite frequently made an overpowering impression. Added to this was the fact that this direct revelation of God in a dream was the first Daniel received. When we read the first six chapters consecutively, we easily get the impression that Daniel was accustomed to the wonders and revelations of God, but actually the fact was that during the time of about half a century he had beheld the wonders of the Lord for only a few days. Add to this that he found himself in a painful uncertainty regarding these ministrations, and a fearful premonition must have told him that they spelled little that was good for his beloved Israel, and then we can readily understand how he was totally shaken and upset by these things.

But Daniel followed the right course of conduct in this matter.

He made known his ardent desire to obtain certainty (Dutch version) or the truth of all this. That is what God's children always ought to do when they are in uncertainty about some part of Scripture. They must not want to remain uncertain but allow themselves neither rest nor peace of mind until they have obtained the necessary light. And know there is here below not one single means—albeit there are many aids—that explains Scripture. The explanation must come from on high; the Holy Spirit Himself explains His Word through the channel of a sanctified personality. Thus Daniel asked for light from above. It is not said of whom he desired enlightenment. It is stated in general terms that he addressed his request to one of them that stood by, which undoubtedly means one of thousands of saints who surrounded him, as mentioned in verse 10. And angels are always ready to serve those who inherit salvation. Thus this throne-spirit very readily supplied an explanation for all of the four beasts.

The interpretation he gives is very brief, especially when we remember that it concerns a history of many centuries, with even the consummation included. Yet this brief interpretation is of the utmost importance, for it tells us with divine authority that all four monsters are kings (as representatives of kingdoms). Regardless of how greatly Bible exegetes may vary in their answers to the question which kings together with their kingdoms are meant, due to this interpretation they cannot change it into something else. Thus it is also very important that the angel says here that those four kings will arise out of the earth. This does not confront us with a contradiction but with an interpretation of the sea in verse 2. This phrase, in its simplicity, tells us that the great consummation of all earthly life outside of God is nothing but a royal dominion which squarely opposes God and His Christ and converges in the man of sin. Hence this phrase tells us, negatively, that the world outside of God cannot by itself develop a state of happiness or utopia. All worldly dominions are of the earth, earthy. And no more than an earthy man can make himself into a heavenly man, so no more can the world dominion turn into the heavenly kingdom. This brief interpretation teaches us, positively, the poignant truth that the sum total of all the life of the world amounts to no more than what is bestial and anti-Christian. The salvation of man cannot possibly come from below.

Brief as the heavenly interpreter may be concerning the four world powers, he puts all the more emphasis on the saints. That is where for Daniel and for all believers lies the center of gravity or, rather, the pinnacle of all the longing of their souls. It is the good pleasure of the Father to give them the kingdom. On the basis of this comforting truth they can conduct themselves in a kingly and courageous manner and lift their heads aloft in all humility.

Who are these saints of the high places (Dutch version; King James version: "saints of the most High")? Definitely not the great Maccabean warriors; neither the angels; nor the unconverted Jews. The question is whether our [Dutch] States translation has hit upon the right translation here. The Greek, Latin, English, French and German translations all have "saints of the most High." Van der Palm translates, "the sanctified ones of the highly exalted One." Van Hamelsveld has "the saints in the high dwellings." If that is what is intended here, then we are to think of the glorified members of the Body of Christ who with Him will reign from the heavenly places (Rom. 8:17; 2 Tim. 2:10-12; Rev. 3:21; 5:10; 20:4-6). But it seems to us that here we are simply dealing with a plurality of majesty or of excellency, and that we had better translate the phrase as "saints of the most High". If this is what is meant, then we can take it to mean Daniel's people, converted Israel, for Scripture teaches us that the Lord Jesus Christ together with His mystical body will reign over Israel and the nations, and that converted Israel will reign over the nations in the kingdom of peace. The kingdom of the saints as well as that of Christ will be eternal and worldwide.

War With the Saints

Then I would know the truth of the fourth beast, which was diverse from all the others, exceeding dreadful, whose teeth were of iron, and his nails of brass; which devoured, brake in pieces, and stamped the residue with his feet; and of the ten horns that were in his head, and of the other which came up, and before whom three fell; even of that horn that had eyes, and a mouth that spake very great things, whose look was more stout than his fellows. I beheld, and the same horn made war with the saints, and prevailed against them; until the Ancient of days came, and judgment was given to the saints of the most High; and the time came that the saints possessed the kingdom (vv. 19-22).

The angel-interpreter had already given Daniel a clarification of the four beasts, but Daniel was not wholly satisfied with regard to this fourth monster. Hence he asked further questions. What a golden age would dawn for the church of Christ if those who confessed the Lord would also come to the throne of grace with questions in the heart that showed their interest!

Does present-day Christianity still show that it believes all revealed things belong to us and our children forever (Deut. 29:29)? Do we truly believe the Holy Spirit will guide every humble child of God into all truth and also today will teach things to come (John 16:13)? Do we truly believe—not theoretically, but truly—that God gives wisdom liberally to all who humbly ask Him (James 1:5)? Truly, if Christ were to appear to present-day Christendom He would say to them with no less emphasis than He did to the men on the way to Emmaus, "O fools, and slow of heart to believe all that the prophets have spoken" (Luke 24:25). Most godly people have too much reverence for the Word of God to leave it unread or to ignore it, but when do they read Scripture with the firm determination to obtain a clear concept of future things? With the ingrained idea that prophecy is obscure and at best suitable to induce preachers to far-fetched examinations, they read on in the same monotone without concerning themselves with the true meaning of what they read, and that, while the Guide into all truth lives in the church and in the heart of every believer. How different it was with Daniel! This greatly beloved man is here an example to every believer. His faith demanded knowledge.

On verses 19 and 20, see our comments on verses 7 and 8. Verse 19 adds only that the beast had nails of brass. That was not mentioned before. Such claws explain that the beast could tear an awful lot of things to pieces. When our Lord Jesus Christ will reveal Himself in glory in the day of His second coming, He too will have feet like unto fine brass (Rev. 1:15), in order to trample down His enemies with them. Verse 20 adds something not found in verse 8, namely, that the look of the eleventh horn was more stout than his fellows. The question arises how this statement agrees with the name "little horn." The answer is that the eleventh horn was very small, when it first appeared but rapidly grew afterwards and even uprooted and pushed out of the way three other horns, and thus soon obtained greater size and prouder appearance than its fellows.

In verse 21, the prophet once again adds two new features to what was before said about the little horn. The first feature, not mentioned earlier, is that the little horn made war with the saints. This horn did not at once wage war against the believers but only after it had become great in appearance and so bold that it dared to belch forth insulting language against heaven. In our comment on verse 8 we already voiced our opinion that this little horn is no one less than the Antichrist, the man of sin, the man of perdition. Further descriptions of this demonic personality are found in 2 Thessalonians 2 and Revelation 13. We shall meet him again in Daniel, so that it will be sufficient to say here that he will especially sorely vex Israel after it has returned and been restored in Palestine. When the angel spoke here of saints, without further delineation, then Daniel thought, of course, of none other than his countrymen. Two-thirds of Judah was exterminated (see Zech. 13:8, 9).

The second trait given of the Antichrist is that he will triumph. By that is meant that he prevailed against the saints. That is in complete agreement with what we read about him in other places. For a further description of his victory over the saints, see Daniel 8:24; 9:27; 11:36, 39; Revelation 11:7; 13:7. In Revelation 17:14 we are told that he will be conquered by the Lamb and His church. Here verse 22 says the same thing. The Antichrist will not rage long. Openly and most fiercely for only three years and a half years (see 9:27; Rev. 11:2; 12:6, 14; 13:5). Revelation 19:11-21 describes how Christ and His people conquer the Antichrist. See further the comments made on verse 9.

Judgment of the Antichrist

Thus he said, The fourth beast shall be the fourth kingdom upon earth, which shall be diverse from all kingdoms, and shall devour the whole earth, and shall tread it down, and break it in pieces. And the ten horns out of this kingdom are ten kings that shall arise: and another shall rise after them; and he shall be diverse from the first, and he shall subdue three kings. And he shall speak great words against the most High, and shall wear out the saints of the most High, and think to change times and laws: and they shall be given into his hand until a time and times and the dividing of time. But the judgment shall sit, and they shall take away his dominion, to consume and to destroy it unto the end. And the kingdom and dominion, and the greatness of the kingdom under the whole heaven, shall be given to the people of the saints of the most High, whose kingdom is an everlasting kingdom, and all dominions shall serve and obey him. Hitherto is the end of the matter. As for me, Daniel, my cogitations much troubled me, and my countenance changed in me: but I kept the matter in my heart (vv. 23-28).

Verse 23 stresses once again the separate and repulsive nature of the fourth monster. It will eat up, devour, gobble down the whole earth. And that which it cannot gobble up it will trample down and crush with its feet without any mercy. We saw earlier that it represents the Roman empire. To take it for something else leads to all kinds of absurdities. We also mentioned in that connection that the Roman empire apparently goes through a series of three different stages of development:

- The empire as it once was in the past.
- Now in the present as it is not in its full manifestation.
- One day in the future, in the end-time, as it will reveal itself as an anti-Christian empire.

It is evident from this whole description that the angel refers to the empire in its final stage of development, when it will break loose in open rebellion against the Almighty. Later on we shall have an opportunity to see that all this will take place during the final year-week mentioned in 9:27, also called the time of the end (see further 8:17-19; 11:35, 40; 12:4, 7, 9). Just as the great world drama already now unfolds faster by the day, so it will do even faster in the future. Thus the revival of the Roman empire and the destructions it inflicts upon the earth, and the appearance of the ten kings and the Antichrist will all take place very fast.

Just as the fourth beast is different from all its predecessors, so the eleventh horn will be different from all the others, i.e., the Antichrist will be totally different from the ten kings of the restored Roman empire. It will have much more power and might; it will be filled with much more hatred against God and His people than the ten kings, and it will even uproot and abase the other three (see further on this verse the comments on verse 8).

Verse 25 refers to the terrible persecution by the Antichrist. Papal Rome explained this often in connection with the so-called holy wars against the Turks. Rationalistic exegetes explain this as referring to the cruel persecutions perpetrated by Antiochus

Epiphanes during the time of the Maccabees. The Adventists and many Protestant commentators apply it to the pope of Rome. It seems to us that all three explanations contain an element of truth insofar as Antiochus Epiphanes, Mohammed, and some popes were types, shadowy examples of the Antichrist.

Concerning the evil intents of the Antichrist, it is further said that he will "think to change times and laws." The Adventists interpret this as changing the seventh day into the first. According to them, the Roman pope, the eleventh horn, changed the law by making Sunday the day of rest. There is hardly another text in Scripture on which they speak and write more often than this. But the entire papal institution lies outside of the prophet's field of interest. The entire present-day dispensation also lies outside his vision. It was not men who changed this day but God Himself.

If God speaks not only by and through words but also through deeds, then it must be important that Christ rose on the first day (Matt. 28:1, 6; Mark 16:2; Luke 24:1; John 20:1) and that He came in the midst of His disciples repeatedly on that day, and blessed them (Mark 16:14; Luke 24:36; John 20:19, 26; Rev. 1:10). Later on the disciples gathered together on that day to dedicate their thanksgiving offerings to the Lord (1Cor. 16:2), so we can say after David, "This is the day which the Lord hath made; we will rejoice and be glad in it" (Ps. 118:24). Not the pope but the Lord made this day of days.

Some feel the word "times" does not merely refer to the changing of one day, but rather appointed times or the establishing of cultic days. Both expressions taken together indicate the evil purpose of the Antichrist to destroy restored Israel and its theocratic institutions. It is not said, however, that he will succeed but only that he thought or hoped to do this.

The duration of his raging against the saints is indicated in the last part of verse 25. They, i.e., Israel of that time, will "be given into his hand until a time and times and the dividing of time." Even the critics usually take this to mean a time of three and a half years. A time is one year, times are two years, and part of a time is half a year. The critics apply this to Antiochus Epiphanes who, it is claimed, was master of Jerusalem exactly three years and a half and caused the daily sacrifice to cease during that time. Josephus mentions this in his prologue to his *Jewish War*. We may freely view this matter as a temporary, partial fulfillment of this prophecy.

Adventists, too, interpret these terms as three years and a half, but with their year-day theory they then view each day of this period as a year, so that they confound the counsel and become lost in all kinds of calculations. With this theory, which is devoid of all biblical ground, they come to 1,260 years; for a Jewish year, which is taken as the basis for their calculations, contains only 360 days. And these 1,260 years take them to the Edict of Emperor Justinianus by which in A.D. 533 he proclaimed the bishop of Rome as head of all the churches. But when we soberly ask what this fact contributes to the understanding of these words, then the answer is—nothing. Dr. A. Kuyper adheres to a symbolic interpretation and says this concerning this time reference:

> So, then, in this struggle the children of God, the elect, would be delivered into the hands of the Antichrist, and not just for a short while, but for a long-lasting period. The duration of this period now is indicated as consisting of three periods. First a time, then times, and then half a time. Now there have been those who quite rashly have interpreted that time as being three years and a half, three months and a half, or three days and a half, because since they wanted to apply it to Antiochus Epiphanes, they thought they could figure it out in such a way as to account for exactly such a short period in which Antiochus lost his power and went down. That was due to the fact that also with regard to the mention made of these three time periods they did not see the symbolism of it. A "time, times, and half a time" indicates 3 1/2 (1 + 2 + 1/2), and 3 1/2 is the half of seven, the holy number, which is the indication of God's dispensation regarding that which He as God ordains and carries out. The creation of the world in seven days remains here determinative. The Antichrist will try to imitate God by also attempting to accomplish a work in seven days but then to destroy the kingdom of God. But he will not succeed in this. He will not be given a chance to do so in seven days but in three days and a half. Already when he is only halfway, this Antichristian raging will be stopped and brought to nought. As Jesus declared, this antichristian tyranny will be shortened, for if these days were not shortened, even the church of the elect would perish.

With all due respect for Dr. Kuyper, and with all admiration for his inventiveness, we nevertheless cannot possibly accept his interpretation as being correct. For if we are to drag in the creation of the world when interpreting such a simple time designation, of which he himself says that it means "three and a half" and falls within the period of the Antichrist, we must wonder if this symbolical interpretation is not a bit too far-fetched and betrays too great a lack of artlessness and simplicity! For in that case the symbolical interpretation by Vitringa would be just as acceptable when he says:

> Here we have an allusion to the period of 3 1/2 years of famine and barrenness under Ahab, when the heavens gave no rain, when Elijah, the witness of truth who diligently opposed the idolatry of Israel, was fed by the ravens and the widow of Zarephath and the true church was as it were hid in the desert.

And again from the viewpoint of symbolical exegesis, Calvin in his interpretation is just as sure of himself when he interprets the little horn as referring to Julius Caesar and other Roman emperors and expresses as his opinion that here in general is predicted "that at God's determined time at last there will come an end to the disasters." We cannot refrain from observing that such a careful designation of time would be a very strange way of expressing that certain disasters would one day come to an end! The experiences of every day teach us clearly enough, and besides Scripture also teaches us that one day we shall receive a new heaven and a new earth in which righteousness will dwell. Then all calamities will have come to an end for sure!

All historical interpretations that apply this period to Antiochus Epiphanes, Mohammed, the pope, or Napoleon, and all the various symbolical interpretations, that make this exact time designation dissolve in fog, violate in greater or lesser degree the teaching of Scripture (not only here but also elsewhere) and hence we do not hesitate for one moment, regardless of our love for all godly theologians, to reject their interpretations. With regard to interpreting the future (and does not this whole section point to the future?), variations are hardly imaginable. There may be slight differences, but in the main all are in agreement that this time designation points to the second half of the year-week of Daniel, the three and a half years during which the Antichrist will rage most vehemently. Our grounds for this position are as follows:

1. We have here a literal interpretation of the symbols by the

angel himself. Is it not absurd, then, to look for a symbolical interpretation of a literal explanation provided us by Scripture?

2. All time designations have always been literally fulfilled, and hence we not only may but indeed must interpret those that have as yet not been fulfilled the same way. Since the scope of this book does not allow us to prove this extensively, we take the liberty to refer the reader to our book *Maranatha!*[1] Daniel and Revelation repeatedly refer to this event in the form of three years and a half, as it does here, forty-two months in Revelation 11:2; 13:5, half of a year-week in Daniel 7:25, and 1,260 days in Revelation 11:3 and 12:6. According to this phenomenon, time is to be taken literally, the same way we still do today.

3. This interpretation recommends itself by its simplicity and forthrightness, to say nothing of the unity of its defenders.

Verse 26 makes mention of the judgment of the man of sin. The events surrounding his appearing will be as follows. After having raged openly for three and a half years, the Lord Jesus will come down from heaven to destroy him, accompanied by His church which had previously been taken up into His presence. This will be done without hands, i.e., without human involvement (see 2:34; 8:25; 2 Thess. 2; Rev. 17; 19). Without any further ado and without any juridical process he and his helper, the false prophet, are cast into the lake of fire and brimstone.

Finally, verse 27 speaks once more of the glorious Messianic kingdom which commences at once after the extermination of the Antichrist. For that kingdom we pray daily in the petition, "Thy kingdom come!" Originally, it was God's intention that man would be a king upon the earth. After a fearsome struggle which will last for ages and ages, this glorious goal will at last be obtained. The Lord not only delivers His people, but He also makes them kings together with Christ. "The kingdoms of this world are become the kingdoms of our Lord, and of his Christ" (Rev. 11:15). And Christ's people will reign with Him on earth (1Cor. 6:1-6; Rev. 5:10; 20:4; 18 and 20). All dominions, we are told in the last part of verse 27, will then pay homage to Christ, His kingdom and His people, and be subject to them. The dying

---

1. Harry Bultema, *Maranatha! A Study of Unfulfilled Prophecy*. Grand Rapids: Kregel Publications, 1985.

patriarch, Jacob, already prophesied on his deathbed that one day all nations will obey Shiloh. All of creation is still as in travail, but its sighs will soon turn into joyful songs. The nations may still rage against each other, but soon they will be submissive to Christ; they will also have peace among themselves and beat their swords into spades and their spears into sickles (see Isa. 2 and Mic. 4).

A very important but often neglected statement in verse 27 is that the kingdom is given to the saints. That will rule out all Pelagian fanatic attempts at establishing the kingdom of God, and also all arrogance and presumptions of Rome, the Anabaptists, and the Mormons. In principle and by rights all things are ours (1Cor. 3:22, 23), but factually the government of the world will not be given us until Christ Himself has assumed His kingship.

The last verse of this chapter tells us that the dream and the angel's interpretation are ended. Daniel says once more that he was very much shaken by this experience: the loathsome figures of the four monsters, their emergence from the rolling sea upon the beach and their raging, and the crushing judgment upon them. All these things shook the man of God, but especially the persecution of the saints must have touched him to the quick. This was even visible on his face. His countenance changed, that is to say, the color of his face changed on account of what he saw. He turned pale from inner emotion. The same thing was said of Belshazzar (5:9), but how different were the causes in both cases. Different causes may result in the same outward effects. In the king's case it was a sorrow unto death, but in Daniel's case it was a sorrow unto sanctification; for he kept the matter in his heart. The matter itself, namely the dream and its interpretation, he inscribed indelibly on his mind. They became a source of holy reflection. He did not roughly tell these truths to the heathen, for they could easily have ridiculed them. Besides, everything was not clear to himself yet. Hence, he meditated and reflected on it all the more, constantly asking light from on high on the future of his beloved nation. Centuries later a young Israelite virgin did the same thing (Luke 2:19). May we follow their example while studying this prophecy!

Chapter 8
THE PERSIAN RAM AND THE GREEK HE-GOAT

Daniel at Shushan

In the third year of the reign of king Belshazzar a vision appeared unto me, even unto me, Daniel, after that which appeared unto me at the first. And I saw in a vision; and it came to pass, when I saw, that I was at Shushan in the palace, which is in the province of Elam; and I saw in a vision, and I was by the river of Ulai (vv. 1, 2).

With this chapter the prophet again resumes writing in Hebrew. The things concerning and referring to the Babylonians more than to Israel he wrote in their language; the things which were of more concern to the Hebrews are written in Hebrew. The first half of Daniel deals more with the realm of common grace, while the second half deals more with particular grace.

The time at which Daniel received this vision was during the year of the frivolous king Belshazzar. Hence, that was two years after his remarkable dream visions concerning the four world dominions described in the previous chapter. Before, Daniel had always acted as the interpreter of the visions others had received.

He says he was at Shushan in the province of Elam. Shushan was the capital of Elam and the place of residence of the Persian kings. This city is well known to us, for the whole history of Esther, Mordecai, and Haman transpired there, and the noble man Nehemiah served there as the butler of the king (Neh. 1:1). The city was built along the river. The so-called mausoleum of Daniel is allegedly still found there. Shushan lay in the land of Elam, the old name for Persia, as Elam was the most important province of Persia. According to the table of nations in Genesis 10, the Elamites were descendants of Elam, Shem's oldest son.

It deserves notice that the prophet tells us three times in these verses that he saw a vision. This time he did not receive a dream but was in a state of wakefulness. So he did not receive a dream in a state of unconsciousness but a vision in a wakeful state. Hence there is some difference between his earlier vision and now, both as to form and contents. Then he dreamed; now he was awake; then he saw wild beasts, now only tame animals; then he saw all four world monarchies, now he received a further description of the second and third world powers. The tenor of both was the same, however, namely the instruction and comfort for the people of the Lord—in the first place for Israel, but still for us today.

He pinpoints the place still further when he says he was by the flood or the lake of Ulai (Dutch version; King James version: "by the river of Ulai"). Some people think he was there only in the spirit, like Ezekiel who lived in Babylon but was frequently in the spirit in Jerusalem; but there is nothing which compels us to think this. There is nothing that forbids us to believe he really tarried there bodily. The Ulai or Euleus is a river which flows beside Shushan and joins a little further down with a few other streams and thus forms a lake. The banks of rivers seemed to be suitable places to receive visions (see Ezek. 1:3 and Dan. 10:4).

If we, with many other exegetes, prefer to think Daniel was not really at this place, but that he merely saw himself transported there in the spirit, then we cannot advance sufficient objections against it. It can even be said in favor of it that this indeed occasionally happened to other prophets; and quite often to Ezekiel who in a state of prophetic ecstasy saw himself transported from Babylon to Jerusalem. In the same way Daniel could have found himself in Babylon, while his spirit was transported to the fortress of Shushan. There is no certainty concerning this matter.

Two Horns—Two Great Powers

Then I lifted up mine eyes, and saw, and, behold, there stood before the river a ram which had two horns: and the two horns were high; but one was higher than the other, and the higher came up last. I saw the ram pushing westward, and northward, and southward; so that no beasts might stand before him, neither was there any that could deliver out of his hand; but he did according to his will, and became great (vv. 3, 4).

"Then I lifted up mine eyes, and saw, and, behold." This is an example of the peculiar style of the Bible which usually depicts things in a lively manner and puts them so before our eyes. Dry descriptions are not found in the Bible; its holy authors always place the facts before our eyes as a painting. That is why it uses the word "behold" so often, and expressions such as "He opened his mouth and said;" "She lifted up her voice and wept;" "He inclined his ear," etc. "An Easterner saw and described facts preferably as already done in the past, but as incomplete, as still taking place. In his mind he relived the past once again with his readers" (L. Berkhof). That is why we find the word "seen" in this short sentence up to three times. At the same time it contains a hint that we, too, must rivet our own eye with him on the ram. Apparently, the ram was standing at the bank on the other side of the river, across from the prophet, so that he cast an eye first on the long horns of the animal.

We already came across horns in the preceding chapter as symbols of power and dominion (7:24). Israel was a people of herders and for that reason horned animals and horns appear often in the symbolism of Scripture. Thus the often-used expression "to exalt the horn to honor," make powerful and courageous (1 Sam. 2:1, 10; Ps. 89:17, 24; Ps. 92:10; Ps. 112:9); "to cut off the horn," to disarm, make defenseless, humble (Jer. 48:25; Lam 2:3); "to make the horn to bud" indicates to supply victory, deliverance, salvation. Thus in the Old Testament the Messiah is frequently presented as a budding horn (Ps. 132:17; Ezek. 29:21; Luke 1:69).

So when it is said that this ram had two long horns, we can conclude from it that they symbolized two great powers. Among the exegetes there is great unanimity that this ram represents the second or Medo-Persian monarchy, and that these two horns point to the combined power of this kingdom. This is emphatically told us in verse 20.

When it says that the one horn is longer that the other, we see how beautifully the one part of Daniel's prophecy agrees with the other. In the world statue of Nebuchadnezzar, the union was indicated by the two sides and the right and left arm. In the dream vision of the preceding chapter, the bear lifted himself up on one side. Thus we find here the one horn higher than the other. That is an indication of the greater power of the Persians over the Medes, for in the prophecies of Isaiah and Jeremiah, Cyrus is always presented as the conqueror of the world who will put an end to Babylon's power.

When it says that the higher came up last, this agrees perfectly with history, for it was not Cyrus and the Persians who were the mightiest at first, but the Medes. We need not wonder that the critics transpose this prophet to the time after the downfall of the Medo-Persian monarchy, for if they accept that he lived during the exile, then they are forced to accept the reality of literally fulfilled prophecy, and they do not want to do so at any price. So they much rather consider this prophecy not to be genuine and declare Daniel to be a falsifier, even though no one less than Christ Himself called him a prophet.

Daniel saw further that the ram was pushing with his horns, i.e., waging war. The ram is said to come from the east and this agrees completely with what Isaiah says of Cyrus. In Isaiah 41:2 Cyrus is presented as "the righteous man from the east." In Isaiah 46:11 we read, "Calling a ravenous bird from the east, the man that executeth my counsel from a far country," which also means Cyrus. Persia lay east of Babylon and consequently all Cyrus' conquests spread to the west as far as the Mediterranean Sea. Cyrus did not make many conquests to the north. But then the ram is not a representation of Cyrus but of the Medo-Persian monarchy, and Darius Hystaspes waged war against the northern Scythes and the Armenians, so that here it can also be said that the ram pushed northward. When it is said the ram pushed southward, this undoubtedly refers to the martial activity of Cambyses, who conquered Egypt and Ethiopia, so it could be said of Ahasuerus that he ruled from India to the land of the Moors (Esth. 1:1).

The result of all this bucking by the Medo-Persian ram was that no beasts, i.e., no nations, could stand before him. As conqueror of the nations this animal made himself very great. The book of Esther tells us something of the greatness of this monarchy. At the time of Ahasuerus, his realm contained 127 provinces (Esth. 1:1).

Alexander the Great

And as I was considering, behold, an he-goat came from the west on the face of the whole earth, and touched not the ground: and the goat had a notable horn between his eyes. And he came to the ram that had two horns, which I had seen standing before the river, and ran unto him in the fury of his power. And I saw him

come close unto the ram, and he was moved with choler against him, and smote the ram, and brake his two horns: and there was no power in the ram to stand before him, but he cast him down to the ground, and stamped upon him: and there was none that could deliver the ram out of his hand (vv. 5-7).

This section describes the Greek he-goat and his victory over the Medo-Persian ram. Both history and Scripture tell us this can mean only the Greco-Macedonian world power under Alexander the Great. See verse 21 of this chapter which gives an interpretation of this he-goat. It is well-nigh incomprehensible that some exegetes want to identify him with someone other than Alexander.

Daniel had watched this bucking ram with keen eyes. Observant and with rapt attention he had become engrossed to the depths of his soul in this vision which was still puzzling to him. We must not forget that the first world monarchy was still extant when he saw this ram coming from the east and heading for the west, hence also for Babylon, with leveled horns. But when his soul was still contemplating this ram, he saw still another animal approaching.

A he-goat came running from the west. Greece lay west of the Medo-Persian kingdom. In the East he-goats usually headed the flocks, according to Jeremiah 50:8, and for that reason they appear often in Scripture in a figurative sense as symbols or images of imperious rulers (see Prov. 30:31; Ezek. 34:17; Zech. 10:3; Matt. 25:32). The symbol of a he-goat was particularly fitting for the Macedonian conqueror, because there were numerous flocks of goats grazing in Macedonia. The Greeks were called Aegeans or goat people, and a he-goat was represented on their national coat of arms and escutcheon. Alexander called his own son Aegus, He-goat, and the sea that washed the shore of Macedonia was called the Aegean Sea or He-goat Sea. Most recently coins have been found which carry the image of a he-goat. Hence for several reasons the he-goat was a very fitting symbol of the Greco-Macedonian world empire under Alexander the Great.

The he-goat crossed the whole earth and ran so lightning fast that his feet did not seem to touch the ground. We must be amazed that again and again Scripture in this prophecy succeeds in describing in so few words and accurate manner great and awesome events. As in the preceding chapter, the four-winged leopard indicated the great swiftness of Alexander, so in this brief clause is told again that Alexander, quick as lightning, flew across and subjugated the world. Much later another great commander said of himself, "I came, I saw, I conquered"—this applied in an even greater measure to this world conqueror.

Humanly speaking, the swift conquering of the world was a sheer impossibility. For in the spring of the year 334 B.C. there advanced across the Hellespont, to fly at the throat of Asia, a young man of a little over twenty years of age with a small army of some 30,000 men and few supplies of arms and food. Soon the extremely rich king of Persia with his immense armies was confronting him (11:2), but the Greco-Macedonian he-goat was destined by God to conquer the Medo-Persian ram. And when God works, who can prevent it? He is great in counsel and mighty in deeds. "None can stay his hand, or say unto him, What doest thou?" (4:35). How often has He shown in the history of the world that He can conquer by means of little as well as by means of much. He does not need to be served by the hands of men as though He were lacking anything.

> The Persian world power is not accompanied by a Persian world culture; the dominion of the Persians is of a political and not of a religious nature. Only to Alexander the Great it would be granted to combine both aspects in his world dominion and thereby to lay the foundation for the universal cultural unity which kept the peoples from east and west together (H. Woltjer).

It is generally thought—and stated in verse 21—that reference is made to the person of Alexander himself in the words, "the notable," or protruding, sharp, pointed, horn. Just as a he-goat has all his defensive power in his horns, so the Greco-Macedonian world dominion owed all its strength and victory to Alexander, who may be considered both the founder and the embodiment of this monarchy. When it is said that the horn stood between his eyes, this may be a reference to Alexander's great strategic talents and political acumen. He had been instructed by the renowned philosopher, Aristotle, in all the sciences of that time. Maybe the reference includes all his wise advisers as well.

The prophet further describes the battle against and the victory over the he-goat. With great fury and vehemence he came charging at the ram. There existed an irreconcilable hatred between the

Greeks and the Persians. Daniel saw that he inflicted stab after stab until he broke both horns of the ram and rendered it completely defenseless. After that he had an easy task; he threw the ram to the ground and stamped and trampled him into the dirt so none could deliver him out of the goat's power. Familiarity with Alexander's military pursuits shows how literally this was fulfilled.

Josephus records that after the conquest of Tyre, Alexander came marching to Jerusalem, because the Jews had refused to help him at the siege of Tyre, which had cost him more time and troops than the conquest of all of Persia. After the conquest the high priest Jaddua (most likely the same person as mentioned by name in Nehemiah 12:11) together with another priest went to meet Alexander in a festive parade and showed the world conqueror the biblical prophecy referring to him. This took away Alexander's furious anger, so that he entered the city in a peaceful manner and told the priests to bring sacrifices according to their laws; and he bestowed various favors on them.

The veracity of this story is beyond doubt and ought not be questioned. Zechariah 9:1-8 refers to the same event. In the battle of Arbela in the fall of 331 B.C. the lot of the Medo-Persian kingdom was finally and definitely decided. Alexander with his small and seemingly underpowered army gained a great victory over Darius Codomanus' army which was allegedly twenty times stronger than Alexander's.

Fall of Alexander

Therefore the he-goat waxed very great: and when he was strong, the great horn was broken; and for it came up four notable ones toward the four winds of heaven (v. 8).

In this single verse mention is made of the pinnacle and the decline of Alexander's world monarchy. Alexander's greed for conquest knew no bounds. It is said he wept because there were no more worlds to conquer than the one he had already conquered. His insatiable thirst for military fame even made him undertake an expedition to India. With an army of 120,000 men he crossed the Indus, but at the Ganges his Greek warriors were sick and tired of the campaign and refused obstinately to continue their expedition. At that time it was not the will of God that India also would experience the enlightening influence of Greek culture.

So Alexander had become exceedingly great. He gained greater and more extensive victories than either Nebuchadnezzar or Cyrus. In history he is recorded as a unique and unequaled war hero.

But when the Greco-Macedonian he-goat was at the pinnacle of his power and dominion, his great horn broke. It is not said, as in the case of the Medo-Persian ram, that his horn had been broken by someone else, because Alexander was not brought down by another world conqueror, but was cut down in the midst of his years by the hand of God and his own dissolute way of life.

The man who in the span of some twelve years subjugated the world to himself could not control his own temper and passions. The winged panther was sometimes horribly cruel and his excessive drinking caused an early death. From his history it is very obvious that he, like Nebuchadnezzar and Cyrus, was an instrument in God's hand to carry out His counsel.

> The voice said, Cry. And he said, What shall I cry? All flesh is grass, and all the goodliness thereof is as the flower of the field: The grass withereth, the flower fadeth: because the spirit of the Lord bloweth upon it: surely the people is grass. The grass withereth, the flower fadeth: but the word of our God shall stand forever (Isa. 40:6-8).

There had been no one like Alexander. And being aware of that, he even called himself the son of the gods and the son of Jupiter, but the scythe of death mowed him down like grass. With his death the unity and the glory of his world monarchy was done for.

The second part of verse 8 points out that after his death his kingdom was divided into four parts. In the place of the one great horn four notable horns appeared, pointing in the direction of the four points of the compass. The realm was divided among Alexander's generals:

- Seleucus received Babylon, Syria, and the realm bordering India in the east.
- Ptolemaeus received Egypt, Libya, Arabia, Palestine and Coel-Syria in the south.
- Cassander received Macedonia and Greece in the west.
- Lysimachus received Thracia and Asia Minor in the north (see further v. 22 and 11:3, 4).

The Little Horn

And out of one of them came forth a little horn, which waxed exceeding great, toward the south, and toward the east, and toward the pleasant land. And it waxed great, even to the host of heaven; and it cast down some of the host and of the stars to the ground, and stamped upon them. Yea, he magnified himself even to the prince of the host, and by him the daily sacrifice was taken away, and the place of his sanctuary was cast down. And an host was given him against the daily sacrifice by reason of transgression, and it cast down the truth to the ground; and it practised, and prospered (vv. 9-12).

Here we are confronted again by one of the crosses in Daniel's prophecy. Who is this little horn of Daniel 8? The great majority of exegetes view it as a designation of Antiochus Epiphanes. The smaller half of them are divided into those who identify it with Antiochus the Great, the papacy, Mohammed, Antichrist, and the king of the north mentioned in chapter 11. A few, such as Bettex and Haldeman, identify it with great peremptoriness with the Antichrist. The latter says:

> The attempt of a certain school of expositors to make the little horn of Daniel 8 distinct from the little horn of Daniel 7 is a piece of disastrous contradictory and confusing exegesis conceived in absolute error and certain to darken counsel with words without knowledge.

For various reasons this is put far too strongly. It seems to us that here we do not have the same thing as there. To mention but one thing: no little horn comes up at the end of the fourth world monarchy, whereas this one comes up out of one of the four main kingdoms of the third world monarchy, the Greco-Macedonian. Whereas there a description is given of the judgment by which the little horn is destroyed, here such a description is missing completely. We believe, then, that here we are definitely to think in the first place of the Syrian king, Antiochus Epiphanes, who perhaps more than any other ruler oppressed the holy nation of Israel. No more than the ram and the he-goat are wild, predatory animals have the Medo-Persian and Alexander's empire ever conducted themselves as predators over against God's people; but this horror which came up out of the third world monarchy raged all the more against Israel. Josephus and the first book of the

Maccabees tell us about the persecution and the contumely the Lord's people suffered at the hands of this king, and Hebrews 11:35 alludes to it. The first book of the Maccabees, although not infallible like Scripture, is generally considered a trustworthy story. Although our forefathers introduced the Apocrypha with a note of warning, they nevertheless included them in one binding in the [Dutch] States Bible. The books of the Maccabees deserve far more attention than they commonly receive. Especially the first chapter of the first book, which sheds light on these verses.

However much everyone must agree that the first chapter of Maccabees shed some light on these difficult verses, yet, it seems to us, everyone can be convinced that they cannot be the complete fulfillment of what we are told here. We at least are convinced that they do refer, first of all, to Antiochus but that they do not stop there. We must view him as a type, a shadowy prophecy of the Antichrist. We base this on the following considerations:

1. Antiochus Epiphanes was a far too insignificant figure for his being the fulfillment of these verses. The name Epiphanes, which means (the) brilliant or shining (one) was changed by the people to Epimanes, (the) crazy (one). He could not be called exceeding great, magnified even to the prince of the host. All these expressions point to a very unique greatness.

2. It seems to us verse 17 contains the key to these verses, where the angel says, "Understand, O son of man: for at the time of the end shall be the vision," which means that the fulfillment of this vision will commence in the end-time, as the Latin, German, Dutch, and other translations have it. Furthermore, this chapter constantly points to the time of the end (see vv. 19, 23, 26). "The time of the end" is a standing expression in Daniel for the time of the Antichrist (see 9:26; 11:35, 40, 45; 12:4, 6, 9). It is the time of the last year-week of Daniel and particularly the second half of it.

3. The description given here is strongly reminiscent of those which we find elsewhere in Scripture of the Antichrist:

- He will come at the time when the transgressors are come to the full (v. 23; cf. 2 Thess. 2:3).
- Here again the success of this horn is pointed out. It prospered (vv. 7 and 24; cf. 7:21).
- His self-magnifications exceeded all bounds, according to verse 25 (cf. 2 Thess. 2:3ff).

4. We can point to the general rule that prophecy never stops with the historical events but always, even if it is only in a typical manner, points to the great end event. World and church history simply are not subjects of divine predictions. On these grounds we believe that here is found a partial fulfillment in Antiochus Epiphanes, but that the full event will take place with the Antichrist.

Thus Antiochus is a type of the Antichrist. Just as the Old Testament contains numerous shadowy types who point to Christ, so in all of Scripture and in history there are many persons who were adumbrations of the Antichrist, because they greatly opposed the Lord and His people. We mention some of them: Cain, Lamech, Nimrod, Chedorlaomer, Saul, Absalom, Rabshakeh, the Assyrian kings in the Old Testament, Antiochus Epiphanes in the intertestamentarian time, and Herod, Pilate and Judas in the New Testament. In history such types are to be found in the Roman emperors, specifically Nero, and further Mohammed, the popes, Napoleon, Nietzsche, and others. From this phenomenon can be concluded that the Antichrist is not a single personality but a series of personalities or even a system. Nay, one day the many antichrists will converge in the one superman, the man of sin.

We will see more in chapters 9 and 11 about this, but the observation here is not superfluous that the Antichrist will most of all persecute restored Israel in Palestine, as the words sanctuary and sacrifice clearly indicate.

Desolation—How Long?

Then I heard one saint speaking, and another saint said unto that certain saint which spake, How long shall be the vision concerning the daily sacrifice, and the transgression of desolation, to give both the sanctuary and the host to be trodden under foot? And he said unto me, Unto two thousand and three hundred days; then shall the sanctuary be cleansed (vv. 13-14).

The man of God had to behold terrible things. We had seen that one enemy of his nation devastated the beautiful land, Palestine. He cast down to earth the stars—the priests and rulers of his people—and trampled them under foot. He disrupted the temple and its sacrifices. Daniel had seen that this proud enemy opposed and resisted Israel's God Himself as well as His truth, and succeeded only too well in his devilish work. On account of the apostasy—for this is the meaning of the first part of verse 12— many were given over to him as a prey, as victims.

All these things upset Daniel terribly, and now it was inevitable that the question arose as to how long all this would last. To this unspoken question of his soul an answer is given him in these verses. The Lord in His Word answers many questions which he sees lying on the bottom of our souls. Thus here, too, He satisfied Daniel's secret wish even before he formulated a prayer.

The Lord reveals His truth to us by means of our senses of sight and hearing. All the shadows, types, and visions and the two sacraments are geared to our sense of seeing. But there are many truths less suitable or, rather, unsuitable to the sense of sight, and then God does not let us see but hear. This is true of all of the preaching of the crucified One, who must be depicted in pure preaching rather than in beautiful pictures. At least that was Paul's conviction (Gal. 3:1).

In this prophecy God is not only the hidden One to His people but also the silent One. Here we do not hear His voice itself, for He always makes use of intermediaries; of watchmen, saints, and angels. Thus Daniel overheard a conversation between a saint and an unknown person. There is no doubt that we must think of the saint as an angel (see also 4:13; 10:5). God's angels are extremely interested in the salvation and holiness of men (Luke 15:7; 1Cor. 11:10; Eph. 3:10; 1Peter 1:12). And this unknown person asked how long a period was covered by this vision concerning the daily sacrifice and the transgression of desolation, and how long the sanctuary and the host would be trodden under foot.

It is not said who this unknown person was. In the original language we find the name *Palmoni*, which means wondrous calculator or discoverer of wonders. This is the only place where this word appears. There are some who take it to mean Christ Himself, who in Isaiah 9:6 is also called "Pele," or Wonderful and who is also the Revealer of the secrets of the Father. We do not wish to deny with any degree of certainty that we have here a shadowy reference to the Lord Jesus Christ, for we do know that the Old Testament is filled with such allusions.

With regard to Messianic prophecy there are two extremes which must be scrupulously avoided. Some commentators see

Christ nowhere in the Old Testament; others see Him referred to everywhere. In our opinion the truth lies somewhere in between. We find shadowy and mysterious references to Him everywhere, and in our opinion here also. For if this were an allusion to an ordinary angel, there would have been no reason at all to refer to him with such a unique name. The view that the next verse shows that Daniel is meant by the unmentioned one (Dutch version; KJV: "that certain saint") is in any case something we cannot agree with at all.

Verse 14 contains the answer to the question by the unmentioned one. He obviously had asked that question for the benefit of Daniel, for the answer is given to Daniel. It is not too clear who of the two gives this answer, the first saint or the unmentioned one. The natural deduction seems to be that it was the first one. The answer itself is, "Unto two thousand and three hundred days; then shall the sanctuary be cleansed." Practically infinite is the number of interpretations given of these words. We come across the wildest reflections on this matter and by far the most of these speculations have done incalculable harm to a calm, sober treatment of prophecy.

William Miller, the father of Adventism, with the aid of his year-day theory, calculated on the basis of this text the end of this world which, according to him, would take place in 1843. He calculated this from the time reference given in Daniel 9:25 plus 2,300 years to the year mentioned. He viewed the cleansing (that is to say, the restoration, sanctification, purification) of the sanctuary as the burning of heaven and earth. The whole theory, which makes a day into a year, is false. It is based on only two exceptional and symbolical texts, namely, Numbers 14:34 and Ezekiel 4:6. And what is mentioned there as an exception they make into a standard rule which they allow to govern the interpretation of all prophecy. But even granted that this theory could be applied elsewhere, in any case it cannot be done here, for days are not even mentioned here but evenings and mornings (Dutch version; King James version does have "days"), to wit, evening and morning sacrifices. And even if we were to translate this clause as days, then this would still mean ordinary days, for when Hebrew uses the terms evening and morning in connection with the word day, it always refers to an ordinary day.

Miller and the so-called Millerites were proved wrong. Christ did not return in 1843 and the world was not burned then. But instead of acknowledging that Miller was a false prophet in this regard, and that his whole calculation and the basis it rests on is absolutely no good, the Seventh-day Adventists appealed once more to this text for their so-called sanctuary theory. This theory maintains that Christ came again in 1843 but that He did not come to earth, but rather to the heavenly sanctuary which He is now cleansing. As soon as He is finished with that He will come down to the earth, according to them. But Scripture teaches us clearly that Christ has been in heaven for over nineteen hundred years and, sitting at the right of God, has already brought about the cleansing (see Mark 16:19; Luke 25:51; Acts 1:9; Heb. 1:3; 8:1; 10:12; 12:2). Adventism is completely unbiblical, although it must be said in defense of Miller that he did not know of the sanctuary theory at that time. The fact that people preferably, if not exclusively, pounce on difficult texts like these while often ignoring the Gospels and Epistles is already very suspect in itself.

The able student of prophecy, Dr. Scofield, says of Daniel 8:10-14, "This passage is confessedly the most difficult in prophecy." Maybe not everyone agrees with that, but it is a fact that it is very difficult. The explanation which may be called the simplest and agrees most exactly with other unfulfilled prophecy is this: These 2,300 evening and morning sacrifices, figuring two sacrifices per day, point to a cessation of the temple service, or 1,150 days, hence three years and two months. Rounding this figure off, this would be about three years and a half. According to Josephus this is the time during which the temple service was interrupted due to the raging of Antiochus Epiphanes. First Maccabees 4:36-61 gives a description of the cleansing of the temple. Thus, according to many commentators, this prophecy already obtained its literal fulfillment at that time.

We feel this was only the temporary fulfillment, and the complete fulfillment will not come until the time of the Antichrist. Just as in Matthew 24 and Luke 21 the destruction of Jerusalem and the return of the Lord are intricately connected and even imperceptibly flow together, so here also the raging of Antiochus and of the Antichrist run together. The Antichrist will rage during the second half of Daniel's year-week (see 9:27). That will be the time of the Great Tribulation (Dan. 12:1; Matt. 24:15-28; Rev. 3:6–19). Israel, which then will have returned but is still not converted, will see the temple service being suspended. But after that specified time, Christ by His coming will "justify" (Dutch version; KJV: "cleanse") the sanctuary by His entering it (Hag. 2:10; Mal. 3:1).

Make This Man Understand

And it came to pass, when I, even I Daniel, had seen the vision, and sought for the meaning, then, behold, there stood before me as the appearance of a man. And I heard a man's voice between the banks of Ulai, which called, and said, Gabriel, make this man to understand the vision. So he came near where I stood: and when he came, I was afraid, and fell upon my face: but he said unto me, Understand, O son of man: for at the time of the end shall be the vision. Now as he was speaking with me, I was in a deep sleep on my face toward the ground: but he touched me, and set me upright (vv. 15-18).

Daniel is the total opposite of many Christians, for his soul never had rest until he understood the meaning of the prophecy; but many Christians consider a person not quite normal when he applies himself with all seriousness to the study of unfulfilled prophecy. Although the Lord in His condescending goodness has given us the light of prophecy that shines in a dark place, many people warn us against it as a dangerous area or as belonging to the secret things which belong only to the Lord God. And there are very many who think that the prophecies are very impractical since, according to them, they will not be understood until they are being fulfilled. Daniel, however, had the constant desire to understand them. And his writings supply us with many a glorious example of how God always fulfills that desire. This is also the case here.

Suddenly there stood before him "the appearance of a man." The text does not say who this man was. He may have been a common angel, the archangel Michael, or even the Christ before His incarnation. It seems to us the last-mentioned idea is most likely a veiled appearance of the coming Savior. Hence we find throughout all of Scripture similar references to a Man, who with more or less clarity indicates the Savior (see Isa. 53:3; 32:2; Ezek. 9:2, 3, 11; 22:30; Zech. 6:12; 13:7). Also in the New Testament the name Man is often used with reference to Christ (Rev. 12:5). Theologians hold the opinion that this name contains an allusion to the fact that it was not the disobedience of the woman but of the man that was determinative for the fall of the whole human race, and that now the Man is the second Adam who obtains for Himself a new mankind by his incarnation, suffering, and death. In all of the Old Testament it is evident that God looks for a Man who can wall up the breach sin has struck.

Daniel hears further the voice of a man who exclaimed, "Gabriel, make this man to understand the vision!" When it is said that the voice came from between "the Ulai" (Dutch version), this means from between the banks of the river, hence as floating over the stream or hovering on it. The text does not say whose voice it is, but it appears to us it is the unmentionable one of a while ago, the appearance of a man, and the man's voice all point to one and the same holy person. For that this voice did not come from an ordinary angel is evident from the fact that he gives commands to Gabriel, the prince of God. The critics have the opinion that Daniel was afflicted with Chaldean superstitions and for that reason he thought to see so many angels and to hear so many voices, but we believers in Scripture know that the Lord has a rich world of mighty spirits who obey the voice of His Word and who are sent to serve those who inherit salvation. Thus here a prince of God is given the command to satisfy the longing of Daniel and give him the desired interpretation of the vision. Kuyper says:

> Concerning this Gabriel there have been of old three opinions in the church. By far the most exegetes view him as a "created angel" who belongs to the seven most eminent angels and is called Gabriel. On the other hand there are those who although they also consider him a "created angel" deny that Gabriel is a proper name. Gabriel means, they say, "man of God" and they would prefer to translate Daniel 8:16 thus, "Thou man of God, make Daniel to understand the vision." Finally, still others view Gabriel as an "uncreated being" and venture the opinion if Gabriel might not be the Holy Spirit, as Michael then would be the second Person in the holy Trinity.

The last-mentioned opinion is no longer held by anyone. The idea that Gabriel is not a proper name but a generic name also finds few defenders. Almost all conservative, orthodox exegetes are agreed that he indicates a special strong angel by the name of Gabriel, the prince of God.

Gabriel obeyed. He came closer to be able to speak to Daniel. But man, in the state of his humiliation, cannot have familiar intercourse with the higher world. Manoah and his wife and the godly shepherds in Bethlehem's fields were deathly scared when an angel visited them. Jesus' most beloved disciple who had often lain at his bosom fell as one dead at the feet of his glorified Master. That which is corruptible must first have put on incorruption, and that which is mortal, immortality, before the full communion between that higher and this lower world can exist. We see also that this greatly beloved man was so terrified that he crashed down to the earth on his face (cf. 10:7, 8; Ezek. 1:28; Rev. 1:17).

The angel had been charged, however, to give Daniel the interpretation, and he obeyed that command: "Understand, O son of man: for at the time of the end shall be the vision." We already gave as our opinion that this verse contains the key to the explanation of this vision. In the Book of Daniel the time of the end is the standard expression for the time of the Antichrist. We might also translate it, "This vision will be interpreted in the end-time." This expression alone already forbids us to stop at the time of Antiochus Epiphanes.

When the angel was speaking thus to Daniel, the latter fell down, totally stupefied from dismay, before the angel of God. Here we need not suppose that Daniel had a very weak constitution, nor that this was a preventative measure against pride on account of this vision. We need only recall the scare mentioned in the preceding verse with regard to the higher world, and in addition the fiery love of Daniel for his people, which upon hearing about this unheard-of and long-lasting suffering received a terrible shock (see also v. 27). This fainting spell of Daniel is called by Bishop Newton "an irrefutable proof that the persecutions under Antiochus cannot possibly be the main contents and sole meaning of this prophecy." If it may not be an "irrefutable proof," it is in any case a strong allusion to a much more terrifying time than that of the foolish king Antiochus. The end of verse 18 tells us that Gabriel took pity on the swooning prophet. He touched him lightly, brought him back to consciousness, and placed him on his feet so that he could continue his explanation.

A King of Fierce Countenance

And he said, Behold, I will make thee know what shall be in the last end of the indignation: for at the time appointed the end shall be. The ram which thou sawest having two horns are the kings of Media and Persia. And the rough goat is the king of Grecia: and the great horn that is between his eyes is the first king. Now that being broken, whereas four stood up for it, four kingdoms shall stand up out of the nation, but not in his power. And in the latter time of their kingdom, when the transgressors are come to the full, a king of fierce countenance, and understanding dark sentences, shall stand up. And his power shall be mighty, but not by his own power: and he shall destroy wonderfully, and shall prosper, and practise, and shall destroy the mighty and the holy people. And through his policy also he shall cause craft to prosper in his hand; and he shall magnify himself in his heart, and by peace shall destroy many: he shall also stand up against the Prince of princes; but he shall be broken without hand. And the vision of the evening and the morning which was told is true: wherefore shut thou up the vision; for it shall be for many days (vv. 19-26).

Before the angel began his interpretation, he reminded him once again of what was emphasized in verse 17 and what we called the key to this vision. His purpose was not merely to say that God's wrath will not last forever, and that one day there will come an end to Israel's miseries. According to many exegetes that is all that is meant here, but such an exegesis does not do justice to the words. For verse 19 literally says Gabriel will make known what shall be in the last end of the indignation. That is also the way the Greek, Latin, and other translations have put it. Luther has, "how it will go at the time of the last anger," and the French translation by G. Martin, "that which shall come to pass at the end of the indignation." Van Hamelsveld has "what will happen at these last calamities and rage." Van der Palm translates the expression in question as "in the last days of the wrath." And this learned translator renders the last clause of verse 19 thus: "for it is to the appointed time of the end," and makes the following note, "The manner of speaking is completely of the same meaning as the expression in verse 17, "the time of the end," and it would be arbitrary to translate here, "at the appointed time the end will be." Especially in the prophets the word *moeed* often refers to far-off times (see 11:27, 35; Hab. 2:3). Hence without wishing to deny that with this expression here the thought is first of all the evil times of Antiochus Epiphanes, we nevertheless wish to maintain our opinion expressed previously, being based on the words themselves, that here we are to think of the time of the Antichrist, when the times of the Gentiles (Luke 21:24; Rev. 16:14) have sped by and the course of Israel's history will be resumed.

Verses 20, 21 give us a very brief interpretation of the vision of the ram and the he-goat. Hence concerning these two world powers there can in the main be no difference of opinion. For an exposition of these verses we refer to our remarks on verses 3-9.

We must keep in mind that the word "king" in the book of Daniel means not merely a high-ranking head of government but, the majestic head, the embodiment of his entire kingdom. Consequently, it is often used, as in this case, for the kingdom itself. The prophets know nothing of constitutional monarchs who rule by the fiat of the people, except maybe in the case of the ten kings of the ten toes of the world image. Hence, the hairy he-goat is not merely Philippus, the father of Alexander, but all of the kingdom of Greece.

Just picture the situation. Greece at that time was at the pinnacle of its glory. Poets and philosophers looked back with ardent longing to the eminent culture of old Hellas. In all high schools and colleges the golden age of Pericles is conjured up and depicted in brilliant colors before the students. But when we soberly ask the question, What does God say about it, then the answer is, all of Greece was a rough, hairy, stinking he-goat, a loathsome creature! Christians are called to be like dear children, followers of Christ (Eph. 5:1). That means in their evaluation of Greece's culture they are to follow Him. All that is high in the estimate of men is an abomination to God. That is what the hairy goat teaches us.

Nobody lingers near a butting and a rough ram, and, therefore, the divine interpreter hurried to get on with his explanation. In our remarks on verse 8 we already pointed out the fulfillment of verse 22. All Christian commentators view the four kingdoms after Alexander's death, which never attained the extent and power of Alexander's kingdom, as the literal fulfillment of these words.

The explanation of the little horn takes up the greatest place in Gabriel's interpretation. He paid more attention to it than to the second and third kingdoms. That, too, indicates someone greater and more terrible than Antiochus Epiphanes.

Verse 23 first makes two allusions to the time of his appearance. He will come on the scene in the latter time of the four kingdoms. The Latin translation has *et post regnum.* Luther translates, "After these kingdoms," which undoubtedly reflects the meaning well. The second allusion to the time of the little horn then is when the transgressors are come to the full. Again, that cannot merely refer to the time of Antiochus, but must also point to the end of the times of the Gentiles, concerning which Scripture also teaches elsewhere that they will be extremely wicked (see 2 Tim. 3:1-9).

This expression points also to the time of the divine judgment, for when the measure of sin is full, the Lord will come with judgment. Scripture points out the idea that the development of sin will not be stopped in its course but will obtain its full measure according to the longsuffering of God. But once this measure is full, the longsuffering and forbearance of God will have been exhausted and His judgments will be poured out without mercy. That is what the Amorites of old experienced (Gen. 15:16); that is what happened to Israel (1Thess. 2:16); and that is what will happen to apostate Christendom (see Rom. 11:22-25; 2 Peter 3:9, 10; Rev. 3:10; 18:5). The time of Antiochus Epiphanes was very wicked indeed, and there were, as 2 Maccabees tells us, many apostate people, but at that time the apostasy and wickedness had not reached its culmination point. That is reserved for the end of this dispensation and the time of the Antichrist in particular. So much, then, for the time of the little horn.

Gabriel further pointed out the nature of this little horn. He tells us it will be a king. Then, of course, not as some John Lackland but as the head and embodiment of a kingdom, and we saw earlier that this will be the fourth world monarchy in its third or revived phase. Concerning his character, it is said he will be of fierce countenance. Already Moses referred to the Romans as the enemies of the Jews in the same words (Deut. 28:50). This expression indicates great brutality that cuts down everybody without any regard. "And understanding dark sentences" refers to his demonic cunning and infernal wiles, so that he will outsmart everybody and seem unfathomable in all his tactics.

These two characteristics depict him as a true son of perdition. He will be acquainted with the mysteries of Satan himself. Even the great fiery dragon himself will put such great confidence in him that he will give him all his power and royal authority (Rev. 13:2). The man of sin will truly be a superman, a unique genius, so that the whole apostate world will admire and worship him. Antiochus Epiphanes is no more than a pale adumbration of him.

Verse 23 pointed out his brutality and cunning. Verse 24 further points out his great power, his prosperity, and his persecuting of the saints. "And his power shall be mighty, but not by his own power." This means that he will obtain great royal power less by his inner strength than by cunning and infernal deceit, which was mentioned earlier. We are not dealing here with an allusion to Alexander as some think, but much rather to the terrible fact spoken of in Revelation 13:2 and other places. The Antichrist will work with the energy of Satan himself. His coming will be after the working of Satan (2 Thess. 2:9). He will be active not by his own but by Satan's energy. So it need not amaze us that it is further stated he will destroy wonderfully. In the beginning his strength was little; he was but a little horn; but when Satan entrusts him with his power and throne and great authority, and when also the ten kings of the restored Roman empire unanimously give him their power (Rev. 17:13), then the Antichrist will have the power to inflict the most horrendous destructions upon the earth, miraculous works of destruction.

And in everything he does he will succeed for a time; he shall prosper. The whole world, infused by the power of erroneousness, will even believe that he is God and worship him. From Revelation 13 we can learn that he will have control over the military, the commercial, and, with the help of the false prophet, even the religious powers. And because he works with Satan's power, he will even display supernatural power in signs and wonders. See further on his success and prosperity in verse 12.

Gabriel pointed out in the third place that this person would be a persecutor and destroyer. He will destroy the mighty and the holy people. Again this cannot be said of Antiochus, but it can be said of the Antichrist, for in the preceding chapter we already saw that the eleventh little horn pulled up and destroyed three of the ten kingdoms. For the mighty here means the powerful ones, kings. And the holy people refers to Israel. Daniel knew nothing of the church as the Body of Christ. At that time the church was still the mystery hidden in God, as Paul teaches us in many places.

Verse 25 indeed has, as did both preceding verses, obtained a partial and temporary fulfillment (see 1 Macc. 1:29, 30), so that Israel at that time could already use this prophecy by way of application. But the full and final fulfillment will not come until the time of the Antichrist. The first part of this verse supplies a further development of verse 24. Through his policy, i.e., his wickedness and craft, he will prosper in all his undertakings, especially his persecutions. The verse further points out his satanic self-exaltation (see on this v. 11; 11:36; 2 Thess. 2:4). In his wicked boldness he will even measure himself with Christ. He shall stand up against the Prince of princes. He will take up the battle not only against the Jews, but also against their legal King.

But whereas in everything he succeeds and prospers as far as Israel is concerned, he experiences something quite differently with regard to Israel's King. In this connection we do not read that he was successful, but we do read that he will be broken without hand. This is again a striking indication that he is the Antichrist, for how beautifully Scripture corroborates the description of his final end (see 2:34; 7:21; 2 Thess. 2:8; and Rev. 19:20). In all these texts we see that he perishes suddenly and without any participation by any human power. According to the last-mentioned text he will not even die but be cast alive into the pool of fire, into hell.

Many exegetes have thought to find in verse 26 a prooftext for their idea that prophecy in general is not meant to be understood until it is fulfilled. Disregarding the absurdity of this viewpoint, it certainly cannot, to say the least, be deduced from this verse. For this is partly evident from the angel's assurance that this vision is the truth. When we may not hide the truth under a bushel, we can bank on it that neither does God not hide it after He has once revealed it. Furthermore, when the angel said that this vision was the truth, he thereby indicated it must be understood literally.

Finally, when we compare this expression with Isaiah 8:16 it is quite obvious that the shutting up of the vision means that Daniel must preserve and keep it. This expression is derived from the rolling together of the loose sections of a scroll. These loose parts of an unbound scroll might easily get lost, but if they were carefully bound into a scroll, this would not happen very easily. Thus understood, we have here a divine command to write down this remarkable vision and to preserve it carefully in a scroll, because there was an urgent need that this revelation of God be immortalized, for there would be many days before the final fulfillment. Hence the reason for this shutting up was not its alleged incomprehensibility, but, indeed, its comprehensibility and great importance to Israel. And Israel would not have to wait until its fulfillment to understand it, for she must already from that time on read and comprehend it before everything was fulfilled.

The many days refer back to verse 17. In the prophets this expression usually points to times that are still far in the future (see 10:14; Ezek. 12:27; Hos. 3:4, 5). This expression is another proof that this vision does not exclusively refer to Antiochus Epiphanes as the horrible king, for in that case it would have to wait less than four hundred years before it was fulfilled.

We can state here that we agree with the viewpoint of many exegetes that the Chaldeans and Medo-Persians were not allowed to know about this vision, for it would have especially angered the Persians very much if they had learned of the downfall of their kingdom. Such displeasure would have resulted in an untimely revenge upon Israel, whereas the Lord's intent was to deliver Israel soon by means of the Persian king Cyrus.

Daniel Fainted and Was Astonished

And I, Daniel, fainted, and was sick certain days; afterward I rose up, and did the king's business; and I was astonished at the vision, but none understood it (v. 27).

It struck him down and made him weak and sick. Verse 18 already mentioned something about it. The preceding chapter contained great horrors as well, which would be poured out upon his people in the future, but at that time the vision had ended in the glorious victory of his people; but here everything is entirely different. It seemed that Israel would go down. True, it is said that the cruel king will be broken without hand, but not a word is mentioned about the triumph of the holy nation.

The love of a godly Israelite for his nation is something we Westerners do not understand. It was not an ordinary love of country but a commingling of his love of God, His glory, His country, His people, and His Word and covenant. These things were interconnected in his soul as in the essence of the matter. But then try to imagine the condition of the soul to whom it has all the appearance that a link in this chain is removed, and then you can form some idea of his sadness; then you can to some extent imagine this thought must have been well-nigh unbearable and overwhelming to Daniel, so that it seemed for some days his body would break down under it. Moreover it seems at that time there was apparently nobody who could comfort and encourage him. This verse gives us the impression he was a very lonely man.

Alas, it is the lot of many a godly person to be lonely and alone and so spread his days and fight his battles. Noah built and sailed alone; Abraham wandered about alone as a stranger in a strange country; Jacob wrestled alone at the river Jabbok; Elijah lay alone underneath a juniper tree; Jeremiah wept and lamented all by himself; Paul had to complain, "At my first answer no man stood with me, but all men forsook me." And so, too, Daniel was left alone with his grief—and his God—for soon he took courage again and in all faithfulness did his work for the king. His sorrow was not a sorrow of the world which results in death, but a sorrow after God. It seems to us that the condition of the soul of this greatly beloved man cannot be more accurately expressed than in the words of Psalm 102.

Chapter 9
THE SEVENTY YEAR-WEEKS

Daniel Understood by the Books

In the first year of Darius the son of Ahasuerus, of the seed of the Medes, which was made king over the realm of the Chaldeans; In the first year of his reign I, Daniel, understood by books the number of the years, whereof the word of the Lord came to Jeremiah the prophet, that he would accomplish seventy years in the desolations of Jerusalem. And I set my face unto the Lord God, to seek by prayer and supplications, with fasting, and sackcloth, and ashes (vv. 1-3).

It is obvious the prophet did not intend to be strictly chronological in his prophecy, for we met this Darius already in chapter 6, and there Daniel spoke of his experiences during the time of the Medo-Persian world monarchy. Chapter 7 took us back to the first year of Belshazzar, the last king of the first chapter. The vision of chapter 8 took place two years before. And here we are again in the time of the second or Medo-Persian world monarchy.

On this Darius we have already commented in 6:1. Most likely he was the person called Gobryas of the inscriptions. The fact that he was not an independent person is evident from the brief description Daniel gives of him in 6:1 and here. There it was said he "received" the kingdom, and here that he was made king. Apparently he was of royal blood, for his father, Ahasuerus, had the title of king. Cyrus was the great general who as yet did not want to rest on his laurels, and God had destined him to be a world conqueror. Thus he had made the aged governor-general a king for the time being, with the intent of taking on the government himself after his expeditions. Darius, who apparently was more a statesman at heart than a general, had soon noticed the excellent qualities of Daniel and had therefore given him a high position of honor in the state. What is mentioned in this verse apparently took place in the same year when the faithful man of God had been thrown into the den of lions as a result of the envy of the great men in the realm.

In the second verse, the prophet says once again that it was in the first year of Darius' reign, after having just said that the latter was of the seed of the Medes. He apparently wants to give us a silent hint that Babylon had fallen and that he, therefore, expected the deliverance of his nation. For it was by no means unknown to him that the prophets connected Israel's deliverance with the downfall of Babylon. He knew Nebuchadnezzar's world monarchy would be destroyed after seventy years (Isa. 23:17; Jer. 25:12; 29:10-14). Nor can it have been unknown to him that his nation would be delivered as a result of this downfall (Jer. 50:18, 19, 33, 34; 51:1-10). Indeed, about a century before Babylon's fall Jeremiah had symbolically doomed it to its ruin by sinking the small scroll describing Babylon's judgments in the middle of the Euphrates by means of a stone attached to it.

Now Babylon was really fallen and all its glory had been given into the hands of its conquerors. The prophet, who himself searched the writings of other prophets and, therefore, knew about the threatenings upon Babylon, must also for a long time have seen the approaching judgment, for had not Belshazzar been busily engaged in filling the measure of unrighteousnesses? He, Daniel, had been a witness, yea more, the interpreter of the flaming condemnatory writing in Belshazzar's palace. Thus the infallible word of the Lord was fulfilled and a new period in world history had commenced. One world monarchy had sunk away and another had emerged, exactly as the Lord had predicted.

But now it was inevitable that the question arose in the prophet's mind as to what would become of the promised deliverance of his beloved nation. With this question burning in his heart, he turned to the holy Scriptures for enlightenment. Apparently, Daniel already had a collection of holy books. Among these scrolls were also the prophecies of Jeremiah in which he could read the words:

> For thus saith the Lord, That after seventy years be accomplished at Babylon I will visit you, and perform my good word toward you causing you to return to this place. For I know the thoughts that I think toward you, saith the Lord, thoughts of peace, and not of evil, to give you an expected end. Then shall ye call upon me, and ye shall go and

pray unto me, and I will hearken unto you. And ye shall seek me, and find me, when ye shall search for me with all your heart. And I will be found of you, saith the Lord: and I will turn away your captivity, I will gather you from all the nations, from all the places whither I have driven you, saith the Lord, and I will bring you again into the place whence I caused you to be carried away captive (Jer. 29:10-14).

Most likely these were the words the prophet read. They speak clearly and unmistakably of a seventy-year exile. Now Daniel may not have known exactly when this period had started, but without doubt he knew that Israel's welfare was most closely connected with Babylon's downfall—and had not Babylon fallen already?

But, lo, when contemplating these things, it became clear to the prophet that his people still by no means met the demands the Lord required of them in regard to their return. For did not the Lord speak in Jeremiah of a searching and a calling upon Him with their whole heart. Where did Daniel find deep humility and a calling upon the Lord by his people? Indeed, nowhere. All we need to do is read Ezekiel.

But lo, that which *Lo-ammi* does not do, the prophet as the representative of the remnant will do himself. He will make confession of trespasses and seek the Lord with his whole heart. He will pray and beseech, plead and wrestle; he will cast himself down in sackcloth and ashes. We cannot refrain from again admiring the spiritual greatness of Daniel. For although he was exalted to high places, he did not forget his despised nation (v. 16). His heart always went out to Jerusalem and his people. Although he was a busy statesman, he nevertheless took time to search prophecy. He did not consider it obscure but as light in a dark time and place. Prophecy did not turn him into an idle dreamer, nor did it put strange notions into his head, but made him bow his knees, lift up his heart to the God of his life, and open his lips to utter words of repentance, confession, and prayer.

If someone had asked him why he was still praying for deliverance, since God had determined the exact time, he would have answered that the Lord always fulfills His promises in the way of prayer. And it was all too clear from the above-quoted words of Jeremiah that the Lord wanted to prepare deliverance of His people in the way of confession and prayer.

Prayer of Confession

And I prayed unto the Lord my God, and made my confession, and said, O Lord, the great and dreadful God, keeping the covenant and mercy to them that love him, and to them that keep his commandments; we have sinned, and have committed iniquity, and have done wickedly, and have rebelled, even by departing from thy precepts and from thy judgments: neither have we hearkened unto thy servants the prophets, which spake in thy name to our kings, our princes, and our fathers, and to all the people of the land. O Lord, righteousness belongeth unto thee, but unto us confusion of faces, as at this day; to the men of Judah, and to the inhabitants of Jerusalem, and unto all Israel, that are near, and that are far off, through all the countries whither thou hast driven them, because of their trespass that they have trespassed against thee. O Lord, to us belongeth confusion of face, to our kings, to our princes, and to our fathers, because we have sinned against thee. To the Lord our God belong mercies and forgivenesses, though we have rebelled against him; neither have we obeyed the voice of the Lord our God, to walk in his laws, which he set before us by his servants the prophets (vv. 4-10).

Although it is difficult to divide prayers into parts, especially such as we have before us, they nevertheless generally consist of three parts. In the section under discussion the chief sins of the nation are confessed and God's mercies are glorified. Verses 11-14 express that the punishment has fully come and was deserved, as it was already threatened in the law of Moses, and they moreover point out the causal connection between Israel's sin and punishment. Verses 15-19 constitute a pleading for mercy upon the holy city and the holy nation.

We are not even considering analyzing this pouring out of the heart. In doing so we would not be clarifying but obscuring it. If we wish to derive practical and spiritual benefit from this prayer, we must read it repeatedly, and in the same condition of soul as Daniel's. That will also bring about a greater spiritual understanding of the seventy year-weeks mentioned later.

The secret of the Lord is with them that fear Him (Ps. 25:14). Fearing the Lord is what Daniel did, as is evident from his entire life and from this prayer. He was great as a statesman, very beloved as a person, and as steadfast as a pillar. But his real power and greatness lay in his prayer and prayerful communication with God. The sins of his people, the raging of the nations, and the words of Moses and the prophets—all these things brought him down on his knees in the upper room before the window facing Jerusalem. And this time he had hardly poured out his prayer completely before the Lord when a messenger from heaven came to grant him his desire. "And it shall come to pass, that before they call, I will answer; and while they are yet speaking, I will hear" (Isa. 65:24). This prayer, which in the kingdom of peace will be fulfilled for all Israel, would soon also for him be glorious reality.

So Daniel prayed to God. This is not mentioned here as something unusual and special, for we know it was his custom to have three prayer sessions daily. On this occasion his prayer is accompanied by extraordinary struggle in his soul, so that he even abstained from eating and drinking, for, according to verse 3, he was fasting. Fasting originally indicated a bowing down and humbling one's soul before God.

In the law of Moses there was originally only one day a year set apart for fasting (Lev. 16:29ff.; 23:27ff.; Num. 29:7), and this is still observed by Jews as an eternal institution. Afterward, however, Israel commenced to fast at every occasion of deep feelings of sadness and mourning. This was often accompanied by other manifestations of sorrow, such as the donning of a narrow, black sack, the sprinkling of ashes and dirt on the head, lying stretched out and flat on the ground, the rending of one's clothes, the shaving off of the beard, the cutting and pulling out of one's hair of the head, walking barefoot, and refraining from washing and anointing oneself. In Ezra 10:6 and Joel 2:12 we find fasting, as we do here, a means of doing penance for national sins. Hence we have here no ordinary prayer of Daniel, but a very special wrestling of the soul, accompanied by signs of deep sorrow and mourning. He prayed to Jehovah, his God.

The name Jehovah is not found in this prophecy except on the lips of Daniel. In his mouth, the name Jehovah is especially glorious. He expresses at once that, as a member of the covenant, he turns to the Lord as his covenant God. This name is the profoundest and most glorious of all the names the Lord gives Himself in His Word. It contains the three glorious ideas of eternal, unbreakable, covenant faithfulness with regard to His Israel. The fact that he dares to call this Jehovah his God, shows his courage of faith and his confidence of faith. He further addresses God as Adonai, the almighty Ruler, and El, the mighty God whom he further calls dreadful and awe-inspiring. However much he knows God as great of majesty and greatly to be feared on account of His righteousness and holiness, he, nevertheless, dares to address the Lord as a God keeping the covenant and mercy to them that love him, and to them that keep his commandments. Compare this striking appellation with the opening words of Nehemiah's prayer and also Exodus 20:6 and Deuteronomy 7:8, 9.

Whereas in verse 4 he indicates confession must take the predominant place in his prayer, in verse 5 he actually commences with it. He was obviously deeply convinced that the Lord demands in the first place heartfelt confession of sin. Let God's children never forget that after every form of trespassing the Lord demands first of all a humble confession of guilt, for only he who confesses and forsakes his sin will obtain mercy, while on the other hand he who hides his trespasses will not prosper. Thus Daniel piles one term of confession of sin and self-loathing upon another. And he does not exclude himself from all the wickedness of his nation, but considers himself one with all of faithless and covenant-breaking Israel; he identifies himself with it and stands here as it were the priestly substitute before the countenance of the Lord.

Auberlin says Daniel's prayer is one of those biblical prayers that cannot be explained, and of which we feel that the words must explain themselves in our hearts if we wish to comprehend the meaning and the purpose. Daniel, the faithful and righteous servant of God, submerges himself totally in the sin and guilt of his people; his priestly disposition identifies himself with them to such an extent, and he makes such a heartfelt confession in the name of all of Israel, that we feel something here of what went on in the innermost being of Him who in our stead made confession; so that we look beyond Daniel at the sacrifice of prayer in Gethsemane and on Golgotha. Daniel in his prayerful suffering is an example of, and represents that High Priest who, when He was put to death (verse 26), caused the burnt offering and the meat offering of the Old Covenant to cease, since He himself made reconciliation for sin and brought about eternal righteousness. Exactly now, when Daniel assumed the office of a priest, he must have been specially receptive to this revelation of the New Testament high-priesthood.

Whereas the main thought in verse 5 is that Israel rebelled

against the Lord as a rebel, in verse 6 Daniel makes confession of Israel's sin of not having hearkened to the Lord's prophets. That was indeed a horrendous sin, for if prophecy is a light, then the prophets were the bearers of that light to kings, rulers, governments ("the fathers"), and all the inhabitants of the land. Hence they had clearly manifested that they loved darkness more than the light. And the prophets were the servants of the Lord.

They had also rejected the King Himself, for what Christ later said of the apostles applied no less to the prophets, "He that heareth you heareth me; and he that despiseth you despiseth me." The story in 2 Samuel 10 can teach us how earthly rulers regard disrespect to their ambassadors, and Amos 2:11-16 and 7:12-17 gives instructive examples of God's displeasure with sin. One of the reasons Jerusalem lay deserted for centuries was that it was the city of prophet killers (Matt. 23:37, 38).

Verse 7 expresses the twofold thought that the Lord has treated Israel according to His unimpeachable justice and their desert when He dispersed them throughout all the provinces of Babylon. He justifies the Lord in His severe punishment and puts the blame for it on Israel. When he says "unto us [belongeth] confusion of faces," he wishes by no means to claim that Israel is really ashamed of its sin, but that it should be ashamed of its evil misdeeds. And he pronounces all of Israel guilty. He spells it out in toto by mentioning separately Judah, Jerusalem, all Israel, and those that are far off; indeed he includes himself. Although he had already left his country when still a young man and had always lived conscientiously before God and man, he nevertheless felt himself to be one with his guilty people, so he testifies also of himself that he should be ashamed. The law of solidarity or unity with regard to sin is little felt today. Nevertheless, Scripture clearly teaches it. When Achan had sinned, it was said that Israel had sinned and there was an accursed thing in the whole camp (Josh. 7:1, 11). Due to the abominable sin of Gibea the entire tribe of Benjamin was considered guilty.

In verse 8 the man of God continues to point out those who ought to be ashamed when he once again names the kings, the princes, and the fathers. In verse 6 he already accused these three classes of disobeying the prophets, but here he says these great men also must be ashamed of their sins. When we examine the prophets, it soon becomes evident to us that these three classes were often the most disobedient and the guiltiest of all.

Verse 9 completes the contrast between God's just punishment and the deserved punishment of Israel mentioned in verse 7. To the Lord our God belong mercies and forgivenesses, he exclaims exultantly. It sounds as though we hear the echo of Jeremiah's exultant language, "It is of the Lord's mercies that we are not consumed, because his compassions fail not. They are new every morning: great is thy faithfulness" (Lam. 3:22, 23). For just as dark as the future of Israel looked then, so it looks now to Daniel, yet he still boasts of God's mercies and forgivenesses.

Daniel undoubtedly saw the abundant mercy and multitude of forgiveness, as did Jeremiah, in the fact that Israel had not been consumed, and further in the fact that God for seventy years had kept His people while in exile and was at the verge, according to His promise, of returning them again to their country. There is no other nation on earth that can boast of God's mercies and forgivenesses in a similar manner. Besides, this nation was formed for the purpose of showing forth His praise. For that reason, one day *Lo-ammi* will become *ammi* and *Lo-ruhamah*, *ruhamah* again, and this people as a nation will say more emphatically than ever before, "O, my God!" (see Hos. 2:23).

In verse 10 the prophet makes clear that Israel, by rejecting the prophets, had not listened to the voice of the Lord. He obviously includes Moses among the prophets when he speaks of the laws given by the prophets. At the same time this expression indicates that the admonishments and warnings of the prophets had the power of laws. By not hearkening to the admonishments of the prophets the people transgressed the divine laws. When the prophet says here that these laws had been given before the countenance of the people (Dutch version), he implies that the trumpet of the prophets had not produced an uncertain sound, that these ambassadors of the Lord had passed on their message loud and clear, so that Israel could not hide behind the shield of ignorance. Israel was acquainted with the way of life, for it had as it were been painted before their eyes, but Israel had refused this way. They had known but refused it. And that is why Israel was so deeply guilty in the sight of God.

Israel's Sin and Punishment

Yea, all Israel have transgressed thy law, even by departing, that they might not obey thy voice; therefore, the curse is poured upon

us, and the oath that is written in the law of Moses the servant of God, because we have sinned against him. And he hath confirmed his words, which he spake against us, and against our judges that judged us, by bringing upon us a great evil: for under the whole heaven hath not been done as hath been done upon Jerusalem. As it is written in the law of Moses, all this evil is come upon us: yet made we not our prayer before the Lord our God, that we might turn from our iniquities, and understand thy truth. Therefore, hath the Lord watched upon the evil, and brought it upon us: for the Lord our God is righteous in all his works which he doeth: for we obeyed not his voice (vv. 11-14).

Verse 11 forms a contrast with verse 10. For far from listening to the voice of the prophets and hence to the voice of the Lord, Israel had transgressed the law and discontinued all obedience to the Lord. The law of Moses had already taken into account the possibility that Israel would break the national covenant and as the people of the Lord, the chosen nation, would depart from Him body and soul. For that reason Moses in the name of the Lord had held before their eyes both life and death. In Leviticus 26 and Deuteronomy 27 to 32 he had depicted in the most terrible of terms the fearsome way of suffering Israel would have to walk after its disobedience. And this curse had been confirmed by a divine oath. When Moses called heaven and earth to witness, this had the power of a divine oath. The prophet means to say that God's threatenings had been literally fulfilled. The judgments with which Israel was threatened have been fulfilled, not figuratively but literally; that is something about which all expositors agree.

This furnished strong proof that when Israel's fearful history of suffering has finally come to an end, all God's further promises will also be fulfilled to the letter. Both the threatenings and the promises have been pronounced in the same breath, by one person, in the same manner and in the same place, and before the same persons. Since Scripture itself frequently points out that these threatenings have been literally fulfilled, we can count on it that it will not be any different with the promises. There are some exegetes who like to carry these promises over to the realm of the church, but that is not only robbing them from Israel but runs into repulsive absurdities and even ends in secularization of the church. If we want to retain Israel's blessings we must also accept its curses. That is being consistent.

By "judges" are generally meant the rulers and heads of government, such as kings and lower officials. Israel's sin had been committed by both its head and its members, and on head and members punishment descended. God's acts are always just and He gives to everyone what he deserves without respect of persons.

The prophet further points out that the devastation which had struck Jerusalem was unequaled anywhere under heaven. The question might be asked whether the cities of the Canaanites, which were totally destroyed and razed to the ground, had not received at least as severe a judgment, and if Sodom and Gomorrah had not been punished much worse. We must keep in mind, however, that no city had been as privileged as Jerusalem. It was the city of the great King which the Lord had chosen to dwell in forever. That made the punishment of Jerusalem unequaled and different from all others under heaven.

Verse 13 calls to mind once more the literal fulfillment of the threatenings in Moses' law, and Daniel further points out the terrible sin of omission when he prayerfully confesses, "yet made we not our prayer before the Lord our God." Prayerlessness is a general and God-dishonoring sin of omission. The Christians in James' time were desperately poor and lived in strife and enmity with each other because they lived a prayerless life; "because ye ask not" (James 4:2). Whoever does not pray will sooner or later end up cursing God with his whole life. "Therefore, O man, draw nigh to God, and He will draw nigh to you" (James 4:8).

Not coming to God in prayer is a slap in His face and has always dire results. One result for Israel was that it blindly rushed headlong on the pathways of sin, not returning from its wicked works and not paying heed to the execution of God's threatenings. For examples, read the prophets Isaiah, Jeremiah, and Ezekiel, especially Jeremiah.

Israel rushed blindly toward judgment and had not the least idea that God was carrying out His harsh judgments. But even if Israel was sleeping and slumbering on its way toward God's judgment, with God matters were totally different. Israel's Watchman never sleeps or slumbers, neither in keeping His people nor in chastising them. That is what verse 14 makes clear. The prophet says, "the Lord watched upon the evil." That is a strange expression. It does not tell us that He allows no evil to come upon His people because He is half asleep or has His eyes half shut, but that

He does so consciously as a watchful Judge who does not allow anyone to escape His hand. Thus the Lord says in Jeremiah 1:12 and 31:28:

> For I will hasten my word to perform it. And it shall come to pass, that like as I have watched over them, to pluck up, and to break down, and to throw down, and to destroy, and to afflict; so will I watch over them, to build, and to plant, saith the Lord (Jer. 32:28).

Daniel Pleads With God

And now, O Lord our God, that hast brought thy people forth out of the land of Egypt with a mighty hand, and hast gotten thee renown, as at this day; we have sinned, we have done wickedly. O Lord, according to all thy righteousness, I beseech thee, let thine anger and thy fury be turned away from thy city Jerusalem, thy holy mountain: because for our sins, and for the iniquities of our fathers, Jerusalem and thy people are become a reproach to all that are about us. Now therefore, O our God, hear the prayer of thy servant, and his supplications, and cause thy face to shine upon thy sanctuary that is desolate, for the Lord's sake. O my God, incline thine ear, and hear; open thine eyes, and behold our desolations, and the city which is called by thy name: for we do not present our supplications before thee for our righteousness, but for thy great mercies. O Lord, hear; O Lord, forgive; O Lord, hearken and do; defer not, for thine own sake, O my God: for thy city and thy people are called by thy name (vv. 15-19).

In this third and last part of this deeply touching prayer we can hear how this very beloved man can plead as a penitent. After the prophet has called God's attention to Israel's great guilt and to the connection between its guilt and its punishment, he now beseeches Him for turning away His wrath, the withdrawal of the punishment, and the restoration of His sanctuary.

In the opening words of this part of his supplication he points out that the Lord brought Israel out of Egypt and that thereby He obtained renown and glory which the men of his day still remembered. The glorious deeds and great miracles the Lord performed at that time had been indelibly retained in the memory of the heathen nations. Scripture often recalls that glorious act of deliverance. And so Daniel mentions it here with the purpose that the Lord might stretch out His hand again in the same way unto deliverance of Israel, and thus to deliver His people from Babylon. The deliverance from Egypt was already an example and a guarantee to Israel of future deliverances, as Scripture teaches in many places (see Ps. 80:8, 9; Jer. 16:14; 23:7, 8; 32:20-44). From this prayer it is evident that Daniel had read much, especially in the prophecy of Jeremiah, for he alludes more often to words from this prophet than to those of any other.

> The exodus from Egypt was to Israel a raised banner to which all believers of all times in Israel looked back as to the eternal monument to the faithfulness of God. To believers under the New Testament, the cross of Christ is such a banner, the infinitely more glorious monument of divine grace, for on it our eternal salvation was accomplished. To look unceasingly back to that cross is the task of our faith, the foundation of our hope, the mainspring of our love (Da Costa).

In verse 16 the supplicant of Babylon beseeches God to turn away His anger and fury; and he makes all the righteousness of God the solid foundation of this plea. The righteousness of God often appears in the Old Testament as the principle and the source of the deliverance of God's people (see the second part of Isaiah). Daniel apparently means to say that since God's avenging anger had been satisfied by the seventy-year exile, now God by right must fulfill His promise of restoration. The expression "all thy righteousness" indicates that there is not only an avenging righteousness that demands punishment, but also a rewarding righteousness. Thus the word "righteousness" often appears in the sense of mercy, faithfulness, favor, grace (see 1Sam. 12:6; Ps. 23:3; 32:2; 143:1; Mic. 6:5).

Although Jerusalem was still a heap of black ruins, Daniel nevertheless dared to call this city, namely, Zion, a holy mountain, i.e., a mountain the Lord had set apart from the other mountains and had sanctified for a special purpose. He knew on the basis of Scripture—and believed it—that God had desired Zion for His dwelling place and will dwell there eternally (see Ps. 68:16; 87:1, 2; 125:1; 132:13,14). Where are the Christians today who dare believe this of Jerusalem since it again was delivered from the hand of the heathen, according to prophecy?

Alas, by far the majority of believers always identify Zion's holy mountain with the church from all nations. And thus in this respect they make a lie out of Scripture and defile God's holy mountain where He wishes to dwell forever. From the last part of verse 16 it is evident that not only the Jews of our day but also already those at that time were a reproach to all the nations around them. That, too, was a literal fulfillment of the threatenings of God predicted to Israel by the mouth of Moses and the prophets.

Anti-Semitism has been predicted by the Lord and is to Israel and the nations a judgment of God. "And will deliver them to be removed to all the kingdoms of the earth, to be a curse, and an astonishment, and an hissing, and a reproach, among all the nations whither I have driven them" (Jer. 29:18; read and reread further Deut. 28:25, 37; 2 Chron. 7:20; Jer. 15:4; 29:18; 34:17; 42:18).

By its wanderings on the earth, Israel is an eloquent witness to God's severe justice and faithfulness and to the truth of God's Word. This nation can make us understand a large part of holy Scripture and the signs of the times. But this reproach, this contempt, had still another meaning to Daniel. He calls it to God's attention as if to say, "Lord, does this not violate Thy honor?" He finds it very grievous that the scorn poured out on Israel is a scorn by Jehovah Himself. For that reason he wants the Lord to restore His people again and give them honor to the confusion of these uncircumcised enemies, so that to this end Israel's glory may magnify the majesty of His name among the nations.

The soul's struggle of the praying servant of the Lord increases as he continues to pray. Helpless and miserable in himself, he casts his soul upon the Lord. In verse 17 he beseeches God to cause His face to shine upon the destroyed sanctuary. To lift up one's face or to cause it to shine was a standard expression in Israel for favorably remembering someone or something. This expression is the opposite of to hide one's face in the sense of forsaking, leaving, chastising someone. So it is Daniel's prayer here that the Lord may again look in mercy on Israel's temple, as He did in days of old. Daniel does not ask this on the basis of his own righteousness, but for the Lord's sake.

Because this verse contains the name of the Lord twice, Calvin and many other expositors with him thought this to be an allusion to the second Person of the holy Trinity, and in our opinion not incorrectly so. Not alone do we know that all promises are yea and amen in Christ, and we must go to the Father through the Son. We also come across the same idea in Psalm 80, which was clearly composed in the days of the exile. Also noteworthy is that in verse

19 the word "Lord" is repeated three times, which many exegetes and dogmatics consider a faith allusion to the mystery of the holy Trinity. So it seems to us that here we have, if not a clear Messianic prophecy, then at any rate certainly a faint allusion to the Messiah. Polas says this was the unanimous testimony of the best exegetes as well as of the Synod of Sardis.

Daniel does not let go of the thought of the glory of God. That to him is especially the crux of the matter, and therefore, in verse 18 he emphasizes it even more. Whereas in verse 15 he only spoke of the glory the Lord obtained unto His name in the deliverance of Israel from Egypt, and whereas in verse 16 he spoke only three times of "thy city," "thy holy mountain," "thy people," in this verse he goes one step further and says emphatically that Jerusalem is named after God's name. Hence Jerusalem is His possession in a very special sense. He has called Himself after this city. If He let this city lie in bare ruins, then the heathen would say He was too weak to defend His city against the gods of the nations. Thus Daniel in his supplication reduces everything to the question, not of whether Jerusalem will be rebuilt, but whether God will maintain His name, His glory, His virtues.

A second ground to plead upon in this verse is contained in these words, "for we do not present our supplications before thee for our righteousnesses, but for thy great mercies." Scripture sometimes represents our prayers as being lifted up and rising up on high; then again, as is the case here, as being cast down before His face or throne. Both representations are very striking, for where faith ascends as on wings, there humility casts us in the dust, as we find here with Daniel. The weary and burdened soul casts its burden from itself and upon God. Thus Peter says, "Casting all your care upon him, for he careth for you" (1Peter 5:7). The ground on which the man of God expects mercy and deliverance is not his ardent prayer, nor any righteousness or good work, but the mercies of God. He has learned by experience that all our righteousnesses—note well: not only our sins, but our best works—are as filthy rags, as torn and moldy old rags.

Thus resting himself completely on these great mercies of God, he groans on in verse 19, "O Lord, hear; O Lord, forgive; O Lord, hearken and do; defer not," i.e., do not postpone. It seems to us that we can justifiedly consider this thrice-repeated appellation "Lord" an allusion to the holy Trinity, for the context favors this idea, and we often find in Scripture this mysterious trio conspicuously mentioned. But those expositors go much too far when they draw all sorts of Christological conclusions from it, for Daniel himself had no clear concept of this mystery.

At the end of verse 19 he reminds the Lord once more that Jerusalem and Israel are called after God's name. Israel, the city, and the sanctuary are to Daniel the three glorious things most closely connected with the glory of God's name. When the prophet repeatedly says Jerusalem is called after God's name, he undoubtedly was thinking of such texts as Psalm 48:1 and 2, "Great is the Lord, and greatly to be praised in the city of our God, in the mountain of his holiness. Beautiful for situation, the joy of the whole earth, is mount Zion, on the sides of the north, the city of the great King." Especially also Jeremiah 25:29, where the Lord says the city is called after His name (see also Ps. 5:2; 2 Chron. 6:6). It is probably the oldest city in the world, and no other city has been besieged and destroyed more often. It has been the apple of discord of the nations for centuries and still is.

A Man Greatly Beloved

And whiles I was speaking, and praying, and confessing my sin and the sin of my people Israel, and presenting my supplication before the Lord my God for the holy mountain of my God; yea, whiles I was speaking in prayer, even the man Gabriel, whom I had seen in the vision at the beginning, being caused to fly swiftly, touched me about the time of the evening oblation. And he informed me, and talked with me, and said, O Daniel, I am now come forth to give thee skill and understanding. At the beginning of thy supplications the commandment came forth, and I am come to shew thee; for thou art greatly beloved: therefore understand the matter, and consider the vision (vv. 20-23.)

Daniel strongly stresses the point in the first two verses that Gabriel appeared when he was still praying. He had not finished his wrestlings of the soul. The Lord does not always show so speedily that He has heard and answered our prayers. Even in the next chapter we see that Daniel at times had to wait a long while for an answer. We know the Lord always has a wise reason for everything, but we see there may be second causes outside of us why our prayers sometimes are not answered for a long time.

For comment on Gabriel himself, we refer to Daniel 8:15, 16. Verse 21 briefly calls our attention to the manner and time of his coming. Concerning the manner it says that he was "caused to fly swiftly." There are many who translate this "when I lay in a swoon," and connect it then with the preceding time as an indication of the previous vision, but the meaning is obviously that the angel had flown so fast that it had made him tired, because for swooning a totally different word is used in the preceding chapter and elsewhere. Whether angels can get tired is a totally different question which we dare not answer quickly. Most certainly their power is neither divine nor unlimited, and in the state of rectitude God created already a day of rest in the heart of man. If man in the state of rectitude could get tired, then the angels can too. There is not a single creature that is a source of strength in itself, and so after some exertion of strength there must follow to a greater or lesser degree some exhaustion of power. Besides, we read only of God that He, as the Creator of the ends of the earth, neither faints nor is weary (Isa. 40:28). In any case, the angel had hurried to get to the greatly beloved man.

Concerning the time, we are told he came about the time of the evening oblation. This was a very remarkable time. The evening sacrifice was like the morning sacrifice, the daily sacrifice of a lamb prepared with some beaten oil and wine. It was prepared in the morning at six o'clock and in the evening at three o'clock. At the institution of it the Lord had connected glorious promises:

> This shall be a continual burnt offering throughout your generations at the door of the tabernacle of the congregation before the Lord: where I will meet you, to speak there unto thee. And there I will meet with the children of Israel, and the tabernacle shall be sanctified by my glory (Exodus 29:42, 43).

It is most certainly a remarkable fact, but totally in agreement with the glorious promises attached to it, that the Lord Jesus Christ cried, "It is finished," at the time of this evening burnt sacrifice. In the history of Elijah in 1 Kings 18:36-38 and in Ezra 9:4 we see that the godly Israelites always kept this hour of the sacrifice in mind. It may especially not escape our attention that Gabriel came flying so fast here with the important intent of making known to Daniel the hour of the death of the Messiah.

Gabriel approached Daniel and told him first of all the goal of his coming. To put him at ease, he called the man of God by his name. The purpose of his coming was, according to Gabriel, to increase Daniel's knowledge concerning Israel, Jerusalem, and the temple. It was concerning these three matters that Daniel had wrestled; now he would receive light on them. He further told Daniel that already at the beginning of the latter's supplication the command had been issued. It does not say by whom, but the meaning is by the Lord who Himself does not mention His own name in Daniel's prophecy; He is the God who keeps Himself hidden. Nor is it said which command is meant or to whom it was given. Some exegetes hold the opinion that Gabriel meant the command given him to go to Daniel; others think the command had already been given to the Medo-Persian monarchy to free Israel; but the best thing is maybe to think that it means the announcement in heaven of Israel's liberty to the teeming world of angels who are so very interested in the people of the Lord. The second idea is at any rate impossible since Cyrus did not reign as yet and the edict of Israel's release was issued in the first year of his reign.

He called Daniel a greatly beloved man, i.e., a man much-loved. Just as the critics have argued against the authorship of the five books of Moses because of the favorable descriptions concerning Moses' character they contain, so they have done in the case of this prophecy on the basis of this expression. What a petty argument this is! It would have some value only if he had given this name to himself. Now that this name was given him from heaven, it is only natural that Daniel wrote it down. But that is exactly what the critics do not believe—that this name was given him from above. Fuller writes so correctly concerning his name:

> It was not for Daniel himself that he is represented as a jewel in God's sight, not because of what he was as a person, but as the representative of that Israel which was faithful to God's covenant. Israel was this jewel in the first place because God had chosen the nation unto Himself from among all the nations of the world to be His possession, which He keeps through all ages as a jewel, and which He courts like a man courts his bride, even when she is unfaithful to Him. At present this nation finds itself under the chastising hand of its God, but the Lord sees in Daniel the representative of His nation, which is godly and faithful to the covenant. Just as the nation as it should be is concentrated in him, so also concentrates God's love on its representative.

"Therefore understand the matter, and consider the vision," Gabriel says to Daniel. Not only to Daniel, this is also said to us. This brief command is still not superfluous and unnecessary today. Let us not despise prophecy but give diligent heed to it. Maybe our Savior was thinking of this command of Gabriel when He says in Matthew 24:15, "Whoso readeth, let him understand."

Not one but two matters are mentioned to which the prophet must pay heed. Gabriel is not simply using two different words for one and the same thing, as Scripture often does, for the following verses are indeed a word of the Lord, but they are not a vision. It seems to us there are some indications which tell us that Gabriel was referring to the vision in the preceding chapter. In the first place it is remarkable that the preceding vision said so little about Israel. So what was not said there is apparently revealed to Daniel only a few months later. In the second place, it is not without significance that the same angel who gave Daniel the vision of the preceding chapter also comes and gives this revelation, whereas we know that Gabriel seldom if ever gives revelations. In the third place, in verse 21, this revelation is to some extent connected with the vision in chapter 8. Finally, concerning the meaning of these words, they can become clear in Van Hamelsveld's translation, "so understand this command and compare it attentively with that vision." It seems to us that this very well reflects the meaning of these words. If viewed that way, then the remarkable words in verses 24 to 27 are a continuation of the previous vision.

Gabriel was aware that he came to bring a message of great importance to Daniel and to Israel and the saints of all times. Hence he did not enunciate his message until he had evoked the necessary attention and had urged Daniel to examine this prophecy and to compare it with other parts of Scripture. His inestimable prediction is contained in the last four verses of this chapter.

The Seventy Weeks

Seventy weeks are determined upon thy people and upon thy holy city, to finish the transgression, and to make an end of sins, and to make reconciliation for iniquity, and to bring in everlasting righteousness, and to seal up the vision and the prophecy, and to anoint the most Holy. Know, therefore, and understand, that from the going forth of the commandment to restore and to build Jerusalem unto the Messiah the Prince shall be seven weeks, and

threescore and two weeks: the street shall be built again, and the wall, even in troublous times. And after threescore and two weeks shall Messiah be cut off, but not for himself: and the people of the prince that shall come shall destroy the city and the sanctuary; and the end thereof shall be with a flood, and unto the end of the war desolations are determined. And he shall confirm the covenant with many for one week: and in the midst of the week he shall cause the sacrifice and the oblation to cease, and for the overspreading of abominations he shall make it desolate, even until the consummation, and that determined shall be poured upon the desolate (vv. 24-27).

We have now come to the much-disputed prophecy of the seventy year-weeks of Daniel. We could call this the heart of Daniel's prophecy as well as the backbone of all predictions. It is the unanimous opinion of all students of prophecy that whoever does not understand these four verses cannot possibly obtain a clear concept of unfulfilled predictions. For that reason we wish to dwell on the passage rather extensively, and before we commence with the commentary to make a few preparatory remarks.

1. This prophecy must not be understood and interpreted symbolically but simply and naturally. There are mountains of literature on these four verses and we have counted no less than fifty different commentaries. This can easily lead to a certain measure of prejudice so that the simple reader may come to the conclusion that it is better for him not to get involved in it, since the words on which the learned people are so much in disagreement must simply be considered inexplicable or at least way above their comprehension. By saying right now that this section must be understood literally or, if you will, verbally, we are excluding a great number of interpretations as being incorrect. All the symbolical, mystical, and cabalistical interpretations may safely be ignored. Following are our bases for a simple verbal interpretation of these verses:

- The angel Gabriel emphatically commands that the word, and not merely the spiritual underlying causes or the principle or something of that nature, must be understood.
- The angel himself gives a literal explanation and it would be nonsensical to insist on giving a symbolical interpretation of

a literal explanation. If the exegetes had always obeyed the angel's command and had accepted his explanation as a literal interpretation as is evident from practically every word he speaks, then this text would never have been so obscured by all kinds of human conjectures and imagined "deep" insights.

- There is absolutely nothing here that forces us to depart from the simple literal explanation, and it is a standing rule in hermeneutics that words must be taken as they appear unless this leads to palpable absurdity.
- It was the obvious intent of the angel to be understood literally by Daniel.
- These verses contain many predictions which have been literally fulfilled in the past.

2. The purpose of this prophecy is to show what will take place with Israel during the time of the Gentiles. This is the same as saying that here we are absolutely not to think of the church of Christ. Many believers always look for themselves in prophecy and for the church and the state of the church, whether it be languishing or flourishing. If we approach prophecy with such presuppositions we shall make no advances in the knowledge of unfulfilled prophecy. And so, too, it will be impossible to interpret this section if we are obsessed with the church, which never is a subject of Old Testament prophecy. Does not the angel emphatically say, "Seventy weeks are determined upon THY people and upon THY holy city?" It is Daniel's people, Israel, and Daniel's city, Jerusalem, to whom these times refer most of all. Was it not for Israel and for Jerusalem and the temple that Daniel had poured out his supplications? Whoever ignores this indication and wants to explain these words outside of Israel will end up with nothing but a mass of absurdities. Chapters 2 and 7 described the times of the Gentiles; now here Daniel is told what will happen to his people during these times.

3. We must interpret this prophecy in the mood in which Daniel received it. Alas, there are many believers who merely look at unfulfilled prophecy coldly and intellectually. But this intellectual way is nevertheless not the wisest. We must learn from Daniel how to view with the heart the holy secrets regarding the future.

All mere curiosity was far from him. He had studied prophecy with a prayerful heart. He had wrestled with his God and only afterward received the answer in this prophecy. And just as this prophecy was received upon prayer, so can it also only be understood and explained upon humble examination and prayerful supplication to God. The secrets of the Lord are for those who fear Him. On the basis of Scripture we dare make the statement that the simple day laborer, who approaches this prophecy in the same frame of mind as Daniel's, will soon understand more of it than the most learned professor who approaches it coldly and intellectually.

After these brief preparatory remarks, concerning which we hope the kindly disposed reader will not ignore, we turn to a brief explanation of these verses.

Verse 24 describes in general terms the broad scope of this prophecy, while the following verses indicate more particularly the division of the seventy year-weeks. The fact that exactly here the number 7 is again so prominent is not without significance. In Leviticus 26:24 and 28 the Lord had foretold that He would punish Israel "seven times" for sinful disobedience. The whole history of the suffering of Israel stands in the sign of the number 7.

These seventy weeks are not day-weeks but year-weeks; the original says "seventy sevenths." Pronouncing this word in Hebrew results in a peculiar play of sounds, known as paronomasia (*shaw-voo-eem shi-veem*). Now it does not say at all whether this means sevenths of days, weeks, months, years, or centuries. The context must determine the designation, and this shows clearly enough that it speaks of year-weeks. For had not Daniel just read in the prophecy of Jeremiah about seventy years?

The following context points in the same direction as well, for in contrast with these year-weeks 10:3 speaks emphatically about three whole weeks. Apart from a few exceptions, all expositors speak here of year-weeks. They fully realize that if they were to abandon this idea, then the rich Messianic prophecy contained in these verses would be lost. The only objection advanced against the "weeks of years" is that this manner of expressing time was unknown to the Jews. But this objection is invalid, for in Leviticus 23:15; 25:2, 4, 5, 6, 8 and other places we have the same way of indicating time. Therefore, this cannot have been unknown to

Daniel. Besides, seventy day-weeks would be no more than the brief period of a year and a half.

Thus here we have 70 x 7, which equals 490 years. These, as we shall see shortly, are divided into three parts, and these years are determined upon Daniel's people, upon Israel. The word translated as "determined" actually means cut off. This word, which is only found here in the Bible, means a careful shortening, measuring, and so a deciding of something. The Lord has determined Israel's time carefully. Just as a wise person never cuts or snips at random, the Lord as the all-wise God does so even less. All His works are determined from eternity, and the times also are only in His hands. The seventy year-weeks are envisaged as a unit here, as is evident from the usage of the verb in the singular.

It deserves noticing that it says here "thy people" and upon "thy holy city," and not MY people. That is wholly in keeping with the nature of Daniel's prophecy, in which the Lord hides Himself from Israel, which He considers as *Lo-ammi*. It is for that reason that He does not say here my people and my holy city. In his supplication Daniel had used the expressions "thy people" and "thy holy city" (vv. 18, 19). But God cast this name from Him; He did not want to say *ammi* to Israel at that time. God spoke in a similar vein to Moses after Israel's sin with the golden calf (Exod. 32:7). Those people are going much too far who want to deduce from these expressions that Israel is now no longer God's people and consequently have no longer any future. A glance at 12:1 teaches us differently. Israel will be *Lo-ammi* for many days, but not forever (see Hos. 3:4, 5).

"To finish the transgression." The word translated as "finish" actually means keep back, push back. Hence Luther translates, "thus the transgression is prevented." The idea of resisting, pushing back leads to the derivative meaning of locking up, enclosing, in order to make it come to an end. Transgression here means apostasy, uprising, rebellion. In 2 Kings 8:20, 22 the word appears in its original meaning in connection with the revolt of Edom and Libya against the kingdom of Judah; in 1 Kings 12:19 it is used in the same sense of the northern tribes (see Job 34:37; Isa. 1:2). The meaning of this expression is that Israel's defection from Jehovah will end at the end of the seventy year-weeks.

"And to make an end of sins." Hebrew is not a rich language, but it contains many different words to describe the reprehensible nature of sin. Here the idea is less the sinful acts than the sinful walk of life outside of God. The original meaning of the word indicates the hollowness, the vanity, the purposelessness of sin by which the sinner must forego the glory of God and become most wretched in the end. But Israel's transgressions will be finished, they will be covered, for when something is sealed (Dutch version), it is covered, whether it be a scroll or a den of lions.

"And to make reconciliation for iniquity." For the third time a brief clause is used here to indicate the removal of sin. The word translated as reconciliation has also the meaning of covering. It indicates that God will cover Israel's sin in such a way that He Himself does not see it any more. When His all-seeing eye no longer sees sin, then it does not exist any more, then it is reconciled. This is effected by the blood of Christ, which is called the blood of reconciliation. This is an allusion to the Mercy Seat. Christ is the great and actual Mercy Seat. Hence sin would be locked up, sealed, completely covered from the holy eyes of God.

Whereas the first part of verse 24 consists of three clauses referring to the removal of sin, the second part contains three matters pointing more positively to the salvation God will provide.

"And to bring in everlasting righteousness." This clause refers to the state of bliss Israel will enjoy after the seventy year-weeks. The prophets are full of similar promises to Israel; but these promises will not be fulfilled until at the end of its woes and at its last reacceptance, when *Lo-ammi* will be *ammi* again. Converted Israel will then with joy make mention of Him by whom all its sins have been reconciled and an eternal righteousness has been effected. Hear the inhabitants cry out, "All we like sheep have gone astray; we have turned every one to his own way; and the Lord hath laid on him the iniquity of us all" (Isa. 53:6; also Isa. 51:6-8; 45:17; Jer. 23:6; 31:3; Mic. 7:18-20; Luke 1:74, 75).

"And to seal up the vision and prophecy." "Prophecy" does not refer to Christ here but to prophecy in general. The "vision" this verse speaks of is not a reference to this vision nor to any of the other visions Daniel received, but together with the word "prophecy" refers to all predictions. A scroll was not complete until it was completely filled. Thus this sealing of a scroll became a symbol of fulfillment (Isa. 8:16). So also here it indicates a complete fulfillment of all prophecy. The old rabbis interpreted this expression this way, since they lived in steadfast expectation that all prophecy would be fulfilled at Messiah's coming.

"And to anoint the most Holy." We have here a historical allusion to the dedication of the tabernacle and the temple (Dutch version has the most holy place). This expression is never used of a person. So it is not a reference to the Messiah. Nor to the church, for the church is nowhere mentioned or found in the whole prophecy of Daniel. It refers to Daniel's people, Israel. Hence we are neither to think of its referring to the outpouring of the Holy Spirit or the founding of the church. Because this prophecy places us in the time of the end of Israel's history, we prefer to think it is a reference to what the prophet Zechariah describes in the last verses of his prophecy—"In that day shall there be upon the bells of the horses, HOLINESS UNTO THE LORD," etc. (Zech. 14:20, 21; cf. Ezek. 40 to 48). It refers to the state of bliss and holiness of all Israel after the Savior has come to Zion and has turned away the ungodliness from Jacob (Rom. 11:26). After this verse, which considers Israel's future in general, the angel Gabriel goes into more details in the following verses.

Verse 25 speaks of two parts of the seventy year-weeks, consisting of seven and sixty-two weeks. The fact that Gabriel wants Daniel and all of us to understand this prophecy is evident from his repeated admonition to know and understand it. Verse 25 contains two main subjects. We must answer two questions: which time is meant by "the going forth of the commandment"? and who is meant by "Messiah the Prince?"

The first question would not be so difficult to answer if it were not known that four different commands must be met before Israel could return. There have been those who thought that they had found all these four different words or commandments regarding Israel's return promulgated at very different times and referred to in this expression. The first command to Israel to return is found in the edict of Cyrus, as described in 2 Chronicles 36 and Ezra 1. But this cannot be meant here since it speaks only of the rebuilding of the temple and does not say a word about rebuilding Jerusalem, as this verse does. The second command is found in Ezra 6 and here, too, only mention of Israel's religion is made and not of its streets and walls, as does this verse. And again the same objection can be made against the third command in Ezra 7. In this proclamation also, given by king Artaxerxes to Ezra, not the city as such is referred to but only the temple service, as is very evident from the heartfelt prayer of thanksgiving of Ezra 7:27, "Blessed be the Lord God of our fathers, which hath put such a thing as this in the king's heart, to beautify the house of the Lord which is in Jerusalem." For reaching this goal not a political person but a "ready scribe" like Ezra was sent.

A further objection against these three edicts just mentioned is that chronologically they do not coincide with the death of the Messiah, which, according to verse 25, is required. So there is nothing left but to refer to the fourth command mentioned in Nehemiah 2. The request of Nehemiah to king Artaxerxes was, "If it please the king, and if thy servant have found favor in thy sight, that thou wouldest send me unto Judah, unto the city of my Father's sepulchres, that I may build it." This took place in the twentieth year of Artaxerxes Longimanus. These seventy year-weeks then commence in the month of Nisan of the year 445 B.C. The entire book of Nehemiah is proof that this godly governor built Jerusalem and its streets and walls, and that, as this prophecy says, in troublous times. According to qualified chronologists this also agrees with the needed chronology set forth in Daniel.

It took seven year-weeks or forty-nine years to rebuild the city. Adding to them sixty-two years of weeks leads (with the necessary limitations) exactly to the death of Christ, as the following verse demands. For a further study on this we refer the reader to Sir Robert Anderson's, *The Coming Prince* (Kregel Publications).

The second question which demands a definite answer is, who is this "Messiah the Prince"? Those who deny the authenticity of Daniel think of all kinds of known and unknown historical persons, except the Christ: Alexander the Great, Seleucus, Philopater and Onias 3 are given the honor of being suggested. Especially the last-mentioned one is frequently considered as the person meant here. This Onias 3 was a godly high priest in the time of the Maccabees, who was treacherously murdered by the Syrian governor, Andronicus. Quite correctly Auberlin calls this a "meaningless fact." Many people of the critical school translate here "an anointed prince."

The Jews also always considered this prophecy very important. Josephus seems to have thought that this Messiah the Prince meant Ananus, a high priest who was murdered by the Idumeans. Shortly after the beginning of the Christian era the Jews found in this prophecy a prediction of the destruction of Jerusalem. The Messiah, who is killed (v. 26), was Jesus, who has no right to the rulership, as they translate the words "but not for himself." During the Middle Ages the Jews had other ideas. Then some of them applied the words "Messiah the Prince" to Cyrus, others to Nehemiah, Joshua the high priest, or even Darius Hystaspis.

In recent years they seem to be afraid of this prophecy. Many orthodox Jews, like many Christians, consider it so obscure that no interpretation is certain and effective. A famous rabbi (Simon Luzatto) gave his opinion that a prolonged and thoroughgoing study of this prophecy might result in all Jews becoming Christians, as it was his view that it could not be denied on the basis of Daniel's chronology that the Messiah had already appeared. Whether Jesus of Nazareth was the true Messiah he dared not say with certainty.

If there is not much agreement among the Jews and rationalistic interpreters, there is no less agreement among the conservative exegetes of all denominations. They are all agreed that here is found one of the clearest Messianic texts in the Old Testament, even unique by the fact that it affords a chronological indication. That this view is also ours needs no confirmation. All non-Messianic interpretations run into inexplicable absurdities.

Verse 26 is a strong proof for this view. There it is said that the Messiah will be cut off. This would take place after sixty-two year-weeks. The seven year-weeks mentioned earlier must be included in them, so that it says here that from the command for Nehemiah to rebuild Jerusalem until the death of the Messiah would be sixty-two year-weeks or 483 years. Excepting those who deny the miracle of prediction, practically all exegetes are agreed that, taking into consideration the necessary limitations (such as taking the forty-nine years of the rebuilding of the city together with the 434 years) take us up to the death of Christ. For that reason we can view this is incontestably certain.

"The Messiah would be cut off." The word used here for the killing of Christ is that of the hewing down of a tree. In Isaiah 44:14 it is used for the hewing down of cedars. In the Old Testament it is also the standard expression for cutting off by capital punishment (see Exod. 12:15; 30:33, 38; Lev. 18:19;

20:17; Ps. 37:34). Thus we have here, as we do in Isaiah 53:8, a striking prediction of the violent death of Christ. In their blindness even the Jewish scribes did not know that by murdering Christ they literally fulfilled their Scriptures.

"But not for himself." These words are translated and interpreted in greatly different ways. As it is translated here, it is usually applied to the mediatorial suffering and death of Christ, and that in itself is, of course, a natural and glorious truth taught us by Scripture in many places. But the question is whether this is taught here. Others translate, "although nothing [of guilt] was in him." Again others, "he will be nothing," and apply this to His being totally forsaken by God and men. Some translate, "although not against him," namely, not against His will and intent, and that would refer to His voluntary self-sacrifice.

Literally it says, "but nothing for him." The meaning is obviously that nothing was for Him. When we ask in which sense He had nothing, the answer must be: He had no glory, no kingdom, no people that threw themselves at His feet. "He came to His own, but His own received Him not" (John 1:11). Ever since Hengstenberg, many exegetes take it to mean that Christ would not assume the royal government over Israel immediately after His death (cf. Acts 1:6).

"And the people of the prince that shall come shall destroy the city and the sanctuary." This is a clear prediction of the destruction of Jerusalem after the execution of the Messiah. All orthodox exegetes agree on this. The opinions vary greatly, however, concerning "the prince that shall come." Some think it refers to Christ, since He used the Romans as His instruments against the city of prophet killers (Matt. 22:7). This interpretation loses sight of the fact that it has just been said that Christ was cut off. Others think it is a reference to Vespasian or Titus under whose command Jerusalem was destroyed. There are some who take this clause to mean nation of princes, in the sense that every Roman citizen considered himself to be like a king.

Finally, there are many exegetes who think it refers to the Antichrist. This is indeed according to the rule of prophetic writings, according to which the Antichrist is the fourth or Roman empire. Just as Nebuchadnezzar, Cyrus, and Alexander, respectively, were the head of the first, second, and third world monarchy, so in Daniel and Revelation the Antichrist is considered the head and embodiment of the fourth and final world power. The translation, "people of the prince that shall come," makes this interpretation much more acceptable. This is the translation that presently is generally accepted.

The following verse confirms this interpretation: "And the end thereof shall be with a flood, and unto the end of the war desolations are determined." The question is who is meant by "thereof." The most obvious interpretation, and hence the most acceptable one, is that here is meant "the prince that shall come," namely, the Antichrist. Already mention is made here of the destructions which the man of sin will cause among Israel. Just as Christ had said to the apostate city, "Behold, your house is left unto you desolate" (Matt. 23:38), so the same thing is already made known here. The last part of verse 26 no longer speaks exclusively of the destruction of Jerusalem but of the terrible destructions which the head of the fourth world monarchy, "the prince that shall come," will cause among Israel.

Until now there was still one week of the seventy year-weeks, of which nothing had been said. Now the last verse of this remarkable prophecy is going to say something about this one year-week—a period of seven years. It is important to realize that this one week can nowhere be placed in history naturally. The great mistake often made regarding this verse is that the "he" is thought to refer to Christ, whereas it refers to the Antichrist, because:

- Of Christ it has already been said that He was cut off and had nothing.
- This pronoun "he" refers back to "the prince that shall come," and of him it is said that he oppresses and destroys Israel, which expressions cannot very well apply to Christ.
- Christ never made a covenant for "one week."
- Our Savior never caused the sacrifice and the oblation to cease in the middle of a year-week.
- Christ Himself interpreted this text as referring to something in the future (Matt. 24:15): "Whoso readeth, let him understand." This is specially important and by itself sufficient proof.

Between these sixty-nine year-weeks, which come to an end with the death of Christ, and this one year-week lies this entire present dispensation. We have a clear proof here that Old Testament prophecy absolutely takes no account of this dispensation, during which the church as the Body of Christ is gathered from among the nations. Between the sixty-ninth and the seventieth year-weeks lies a period of already more than nineteen-hundred years. The apostle Paul calls this dispensation "the mystery, which from the beginning of the world hath been hid in God" (Eph. 3:9). The present dispensation is a parenthesis. This dispensation of grace is as much hidden to the prophets as is the Body of Christ.

This year-week is the brief period in which all the terrible judgments from Revelation 6 to 19 take place. This week is the period of the closing of the times of the heathen and the resumption of Israel's history and the closely connected establishment of the kingdom of peace. According to verse 27 Israel will be at least partially restored again in Palestine. Then the Antichrist as head of the restored Roman monarchy will make a covenant with Israel. (cf. Isaiah 28:15, 18). At that time Israel is not yet converted and will accept the Antichrist instead of Christ. Possibly Christ was thinking of this in John 5:43.

After three and a half years the Antichrist will break the alliance, cast off his mask, and turn against the apostate nation with all his demonic fury. He will cause the sacrifices of the temple service in the rebuilt temple to cease and reveal himself as a terrible destroyer. He will set himself up in the temple and pretend to be God (see Dan. 11:36 and 2 Thess. 2:4).

The wording of the last part of verse 27 is very mysterious. Two things are clear, however. In the second part of the still future year-week the Antichrist will destroy Israel in a terrible manner, and reciprocally at the end of the week divinely appointed destructions will be poured on her. We quote the translation of Van der Palm as the most generally accepted:

> And on the pinnacle (of the temple) will stand the destroying abomination until everything is demolished and irreparable destruction has been poured on the destroyer.

This translation alludes to the pronouncement of Christ in Matthew 24:15. The Scripture speaks in many places concerning the destruction the Antichrist will bring about one day in Jerusalem (see Isa. 25:7-9; Ezek. 22:19-22; Mic. 4:11, 12; Joel 3:9-17; Jer. 30:7-9; Zech. 12-14; Rev. 11, 12, 13, 17).

Chapter **10**
A MAN CLOTHED IN LINEN

Three Weeks of Mourning

In the third year of Cyrus, king of Persia, a thing was revealed unto Daniel, whose name was called Belteshazzar; and the thing was true, but the time appointed was long: and he understood the thing, and had understanding of the vision. In those days I, Daniel, was mourning three full weeks. I ate no pleasant bread, neither came flesh nor wine in my mouth, neither did I anoint myself at all, till three whole weeks were fulfilled (vv. 1-3).

The last three chapters of Daniel belong together, for they constitute the final and most complete revelation Daniel received. They afford an exact prediction of the pressure which two nations in particular would put on Israel, and in a few words chapter 12 makes mention of Israel's deliverance.

The three present verses indicate the time when and the state in which Daniel's soul found itself when he received this revelation. He obtained it in the third year of Cyrus. On the seeming contradiction between this time reference and that mentioned in 1:21, which says that Daniel remained at the court until the first year of King Cyrus, we commented already with a few words at the time. Some exegetes hold the opinion that here is meant the third year of Cyrus' co-regency with Darius the Mede and not Cyrus' absolute, sole monarchy.

Daniel is mentioned by both of his names. It is somewhat strange that he also mentions his Chaldean name alongside his Israelite one, for this man of God must have detested a name that constantly reminded him of the idol, Bel. Many commentators consider this an emendation from a later writer, but it is better we conclude that this part of the revelation was meant to be made known immediately not only to Israel but also to the Chaldeans, the Medes, and the Persians. In that case, Belteshazzar was the well-known and famous name that would assure interest and acceptance.

"But the time appointed was long." This simple expression has been translated and interpreted in more than twenty different ways. The most correct translation of *tsaba* is wars, afflictions. It is the same word that so often appears in the name Lord (*tsabaoth*) where it is always translated as hosts. Hence the meaning is that Daniel received a revelation concerning great and destructive wars. The following verses indeed point at such afflictions for Israel. The conclusion of this brief introduction says that Daniel understood the vision. Hence this prologue contains the time, the person, the subject, the certainty, and the light of this prophecy.

The psychological condition in which Daniel received this revelation is mentioned in verses 2 and 3. He had mourned for three long weeks. It is a comforting truth that Scripture does not call the lighthearted optimists blessed, but reserves this for those who mourn. Daniel often mourned, and every child of God will have to mourn much when he or she lives a deep, true, and serious life. Did not also the apostle Paul sigh and mourn often during his eventful life? The Westminster/Heidelberg Catechism correctly calls this world a vale of tears. It is a vale full of misery and woe to them who know their citizenship is in heaven, and everyone experiences sooner or later that Moses did not exaggerate in a bout of sadness when he sang of "sorrow, fear, and sore vexations, God's relentless visitations."

Daniel not only had an eventful life but a long life. He was at this time an old gray man of about ninety years of age. He had witnessed Israel's being carried into captivity some seventy years earlier. And now he had seen Israel return again to the land of their fathers. For had not the noble Cyrus the Great issued the famous decree for the freeing of Israel? This edict and its execution is described in Ezra chapter 1.

As is evident from this edict, Cyrus knew the prophecy of Isaiah who had already mentioned him by name two centuries before and had pointed him out as the one who would cause Israel to return (Isa. 44:28; 45:1-13; 46:11; 48:14). Many commentators hold the opinion that Cyrus actually became a true worshiper of the God of Israel, but somewhere the Lord says of him, "although he knoweth me not." Moreover, it has become evident from excavated inscriptions that he was a polytheist. It is generally thought now that he was driven more by political motives than by religious ones in the freeing of Israel.

In the meantime it cannot be denied that this edict exudes an excellent spirit. The Jews have always considered it to be the work of Daniel, although this cannot, alas, be proved. When we consider his soul's struggle as described in chapter 9 and his high and influential position at the court of Persia, the observation in 1:21, and the spirit and wording of this edict, we may at the least speak of a high probability that Daniel had a hand in the freeing of Israel or in any case exerted his great influence regarding this matter. Most probably Daniel pointed out to Cyrus the predictions of Isaiah concerning him.

The question could be asked why Daniel himself did not join Israel on their return to the land of his fathers, which had all the love of his heart. It has been thought that his advanced age was a deterrent, but in Ezra 3:12 we read that other old men returned, and Daniel seemed to have been still quite vigorous at that time. The Lord had given him a special position at the Medo-Persian court, however, so that it was necessary for him to receive a special indication from the Lord to abandon it. And it seems that this indication from God was not forthcoming. It was obviously the Lord's will for him that he was not to labor among His people, like other prophets, but rather in the midst of heathendom in the interest of His people.

If we ask what the reason was for Daniel's deep sorrow, then more than one answer can be given. Most certainly one reason was the little enthusiasm on the part of Israel to make grateful use of the proffered freedom by Cyrus. For by no means all exiles made ready to return to Palestine. In Ezra 1:5 it is said of only the tribes of Judah and Benjamin that they went on their way to Jerusalem. We do not read that the ten tribes, who had been carried off even before Judah and who were now, like this tribe, subjects of the Medo-Persian world dominion, returned as a result of Cyrus' edict. It is true, some people of these tribes joined the returning people, but as a whole they stayed behind to live among the heathen (see 1 Chron. 9:2; Luke 2:36; James 1:1; Acts 26:7). Josephus says that they remained living on the other side of the Euphrates and had multiplied unbelievably in number. Their present-day whereabouts are unknown. People have looked for them all over and there has hardly been a group of people that has not been identified with them. But Scripture teaches us that they are dispersed everywhere among the nations and that they will be gathered together one day and be reunited with Judah (see Isa. 11:11-13; Ezek. 36:16-28).

This indifference of Israel to the holy land and the holy city and dwelling place must have grieved Daniel deeply. Add to this, in the second place, the opposition of the Samaritans to the building of the temple—this, too, must have hurt him deeply. Finally, by this time Daniel knew only too well that his beloved people were only at the beginning of their long and bitter suffering. All these things must have been vexing and oppressive to his soul.

He was mourning three full weeks. This indication is important, since it is obviously meant as a contrast to the year-weeks of which the preceding chapter speaks. The expression implies that here we are not to think of year-weeks, as earlier, but of ordinary weeks.

In verse 3 he tell us how he mourned; he ate no pleasant bread. After the exile, fasting became more and more a custom, and this may be partly explained by Daniel's example. Thus we see here that Daniel fasted for three weeks, in the sense that he ate no desirable food but only the simplest fare. More than seventy years before he had not eaten any pleasant food for three years. Later on he apparently did eat it. We conclude from this that he acted in this manner from principle and not for secondary reasons. Daniel was a man of principle and self-denial. He mastered the art which Paul had made his own by exercise of faith—"I keep under my body, and bring it into subjection." Daniel did not become a servant of his body, but rather made his body serve him.

During those days he drank no wine, from which we can safely deduce that he was not a tee-totaler. Nor did he anoint himself during those three weeks. All these things were manifestations of mourning. On this matter of non-anointing see Matthew 6:17, where Christ says to the Pharisees, who apparently had made non-anointing into something meritorious, "But thou, when thou fasteth, anoint thy head, and wash thy face." Needless to say, Daniel did not ascribe any merit to all this whatsoever. To him it was no more than an aid to prayer. Only when fasting is used as a means to a richer life of prayer does it have any significance.

A Certain Man

And in the four and twentieth day of the first month, as I was by the side of the great river, which is Hiddekel; then I lifted up mine eyes, and looked, and behold a certain man clothed in linen, whose loins were girded with fine gold of Uphaz: his body also was like the beryl, and his face as the appearance of lightning, and his eyes as lamps of fire, and his arms and his feet like in color to polished brass, and the voice of his words like the voice of a multitude (vv. 4-6).

The fact that Daniel gives such an exact description of time and place has a reason. He was fasting and received this vision in the first month, namely, Nisan, called Abib before. This was the month—our month of April—in which Israel had departed from Egypt and concerning which God had said, "This month shall be unto you the beginning of months: it shall be the first month of the year to you" (Exod. 12:2). It is by no means unlikely that the time of the exodus from Egypt and of the Passover was the exact time of Israel's return to Canaan. If we accept this, together with other interpreters, then the mourning of Daniel is all the more understandable as a psychological fact that days of commemoration evoke not only the greatest joy but also the deepest sorrow.

The place where Daniel obtained this vision was the side of the great river Hiddekel. This is the same as the Tigris, which is a broad branch of the Euphrates. Genesis 2:14 and this text are the only times this river is mentioned in the Old Testament. There we see that the Tigris once flowed through the Garden of Eden. On its banks man once walked about without sin and misery, but after the destruction brought about by sin the Tigris and the Euphrates flowed through the world dominions, and on its banks all kinds of abominations were perpetrated. Here the fate of the second world dominion was sealed and with it that of all of Asia, when in the decisive battle of Arbela, Alexander the Great conquered the last king of the Medo-Persians, Darius Codomanus.

The river also flowed past the fortress Shushan, and it seems that the prophet had quietly withdrawn himself there after the freeing of Israel. It seems to us that Daniel provides these exact indications here to show that he received this vision after quiet seclusion and deep wrestlings of the soul, and that it was truly given him in a condition of wakefulness. The wordy expression "I lifted up mine eyes, and looked, and behold" serves the same purpose. See further on this expression our notes on 8:3.

Daniel saw a man. Here again the ideas as to who this man was are threefold. He has been seen as an ordinary angel, such as Gabriel who had already appeared to him before; the archangel Michael, since such a glorious description is given of him; or possibly the uncreated Son of God before His incarnation in the form of a man. The ratio between those exegetes who see in him a created angel and those who view him as the uncreated Son of God is about fifty-fifty. By way of argument that this verse refers to a created angel, albeit a glorious one, it is pointed out that later in the chapter it is said that the archangel Michael had to help him against the king of Persia. But it seems to us that we may safely assume we are dealing here with an appearance of Christ before His incarnation because of the following:

- The description of this Man exceeds all those of all ordinary angelic appearances. There is no other instance when a created angel appeared with such majesty or was described with such majestic words.
- In verse 8 Daniel calls this vision a great vision to distinguish it apparently from ordinary visions.
- John in Revelation 1; 10:5, 6 apparently derived his imagery and description from this text when he depicts the glorified Christ.
- When we assume the Son of God appeared to him, then there is in the prophecy of Daniel a beautifully proportional ascending progression from the lowest form of revelation—that of interpreting dreams—to the viewing of the Son of God, and thus every chapter is to this greatly beloved man a higher rung in the ladder of revelation.
- Chapter 12 obviously speaks of the same Person, and there He is distinguished from the archangel Michael.
- The objection mentioned above does not prevail, since the angel who needed help against the king of Persia was obviously another, ordinary angel.

The strongest proof that we are dealing here with the uncreated Son of God is undoubtedly the description itself. He is called a man. See on this expression the comments on 8:15. In all of the

Old Testament we come across this mysterious man, and God's looking for a man who can stand in the breach in the wall. The heathen Nebuchadnezzar saw Christ as a stone; Daniel saw him as a man. There is hardly a chapter in all of Daniel in which we do not find either a weaker or a stronger allusion to the Son of God.

This man is clothed in linen, pointing to his high-priestly dignity (Exod. 28:4; 29:5). High priests wore such a white, shimmering garment, stitched around with heavenly blue stitches. The color white is the symbol of innocence, purity, immaculate holiness.

He further had his loins "girded with fine gold of Uphaz." Here the girdle is around his middle. In Revelation 1:13 his breasts were girded about as a sign that He had finished the travail of His soul and was now walking amidst the golden candlesticks. When a person in the Near East went out for a walk or a trip he pulled up his garment at the loins and girded himself at the chest. In times past kings wore golden girdles, so that here, as in Ezekiel 9, the Son of God appears in His office as King and Priest. Uphaz is probably the same place as Ophir, which according to experts is the same as Afer, or Africa (cf. Jer. 10:9).

His body also was like beryl. In the original text it literally says like the "tarshish." Tarshish is the biblical name for Spain which was famous for its precious jewels and metals. The merchants of Tarshish were extremely rich. This stone is described as shimmering green and is a nontransparent semi-precious gem. How it got its name is unknown but most likely it was simply named after the place of its origin, Tarshish, or because it was transported on the ships that plied at Tarshish (see also Exod. 28:20; 39:13; Ezek. 1:16; 10:9; 28:13; Song. 5:5, 14).

"And his face as the appearance of lightning." This image of lightning appears often in Scripture with reference to Christ (see Matt. 24:27; 28:3; Rev. 4:5). Just as lightning consumes and purifies the atmosphere, so this image points to His consuming and purifying judgments.

"And his eyes as lamps of fire." These eyes like brilliantly burning lamps point to His omniscience. As the omniscient Judge He searches and examines everything so that afterwards He may pronounce a righteous verdict.

"And his arms and his feet like in color to polished brass." This indicates the strength with which He can vanquish His enemies.

Finally, this grand picture points out the power of His voice. It was "like the voice of a multitude." The idea is that of a multitude of rolling bodies of water. This feature, too, points to judgment when the Lord will appear, roaring from Zion to throw Himself at His enemies. Tender love whispers, but wrath and vengeance cry out with power. Hence, we often find this great voice in connection with judgments, whether by the Lord Himself or the angels of His wrath as the servants of judgment (see Ezek. 1:24; 9:1; 18:2; Rev. 1:10, 15; 14:2, 7, 8, 9; 16:1; 18:2; 19:1).

It must be obvious that these descriptions apply to none else but Him who one day will appear on the clouds of heaven with power and majesty. Undoubtedly, the purpose of this grand vision was in the first place to comfort Daniel. Not long ago he had received the terrifying revelation that Messiah, the Prince, would be cut off and die a violent death. A godly Jew, who saw the promise from afar, and who believed and embraced it (Heb. 11:13), could not imagine anything more dreadful. But from this vision Daniel could now deduce that the Messiah would not be cut off because of powerlessness or wrongdoing, and that one day He would come to quell His enemies. Furthermore, the purpose of this vision was to make known the long road of suffering but also the ultimate deliverance of Daniel's people.

Daniel Is Overwhelmed

And I, Daniel, alone saw the vision: for the men that were with me saw not the vision; but a great quaking fell upon them, so that they fled to hide themselves. Therefore I was left alone, and saw this great vision, and there remained no strength in me: for my comeliness was turned in me into corruption, and I retained no strength. Yet heard I the voice of his words: and when I heard the voice of his words, then was I in a deep sleep on my face, and my face toward the ground (vv. 7-9).

Daniel alone saw this vision. The men who were with him did not. We have a similar situation with the conversion of Paul on the road to Damascus, described in Acts 9:7. It is to this text and similar ones that those who believe in a secret rapture of the Church appeal, of which the children of the world know nothing. In any case this much is evident from such texts, that the relationship of the children of God to the visible world is totally different from that of the people of the world. Although it is not specifically said here that we are dealing with unbelievers, this is nevertheless quite natural in a heathen land.

These heathen men saw nothing but obviously heard something, because they became frightened to death and hastily fled away to hide themselves. This feature, too, strongly reminds us of what will take place on the last day at the return of the Lord. The day will come when not only a few men but also the kings of the earth, the great and the rich and the chief captains and the mighty men and every bondman and every free man will flee from Christ to hide themselves in dens and rocks of the mountains (Rev. 6:15, 16; see also Isa. 2:19; Hos. 10:8; Rev. 9:6).

Daniel was left alone just like Jacob at the Jabbok had to be alone in his wrestling. Is this loneliness of Daniel not a striking image of his entire life? Was he not the great lonely man in all of Babylon? He was always alone and yet never alone, for his God was with him in all his vicissitudes. This lonely man is a striking example of the lonely people of whom the Lord through Balaam told that they would dwell alone and would not be reckoned among the nations (Num. 23:9).

This great vision was also overwhelming to Daniel. Ah, the vile mortal human being in the body of humiliation cannot have full fellowship with heaven except by the prayer of faith. Even the godliest of men drop down like the dead to the earth when heaven opens up to them. We can see it in such men as Moses, Jacob, Samson's parents, Isaiah, Ezekiel, and John on Patmos. The last mentioned was the most beloved disciple of the Lord who had often leaned upon His bosom, but when he saw the glorified Savior on Patmos, he nevertheless fell at His feet as dead (Rev. 1:17). All of Scripture teaches us that we can live heavenly-minded lives but not yet heavenly in these bodies of humiliation. Fanatics, throughout church history who wanted to live "heavenly" ended up in nudism and similar abominations.

Curious man, who is ever thirsting for new phenomena, at times wishes for a visitor from heaven. We must admire God's grace in the fact that He keeps the world of spirits hidden from us, for if a greatly beloved man like Daniel swooned and fainted at such an occasion, what would happen to us who are far more carnally minded? Is it not true that if giants like Daniel and John fainted then we, spiritual dwarfs, would almost die? Let the unconverted sinner learn from this what will become of him in the day of His coming! Who may abide the day of His coming? Who shall stand when He appears? "For, behold, the day cometh, that shall burn as an oven; and all the proud, yea, and all that do wickedly, shall be stubble: and the day that cometh shall burn them up, saith the Lord of hosts, that it shall leave them neither root nor branch" (Mal. 4:1).

When it is said that Daniel's comeliness was turned into corruption, it means that fright and dismay caused his face to turn as white as that of a dead man. Nor did he retain any strength; all his strength left him, and he fell into a dead faint. The reason was not his great age or weakness due to all his fasting; on the contrary, the real cause of his unconsciousness was the tremendous contrast between humiliation and glory, between sin and holiness.

His powerlessness was not complete immediately. First, the voice of the divine figure faintly penetrated his brains, but it was exactly this voice that clinched the matter so that he, completely deprived of all his senses, crashed unconsciously face down to the ground, totally unconscious of what took place around him.

The same thing had happened more than once to Ezekiel when he beheld the glory of the Lord. We do not read of him that he, like Daniel, fell down into a deep sleep, in a complete state of unconsciousness, but nevertheless, several times that he fell down flat on his face to the ground (see Ezek. 1:28; 3:23; 43:3; 44:4). In Revelation 1:17 the same thing happened to John as it did to Daniel. How long the man of God lay there at the bank of the great river we are not told, but judging by the nature of the case, not very long. God did not leave His favorite servant over to his own devices but soon sent a messenger who put him on his feet again as we learn from what follows.

The Prince Withstood Me

And, behold, an hand touched me, which set me upon my knees and upon the palms of my hands. And he said unto me, O Daniel, a man greatly beloved, understand the words that I speak unto thee, and stand upright: for unto thee am I now sent. And when he had spoken this word unto me, I stood trembling. Then said he unto me, Fear not, Daniel: for from the first day that thou didst set thine heart to understand, and to chasten thyself before thy God, thy words were heard, and I am come for thy words. But the prince of the kingdom of Persia withstood me one and twenty days: but, lo, Michael, one of the chief princes, came to help me;

and I remained there with the kings of Persia. Now I am come to make thee understand what shall befall thy people in the latter days: for yet the vision is for many days. And when he had spoken such words unto me, I set my face toward the ground, and I became dumb (vv. 10-15).

Those who think that in the preceding verses a created angel appeared to Daniel assume as a certain fact that the text here still speaks of such an angel. In our opinion that is unjustified.

1. We have advanced proof that the man of verse 5 is none other than the uncreated Word who in the form of a man showed Himself to Daniel. Once we have agreed to this, it would never do to assume He needed Michael's help against the prince of Persia.

2. It is not said here that his hand touched him but that "a" hand did so. Had this been the same person then it would have been logical to expect the text to say his hand.

3. Also the little word "behold" indicates that a new figure is speaking. That which is especially determinative here is found in verse 11. There this person says to Daniel, "For unto thee am I now sent." If we assume that he is the same person, we must then also assume that after Daniel's swoon he had first departed and, while Daniel was still lying unconscious on the ground, received once more a command and so returned again to the fainted prophet.

Such a supposition is foolish and totally superfluous if we assume with such able expositors as Lowth, Kranichfeld, Havernick, Hengstenberg, Klinkenberg, Van der Palm, Kelly, and others that another person is meant here than in the verses mentioned above. Hence we believe we are dealing with an angel, maybe even Gabriel, who under different circumstances had been sent to Daniel more than once (see 8:16, 18; 9:21). Now this angel, whoever he may have been, awakened the prophet and lifted him from the ground on which he lay stretched out flat in such a way that he was now resting on his hands and knees.

In verse 11 we read the angel's soothing words to Daniel. Just as in 9:23, he again calls him the greatly beloved man. From these beautiful words he could at once deduce that God had not cast him down on the ground in anger. The angel further told him he was to listen attentively to the message being brought to him. If we want to absorb the words God speaks to us, we must not be totally or even half unconscious but completely sober and very attentive. For that reason the angel said to him that he must pull himself together and stand up straight, for Daniel had continued to sit on his knees, leaning with the palms of his hands on the ground. Upon hearing these words Daniel, still trembling, got to his feet.

Then, while the prophet was still shaking from dismay and standing before the angel, the latter continued, "Fear not, Daniel." God's children have actually nothing to fear. Since God is for them, nothing can be against them and all things must work together for good. The angel tells him a comforting truth when he says Daniel's words had been heard from the very beginning of his soul's struggle. During those three weeks of mourning it must have looked to Daniel as though God was not listening to him and as if the heavens were of brass. For various reasons, sometimes the Lord lets his children wrestle long, and of one of these reasons we shall hear presently. At the end of verse 12, the angel says he has come now for the sake of Daniel's words. The fact that the angel was standing there in front of him was the result of Daniel's pleas. He had come in answer to Daniel's prayer. So let Daniel rejoice and give heed to the angel's message.

The question must have presented itself to Daniel as to why the angel did not come sooner if his prayers had been heard immediately. What was the reason he had to wait for three weeks? Verse 13 gives the answer. And it throws a flood of light on many a dark problem and many apparently unanswered prayers or prayers which have not been answered for a long time. Also, it sheds light on much opposition to the people of the Lord. The main element of this answer is that "the prince of the kingdom of Persia" faced this angel as an enemy. Who is this prince of Persia?

- Rationalists of every kind think this is a case of superstition on the part of the writer, that it refers to the guardian spirits of the Chaldeans and Persians. Or the writer, knowing better himself, goes along with the Chaldean-Persian ideas and only wishes to convey that there was a corrupt spirit of opposition found at the court of Persia, in the same way as we today sometimes use similar expressions.
- There are many who think it refers to Cyrus who was king of Persia at the time, or to his son Cambyses who temporarily

took the place of his father while the latter had gone out on a march against the Scythes.

• And there are others who think the text speaks of an angel.

This last group is divided into two. Some of them think it refers to a good guardian angel of Persia, while most consider him to be an evil angel. We fully agree with the latter group.

We must take the expression "the prince of Persia" to mean an angel. Since the Man of God wages war against him, he cannot be a good angel, but must be an evil one. He also appears to be a powerful angel, for it is necessary for the Man of God to march upon him to stop him and to rout him; also the title "prince" indicates that he belongs to the higher class of angels. "Prince of Persia"—this title must not induce us to consider him the human prince of Persia; for obviously, he is distinguished from the angelic prince in Daniel 10:13b. Moreover, the contrast here demands that the battle is not waged between angel and man, but between angel and angel. Also, in case the historic prince of Persia were meant, it would have to be Cyrus (cf. 10:1), but whoever remembers how many glorious things Isaiah said of him, and how many good things he did for Israel, will not see in him a prince against whom an angel, indeed someone more than an angel, must do battle in order to prevent evil intents against Israel. But how does this evil angel get the title of "prince of Persia"?

To understand this, somewhat, we must remind ourselves how great is the power of fallen angels in the heathen world. They have not obtained this power in any legal way, but since men separated themselves from God, He abandoned them, up to a certain point, to the power of evil angels. That is why Satan, their chief, could say to Jesus in the hour of His temptation, and that not altogether without any basis, that the kingdoms of the world had been given him. Among the angels there are principalities, powers, dominions. Not all angels were cast into hell immediately after their fall and not all of them forever. Some among them retain their glory/luster and their power as long as God deems necessary. Through them He tests His people, chastises men, causes evil to reach its zenith and carries out His counsel.

Now such an angel was connected with the court of Persia. He tried to antagonize the king of that realm against the people of Israel so that he would forbid the rebuilding of the temple and the fortification of Jerusalem. Actually he wanted to convoke the world dominion to do battle against Israel, and ah! what could such a small nation do against such a superior power? The angel could indeed say many bad things about Israel for, alas, it could not be denied! There was truth in what Judah's enemies wrote to the king Artaxerxes, namely, that Jerusalem had been a rebellious and disloyal city, which did damage to the king and the provinces from of old (Ezra 4:15). But there was one thing the angel did not take into account, namely, the covenant between God and Abraham.

> The realization of this mystery enlarges our insight considerably. Now we know that the battle between these two powers, namely, that of light and that of darkness is indeed fought and determined here on earth, but not between man and man alone. This earth is the battlefield of the universe; here not only men fight with men, but also angels with angels. But not in such a way that both kinds of beings remain separated from each other. From Daniel it is evident that on the contrary Satan and his angels as his advisers and tempters of the nations, especially of the world dominions, take part in this battle. For that reason no battle will be waged against the Church when Satan is bound; the sea of nations will be calm and the storm of the spirits can no longer stir them up (Rev. J. VanAndel).

These words reflect our idea concerning the prince of Persia perfectly. The angel, now standing before Daniel with friendly intentions, has for twenty-one days faced this bad angel of Persia as an enemy. So when Daniel was praying he was already making his way toward him, doing battle all the while. He found his way blocked from step to step in such a way that he was in need of Michael's help, one of the chief princes.

Who is this Michael? He appears here for the first time, and then once again in verse 21 and further in 12:1, Jude 9 and Revelation 12:7, while 1 Thessalonians 4:16 speaks of an archangel, which no doubt refers to him as well. His name means "Who Is Like Unto God?" In Israel this name was very well known and very much loved, for Scripture mentions no less than ten persons having that name. Three opinions have been voiced concerning this Michael:

1. He is the chief of all the angels.

2. He is the Christ.
3. He is the Holy Spirit.

But nearly in every place he is mentioned in Scripture he is distinguished from Christ. Here, too, it is quite clear that he is not the same as the shining figure of verses 5 and 6. Nor is he called the chief prince but one of the chief princes, and that cannot be said of Christ, for He is the Lord and Chief of all angels.

Those who hold the opinion that he is the Holy Spirit arrived at this view because they felt on the one hand that since he was not a created angel he was, nevertheless, different from the man clothed in linen, and it is the Holy Spirit who restores the image of God in our hearts, whereby we become like unto God and share His divine nature. Also, in Isaiah 59:19 the Holy Spirit is presented as the Protector of Israel. According to Daniel 12:1 Michael, the great prince is the guardian spirit of Israel. The generally held view that Michael is the greatest and chief angel, the prince of angels, may be freely considered as being based on Scripture and hence irrefutable.

The words "I remained there with the king(s) of Persia" are translated in various ways. It seems to us the literal meaning of "I remained there" offers the most correct and most beautiful idea. Due to the importance of verse 13 we cannot refrain from quoting a paragraph from the beautiful book by Dr. A. Kuyper on the angels of God. He writes:

For in both these places (Dan. 10:13 and 21) Daniel is given an insight into that which, behind the curtain of the humanly observable events, is fought out in the world of spirits to further the cause of God and to oppose the power of Satan. For the cause of God at that time was embodied in the people of Israel. If, reverently speaking, the cause of Israel succumbed, then also the cause of God on earth would have been lost. Hence at that time the battle between the kingdom of God and the kingdom of Satan was almost completely identical with the battle between Israel and the nations assailing it. From this point of view it is completely understandable how Satan waged war with God in a twofold manner: 1) by causing apostasy in Israel and 2) by strengthening the heathen nations against Israel.

When we keep in mind how such a battle was fought—simultaneously among spirits on high and among men on earth—

then here, too, there were two parallel battles and struggles: one here on earth, the battle between Israel and the nations; and the other, in the spirit world between the demons and the good angels, the battle for Israel's preservation. The angels who headed the armies in this battle are called princes, as is evident from the texts cited above, and that they are also called principalities and powers.

It is apparent that there are many such princes (angels) who in this spiritual battle between Israel and the nations occupy a prominent place, and among these many the one seems to carry out a more important task and service than the other. For this section mentions not only princes among the angels but also some of them who are specifically called the "chief princes" (Dan. 10:13). Among these who are serving in this all-important battle of God and who are at the head of the army is Michael.

The angel continued to say that after this long-lasting battle he had finally come to make Daniel understand "what shall befall thy people in the latter days," or better, in the last days. The same expression Daniel and the other prophets use for the far-off Messianic times is also used here (see Gen. 49:1; Num. 24:14; Isa. 2:2; Mic. 4:1; Dan. 2:28, and other places). In view of the preceding context (8:23) and the following context (11:30-35) we must think here first of all of the last days of the Greco-Macedonian world monarchy and in particular the time of Antiochus Epiphanes. But it is further evident from the sequel to this vision (11:41-45 and 12:1) as well as from the words themselves that the angel is referring here to the end of the times, the time of the Antichrist. From the words of the angel can also be deduced that the man of God had especially agonized about his people Israel, and that it was his ardent desire to know still more about the future of his nation. In this, too, he is an example worthy to be imitated.

When Daniel heard that his people still had to walk a long and bitter road before the Messianic sun of Salvation would arise, he was struck dumb with terror and crashed once more face down to the ground. This proves more the greatness of his love than his weakness. Only the person who, like Daniel, loves much will also sigh and often fall silent.

Who Is This Being?

And, behold, one like the similitude of the sons of men touched my lips: then I opened my mouth, and spake, and said unto him that stood before me, O my lord, by the vision my sorrows are turned upon me, and I have retained no strength. For how can the servant of this my lord talk with this my lord? for as for me, straightway there remained no strength in me, neither is there breath left in me (vv. 16, 17).

Here the difficult question is who is this one like the similitude of the sons of men? There are those who think it is the one and the same created angel who has been talking right along. Other expositors think we are constantly dealing with the eternal uncreated Being, and they refer to similar healings and acts performed by the Lord Himself both in the Old and in the New Testament (Ps. 51:5; Isa. 6:7; Jer. 1:9; Mark 7:33; Eph. 6:9). Still others see in the first majestic person Christ before His incarnation, and in the next three instances, Gabriel. Others again see in the first two instances the same person and in the third and fourth instances someone else. Some even see a different person in each instance. It is extremely difficult to decide.

It seems to us, nonetheless, that the most acceptable explanation is that the uncreated Word, whom we met in verses 5 and 6 in His terrible appearance as He will reveal Himself on the last day, was accompanied by a retinue of holy spirits of the throne. For He is often depicted this way at His return. When He visited Abraham, He was not alone but was accompanied by two other persons who, like Himself, were called men. In Ezekiel 9 we come across the same thing. There He marches up to Jerusalem with a company of six men. In the night visions of Zechariah, we find this representation again and again (see especially the first three chapters). Hence, it appears to us that we are dealing here with the Son of God surrounded by a group of angels who carry out His commands. And we do not consider it absurd that every time we must picture different heavenly spirits, except in verses 10-15 and 20 and 21, where it is obvious the same angel is speaking.

It is further evident from Daniel's question to the angel that the latter is not the same as the one mentioned before and who appeared to him in brilliance and glory. If he was the same figure, then he showed himself at least in a wholly different manifestation, and that possibility is, of course, not excluded, for we hear Daniel himself say that, because of the great sight mentioned above, he is totally undone. (Dutch: had pangs as of a woman in travail.) This expression was one of the most commonly used comparisons in Israel and served to express all kinds of vexation and misery. Hence it appears in many places in the Old and New Testaments as well as in the Apocrypha. The appellation "my lord" is nothing but a title; we cannot deduce from it that this angel was the Lord Himself. In verse 17 Daniel asks the angel how he, Daniel, can still speak to this august Person after the great consternation due to that exalted vision. For there was no strength and breath left in him. With this question he makes a silent request for strength. An open mouth without strength cannot make a person to speak, so further strength is given him.

Fear Not

Then there came again and touched me one like the appearance of a man, and he strengthened me, and said, O man greatly beloved, fear not: peace be unto thee, be strong, yea, be strong. And when he had spoken unto me, I was strengthened, and said, Let my lord speak; for thou hast strengthened me. Then said he, Knowest thou wherefore I come unto thee? and now will I return to fight with the prince of Persia: and when I am gone forth, lo, the prince of Grecia shall come. But I will shew thee that which is noted in the Scripture of truth: and there is none that holdeth with me in these things, but Michael your prince (vv. 18-21).

It is obvious that the fright and consternation of Daniel were extremely great, for he caused the angel a lot of work. Before he could listen to the message he needed another touch and once more a word of encouragement. On the question as to who this angel was, we refer to our notes on verse 16. A definite or definitive answer cannot be given. This angel was condescending and friendly. The splendor of the angelic appearances exceeded all Daniel's capability of perception and the angel took that into account. He strengthened Daniel. It is not said how this took place. After he had strengthened him, he said to him, "O man greatly beloved, fear not." These words bespeak tender love and must have been very comforting to Daniel. Fear not! How often does the Lord say this in His Word to His children. Ah, we are often so very much afraid and burdened down. And we drag this load of grief along without casting it upon the Lord. We are often in the same condition as David when he said, "I shall surely perish one of these days by the hand of Saul;" or as Peter, when he feared that the waves of the sea would swallow him up.

After wishing him peace, the angel said further to Daniel, "Be strong, yea, be strong." Notice this word after he had been strengthened! In the same way all of God's Word exhorts us to manifest the power of our faith after the Lord has given us faith! The Lord especially wants His servants who are called to a special task to show themselves to be strong in His strength. And they do not receive true strength unless they have, like Daniel, died to their own strength first. We find the same thing with the apostle Paul, who had to be pricked by the thorn in his flesh and be pounded by the fists of Satan before he could say, "When I am weak, then am I strong" (2 Cor. 12:10). Thus Daniel was strengthened here.

When the angel was speaking to him, Daniel felt new strength flowed as it were through his veins. Whereas a short while ago he lay on the ground as dead, he now begins to live again and even asks the angel to speak to him as he has received strength from him. We can see here that the Lord lifts up those who are bowed down. "Fear not, little flock; for it is your Father's good pleasure to give you the kingdom" (Luke 12:32).

In verse 20 the angel asks whether Daniel has understood his message and the reason why he has come to Daniel. In his condition of a short while ago the prophet had not been all that receptive and perceptive to assimilate a revelation. Also this question is meant to make him more conscious. The prophet had asked the angel to speak, but the latter did not want to go on until Daniel understood the purpose of his visit.

This also gives us a hint that we must first make sure we understand the purpose of this vision and of all visions. The angel's purpose had been to fulfill Daniel's desire and make known unto him the future of Israel. But it seems to us there was still a higher objective to the angel's visit and speech, namely, that Daniel had to learn to see, and through Daniel's insight that Israel and all of us must also see that not only the world of nations but also even the world of evil angels are arrayed against the people of God. The battle is first brought to a conclusion in the world of spirits, and only then between flesh and flesh in this mundane world. To make this known, the angel in verses 13, 20, and 21 speaks emphatically of his battle against the prince of the Persians. And when he has gone forth, that is to say, has returned from the battle as a victorious conqueror now that the Medo-Persian world monarch will crumble away, "lo, the king of Grecia shall come," i.e., Alexander the Great, who will give this kingdom the coup de grace. The angel means to say he will then have to take up the battle again against this kingdom and against its evil spirits. Indirectly he again tells Daniel about the succession of these two kingdoms.

First, the angel will tell Daniel what is written in "the Scripture of truth." By this the angel means the book of the decrees and decisions of God's counsel in which the future events, namely, the vicissitudes of the nations, are written down. We find similar references often in Scripture (see Deut. 32:34; Ps. 56:8; 139:16; Isa. 65:6; Mal. 3:16). Daniel would learn but a single paragraph from this divine writing, in which no untruths are found. This, too, must afford comfort to Daniel, for in a book or document like this there is found a plan, unity, and order. What blasphemy is committed by the men of criticism when they consider all of this fantasy and pious deceit!

Finally, the angel tells Daniel that "there is none that holdeth with me in these things, but Michael." We cannot consider this statement as a lament, far less that it contains an accusation against the other holy angels who are at all times ready to do battle against all evil in any form. Nor is it plausible to think this statement betrays any concern whatever regarding the outcome of his battle as though he were afraid he might perish in it. It seems to us that this is a reassuring answer to an unspoken objection on Daniel's part. The angel had told him that he had fought against the evil angelic prince of Persia. And since he was now standing before Daniel, the latter might easily wonder whether the evil enemy in the meantime could do as he pleased. In answer he replies that presently there is none at the Persian court to further Israel's cause but Michael, and that he must now make haste to go to his aid again.

Michael is called here "thy prince." That contains a double assurance to Daniel, for Michael is one of the first princes (v. 13) and he is the special guardian spirit of Israel. Also in 12:1 he is called "the great prince, which standeth for the children of thy people." Scripture and history teach us that Satan hates nothing more than he hates Israel, the beloved of God for the sake of their fathers. For that reason he directs his worst attacks on this miracle nation par excellence. But in this evil attempt at destroying Israel, the archangel Michael especially opposes him as we usually find him in the thick heat of battle to fight against the devil and his evil hosts (see Jude 9 and Rev. 12).

Chapter **11**
IN THE GLORIOUS LAND

The Fourth King

Also I in the first year of Darius the Mede, even I, stood to confirm and to strengthen him. And now will I shew thee the truth. Behold, there shall stand up yet three kings in Persia; and the fourth shall be far richer than they all: and by his strength through his riches he shall stir up all against the realm of Grecia (vv. 1, 2).

The people who divided Scripture into chapters have not done this accurately at all times. Thus the first verse of this chapter should have been the last one of chapter 10. Once again the angel presents a chunk of world history to the prophet. He gives a bird's-eye view of the main events in the Medo-Persian realm, and this kingdom existed for about two hundred years. Chapter 10 can be considered as an extensive introduction to the last, long, and difficult revelation given to Daniel.

It was the angel's intent for Daniel to understand first that Israel's battle was not primarily a battle between flesh and flesh, nor between principle and principles. We, too, often represent the battle as though it actually is a battle of principles. This is to greatly weaken the biblical representation, if it does not in fact contradict it, for Scripture reduces the great struggle of the ages, the battle between light and darkness, to a camp of evil and good spirits (Job 1; 2; 1 Kings 22:19-22; 2 Chron. 18:18-22; Zech. 3; 2 Thess. 2:7; Rev. 12 and 13).

The words the angel addresses to Daniel give us a divine interpretation of the bitter opposition Zerubbabel, Ezra, and Nehemiah experienced when attempting Israel's restoration. The Tobiasses and the Sanballats were in the service of Satan himself. It was the struggle between the seed of the woman and the seed of the serpent. It is from this point of view that history is told. History is not mentioned here for its own sake, but it is described to the extent that Israel, representing the seed of the woman, is involved in it. And thus is not only the evil fate of Israel due to evil angels in a causal sense and in connection with its own sin, but also the good things are due to good angels. This is made clear in the first verse of this chapter, when the angel says he had helped and supported Michael in the battle in the first year of Darius.

This year had been a happy one for the Jews. The new ruler of the second world dominion seemed to be especially favorably inclined toward the Jews; he had the greatest regard for Daniel and advanced him even to the highest position in the realm; Daniel was miraculously saved from the den of lions, while his accusers had been devoured in it, and the proclamation, issued to all nations, urged everyone to tremble and fear before the God of Daniel (6:26-28). The angel ascribes this in a causal sense to his and Michael's intervention. These verses could not but broaden Daniel's outlook.

With the assurance that he will tell Daniel strictly the truth, so that he will be filled with undoubted certainty, the angel begins by giving a brief sketch of Persia's history. The angel's presentation is indeed so accurate that ever since Porphyrius, the great adversary of Christianity in the first centuries, this chapter has been the main obstacle to the deniers of the genuineness of this prophecy. Such accurate predictions, which were so literally fulfilled, were thought to be impossible, and so the critics placed the writer in a time after the events; so that he could no longer be considered an infallible prophet but a poetic novelist. No matter how often learned men have shown that such a thing is not possible, the satanic hatred against this book remains just the same. There are even those who dare maintain that the spuriousness of Daniel is a scientifically proven fact and boast that this is one of the most certain facts of criticism. Here, however, is an angel from heaven who speaks as the servant of the Lord, saying that he reveals the truth as it was given him regarding the future.

"There shall stand up yet three kings in Persia." The question may be asked whether this is correct, since in history the list of Persian kings is given as follows:

Cyrus	558-529
Cambyses	529-522

Pseudo-Smerdis	522-521
Darius I	521-486
Xerxes I	486-456
Artaxerxes (Longimanus)	456-425
Xerxes 2	425-425
Longimanus	425-425
Darius 2 (Nothus)	424-405
Artaxerxes 2 (Mnemon)	405-359
Artaxerxes 3 (Ochus)	359-338
Arses	338-336
Darius 3	336-330

However, it is by no means the angel's intent to give a complete list of all the kings, neither does he wish to imply that Xerxes was the last king of Persia. His sole intent is to point at the zenith of Persia's glory, which was at the same time the beginning of its downfall. As is evident from the preceding list the first three kings after Cyrus were Cambyses, Pseudo-Smerdis, and Darius I. Since the false Smerdis reigned only for seven months, he is often omitted by many historians, who then consider Cyrus the first of these three. The intent is specifically to call attention to the fourth who would possess greater riches than all the others.

This fourth ruler, Xerxes is usually considered the king Ahasuerus in the book of Esther. It is evident from the first chapter in Esther that he must have been fabulously rich, far richer than they all, as the prophet predicts here, and money is power. So this Ahasuerus became very powerful due to his riches and started to feel himself strong. Conscious of his great power he began to make preparations for his famous march on Greece. When it says, "he shall stir up all," this obviously refers to his four-year-long preparation for the mobilization of his enormous armies. At the end of his preparations he marched to Greece with an army of two and a half million, and if we include his retinue, a mass of five million people altogether. Until today it could be said there had never been again such enormous armies arrayed against an enemy as those of Xerxes. Further, he had a fleet of no less than twelve hundred ships, but this giant fleet was totally defeated at Salamis.

There are some scholars who translate these words "he will antagonize the entire kingdom of Greece," that is to say, evoke its bitter resentment and rancor. Even when translated this way, these words were fulfilled, for Greece continued to hate the Persians for many successive centuries. Alexander the Great was even motivated, at least in part, by the fire of hatred against the Persians (see 8:6). This campaign was the shining zenith of the second world empire, but at the same time, as we said earlier, the beginning of the end. After severe losses the proud king Xerxes retreated ingloriously to Persia. The power and supremacy of the Persian monarchy passed away with the reign of Xerxes. The last one hundred and forty years of the existence of the empire was a time of weakness and of anarchy. This period was spanned by the reign of eight kings (Meyers).

Scripture looks at Xerxes' expedition as the ruin of Persia. It does not even consider the eight kings who reigned during Persia's decay worthy of any mention. Only one century of its existence was important enough to be mentioned indirectly.

The Broken Kingdom

And a mighty king shall stand up, that shall rule with great dominion, and do according to his will. When he shall stand up, his kingdom shall be broken, and shall be divided toward the four winds of heaven; and not to his posterity, nor according to his dominion which he ruled: for his kingdom shall be plucked up, even for others beside those (vv. 3, 4).

These verses are referring to Alexander the Great. Here Scripture takes a jump from one world power to another, from the year 465 B.C. to 336 B.C., when Alexander ascended the throne of Macedonia. Scripture does not mention him as a brilliant genius or an invincible general, but as the head and embodiment of the third world dominion through whom God made great preparations for the gospel among the nations, and who did many favors to His people but also brought it partially under the dominion of the Greek mind and spirit. The literal fulfillment of this prophecy can be read in any history book on antiquity. We wish only to make the observation that Alexander's greatness was particularly evident from the fact, that after his death no one proved capable of keeping the conquered lands united under one scepter. On his deathbed he had given his signet ring to one of those who were standing by, saying, "To the most worthy," but he had not indicated whom he had in mind. Then a war erupted among his generals, which resulted after the battle at Ipsus in the fourfold fragmentation of his world empire.

Verse 4 points out four things literally fulfilled in history:

1. Upon his death his realm fell apart.
2. It was divided according to the four points of the compass.
3. It was divided among his generals, not his descendants.
4. The four realms did not possess, either individually or combined, the power of Alexander's world empire.

King of the South

And the king of the south shall be strong, and one of his princes; and he shall be strong above him, and have dominion; his dominion shall be a great dominion (v. 5).

To understand this chapter correctly we must realize that the concepts south, north, east, and west in Scripture always mean as referenced from the Holy Land. Egypt lay south of Palestine, so that the king of the south means the king of Egypt. This king is here called one of his princes, i.e., one of Alexander's generals. The person referred to is Ptolemy, son of Lagus, who was the founder of the powerful realm of the Lagides in Egypt.

"And he shall be strong above him." This refers to another of Alexander's generals, the mighty Seleucus Nikator, founder of the Syrian kingdom, which far surpassed the kingdom of Ptolemy in riches, power, and area. He is the king of the north, as Syria lay north of Palestine. On account of the constant wars between these two kingdoms, the Jewish people had to suffer a great deal. The Jews were always the possession of one or the other alternately.

Conniving in the Court

And in the end of years they shall join themselves together; for the king's daughter of the south shall come to the king of the north to make an agreement: but she shall not retain the power of the arm; neither shall he stand, nor his arm: but she shall be given up, and they that brought her, and he that begat her, and he that strengthened her in these times (v. 6).

Everyone agrees that here again we have literal history described beforehand. Only the rationalists believe it was written afterward. This text speaks of the two kingdoms under which

Israel was oppressed by each successively. These two realms were in bitter enmity against each other. In the end of years, after about half a century, Ptolemy, the king of Egypt, and Antiochus 2, nicknamed Theos, "the divine," wished to become friends by intermarriage. The text says the daughter of the king of Egypt would come to the king of the north to make an agreement or, literally, to make everything level or smooth. In so doing they wished to turn enmity into friendship and cause the interminable wars to cease. So Ptolemy gave his daughter Berenice to the afore-mentioned Antiochus of Syria. For that purpose he divorced his wife, Laodice, who was his half-sister, on the condition that the children born from his marriage with Berenice be heirs to the throne.

"But she shall not retain the power of the arm." With these words the text indicates that this marriage of Berenice did not result in a lasting union. It indeed ended in complete failure. Ptolemy died, and soon thereafter Antiochus sent Berenice away to take back his former wife Laodice. Thus Berenice did not remain queen and did not retain "the power of the arm." But neither did Antiochus stand, and his arm, his strength, also crumbled. The reaccepted wife, Laodice, mistrusted the fickle-ness of her husband Antiochus and put an end to his life by poisoning him. In the same way she killed her son. That is what is meant by "he that begat her"—whom she bore or who was born of her.

"And they that brought her." Many of the Egyptian courtiers who had accompanied Berenice from Egypt and who now served her were also killed by her. "And he that strengthened her in these times"—all of them became objects of feminine revenge. The reason why these immoral abominations and assassinations are mentioned must undoubtedly be sought in the fact that these shameful acts laid the groundwork for new and destructive wars between the two kingdoms, and that the people of the Lord were frequently fearfully afflicted during those long wars.

Entering the Fortress

But out of a branch of her roots shall one stand up in his estate, which shall come with an army, and shall enter into the fortress of the king of the north, and shall deal against them, and shall prevail: and shall also carry captives into Egypt their gods, with

their princes, and with their precious vessels of silver and of gold; and he shall continue more years than the king of the north. So the king of the south shall come into his kingdom, and shall return into his own land (vv. 7-9).

"A branch of her roots" means a descendant, a little branch sprouted from the same stump as had Berenice. This is a reference to Ptolemy Euergetes, king of Egypt and a brother to the murdered Berenice. The latter, bent on avenging the death of his sister, organized a campaign against Syria, conquered many strong places, and meted out considerable revenge everywhere he went. He succeeded everywhere, as verse 7 indicates.

Verse 8 speaks of the rich loot which he took along to Egypt. According to old history books, he took to Egypt countless treasures and precious things, besides many prisoners, including the idols which the son of Cyrus the Great had stolen from Egypt many years before. Out of gratitude the Egyptians gave him the name Euergetes or benefactor. The word translated here as "princes" can also mean, in the original, molten images. What is meant, undoubtedly, is golden or, as Van Hamelsveld translates, princely images. As verse 8 indicates, Egypt's king succeeded in keeping Syria at bay for a number of years.

The opinions regarding the meaning of verse 9 vary depending on which of two very different translations is chosen. As it is given here it is merely the concluding verse of what was said before. Another translation has "this king," i.e., the king of the north, "shall invade the kingdom of the south." Even taken in this sense we can speak of a literal fulfillment, for Seleucus Callinicus tried by way of revenge to invade Egypt, but a severe storm destroyed his fleet and he had to return to his country with great losses and in shame, as this verse predicted.

A Great Assembly

But his sons shall be stirred up, and shall assemble a multitude of great forces: and one shall certainly come, and overflow, and pass through: then shall he return, and be stirred up, even to his fortress (v. 10).

The two sons of Seleucus Callinicus were Seleucus 3 and Antiochus 3, who later obtained for himself the epithet "the Great" on account of his successful field battles. Our text calls specific attention to the latter. He fully deserved the sobriquet "the Great," for he was a very regal and prosperous warrior. On the advice of his first minister, Hermias, he marched on Ptolemy Philopater, son of Euergetes, as soon as he ascended the throne of Egypt. His first campaign did not succeed gloriously and is therefore passed over, but the next two, referred to in verse 10, were a great success. In the first, one city after another fell into his hands, and in the second campaign the following year almost all of Palestine was subjugated. The verse refers especially to this last-mentioned fact.

Usually the Lord describes wars (as well as world history) exclusively from the point of view of His people even though it is temporarily *Lo-ammi*. All of the divine plan, made before the foundation of the world, is traced out with His elect people in mind. For that reason the wars of Alexander the Great waged in the Middle East are not mentioned simply because they had no significance for the holy nation. To God there is no such thing as world history. All vicissitudes of the nations are either history of the kingdom of God or not worth mentioning.

A Stirring Up

And the king of the south shall be moved with choler, and shall come forth and fight with him, even with the king of the north: and he shall set forth a great multitude; but the multitude shall be given into his hand (v. 11).

It is said that the king of the south, Ptolemy Philopater, would become angry on account of all the victories won by Antiochus the Great and would do battle with him. Philopater is described as a slow, low, and effeminate king, but now he awakened from his lethargy and laziness and reached for his armor. He put himself at the head of seventy thousand foot soldiers and five thousand horsemen and seventy-three elephants. Antiochus had also put together a great army, as this verse tells us. It was even larger than that of Philopater's, for he had seventy-two thousand foot soldiers, six thousand horsemen, and one hundred and two elephants. The armies clashed near Rafiah and the outcome of the battle was that Philopater completely defeated the Syrian army.

The great multitude of Syrians fell into the hands of the king of Egypt. They lost no less than ten thousand slain and four thousand prisoners, while Antiochus returned to his country and by means of an embassy begged Ptolemy for peace. The latter showed his shortsightedness by not taking advantage of his great victory. He could easily have conquered all of the Syrian realm, but his laziness and sensuality made him choose in favor of the fun at the court rather than the battle on the field. Moreover, he was extremely conceited about the victory he had won. The result of these things are recorded in the following verses:

A Haughty Heart

And when he hath taken away the multitude, his heart shall be lifted up; and he shall cast down many ten thousands; but he shall not be strengthened by it. For the king of the north shall return, and shall set forth a multitude greater than the former, and shall certainly come after certain years with a great army and with much riches (vv. 12, 13).

The third book of the Maccabees is not very reliable because of its palpable exaggerations, nevertheless it clearly describes the literal fulfillment of verse 12. Ptolemy was so vaunted on account of his great victory that he had the evil courage to penetrate to within the holy of holies, disregarding the admonitions of the Jews. By a special punishment of God he was struck down so that he was carried out of the temple, seemingly dead. In anger he had inscribed upon a pillar that he would carry away the Jews as slaves. He also got the crazy idea to let five hundred drunken elephants run loose into a group of imprisoned Jews, but upon the prayer of a godly priest this calamity was averted. One story says God sent two angels who scared the brute animals so much that they trampled down the army of Philopater instead of the Israelites.

Verse 13 tells us that Antiochus recovered from his terrible defeat, and with an even greater army than before returned to Egypt to do battle. After some thirteen years his opponent Ptolemy IV Philopater had died and was succeeded by his little son, aged six, Ptolemy Philopater. Antiochus considered this moment advantageous to invade Egypt with a great army. With awe-inspiring war equipment he advanced, defeated the army of the Egyptians, and conquered Sidon, Gaza, and Palestine. The Jews were sick of the Egyptian dominion and everywhere they joyously greeted the conqueror, who therefore, at the occasion of his entrance into Jerusalem, granted him several privileges.

Rebellion Failed

And in those times there shall many stand up against the king of the south: also the robbers of thy people shall exalt themselves to establish the vision; but they shall fall (v. 14).

This verse informs us that many Jews, extremely tired of the yoke of Ptolemy, revolted against him and welcomed Antiochus into their city with shouts of joy. Some exegetes think this refers to the covenant Antiochus the Great made with Philippus, king of Macedonia, but according to the rule which may not be over-looked when explaining this chapter (that all these wars and events are described for the benefit and from the point of view of Israel) we must interpret this as referring to the rebellion of the Jews against their legal king.

In those days there were many persons who wished to deliver Israel by force from their foreign despots, and here they are called "robbers." The addition of "thy people" shows that Jews are meant. But they will not succeed. As long as the times of the Gentiles are in force Israel has never succeeded and will never succeed to free itself from foreign dominion. The long history of blood and tears which this nation has experienced has proven this beyond the shadow of a doubt. In His time the Lord Himself will deliver Israel with an everlasting deliverance. Hence, here it is predicted that the Jews, by way of confirmation of the vision, would perish. We can further learn from this verse how the Lord hates every form of disobedience and revolution. Many writers may praise these acts by the Jews, but the Lord calls them robbers. Even though Philopater was a cruel oppressor, this did not give them the right to revolt.

Antiochus the Great

So the king of the north shall come, and cast up a mount, and take the most fenced cities: and the arm of the south shall not withstand, neither his chosen people, neither shall there be any strength to withstand. But he that cometh against him shall do according to his own will, and none shall stand before him: and he shall stand in the glorious land, which by his hand shall be consumed (vv. 15, 16).

The "he" at the beginning of verse 16 refers to Antiochus and not to the king of Egypt. This verse is a further description of the victorious advances of the Syrian king. Nobody and nothing could stop him. Josephus gives a rather extensive description of his martial acts. But with God it is especially the holy nation and land which stand in the foreground. For that reason attention is called to the fact that he would stand in "the glorious land" or land of glory, as Palestine is called here. God loves this land above all lands and it has pleased Him to perform nearly all of His wonders on this sacred soil. "When the most High divided to the nations their inheritance, when he separated the sons of Adam, he set the bounds of the people according to the number of the children of Israel" (Deut. 32:8 ; cf. Dan. 8:9; 11:16, 30, 31, 41).

The translation "which by his hand shall be consumed" could have been better and more carefully expressed. It gives the impression that he would fearfully persecute the Jews. He did not do this. On the contrary, he gave them many special privileges. The text literally says he would accomplish or perfect it, which means he would subjugate the Jews so that from that time on they would never serve Egypt again.

Alliance and Treachery

He shall also set his face to enter with the strength of his whole kingdom, and upright ones with him; thus shall he do: and he shall give him the daughter of women, corrupting her: but she shall not stand on his side, neither be for him (v. 17).

This verse is also very remarkable because of its detailed predictions which have been literally fulfilled. "To set one's face" to do something was a picturesque expression in Israel for entertaining an intent and making an attempt at carrying out that determined intent. Thus it was Antiochus' determination to master Egypt, and for that purpose he wanted to pound on it with all his might. Behold, Antiochus did not do so but approached Egypt with fair conditions. To what must this change in tactics be ascribed? To the fact that Antiochus was watching Rome's increasing power with great concern. For Rome had taken on the guardianship over the very young king of Egypt, so Antiochus did not dare challenge Rome's power at that time. For that reason he wanted to affect by ruse what he possibly could not do by power.

To prevent Rome from turning against him, he sought to establish ties of relationship with the Egyptian dynasty. This is a very common trick to which the great men of the earth have always taken recourse. He apparently tried to reach a twofold goal with it; to fend off Rome and to obtain power over Egypt. He gave his daughter Cleopatra I to the youthful king Philopater in marriage. It is she who is indicated by the words "daughter of women." He did not want to corrupt her but use her as a means of corrupting that kingdom. But she would not be steadfast, would not stand, as the text expresses it. It is indeed history that after her marriage she did not serve the interests of her father. With her husband she chose the party of the Romans.

Antiochus Defeated

After this shall he turn his face unto the isles, and shall take many: but a prince for his own behalf shall cause the reproach offered by him to cease; without his own reproach he shall cause it to turn upon him. Then he shall turn his face toward the fort of his own land: but he shall stumble and fall, and not be found (v. 18, 19).

The narrative is still speaking of Antiochus the Great. The Hebrews called all coastlines islands, even the countries bordering the sea. Verse 18 indicates that he fitted out a big fleet to extend his conquests to the west and that he obtained many victories there. "But a prince for his own behalf shall cause the reproach offered by him to cease" means that a Roman general, Cornelius Scipio, would stop the shame of defeats and that he himself would inflict a shameful defeat upon Antiochus. This victory over the Asiatic king caused Scipio to become so famous and so beloved that he was given the epithet Asiaticus.

Verse 19 speaks of the end of this famous king of the north. After having obtained a less than honorable peace he found himself forced to hole up within the borders and forts of his own land. Because of lack of funds he undertook to rob the temple of Jupiter. This act of sacrilege galled the people extremely and made them revolt. In this revolt he was killed, so that once again we are dealing here with pre-recorded history when it says he fell and was no longer to be found.

A Raiser of Taxes

Then shall stand up in his estate a raiser of taxes in the glory of the kingdom: but within few days he shall be destroyed, neither in anger, nor in battle (v. 20).

When interpreting Daniel 11 it is of great importance to read Article 6 of the *Reformed Confession of Faith*. This article deals with the difference between canonical and apocryphal books:

> We distinguish those sacred books from the aprocryphal. viz.: the third book of Esdras, the books of Tobias, Judith, Wisdom, Jesus Syrach, Baruch, the appendix to the book of Esther, the Song of the Three Children in the Furnace, the history of Susannah, of Bell and the Dragon, the prayer of Manasses, and the two books of the Maccabees. All of which the Church may read and take instruction from, so far as they agree with the canonical books; but they are far from having such power and efficacy as that we may from their testimony confirm any point of faith, or of the Christian religion; much less detract from the authority of the other sacred books.

It very correctly recommends the reading of these books as containing instruction. The books of the Maccabees especially contain instructive details to clarify this chapter and these verses. After the death of Antiochus the Great, his son Seleucus Philopater, surnamed Soter or Savior, became king of Syria. Also this verse deals with his relationship with the Jews. The second book of the Maccabees tells us, and this story does partially deserve our credence, that he gave his chamberlain Heliodorus orders to plunder the treasuries of the temple, but the latter seems to have been punished in a miraculous manner. "In the glory of the kingdom" means the glory of Palestine. This expression agrees with what we read in verse 20. The king's life was taken by this extortioner, not openly nor by a war, but secretly killed by poison, exactly as is predicted in this verse.

A Vile Person

And in this estate shall stand up a vile person, to whom they shall not give the honor of the kingdom: but he shall come in peaceably, and obtain the kingdom by flatteries (v. 21).

Verses 21 to 35 deal entirely with Antiochus Epiphanes. Some interpreters think that with the vile person is still meant the treasurer Heliodorus who first tried to steal the glory of the kingdom. Epiphanes means illustrious but he was called Epimanes, crazy. The people had not ascribed royal dignity to him as Demetrius, the son of Seleucus Philopater, was the rightful successor to the throne, whereas Antiochus Epiphanes was only the youngest son of Antiochus the Great. The rightful heir to the throne spent his days as a hostage at the court in Rome. Because of that, and also strengthened by internal riots and external support, Antiochus Epiphanes peaceably, that is to say, unexpectedly, came to the throne (8:25).

The word translated "flatteries" actually means slick or slippery places. There are those who translate it as precarious circumstances. Luther makes it "sweet words," which of course agrees with the King James version. The latter undoubtedly conveys the correct meaning. History tells us that this king vied unashamedly for the favor of the people. Together with Absalom and Napoleon he, too, was in this respect a type of the Antichrist who one day will do the same thing. There are, it seems to us, two main reasons why this chapter dwells so long on this foolish and wicked king:

1. He oppressed Israel in a fearful way.
2. He is one of the clearest types of the Antichrist. He was, so to speak, the Antichrist of the Old Dispensation or, as K. P. Caspari calls him, "the Antichrist of the third world monarchy."

Prince of the Covenant

And with the arms of a flood shall they be overflown from before him, and shall be broken; yea, also the prince of the covenant (v. 22).

"The arms of a flood" refers to the strong Egyptian martial power. Here we undoubtedly have a reference to the inundating arms of the Nile River. But those inundating martial powers of Egypt will be inundated and broken themselves. The term "prince of the covenant" has boggled the mind of many an exegete. It has been suggested that it means:

1. The high priest Onias, whose glorious office was held up for grabs by Epiphanes to the highest bidder.
2. Ptolemy Philopater, the king of Egypt, who had made a covenant with him.

3. Epiphanes himself, who also had made a covenant.
4. The Trinity, who had made a covenant with Israel.
5. The Lord Jesus Christ.
6. Israel, the royal nation of the covenant.
7. Finally, some commentators think it refers to Demetrius, the rightful successor to Seleucus Philopater.

The context seems to point to the king of Egypt. There is a constant reference to the wars and disturbances between the kings of Syria and Egypt. We do know that Epiphanes had made a covenant with his nephew, the son of his sister, Ptolemy Philopater, so that he could be called the prince of the covenant. The authors of the marginal notes in the [Dutch] State translation also have this opinion.

We are also attracted by the idea that Israel is meant, for not only were the Jews extremely oppressed by him but also God, who, in Daniel, keeps Himself hidden from His people and systematically avoids the usual theocratic names. Also, in Daniel *berith* always refers to the holy covenant of grace.

Wicked Deeds

And after the league made with him he shall work deceitfully: for he shall come up, and shall become strong with a small people. He shall enter peaceably even upon the fattest places of the province; and he shall do that which his fathers have not done, nor his fathers' fathers; he shall scatter among them the prey, and spoil, and riches: yea, and he shall forecast his devices against the strongholds, even for a time (vv. 23, 24).

With regard to these verses commentators usually complain about the lack of historical sources that corroborate the literal fulfillment of these words. The difficulty with them is due mainly to the fact that verses 21-24 contain a general overview of the activity of Antiochus Epiphanes. The books of the Maccabees and Josephus describe at length the rein and wicked deeds of this king. Also these verses speak of his duplicity and serpentine character. He was a true child of hell whose greatest ambition was nothing less than to completely destroy Israel. To that end he applied all his cunning and vehemence.

Verse 24 hints at his serpentine slithering upon the fattest places of the province, i.e., Palestine, which again is referred to in a camouflaged manner. He would deal with Israel in a manner totally different from that of his fathers and forefathers. He was very wasteful. That which he captured as prey and spoil in a certain place he strewed in an inebriated condition among the multitudes and gave gold to total strangers. He gave certain cities huge sums of money and organized many festivities and much merry-making for the people. But all these things were only for a certain time.

The Covenant Violated

And he shall stir up his power and his courage against the king of the south with a great army; and the king of the south shall be stirred up to battle with a very great and mighty army; but he shall not stand: for they shall forecast devices against him. Yea, they that feed of the portion of his meat shall destroy him, and his army shall overflow: and many shall fall down slain. And both these kings' hearts shall be to do mischief, and they shall speak lies at one table; but it shall not prosper: for yet the end shall be at the time appointed. Then shall he return into his land with great riches; and his heart shall be against the holy covenant; and he shall do exploits, and return to his own land (vv. 25-28).

The subject of these verses are the campaigns of Antiochus Epiphanes. Verse 25 speaks of a campaign of which little is known with certainty. What is meant must be his march on Egypt in the year 171 B.C. and the great battle near Pelusium. This conquest made it necessary for the king of Egypt to subject himself to Antiochus Epiphanes, who wrapped him up in the finely spun web of his deceits and designs. The latter were one reason why everything in Egypt became confused. The Alexandrians forsook their king Ptolemy Philometor and placed his younger brother Ptolemy Physkon on the throne. Also the former guardians and mercenary troops, who were paid and kept by him, defected exactly as verse 26 indicates.

The last clause of this verse refers to the great victory of Antiochus and the many who fell in battle. Verse 27 speaks of the reciprocal perfidy of Antiochus and Philometor. Sitting and eating at one table was from of old a sign of friendship, unity, peace, and love in the East. We need think only of the Lord's Supper and the prophetic lament in Psalm 41:9, "Yea, mine own familiar friend, in whom I trusted, which did eat of my bread, hath lifted up his heel against me." That is how they are depicted here, as apparently the greatest friends, sitting together at one table, but at the same time entertaining each other with lies and bent on deceiving each other. All men lie, but the greatest among them lie the most. Antiochus tried to get possession of Egypt in a sly manner, but he did not succeed. The last part of verse 27 indicates that the martial activities of Antiochus Epiphanes had not yet come to an end.

Verse 28 tells us Antiochus Epiphanes returned to his country with great spoils after his victories in Egypt, and in passing through Israel demonstrated his hateful acts against the holy covenant. He boldly entered the sanctuary and stole the golden altar, the candlestick and its implements, the table of shewbread, the cups, the basins, the golden censers, the veil, the crowns and golden ornaments of the temple, then smashed everything to pieces. He killed many people and all Israel mourned. After these shameful acts he returned to his own country.

Anger Against Israel

At the time appointed he shall return, and come toward the south; but it shall not be as the former, or as the latter. For the ships of Chittim shall come against him: therefore he shall be grieved, and return, and have indignation against the holy covenant: so shall he do; he shall even return, and have intelligence with them that forsake the holy covenant (vv. 29, 30).

Antiochus' third campaign against Egypt was not as favorable as the first two, we are told in verse 29. A year earlier he had left the two brothers, Philometor and Physkon, behind in a civil war, hoping they would devour each other so Egypt would easily fall prey to him, but this secret hope did not materialize. The brothers united and decided to rule the country jointly. So he again sent a mighty army to Egypt, but this campaign ended in failure.

"For the ships of Chittim came against him." According to Genesis 10:4, the Kittites or Chittites descended from Javan, one of the sons of Japheth. In Scripture the Chittites are considered to be the nations living on the islands of the Mediterranean and on its coasts. See Numbers 24:24 where Balaam predicts, "And ships shall come from the coast of Chittim, and shall afflict Ashur, and shall afflict Eber, and also shall perish forever." Thus here is meant the ships of the Romans.

The fourth world power was beginning to materialize at that time; Rome was beginning to make its voice heard in the orchestra of the world. And so it had also taken an interest in the matters that concerned Egypt and sent its ambassador Caius Popilius Lenas with a few ships to Egypt to straighten things out there. The Syrian ruler met the robust Roman near Alexandria. They had been warm friends at the time when Antiochus had been a hostage in Rome. Antiochus wanted to embrace his former friend, but the latter stepped back coolly and refused the embrace and any other sign of friendship until he knew whether Antiochus was a friend or an enemy of the Romans. At the same time he informed him of Rome's demand that he stop all aggressions against Egypt and return to his own country. Antiochus pretended that he had to discuss this first with his war council, but then the resolute Roman drew a circle around the king with his bamboo stick with the order not to leave the circle before he had made a decision. This daring act of the proud Roman amazed and angered the king, upon which Popilius offered him the hand of friendship. And so Antiochus in his suppressed fury went through Judea back to his country.

He vented his anger against the holy covenant, i.e., against Israel and its institutions. Israel is once again mentioned in a disguised manner because it is *Lo-ammi*. Only by virtue of the covenant Israel is and remains holy, the separated nation, and so it is named here. The unfaithful among Israel are called "them that forsake the holy covenant." Antiochus paid attention to this disloyal scum; he listening to them and uniting with them.

Terrible Persecutions

And arms shall stand on his part, and they shall pollute the sanctuary of strength, and shall take away the daily sacrifice, and they shall place the abomination that maketh desolate. And such as do wickedly against the covenant shall he corrupt by flatteries: but the people that do know their God shall be strong, and do exploits. And they that understand among the people shall instruct many: yet they shall fall by the sword, and by flame, by captivity, and by spoil, many days. Now when they shall fall, they shall be holpen with a little help: but many shall cleave to them with flatteries. And some of them of understanding shall fall, to try them, and to purge, and to make them white, even to the time of the end: because it is yet for a time appointed (vv. 31-35).

These verses speak of the terrible persecutions Antiochus inflicted upon the Jews. Compare these verses with 8:9-12 and the comments made there. "The arms that shall stand on his part" refer to the army corps, the troops. What is meant are the Syrian troops which Antiochus had placed in the fortress of Zion. "The desecration of the sanctuary," "the termination of the daily sacrifice," and the placing of "the abomination that maketh desolate," are spoken of in the first chapter of Maccabees.

The terrible persecution was a judgment of the Lord upon the fearful apostasy in Israel and was partly caused by the unfaithful Jews among them. They allowed themselves to be enchanted by the presents, positions of honor, and beautiful promises by Antiochus. He flattered them and they pretended to be like the heaven. Two people in particular among these renegades made themselves very infamous by assisting him in desecrating and robbing the temple.

In contrast to these renegade hypocrites are the people that do know their God, as the faithful in Israel are called. These faithful ones were called the Chasidim, the godly ones. Verse 32b does not mean they were seized and killed, as our translation might easily suggest, but that godly people must take courage and remain true to the covenant and their God and do His will.

Even then, as is the case in all periods of apostasy, there were still faithful teachers. We need think only of Eleazar and Matthathias, the Maccabean heroes. Those faithful leaders instructed and encouraged the people, although this resulted for them in suffering by the sword, fire, the dungeon, and plundering. In 2 Maccabees 6 we find a description of a martyr's death of the ninety-year-old Eleazar, and in the following chapter the martyrdom by torture of seven brothers and their mother.

Verse 34 is a prophecy of the deliverance effected by the brave Maccabees. At first these warriors constituted only a slight power, a little help; but soon their power increased since many people joined them, whether out of fear or ambition or vindictiveness, even though they did not share their convictions. There are commentators who want to translate "flatteries" by dangerous circumstances of the time. In that case the idea is that many, forced by the circumstances of the time, joined them. This translation is acceptable and contains a good idea.

"And some of them of understanding shall fall." The word

"teachers" does not imply only priests. In a general sense, we can think of all those who were faithful to God and who admonished others to be faithful. Here it is prophesied that some of those faithful leaders would fall, not only through martyrdom but also in the war. This was not to try and purge the already fallen ones, but to try and purge through them; in other words, for the purpose of urging others on to faithfulness to their God by their example. The godly people in those days understood very well that God had a special purpose in mind with all their suffering. The Lord wants to admonish many even to the time of the end through those martyrs. But that time lies still in the future.

The angel had told Daniel that he would tell him what his people would experience in the last days, in the Messianic period. From there on the prophecy is referring to the end-time. The predictions thus far embrace a period of about four centuries. They describe the events with regard to Israel in such a way that it is possible to trace the particulars almost from feature to feature as having been fulfilled. With verse 36 this is changing.

The Antichrist

And the king shall do according to his will; and he shall exalt himself, and magnify himself above every god, and shall speak marvellous things against the God of gods, and shall prosper till the indignation be accomplished: for that that is determined shall be done (v. 36).

The question here is, who is this king? The interpretations vary greatly. We mention the main ideas without refuting them:

- Antiochus Epiphanes, mentioned in the previous verses.
- The power of the Roman empire.
- The papacy.
- Mohammedism or Mohammed.
- Napoleon.
- The king of the north of the latter days.
- The Antichrist.

Those who adhere to the first-mentioned opinion make a strong case for themselves from the context for, they say, the definite article is used for thinking and this points back to the king these verses have been speaking of all along. Then, too, the end of all the kings mentioned in this chapter is recorded, but not of this one yet. And, finally, since verse 35 is still obviously speaking of Antiochus Epiphanes, it would be an unwarranted jump to continue the history many centuries further into the future.

But the definite article is frequently used to indicate the greatness or the extraordinary character of something or somebody, and that is the way it is used here. This verse speaks of a king who leaves Antiochus Epiphanes far behind in wickedness and of whom Antiochus was but a faint shadow. It is perfectly clear that the context here speaks of a Syrian king, but we find other examples in Scripture of sudden great leaps into the future. There is hardly a Messianic prophecy in the Old Testament where we do not find this phenomenon. Also in Daniel it appears more than once (see 2:23, 24; 7:8-11; 8:22-25; 9:26, 27).

So we need not be surprised that we find something similar here. It will become more than evident from the description itself that we are dealing here with none other than the Antichrist. Against the ideas that the text speaks of the popes, Mohammed, or Napoleon can be correctly argued that the prophets knew nothing of the dispensation of the mystery as this entire present dispensation is called. This fact alone topples the whole so-called historical exegesis. That we are dealing here with the Antichrist is further evident from the following facts:

- He will come at the time of the end (see vv. 35, 40, 45; 12:4, 6, 9). In Daniel this expression always refers to the time of the Antichrist (cf. 7:26; 8:17-19; 9:27), the three and a half years of the second half of the last year-week of 9:27 (Rev. 13:5).
- The apostle Paul derived the greatest part of his description of the man of sin in 2 Thessalonians 2 from Daniel's description here.
- The Antichrist shall cause the Great Tribulation of Israel, and that is what this context speaks of (see 12:1 and cf. Jer. 30:7 and Matt. 24:21).
- The context speaks of Israel's delivery (12:1) and it, too, comes only after the return of Christ.
- The context further makes mention of the resurrection (12:2, 3) and it, too, does not come until at the time of the return of the Lord. According to verse 36 the Antichrist will be a self-

willed, self-glorifying, self-deifying, blasphemous, and prosperous king (cf. further what we have already said on 7:8, 26 and 8:10, 11, 25).

• According to K. P. Caspari, "most of the older commentators in the Church" have interpreted this as referring to the Antichrist.

Self Magnification

Neither shall he regard the God of his fathers, nor the desire of women, nor regard any god: for he shall magnify himself above all (v. 37).

This verse says three things of the man of sin. He will not "regard the gods of his fathers, the desire of women, nor any god," as he himself wants to be exalted and lifted up as the only, exclusive god. The expression in the middle of this verse is the most difficult to comprehend. Both the different translations and their interpretations vary greatly, but as a rule they reflect the viewpoint taken by the various exegetes. Again we pass on the main interpretations and after that supply our own understanding of the issue. Those who think the text is still speaking of Antiochus Epiphanes refer to:

• His cruelty, which made him disregard the tears of women.
• The destruction of the temple which contained images the women greatly loved and respected.
• His licentiousness and immorality which caused him to despise the pure marital love of his wives.
• The feminine feeling of his wives that he should not act so tyrannically, and especially of one of his wives, a Jewess, whose desire and request not to harm her people he allegedly ignored.

Those who think the person referred to is the papacy point out in this connection the forbidding of marriage in 1 Timothy 4:3 and see it then as the enforced celibacy of Roman Catholic priests. Those who see in him Napoleon remind us of his repudiating his beautiful wife, Josephine. There are many exegetes who in a general sense think of the inhumanity that makes the Antichrist shake off all pure human feelings so that he has not any human feelings left. The question is whether the text here is speaking of the desire of women or that of men for the woman. Undoubtedly, the former is meant here.

Today a totally different explanation has arisen, first advocated by Faber and Elliot, and afterward by many others. They think the expression refers to Israelite women who desire to be granted to bring the Messiah into the world; and then they apply it to the Lord Jesus Christ whom the Antichrist will ignore. This interpretation appears to us as the most acceptable on the following grounds:

- We are standing here wholly on Israelite soil and hence the strong desire on the part of Israelite women is very natural.
- The expression "God of his fathers" is also an Israelite expression and the Antichrist will most likely be a Jew.
- The New Testament teaches us very clearly that the Antichrist will specifically oppose Christ.
- This shadowy name for Christ is wholly in agreement with the nature of Daniel's prophecy in which, apart from a few exceptions, we find so many veiled references to the Lord Jesus Christ. Hence, we consider this verse to predict that he will disregard the God of his fathers as well as the Messiah, so long and so ardently longed for, as well as any power of this world; he himself wants to be worshiped and glorified as God. He will not be satisfied until he is acknowledged as deity.

The God of Forces

But in his estate shall he honor the God of forces: and a god whom his fathers knew not shall he honor with gold, and silver, and with precious stones, and pleasant things. Thus shall he do in the most strong holds with a strange god, whom he shall acknowledge and increase with glory: and he shall cause them to rule over many, and shall divide the land for gain (v. 38, 39).

Here we have a further description of the character and crimes of the Antichrist. Verse 38 indicates that the Antichrist will still honor some god. The question is what is meant here by "the god of forces." Here again there are many and widely divergent explanations. The exegetes who opt for Antiochus think it refers to Jupiter Olympus, the chief deity of the Romans, for whom he erected a statue in the temple in Jerusalem. Others think it means Jupiter Capitolinus, as the temple in Rome was called and which was at the same time a strong fortress. Then it would refer to Antiochus' admiration for everything Roman. Again others in this camp think of the war god, Mars, because Antiochus waged so many battles and hence must have felt deep attachment to this deity. Still others think it refers to the Greek idol, Hercules, to whom Antiochus paid honor with the plays at Tyrus. Those who interpret all this in terms of the papacy usually think it refers to guardian saints and angels. Those who find a reference to the Antichrist in these verses translate this clause as "god of natural forces" and that would then apply to the completely materialistic character of the man of sin. Dr. A. Kuyper, who also interprets these verses as speaking of the Antichrist, thinks it refers to the god of war in general. This is, undoubtedly, the best translation and interpretation, for the word *mauzzim* means strongholds, fortifications, and hence refers to battles and destruction. We find the same word in verses 7 and 10. The Antichrist will worship, as it were, the destructions of war.

The objection could be made whether it could be said that his fathers had not known wars. That cannot be said, of course, but what can be said is that his fathers had never known such wars and had never known such satanic joy in destruction as he would one day show. In a special sense it can be said of him, "destruction and misery are in his ways: and the way of peace hath he not known." According to Revelation 13:4 he will possess the military power of the entire world and an astonished mankind will cry out: "Who is like unto the beast? who is able to make war with him?"

There are some exegetes in this connection who think of the image of the beast of which Revelation 13:14-16 speaks. I can think of no objection to combining these two ideas. When it says he will honor this god in his estate, this only means he will magnify this god instead of any and all other gods. Verse 38 adds that he is willing to give all his treasures to this god. Does not anti-Christianity also make huge sacrifices for war in our days?

Verse 39 still continues to enlarge on his veneration of this god. The wording of the verse is obscure. The meaning of it is twofold:

1. For this god he will erect strongholds and make wars.

2. He will give great honor and prominence to all who worship this god; he will make them rulers over wide areas and even

divide unto them, in return for money, all of Palestine. The black shadows of all this already fall daily on our pathways through life.

The Great Overthrow

And at the time of the end shall the king of the south push at him: and the king of the north shall come against him like a whirlwind, with chariots, and with horsemen, and with many ships; and he shall enter into the countries, and shall overflow and pass over. He shall enter also into the glorious land, and many countries shall be overthrown: but these shall escape out of his hand, even Edom, and Moab, and the chief of the children of Ammon. He shall stretch forth his hand also upon the countries: and the land of Egypt shall not escape. But he shall have power over the treasures of gold and of silver, and over all the precious things of Egypt: and the Libyans and the Ethiopians shall be at his steps (vv. 40-43).

Here the expositors who think all these prophecies refer to Antiochus Epiphanes become embarrassed and confused, as history contains nothing that corresponds with these things. For that reason from verse 40 on they sought an escape into another explanation and applied this to his son, Antiochus Eupator. That is who is meant here by the king of the north, they claim, while an unknown king of Egypt is meant by the king of the south. This explanation is no good, however, for it violates the express time reference of verse 40.

Many expositors hold the opinion that the king in verse 36 is the same as this king of the north, and then let him appear in the future alongside the Antichrist. A few others think these verses are still sealed. We must admit that we cannot shed any light on these kings. But the following matters are nevertheless certain to us:

- There is nothing in history that corresponds with these kings; as verse 40 emphatically tells us, all will take place at the time of the end. Hence, this precludes every form of a historical explanation. All this will take place at the time of the end, and not before.
- Israel, although not mentioned, stands again in the foreground. The verses are referring to Israel's great tribulation. "The glorious land" means, as before, the land of Israel, and

the terms north and south refer to the directions as viewed from this central country. God considers Palestine the heart, the center of the whole world.

- During the time of the Antichrist there will be two kings, one to the south and one to the north of Palestine, who will have the courage to oppose the Antichrist, the head of the fourth world empire. When the Antichrist learns this, he will march against them like a wild mountain stream. Thus he will enter Palestine where he will overthrow many places.

Only Edom, Moab, and Ammon will escape out of his hand. The countries of Edom, Moab, and Ammon are still there and there are still people living there, so that these words can by no means constitute an objection to an explanation far into the future. He will conquer Egypt, Libya, and the Moors and will take their treasures, and their sons shall be at his steps, i.e., will serve in his army.

Many texts in the prophets tell us in what a terrible manner the Antichrist will rage in Palestine and Jerusalem. At that time Israel will have partly returned to its country (Jer. 3:14; Ezek. 38:7-12; Zech. 12:1-8) and will still be unconverted. When the great tribulation is at its height, the Messiah with His saints will descend on Mount Olivet and the Jews will fall at His feet with great mourning and lamentation. The last three chapters of Zechariah also speak of these same things.

No One to Help

But tidings out of the east and out of the north shall trouble him: therefore he shall go forth with great fury to destroy, and utterly to make away many. And he shall plant the tabernacles of his palace between the seas in the glorious holy mountain; yet he shall come to his end, and none shall help him (vv. 44,45).

When the Antichrist finds himself with his giant armies in the south, suddenly alarming reports from the north reach his ears. At that time he is apparently camped in Egypt. With great fury he goes forth against the enemy in the north "to destroy and to utterly make away many".

His journey back runs once more through the holy land. Maybe the reports came from the holy land as well. We consider it not unlikely that we must understand the reports to mean the tidings concerning the two mighty witnesses who testify in such a miraculous way in Jerusalem as we are told in Revelation 11. There we see, in verse 7, that the beast suddenly appears, makes war with them, conquers them, and kills them.

But we dare not say anything with certainty concerning this matter. This, however, is certain—the Antichrist will pitch his royal tent, "the tabernacles of his palace", between the Mediterranean and the Dead Seas at the foot of the mountain of the glorious land. By this mountain is meant Zion, representing Jerusalem. His huge and destructive army has laid siege around the beloved city.

As the next verse indicates, it will be for Israel such a time of anguish as has never before been in the world. Everything and everybody will for a short time turn against Israel; God Himself will for the last time contend with His apostate people, and all the renegades will be destroyed; the elements of heaven will pour out terrible judgments upon Israel and all of mankind. But especially the Antichrist will carry out the divinely appointed service of executioner in Israel. However, he will rage only for a brief period of three and a half years among Israel. And the believing Jews who will then be living in Jerusalem are admonished by the great Prophet in Matthew 24:16-18 to flee to the mountains as soon as they see that the image of the man of sin, the abomination of destruction, is being erected in the temple.

In the holy land, the place where the Antichrist has carried out his greatest destructions, he will also find his downfall. He shall come to his end. In the battle at Armageddon, in the battle of the great God, he together with his army will be completely defeated by Christ and His saints (see Rev. 16:16; 19:19, 20). When it is said that none shall help him, this apparently refers to the downfall of the false prophet who had been his most important helper, as the second part of Revelation 13 tells us. Both these two enemies are seized by Christ Himself and cast into the lake of fire burning with brimstone (see Rev. 19:20). Will not the heavens above resound with joy at that time?

In the meantime Israel, which at present promises itself mountains of gold in the land of its fathers, is headed first of all for a terrible future. The first beginnings of its great tribulation can already be observed in our days. Recently the "*Judische Rund-*

schau" published a confidential article by the anti-semitic secretary-in-chief Hennigszen, in which an anti-semitic campaign for after the war is announced and recommended, and for which already money is being collected [editor's note: Bultema wrote this in 1918]. In this article it is said that in the year 1915 a meeting had been held for that purpose which had been attended by several important people. Already mention was made there of soon making use of the material the war had provided against Jewry. It was decided to publish several anti-semitic papers, among others the pamphlet *"Ueber die Juden im Weltkrieg"* ("About the Jews in the World War"). The plan is to send out the first edition free of charge to officers, industrialists, agrarians, merchants, doctors, and students. Thus already satanic plans are made against Israel. Yet no power will ever succeed in annihilating Israel, for the Lord calls it His *am olam*, His eternal people.

Chapter 12
THE WISE SHALL UNDERSTAND

Israel Delivered

And at that time shall Michael stand up, the great prince which standeth for the children of thy people: and there shall be a time of trouble, such as never was since there was a nation even to that same time: and at that time thy people shall be delivered, every one that shall be found written in the book (v. 1).

In Daniel we must not expect such beautiful depictions of Israel's glorious future as in the other prophets, for he is not a prophet of theocracy but of the times of the gentiles. It is specifically his task to call attention to Israel's misery and not to its prosperity. Still this chapter makes a few references to Israel's deliverance. This verse tells us when this deliverance will dawn and by whom it will be effected.

Daniel's people will be delivered at that time, i.e., during the time of the raging of the blasphemous king as he was depicted in the verses 36-45 of the preceding chapter. That time is further characterized as a time of trouble such as never was since there was a nation. These expressions defy all description. The persecutions during the time of the Maccabees were terrible, but it seems almost childish to have these terrifying words refer to them. And that here we are not dealing with Eastern exaggeration is sufficiently clear from the fact that we have the same descriptions in both the Old and New Covenants (Ps. 2:5; Jer. 30:7; Matt. 24:21; Rev. 7:14).

In a moral sense this great tribulation is the result of the apostasy of Israel and the nations; in a juridical sense it must be ascribed to the wrath of Almighty God, while the satanic raging of the Antichrist is the immediate cause. The last book of the Bible describes this great tribulation extensively. For further details we refer the reader to this book.

Michael, the archangel, is presented here as the author of Israel's deliverance. We already met this angel in 10:13 and 21. When we check Scripture on this angel we find he has a twofold task. First, he appears as the angel of resurrection. That is how he is represented here in verse 2 and further in Jude 9 and 1 Thessalonians 4:16. Secondly, he is presented in Scripture as the guardian angel of Israel (see 10:13, 21; Rev. 12:7-9).

He is that archangel who is the head of the angelic hosts. Although it is not specifically said here that many angels go to war under him, we may nevertheless safely assume this to be true. For is he not called the great prince, and as such he must certainly have subjects who fight for him and with him. With his hosts he protects and defends the people of Daniel. We saw in chapter 10 that together with Gabriel he fought against the wicked angel of Persia, so that the latter could not cause evil to Israel.

We assume it is not necessary any more to point out that here again the name Israel is purposely avoided. Here they are called "the children of thy people." We would say, your compatriots. Also avoided is the blessed name of the Lord, for we know that here we are dealing with the time of His return. The Great Tribulation is terminated by His coming again (Matt. 24:21, 27, 29, 30); Israel will be delivered by His appearance. As the apostle says in Romans 11:26, "There shall come out of Zion the Deliverer, and shall turn away ungodliness from Jacob." Also the blessed resurrection will take place in connection with His coming again. The King of kings Himself is not mentioned but His chief servant, the archangel Michael, is placed in the foreground. This veiled presentation is wholly in agreement with the rest of Daniel.

The entire Scripture from Genesis to Revelation teaches us that Israel will be delivered from all its tribulations. All prophets have spoken of this deliverance, except for Jonah, who in a typical fashion shows it in his own miraculous deliverance. The fact that many Christians do not believe in the restoration and conversion of Israel can, alas, not be denied. There is great ignorance and tardiness to believe all that the prophets have spoken. As a result, Israel as a rule is indeed considered an enemy for the sake of the gospel but not as beloved for the sake of the fathers, and such Christians simply will not believe that the gifts and calling of God are without repentance. This lamentable unbelief on the part of confessing Christians has been of inestimable detriment to Israel and the Church, and as a result also to the whole world. Here we can do no more than beseech the reader to examine prayerfully the following Scriptures and to compare them with one another:

Genesis 12:7	Ezekiel 11:17
Genesis 13:14, 15	Ezekiel 20:33-37
Genesis 15:18	Ezekiel 22:19-22
Genesis 17:8	Ezekiel 28:25
Genesis 28:1	Ezekiel 36:23, 24, 38
Leviticus 26:33, 43	Ezekiel 37:21, 22
Deuteronomy 26:9	Ezekiel 39:28
Joshua 24:20-28	Daniel 12:1
2 Samuel 7:11-16	Hosea 3:4, 5
Ezra 4:1-3	Joel 3:20, 21
Psalm 102:13-22	Amos 9:9, 14, 15
Isaiah 11:11, 12	Micah 2:12
Isaiah 18:7	Micah 3:9, 10
Isaiah 27:12, 13	Micah 4:7
Isaiah 29:1, 8	Micah 4:11, 12
Isaiah 44	Zechariah 7:7, 8
Isaiah 60:8-21	Zechariah 8:8
Isaiah 66:18-22	Zechariah 10:6
Jeremiah 3:17, 18	Zechariah 12:2-10
Jeremiah 11:10, 11	Zechariah 13:8, 9
Jeremiah 23:3-6	Zechariah 14:1, 5, 9
Jeremiah 29:14	Malachi 3:6
Jeremiah 30:7, 10	Matthew 19:28
Jeremiah 31:2, 10, 23	Matthew 23:37
Jeremiah 31:26-28	Luke 21:24, 29-33
Jeremiah 31:31, 34	Acts 15:14-17
Jeremiah 33:4-16	Romans 11
Jeremiah 50:19	

Israel will be restored and converted as a nation is amply clear from these Scriptures and also from the verse under discussion. Superficially viewed this might lead to the idea that every Jew individually will be restored. This is by no means the case. Also with respect to Israel there is no universalism but rather election, as is evident from the expression "every one that shall be found written in the book." In this instance this book is not the book of recompence which has a causal connection with this life, but the book of life of which we read in Revelation 20:15. In the elect remnant of the nation of Israel in the last days all of Israel will be represented. The people must, according to the promise made to their fathers, be saved as a nation.

We quote here another text dealing with Israel's future, of which the one part is literally fulfilled prophecy and the other part prophecy as yet unfulfilled; Jeremiah 31:28, "And it shall come to pass, that like as I have watched over them, to pluck up, and to break down, and to throw down, and to destroy, and to afflict; so will I watch over them, to build, and to plant, saith the Lord." He, Israel's Watchman, never sleeps nor slumbers, but is ever watchful over His people. And that is the reason the devil, even with the help of the whole world, has never been able to exterminate this nation. The Lord has a grand purpose with this people—He wants to build it up again as His people and plant it in His land, so that in that day many nations may flow to Him and His people (see Isa. 2:1-5; 66:23; Jer. 3:17; Mic. 4:1-7; Zech. 14:16-19).

The First Resurrection

And many of them that sleep in the dust of the earth shall awake, some to everlasting life, and some to shame and everlasting contempt (v. 2).

This text is often made to serve as proof of the general and simultaneous resurrection, but in no way can it be made to serve that purpose. If anything, then we have here a strong indication of a dual resurrection. The many divergent explanations of this text can be reduced to three:

First, many expositors interpret this text as a revival of the Jewish state under the symbol of a resurrection. As proof they refer to Isaiah 26:14-19; Ezekiel 37 and Hosea 6:2 for similar comparisons. These expositors can be classified into two groups which differ greatly on the time when this symbolical resurrection will take place. Some apply it to the heyday of the Maccabees; others to the restoration of Israel at Christ's return.

Second, most expositors see in it a reference to the one, simultaneous resurrection. In this respect they are like W. E. Barnes, who first remarks on this text, "The natural and obvious meaning of the word 'many' is that a great multitude of men will arise, but not all. That is the way we would interpret the word if it were used for other things." And yet this expositor makes this word "many" to mean "all," with a reference to Romans 5:19. But this appeal is not valid. For if we agree that the word "many" in Romans by way of exception and for valid reasons (the original there has "THE many") is used instead of "all," then this is not conclusive by a long shot, for the two situations are not identical. Here it does not merely say "many," as it does there, but "many of." Supposing that "many" can mean "all" in certain cases, this could definitely not be said in this expression.

Third, nowadays there are many expositors, and their number is growing, who interpret this verse as referring to a twofold, dissimilar resurrection. In our opinion this interpretation is the only true one, but on the understanding that it is seen in the closest connection with Israel's national revival. In support of this conviction we point out the following matters:

- The *min partitivus* here suggests that a separation will take place. We do know that the Lord at His coming will separate the goats from the sheep. "Many of" indicates a multitude which leaves another multitude behind.
- The indicative adjective as it is used here has a distributive meaning; these (who are well known), and those over there (who are totally different and will be dealt with later).
- The metaphor of sleep for death is used in Scripture exclusively of deceased saints. The wicked are not said to be sleeping but are merely referred to as those "over there."
- Scripture teaches nowhere a general resurrection, not even in the two places that are most often quoted as prooftexts, John 5:28, 29 and Acts 24:15. There the believers are specifically distinguished from the wicked and are mentioned first.
- Scripture clearly teaches a first and a second resurrection (see and compare the following places: Luke 14:14; 20:35; John 6:39-54; Rom. 8:11; 1 Cor. 15:23; Phil. 3:11; 1 Thess. 4:16; Heb. 11:35; Rev. 20:5).

Hence, it is clear that this text is not the only one that teaches a first resurrection. If this first resurrection were indeed the spiritual resurrection, as so many people think, then we might ask ourselves why it is connected with the coming of the Lord. For that is surely not the time when we are born again. Peter says that we are already begotten again unto a lively hope (1 Peter 1:3). When we make a symbol of the first resurrection in Revelation 20:5, why not also of the second death in verse 15? That which is taught us so clearly in the New Testament is not wholly unknown in the Old Testament (see Isa. 24:22; 26:14, 19; 66:24; Job 19:25, 26; Hos. 6:2; Ezek. 37:1-14). For that reason the rabbis, the Maccabees, and Jesus' contemporaries expected nothing else but that godly Israel would rise from the dead long before the wicked.

Someone might argue against the above-mentioned exposition that the different kinds of resurrected people are nevertheless mentioned in one breath and this strongly points to the one, simultaneous resurrection. In refutation we observe that Daniel does things like that frequently (9:26, 27; 11:2, 36). Not only does Daniel easily make a jump of many ages, all the prophets do. In the Messianic prophecies we often find that the first coming of Christ is mentioned in one breath together with His return (see Isa. 61:2; Joel 2:29-31; Mal. 4:1, 2).

It needs no clarification or argument that verse 2 contains a strong proof of eternal punishment. If the contempt were not everlasting then neither would life be.

Rewards for the Faithful

And they that be wise shall shine as the brightness of the firmament; and they that turn many to righteousness as the stars forever and ever (v. 3).

It is clear that we must translate here "teachers" and not, as the King James version does, "they that be wise." True, the Hebrew word *maskilim* does indeed mean in the first place the wise, but as a rule it further implies the class of wise men who also instruct others. That is how the word appears in this context. In 11:33 and 35 we find the same word and with the meaning of the wise, spiritual leaders or ministers who incite others to faithfulness to God and a courageous witness before God. For that reason most translations have the word "teachers" or a word of similar meaning.

At the blessed resurrection of the believers the reward of grace is handed out, and that is what this verse is speaking about. There are two reasons why mention is made of teachers. First, this was a great comfort to Daniel, the wise teacher. Second, Scripture gives us the impression that the witnesses of and martyrs for Christ will receive a special measure of reward of grace and glory. So we can also say this verse speaks of an extraordinary glory, not excluding but in addition to the glory all faithful believers will receive.

Of such spiritual leaders who in times of oppression and persecution have urged others on to be faithful it is said that in the day of the blessed resurrection they will shine as the brightness of the firmament. From the preceding verse it is clear that this is not merely a reference to eternal bliss, because eternal life was already there promised to all the believers. One day eternal bliss will be the same for all believers, but not so glory. That will constitute the greatest difference of graduation according to the measure of their service of love to the Lord on earth.

Possibly the beautiful metaphor used here to indicate their glory is an allusion to 8:10, where the little horn is depicted as casting the stars to earth and trampling them. Now it is said they will not remain lying on earth to be trodden down but will be restored to their former places. In the second part of this verse they are specifically called stars. Essentially, these words do not say anything different from the first part. To think here of voluntary custodians is totally baseless. The idea is added, however, that those who were already shining lights and by their words made many people righteous will eternally reap the benefits of their labor and testimony. The idea is that they will eternally shine beautifully, dazzlingly, and enlighteningly. The word "righteous" reflects less righteousness by faith than righteousness of life as being the fruit of the former.

Seal the Book

But thou, O Daniel, shut up the words, and seal the book, even to the time of the end: many shall run to and fro, and knowledge shall be increased (v. 4).

This verse is considered to be one of the most difficult in all of Daniel. It contains mainly three difficulties: What does the shutting up and sealing of the book mean? How must the expression "many shall run to and fro" be interpreted? Which knowledge shall be increased? We wish to look at these three questions more closely.

According to many expositors, the answer to the first question is that Daniel must indeed make this vision inaccessible so that none could obtain any knowledge concerning it. However, this cannot be the intent, for:

- "Whatsoever things were written aforetime were written for our learning" (Rom. 15:4; 2 Tim. 3:16).
- A revelation cannot be at the same time a covering. So Bettex is quite incorrect in his opinion that the last five chapters of Daniel are still sealed, and hence his warning is quite misplaced; "That which is still hidden and sealed we must not prematurely want to uncover and unseal, lest we fall into detrimental errors."
- If God had indeed hidden the meaning of this vision then the wise of verse 10 could no more understand it than the wicked.

It seems to us this expression is first of all meant for Daniel. This can be deduced from the words "But thou, O Daniel." He may first of all consider this vision as a special favor received from his God. This prophecy could be taken as a proof that his God considered him a man greatly beloved. And that which God had given him he must not reveal to the blind heathen, for that could put his people in great jeopardy. Moreover, this vision was specifically given with Israel in mind, and the last part of it with Israel at the end of time in mind. So the first concern of Daniel must be to safeguard it well and confirm it as a divine revelation by ratifying it with his seal rather than making it known immediately to Israel.

This implied at the same time that the vision had come to an end and that he could close it up with a kind of fine clay, as was customary, and finally to put his name on it, as the prophet of the Lord, as a sign of authenticity. The writing had to be kept for a long time, and hence it had to be kept in a safe place. Its contents were precious, especially with regard to the end of time.

We readily agree that indirectly this contains an intimation that the full meaning and the purpose of this vision cannot be completely understood before the time of the end, but that is something entirely different from thinking that everything is deliberately hidden, and hence that it would be a sin to search and examine this Scripture or would give rise to detrimental errors (cf. further the notes on 8:26). It may not escape our attention that the man greatly favored in the new dispensation is told, "Seal not the sayings of the prophecy of this book." (Rev. 22:10). The reason for this command is that the time was at hand, just as the main reason here for the command to seal it is the great distance of the time of the end. The Jews were forever searching for signs that usher in the establishment of the Messianic Kingdom, and in this they had to be toned down. The New Testament church, on the other hand, as a rule places the things to come far into an uncertain, faint, nebulous future, and for that reason God wants to impress on us the idea of brevity.

The second question is how the expression "many shall investigate it" must be translated. In the King James version we read, "many shall run to and fro." Luther translates, "so many will come over it." Van Hamelsveld translates the second half of this verse thus: "at that time many will without any difficulty increase their skills." Adventists place all emphasis on the common English translation and consider this a clear prophecy that at the time of the end there will be much traveling across the length and breadth of the earth. In that case we see this prophecy already being fulfilled in the fast means of transportation today. The warm friends of missions see in this a clear prophecy of the fast expansion of missions as we can observe today. If that translation is correct, then these conclusions are also correct and in that case we can combine these two ideas very well into one prophecy. It seems to us, however, that our translation is the correct one and that we must retain "investigate and examine thoroughly."

The movement of to and fro may refer to that of the eyes through leaves. In Job 1:7 the same expression is used with reference to Satan who answers God's question regarding where he came from by saying, "from going to and fro in the earth and from walking up and down in it." Satan had done this with the intent to watch Job's life carefully and to see whether he could possibly find a basis of accusation against him. Thus considered it seems to us that the text here speaks of the diligent search of Scripture at the end of time. Also if we view it this way we have here a prophecy that will obtain a marked and literal fulfillment in the end-time.

When we take this expression in this sense, then the answer to the third question is already partially supplied, namely, which knowledge will be increased? Judging by the definite article, it is obvious that this is not a reference to science in general. Calvin undoubtedly hits the nail on the head when he says that the knowledge of God's plan, his counsel, will be increased by the study of prophecy. "The hand of the diligent maketh rich," Scripture says—that applies especially to the study of prophecies.

This prediction has already come to fulfillment in a glorious way during the last years. Science in general may have made giant progress, but the knowledge concerning divine predictions exceeds it by far. In our dark days it is one of the most gladdening signs of the times that believers in increasing numbers and measure pay heed to the light of prophecy.

How Long Till the End

Then I, Daniel, looked, and, behold, there stood other two, the one on this side of the bank of the river, and the other on that side of the bank of the river. And one said to the man clothed in linen, which was upon the waters of the river, How long shall it be to the end of these wonders? And I heard the man clothed in linen, which was upon the waters of the river, when he held up his right hand and his left hand unto heaven, and sware by him that liveth forever that it shall be for a time, times, and an half; and when he shall have accomplished to scatter the power of the holy people, all these things shall be finished (vv. 5-7).

With mounting amazement Daniel has listened to the words of the man floating between the banks of the Hiddekel or standing on the waters of the river. What must have passed through the soul of this righteous man when he heard about all these abominations to which his beloved people would be subjected in the days to follow? While thus his thoughts multiplied he suddenly saw two other figures on the banks of the river, one on each side, so that the man clothed in linen stood in between them. The man clothed in linen is the same One who is described in such glorious terms in 10:5, 6. There we have already advanced our grounds for believing that we are to see Him as the second Person of the holy Trinity before His incarnation. In this connection we pass on only two more thoughts which may fortify us in this belief.

First of all, it is remarkable that He occupies here the place Christ is always given, namely, in the middle. These verses call attention to this by saying that someone was standing on both sides of the river. We consider this by no means accidental, for our Lord Jesus Christ always ought to be the center and is always presented as such in Scripture. During His life He was in the midst of them as one who served. In His suffering and death He hung on the cross in the middle. After His resurrection he stood in the midst of the disciples and blessed them with His peace (John 20:19). And even in glorious heaven He retains that place, which is by no means accidental but appointed by God. John saw Him as the slain Lamb in the midst of the throne and among the four beasts and in the midst of the elders (Rev. 5:6). So we find here, as we do in Ezekiel 9, the man clothed in linen amidst the angels of God. Hence, here again we find a silent indication in the richly symbolic language of Scripture that we are dealing here with the central personality, the eternal Word of God.

Another indication that points in the same direction is that we find this linen-clad man above the onrushing waters of the Hiddekel. Seas and rivers are frequently symbols in Scripture of the raging of nations and of swiftly moving, destructive armies (see Isa. 17:12; Jer. 47:2; Ezek. 26:19; Rev. 17:1, 15). Hence it seems to us we have here the same representation as in Revelation 10:2, 5, 6 and there is hardly any doubt that the strong angel in Revelation 10 is the Lord Jesus Christ Himself. What does this symbolism signify? What else but that the Lord Jesus Christ reigns over the raging of the sea of nations, that He reigns over the world empires which want to destroy His Israel, and that even the mightiest armies are powerless against His divine will.

One of these angels asked Him how long these wonderful things which He had just mentioned would last. The question obviously alludes to the terrible time of affliction mentioned in verse 12. He (or maybe both angels asked the same question) wanted to know this very badly. Angels have great knowledge, but they are by no means omniscient. In fact, they seem to be rather ignorant especially with regard to future things (Matt. 24:36; Mark 13:32; Eph. 3:10). Like us, they can obtain knowledge concerning the mysteries of salvation in no other way than by the revelation of God. But these great celestial spirits also act according to the rule that one becomes wise by asking questions. They investigate, ask questions, and worship—the royal way that leads to true wisdom.

Let us continue and hear the answer that is given them. The man clothed in linen raised both hands and swore by the ever-living God. A godly oath may be made. Today an attempt is made to limit this divine ordinance or to replace it by a promise, but this deserves the strongest disapproval. In the state of glory an oath will no longer be necessary, but here it is still necessary on account of our mendacity and unbelieving nature. This man in his priestly garment swore not on his own behalf or on that of the two angels on either bank of the river, but for Daniel's and our sake. We are not dealing here with an oath of purgation but an oath of faithful promise. He appeals here to God's eternality, whereby the Lord even in the furtherest future eons will by no means have forgotten this promise. He as the Almighty still can, and as the Faithful One still will fulfill it. The raising of the hands to heaven was in times of old the most common form of an oath. Thus even the stretching out of the arm obtained the meaning of swearing an oath (Exod. 6:7; Num. 14:30). As a rule, however, it was done with one hand (Gen. 14:22; Deut. 32:40; Rev. 10:5). Why here both hands are raised cannot be said with certainty. It may be in order to give greater assurance, since the fulfillment was so far in the future, or more probably because there stood an angel on either side of Him.

What did this man swear? From the answer he gave we can deduce that the meaning of the question was to know how long the tribulation would last. It is generally thought we must take a "time" to mean a year, "times" two years, and an "half" being half a year. There are indeed those who hold the opinion that each day must be taken as a year. And on the unscriptural basis of the year-day theory all kinds of wild speculations have been made with regard to these words. All such calculations have never done anything but scare off the simple people from studying the prophets and filled decent-minded students with aversion. Calculations with regard to the coming again of the Lord are definitely not permissible (Matt. 24:36; Mark 13:32). Those who engage in calculations want the impossible, for Scripture supplies no basis whatsoever for them with regard to the return of the Lord. There is not a grain of scriptural proof for the noxious year-day theory, from which all calculations proceed. Times and moments in Scripture are always meant literally, unless the Lord Himself gives an indication that they must be interpreted differently. To the practiced and prayerful reader of Scripture it is not difficult to understand such indications.

The time mentioned here is the second half of the last seven years of 9:27. That is the time of the great tribulation, during which Israel is delivered over into the hand of the little horn (7:25). During this period the holy city will be trodden down by the Gentiles in a special way (Rev. 11:2), and the two witnesses will preach (vv. 3, 9, 11; Rev. 12:6, 14). In the middle of the year-week of Daniel, the Antichrist will erect the abomination of desolation in the temple (Matt. 24:21, 22) and immediately thereafter the great tribulation commences, which is extensively described in Jeremiah 30:3 in the same context as here. We also find it described even much more extensively in chapters 12, 13, and 14 of Zechariah, and finally most fully in Revelation 6 to 19. Hence the biggest part of the last Bible book deals with this horrible period. It is the time of judgment upon the nations by the Roman empire and upon Israel; the time in which the times of the Gentiles are terminated and Israel's history is resumed. It is already evident from the fact that the time is expressed in days, months, and years in Daniel and Revelation that it must be taken literally. Jeremiah 30:2-11 is another key section of Scripture to consider in this regard (see also Zechariah 12:2, 3; 14:2; Ezekiel 39:6, 19-22; Revelation 16:18-21.

It needs no further argument that by "the holy people" Israel is meant. The Old Testament knows of only one holy people, and that is Israel. The last part of verse 7 is somewhat obscure in its wording. The meaning is undoubtedly that after the scattering of the power of all of Israel is complete, there will be an oppression for three and a half years. After that everything will be completed by the coming again of Christ and His angels (see Zech. 14:1-5).Then the times of the Gentiles (Luke 21:24) will have been fulfilled as we are told here in the language of the Old Covenant.

Closing and Sealing

And I heard, but I understood not: then said I, O my Lord, what shall be the end of these things? And he said, Go thy way, Daniel: for the words are closed up and sealed till the time of the end. Many shall be purified, and made white, and tried; but the

> **wicked shall do wickedly: and none of the wicked shall understand; but the wise shall understand (vv. 8-10).**

Daniel had heard the solemn oath but he had not understood it; hence he asks here for further information. That oath contained two matters. First, the exact delineation of the time of three and a half years for the great tribulation. Second, the general time setting. All these things would take place after the return of Israel from its extended dispersion.

It was obviously Daniel's desire to know when the end of all this would be. He was not in the first place so much concerned with the beginning and duration of all these things as he was with the end, for in his heart there was the strong desire for the complete future glory of his people. He wanted to know what lay behind this bitter suffering of his people. Hence, there is a difference between the angel's questions and Daniel's question. Whereas the former asked about the duration of the tribulation at the time of the end, Daniel wanted to know the end, the outcome of it.

Here we have a striking example of what Christ said in Matthew 13:17 and the apostle Peter in 1 Peter 1:10-12. From these texts it is quite evident that to the mind of the holy people there remained much that was puzzling. He did not receive satisfaction for his ardent desire to know something of Israel's complete deliverance. He was not the prophet of Israel's glory but of the times of the Gentiles. God dealt with him as He did with Moses, albeit not for the same reasons. Like Moses, he was granted to be a light and leader in the wilderness of the exile for many centuries, but he himself was not allowed to share in Israel's deliverance nor even in the knowledge as to when it would take place. The Lord told him to go his way, that is to say, to be satisfied with the knowledge the Lord had granted him. On 9b see verse 4 and the comment on it. At the end of time all will be fulfilled and understood. Also Daniel must know in part so that he might live exclusively by faith. In his mind there remained much that was mysterious.

In broad but significant terms, the Lord in verse 10 points out to him the moral quality of the long periods of the nations. These words contain the reason why the Lord would not go into details regarding the future. For this would more or less dictate the voluntary acts of the children of men in a manner He does not want to do. He gives man a certain leeway. If He had described the future in minute details, He then would have eliminated man's responsibility to a certain extent. He wants to leave room for serious research, holy desire, constant prayer, work, watching, and waiting. Adventists reject this wise decree out of hand, as they seem forever to be bent on telling people exactly what time it is on the great clock of the universe.

Many sinners will be purified by the cleansing blood of the Lamb and made white by the shining fine linen of Christ's righteousness. Many of God's children will also be purged as gold and silver is purged. The Lord will do all this by His invincible grace, for it is stated emphatically that they will be purified and made white and tried. Who can do all these things to a leprous sinner except He alone?

The wicked, on the other hand, will continue to do wickedly. Another word for wicked is godless, which in essence means loose from God, not yet united with Him through the Mediator. Such people naturally act contrary to the will of God, and so we can say that they act in a godless manner. Although the Lord reveals His wrath from heaven against all ungodliness and unrighteousness of men (Rom. 1:18), this does not prevent them from continuing to do wickedly, nor does it cause them to repent.

It is also said here that the ungodly will not give heed to prophecy nor, consequently, to the signs of the times, which is an ever-present characteristic of the wicked. They are characterized by spiritual blindness. We learn from this that Scripture knows man and depicts him correctly with one stroke of the brush. Who would dare to claim this portrait, painted thousands of years ago, does not give an exact sketch of our wicked contemporaries? And finally, we learn from it that Scripture offers no hope of a converted world before Israel is first redeemed. First, Israel's conversion will come, Paul says, and that will be as life from the dead (Rom. 11:15); but before that time only an unscriptural postmillennialism can expect a converted world.

In this dispensation there will always be one church and one world, and between them is a chasm that can never be bridged. There will always be a seed of the woman and a seed of the serpent, and between them an irreconcilable and unremitting battle.

One characteristic of the wise, the prudent, the God-fearing will be that they understand prophecy. Here we find a ground rule with regard to the study and understanding of prophecy. We must obey the command to take off the shoes of the carnal mind before we enter it, and here we must have spiritual eyesalve. Scripture constantly points out this basic rule for studying prophecy (see Isa. 6:9; Hos. 14:9; John 8:47; 10:27). The highest wisdom consists in this, that we have a childlike faith and belief in all that the prophets have spoken. The simple cottage dweller who has such faith knows more about the future than all the wise men of the world together. And he will obtain not only knowledge but also the greatest comfort when walking in that way of faith. On the other hand, everyone, regardless who he is, will walk in darkness if he pays no heed to the light of prophecy.

The Abomination That Maketh Desolate

And from the time that the daily sacrifice shall be taken away, and the abomination that maketh desolate set up, there shall be a thousand two hundred and ninety days. Blessed is he that waiteth, and cometh to the thousand three hundred and five and thirty days. But go thou thy way till the end be: for thou shalt rest, and stand in thy lot at the end of the days (vv. 11-13).

It is obviously the intent of verse 11 that Daniel should not misunderstand the time of the great tribulation, so it is once more repeated in this form. We do not understand why thirty days are added. The brief period mentioned in verse 7 is expressed in days. And the time is even more closely delineated here. From these indications it is clear that the Son of God who by His omnipotence kept Himself on or above the water was not unwilling to clarify for Daniel what the latter had already heard; He simply did not wish to give him an elaborated account of Israel's future glory.

"The abomination that maketh desolate" is a frequent expression in Daniel. It appears in two different ways. One, in comparing it with the abominations committed by Antiochus Epiphanes in the temple (8:11, 12 and 11:30, 31). And two, in referring to it with regard to the time mentioned here, the time of the Antichrist.

Israel will then have its temple again, as is clear from Ezekiel 40 to 48; Matthew 24:15; 2 Thessalonians 2:4, 8-12. What Daniel and Christ mean by "the abomination of desolation" cannot be said with certainty. Maybe all it means is the presence of the Antichrist in the temple. Maybe it refers to the image which his first minister, the false prophet, will erect for him and which will be able to speak because a demon will take possession of it. We prefer to believe the latter although both ideas may very well be combined.

Those people are called blessed who patiently and submissively wait for the denouement of all things. The weary heart of those who fear God may experience hard longing at times, so that they almost begin to lose patience, but then a promise like this is calculated to urge them on to submissiveness and to comfort them.

What the expression "and cometh to the thousand three hundred and five and thirty days" means is no more clear to us than it is to any other exegete. A short while ago thirty days were added to the time of the great tribulation and now forty-five days are added, so in all we exceed the time of the great affliction by seventy-five days. The meaning of the words are "blessed is he who with his life reaches thirteen hundred thirty-five days," and not blessed is he who with his calculations reaches that number of days. Scripture contains no beatitude for masters of prophetic calculations. We may safely conclude from this beatitude that after these days the full glory of Israel will commence. Scripture tells us nowhere what will be done during those seventy-five days, but from the nature of things, we can deduce that it is the brief period that will elapse between the battle of Armageddon and the establishment of the glorious kingdom of the Lord Jesus Christ. The stone that struck the world monarchy needs some time to grow into a mountain, a glorious kingdom, that will fill the whole earth (see 2:34, 35, 44).

In any case it is clear from this beatitude that it cannot very well be applied to the papacy or Mohammedanism or the days of Antiochus Epiphanes. On the other hand, in Revelation we find many beatitudes in connection with the blessed coming of the Lord and its attendant events.

Finally, the concluding verse of this prophecy says that the prophet must now be satisfied with the revelation he has received and that he must prepare himself for the end of life. Daniel was already very old and would, therefore, soon have reached the end of his earthly pilgrimage, just as he now had come to the end of his prophetic career. He himself would not experience any of these times of affliction. Soon he would softly and calmly sleep away in his Lord. He belonged to those who did not obtain the fulfillment of the promise but who had nevertheless seen it from afar and had believed and embraced it. It had also been his confession that he had been a sojourner and stranger on earth. He had clearly shown that he was seeking a country, and he must undoubtedly, like any one of the patriarchs, have died in the belief of the perfect fulfillment of the promise (Heb. 11:13).

The faithful man of God will stand in "his lot." What does this mean? The word lot refers to Israel's casting of the lot so that everyone could obtain his own inheritance in Canaan. Some expositors think it is a reference to the first resurrection of which Matthew 27:53 speaks. Others think it refers to the Messianic kingdom, the kingdom of peace. Many others think it refers to the reward of grace. Just as Paul speaks of that good thing which was laid up for him, meaning the reward of grace, so in that sense we could here speak of Daniel's lot.

There is much to be said in favor of this interpretation. The context favors it, and Scripture teaches us that the reward of grace must comfort and encourage God's children, just as it does the prophet here. It seems to us this refers to Daniel's blessed resurrection, inclusive of the reward of grace. He will arise to receive his glorious lot, his inheritance, his reward in the Messianic kingdom. Hence Daniel was told three things:

1. He must be satisfied with what he was given and calmly go his way.
2. He would rest after a life of many vicissitudes.
3. One day, at the end of days, he would rise up from the grave to receive his apportioned inheritance in the Messianic kingdom from the hand of the Lord.

Although the man greatly beloved of God did not fully receive in this life what he longed for, he nevertheless will behold the fulfillment of his holy desire. This constitutes a striking conclusion of this vision and of the whole book. Our curious minds would like to know something about the end of this great one in the kingdom of God, but let us also be satisfied with what the Lord has given us, and let us be found ready one day to receive our inheritance from the hand of the Lord at the end of time!

INDEX OF NAMES

INDEX OF SCRIPTURE TEXTS

INDEX OF SUBJECTS